The

HEIRLOOM FLOWER

GARDEN

OTHER BOOKS BY JO ANN GARDNER

The Old-Fashioned Fruit Garden (1989)
The Heirloom Garden (1991)
Living with Herbs (1997)
Herbs In Bloom (1998)

The
HEIRLOOM FLOWER GARDEN

Rediscovering and Designing with Classic Ornamentals

❧

Jo Ann Gardner

CHELSEA GREEN PUBLISHING COMPANY

White River Junction, Vermont

The recipe for Currant Jam was adapted from my book, *The Old-Fashioned Fruit Garden* (Nimbus Publishing, 1989).

Directions for making a child's arbor were adapted from directions courtesy of Christie White, lead interpreter for horticulture, Old Sturbridge Village, Sturbridge, Massachusetts.

Quiggly fence directions were adapted from directions courtesy of Bernard S. Jackson, curator, Memorial University Botanical Garden.

Louise Hyde's "Sweet Cicely Coffee Cake" and directions for making detergent from *Saponaria officinalis* are courtesy of Louise Hyde and Rita Buchanan, respectively, and Timber Press where directions for both first appeared in *Herbs In Bloom* (1998). The original directions for making detergent appeared in *A Weaver's Garden* by Rita Buchanan (Interweave, 1987).

Brief quotations throughout the book from Louise Beebe Wilder and Mrs. Francis King come from the following sources, unless otherwise indicated:

Louise Beebe Wilder, *The Fragrant Garden* (Dover, 1974); *The Garden in Color* (Macmillan, 1937).
Mrs. Francis King, *From a New Garden* (Alfred A. Knopf, 1930).

Designed by Andrea Gray.

Printed in the United States.
First printing, November 2001
04 03 02 01   1 2 3 4

Library of Congress Cataloging-in-Publication Data

Gardner, Jo Ann, 1935-
    The heirloom flower garden : rediscovering and designing with classic ornamentals / Jo Ann Gardner.
        p. cm.
    Rev. ed. of: The heirloom garden. c1992.
    Includes bibliographical references (p.).
    ISBN 1-890132-62-4 (alk. paper)
  1. Landscape plants—Heirloom varieties. 2. Flowers—Heirloom varieties. 3. Landscape plants—Heirloom varieties—North America. 4. Flowers—Heirloom varieties—North America. I. Gardner, Jo Ann, 1935- . Heirloom garden. II.
    Title.

    SB407 .G345 2001   2001047671
    635.9—dc21

Chelsea Green Publishing Company
P.O. Box 428
White River Junction, Vermont 05001
800-639-4099
www.chelseagreen.com

To my grandparents, who never had a garden:

Rebecca, Jacob, Rose, and Sam.

And to our adopted granny, Florence Burnham.

CONTENTS

Landscaping with Heirloom Flowers   31

Period-Inspired Garden Designs   41

A TREASURY OF HEIRLOOM ORNAMENTALS, 1600–1950: FLOWERS, HERBS, SHRUBS, AND VINES

SOURCES AND RESOURCES

Preface to the New Edition

Since colonial times, Americans have grown the flowers they love because the old favorites are beautiful and reliable, like old friends you look forward to seeing every season from year to year. Cherished by generations of gardeners, easily passed on from root, seed, or cutting, they are by now inextricably bound to our past, to people and places and to thoughts and feelings in a dense web of associations not invoked by the latest hybrid or mass-produced disposables in the bedding plant line. Although there are fine new plant introductions like *Veronica* 'Sunny Border Blue' and *Hemerocallis* 'Stella D'Oro', they have not been around long enough for us to care about them in the same way we care about older types. We may grow them for their superior forms, stronger stems, and longer bloom, but it will take decades before they, too, assume the mantle of "heirloom."

It may be in their very imperfection that some heirloom flowers have their greatest appeal: their more natural, more untampered forms, their freely wafted scents, their quirky individuality—these characteristics speak directly to us, reminding us of the fallible human condition and of ourselves as part of the natural world. Unlike more tailored, highly bred flowers, most of which demand pampering to perform their best, the old easy-going favorites are closest to the wild, as far away from what is artificial and synthetic in the modern world as it is possible to be among plants grown primarily for their good looks. More than ever before, as technology dominates our lives, we need the refuge and solace that these plants offer. On any sunny day we can stand among their colorful blooms and watch the work of nature, as assorted insects, butterflies, and hummingbirds come to feed on their sweet nectar.

In this updated and revised edition of my 1992 book, *The Heirloom Garden,* I have added several new features, including more of an emphasis on preserving and self-reliance. In practice this means a detailed section on growing and propagation, from seed germination to seed saving, for if we want to preserve—save for the future—the flowers we love best, we need to understand their basic needs. To be self-reliant in this context means to learn about simple, low-tech ways to deal with drought and limited water resources, ward off disease and problem insects, improve soil, and create favorable microhabitats in unfavorable conditions. Self-reliance is a vanishing virtue in contemporary life, and, like the old plants themselves, needs to be encouraged. Gardening is one of the few activities left that offers us this opportunity.

The landscaping section is greatly expanded to include a wealth of suggestions for grouping heirloom plants, for transforming dry banks and wet meadows through the art of naturalizing, for creating themed gardens that feature butterfly and hummingbird flowers, scented plants for the evening garden, and dressed-up dooryards that star authentic Old World flowers and bulbs. There is a wider palette, too, with the inclusion of the choicest antique Tulips and Hyacinths, Victorian favorites like Canna (now enjoying a revival), old-fashioned Dutchman's Pipe among vines, and Spireas and Wiegela among shrubs. And then there is the irrepressible Policeman's Helmet *(Impatiens glandulifera),* a plant on the wild side that in my experience has broad appeal among every type of gardener, from the the novice to the most sophisticated. It survives because gardeners continue to grow it and pass it along over the garden fence (though a few places still carry seeds—see the *Impatiens* entry). We need Policeman's Helmet in our gardens, for in full bloom, ashimmer with bees on its

lightly freckled, perfumed "hats," it is unrivalled for exuberance and beauty, for utter cheer.

Throughout, the reader is invited to participate rather than observe the garden by using heirloom plants to create flavorings, teas, foods, fragrance, even detergent—not out of need, but for the sake of curiosity, from the desire to experience everything these multifaceted plants (many originally grown for their practical uses) have to offer.

One thing has not changed. This is still a gardening-oriented book, written from the perspective of one gardener to another. I have grown nearly every plant I describe. Like many others, I struggle and try to learn from my mistakes. I have grappled with all the problems that ordinary gardeners experience from seed germination failure to "where can I stick this plant?" I hope that my efforts to act as a friendly guide to growing and landscaping with heirloom plants (helped by other gardeners' experience and comments along the way) will encourage a new generation of readers to continue to grow and celebrate our floral heritage.

In the most basic way, nothing has changed for me since I wrote the original *Heirloom Garden* nearly a decade ago. I still love the old plants for their easy, tolerant, robust ways, their endurance, their irreplaceable beauty, their extraordinary variety. What has changed is that the Three D's on this remote island—the Deck, the Dozer, and the satellite Dish—have in many instances displaced and destroyed many of the plantings I discovered and wrote about. But, at the same time, I have witnessed a revival of interest in heirloom plants from a new generation of local gardeners, eager to know all about "Grandmother's Shrub Rose" and other treasures from their family's past.

This interest in plant heirlooms is everywhere across the land, not only in the efforts of plant preservationists, say, to rescue antique sweet peas and reintroduce them to the public, but through the actions of ordinary backyard gardeners who share seeds of open-pollinated flowers through seed exchanges and make them available to commercial sources. Where a decade ago Essential Petunias—small-flowered, sweetly scented trumpets—were flowers to dream about, they are now available from specialty seed sources and noncommercial seed exchanges in a variety of forms including vining types. "Where have all the flowers gone?" I wondered a decade ago. In some ways I feel like Rip Van Winkle, waking up after a decade to find a transformed world of heirloom flowers in full bloom.

Acknowledgments

MY THANKS to the following enthusiastic gardeners and organizations for their generous help: Heather Apple, Heritage Seed Program; Verna Laurin, Historic Iris Preservation Society; Grant Wilson, general editor, Canadian Gladioli Society; Walter Oakes and Charles Holetick, International Lilac Society; Lily Shohan, Heritage Rose Group; Jeanette Lowe, Marigold Society of America; Arthur Haskins, Nova Scotia Dahlia expert; John Moe, Washington State Lily connoisseur; the late Audrey O'Connor, former editor, *Cornell Plantations,* and discerning gardener; Meg Yerger, Maryland Poeticus Daffodil collector; Robert Martin, membership secretary of the North American Gladiolus Council; Jim and Dotti Becker of Goodwin Creek Gardens for Lavender research; Rita Buchanan for plant dyeing information; Scott Kunst for permission to quote liberally from his Old House Gardens antique bulb catalog.

Thanks, too, to Ben Watson, my editor at Chelsea Green, for his continued support and faith in my work. Thanks are insufficient for my husband, Jigs, partner-in-all-things, whose double duty in the barn, the field, the buttery, and the study (sans computer) enabled me to write this book.

PART I

The Home Gardener's Guide to Growing, Preserving, and Landscaping with Heirloom Flowers

THE EDUCATION OF AN
HEIRLOOM FLOWER GARDENER

IN 1970 WE MOVED a Noah's ark of animals—two horses, two cows, miscellaneous chickens, cats, and a dog—750 miles northeastward to a 100-acre farm at the end of a dirt road on a remote peninsula on Cape Breton Island, Nova Scotia. After we had rebuilt the barn, plowed and planted the fields, restored the fences, and established vegetable and fruit gardens, I turned my attention to the ornamentals I'd inherited with the property: herbs, flowers, and shrubs planted close to the house on a knoll just beyond the front door. There were Lilacs, purple and white, their aging limbs spread over a wide area, almost touching one another. At the base of one, the ground was entirely covered with spotted-leaved Lungwort *(Pulmonaria officinalis)*—clusters of small pink and lilac-blue trumpets in the early spring—and nearby was an impressive clump of Tawny Daylilies *(Hemerocallis fulva),* once described as the floral symbol of our gardening past.

Struggling to survive on the same piece of ground were a few Mock Orange bushes and a group of Daffodils, known locally as the "French Lily" or "White Lily," most of whose buds never opened but expired within their papery covering. The few flowers I saw, though, were unforgettable: tight clusters of intensely fragrant, double white blooms.

A Rosebush sprawled in front of the house just under a window, its suckers spreading in every direction. I knew virtually nothing about Old Roses then. This one, I later learned, was 'Banshee', also known as the "Loyalist Rose," one of the most common at colonial sites all over the Northeast. (First described in 1773 and named by the Rose Society of America in 1928, it is thought to be a natural hybrid between the Alba Rose and a native species. 'Banshee' is available from a few specialty Rose sources, but is more easily obtained from an old garden.) When the flower opened, I discovered Old Rose essence for the first time, deep within the layers of blush pink petals.

Yellow Flag Iris *(Iris pseudacorus)* flourished in a large colony by the back door—

swordlike green leaves and small fleur-de-lis blossoms in a classic design I'd never seen before. I'd never seen the like of *any* of these plants, having grown up in the suburbs and spent my gardening time hoeing rows of string beans to feed my family. This small collection of ornamentals opened up a new world to me. I was attracted to the plants' pronounced scents, variety of forms (somewhat on the wild side), and charming, often quirky ways. Gradually I began to explore the area for other remnants of old gardens and plants.

The peninsula proved to be a rich hunting ground. Because of its isolation from the mainstream, untouched by fashion or development until relatively recently, old plantings here have remained undisturbed for many years. On deserted farms, up lonely glens and mountainsides named for the places the early 19th-century Highland Scottish settlers had left behind—Lewis, Skye, Barra—I found Foxglove, naturalized at the edge of woodland roads where no one had lived for at least fifty years; Peonies, growing among old spruce trees; the double-flowered Bouncing-Bet *(Saponaria officinalis* 'Flora Plena'), once a garden plant, now a roadside weed.

One midsummer day, a friend came by to tell me I'd better get over to see his folks' place before it was leveled by the 'dozer. (Even as I was discovering them, old gardens and plants were beginning to disappear.) Rounding a bend past Blackberries, wild Roses, and Jerusalem Artichokes, I found the house, built in 1878, the third one for a family of settlers from the Isle of Lewis in the early 1800s. The first settlers had spent the winter under a boat by the shore of the nearby lake. I stood on the falling-down porch and looked at the clear signs of a gar-

den: Daylilies, Yellow Loosestrife, Lilacs, Roses, the inevitable Rhubarb, and, at my feet, mats of Forget-me-nots and Columbine, long past blooming. Looking up, I saw the luxuriant Virginia Creeper adorned with clusters of small purple berries, the vine soaring to the peak of the house, past broken windows through which no one would ever look again, the house of my friend's parents, Dan Frank and Katie Flora, who had flailed oats till midnight and milked cows at dawn, yet had planted gardens of "use and delight."

These early experiences shaped my ideas about heirloom plants, which I then defined in a general sort of way as "the ones our ancestors grew." These plants, I thought, with their simple grace and charm, were close to the wild, unspoiled by human intervention. But as I became more involved with the subject of old ornamentals, I realized that curious gardeners had been tinkering with nature for centuries, that the subject was much broader and more complex than I had imagined. It was, ironically, the plight of a modern Hybrid Rose that put the designation "heirloom ornamental" in perspective for me, that made me confront the word *old* when applied to plants. What is old in this context? We have no trouble with plants introduced before the modern era, say 1900. But in the modern era, plant breeding, burgeoning as never before, has created thousands of new plants, and the pressure for their survival has been enormous. The market, in responding to ever-new offerings, tends to cast aside many worthy plants. In a way, we can say that the aging process in plant longevity has been speeded up. Plants enjoying tremendous popularity today may be on the preservationist list thirty years hence.

'Ma Perkins' was introduced to the world in 1952, the creation of the well-known plant breeder Gene Boerner. It is described in Peter Beales's English Rose catalog as "a superb Floribunda which must not be lost. Globular buds opening to cupped flowers of shell pink with salmon shading in well-spaced clusters on a bush with good and ample dark green foliage," and fragrant to boot.

I asked Mr. Beales, a noted Rose authority and author of *Classic Roses* (Collins/Harvill, 1985), if there was anything wrong with 'Ma', any blemish on her evident beauty that would explain why such a quintessential American Rose (bred in America, AARS winner, named after the 1940s folksy soap opera) had vanished from the American marketplace. Was 'Ma' a carrier of some dread disease, a poor performer in American gardens?

Mr. Beales responded that he was frequently baffled as to why Roses of such caliber disappear from commercial circulation. The only possible explanation, he suggested, is that, with sharpened marketing techniques, the public is led to believe that anything new must be better, and when sales drop off to a certain level, the older introduction is quickly dropped.

I began to understand that what constitutes an heirloom ornamental is open to interpretation. Heirlooms change over time and are not fixed absolutely, but represent valued possessions at different periods in history. Those plants that deserve our attention as heirloom gardeners can be as varied as the truly antique 16th-century double-flowered Dame's-rocket (where is it now?)—a naturally occurring sport of nature probably selected and reselected by generations of keen-sighted gardeners—as well as hybrid creations such as 'Ma'—deserving of attention, increasingly rare, and in danger of being lost to future generations of gardeners.

As I was drawn into the effort to find and preserve heirlooms, I met extraordinary heirloom gardeners such as Verna Laurin, then secretary of the Canadian Iris Society, who never intended to collect older Iris, she wrote, but "just grow ones that I like," which turned out to be more than one hundred varieties in a city backyard. From Maryland, I learned about Meg Yerger, who began growing Daffodils for an all-white garden many years ago and eventually had one of the largest collection of Poeticus-types in the world. "It would be nice if you could mention the names of the older Poets, so people will ask for them by name at specialist nurseries and so those places may unearth sources—'Dulcimer' (1913), 'Hexameter' (1927), 'Homer' (1898), 'Lights Out' (1938)"—all of which she described as beautiful and fragrant.

Locally, I found lovely Garden Phlox, developed from our native species, some of which couldn't have been more than thirty or forty years old. They were carefully tended, regarded as one of the family. I found Dahlias, passed around from hand to hand, from garden to garden, whose names were long forgotten but whose fat, homely roots were cherished by people who regarded them as "survivors," although they were probably introduced no earlier than the 1960s.

Just as my earlier experiences had shaped my idea of *heirloom*, my expanded knowledge contributed to a new vision, aptly summed up in Edward Hyams's description of worthy Lilies: easy, tolerant, robust, and enduring—to which I would add beautiful in some irreplaceable way, like 'Ma Perkins'.

> The market, in responding to ever-new offerings, tends to cast aside many worthy plants.

This is the vision that stands behind the wide selection of plants I have chosen to describe. I hope that those just becoming interested in the subject of heirloom ornamentals can experience their diversity as I have and make informed choices about what to grow and which aspects of heirloom plants to explore in more depth.

I believe that qualities such as easy, tolerant, robust, and enduring are virtues that appeal to many gardeners and that these values are most in tune with the kinds of gardens they want to create: informal, low-maintenance, attractive landscapes in harmony with the surrounding environment. As I have learned, the plants that fit this description include the silver-leaved Lungwort, tending to itself under the filtered shade of my old Lilac tree; the broad border of colorful Hybrid Dahlias that thrive at the edge of my neighbors' potato patch; and the 1942 'Blue Shimmer' Iris, an indestructible bearded type that I acquired in the 1970s and have moved more times that I care to remember, now regarded as an old favorite and antique in the world of Iris fanciers.

If one of the greatest pleasures of gardening is sharing, then how much greater is that pleasure when the sharing includes such a rich world of interesting and varied plants, our collective valued possessions.

The Heirloom Flower Garden Book

This book is designed to define the world I discovered—and thereby make it accessible to ordinary gardeners, while also enlarging the possibilities for the committed enthusiast. Both will enjoy meeting old garden friends and getting to know new ones.

The definition of *heirloom ornamentals* here is as follows: those plants introduced to American gardens from 1600 to 1950 (and a little beyond, to accommodate Iris and other plants defined as "antique" if they have been introduced in the past fifty years). This is a diverse group of herbs, flowers, shrubs, and vines, native flora and plants from around the world. It is broken down into two categories: (1) *Ancient* and *antique* types (the terms are almost synonymous, with *ancient* suggesting older), known and described as early as classical times. The plants in this group include many very hardy, nearly wild types that we associate with English cottage gardens. (2) *Middle-aged* types. These are hybrid variations on ancient and antique themes that began to appear in great numbers as the result of expanded knowledge about plant breeding toward the end of the 19th century.

Strictly speaking, *hybrids* are the result of cross-fertilization between two plant species, sometimes occurring naturally, but usually done on purpose. The horticulturalist uses the term more loosely to apply to any cross-fertilization between variant parents, such as the thousands of Glads and Iris created by crossing and recrossing cultivars. A *cultivar*, or *variety*, is any plant that arises from cultivation and is significant enough to name, as distinct from naturally occurring variations. You've probably heard the term *open-pollinated* (OP to the initiated). This means that the blossoms from the plants have been pollinated "in the open" by nature. Plants from any of the groups I have described are variously referred to as "antique" or "old-fashioned."

If you've grown only tamed types in your garden, you might like to become familiar with easily naturalized wild (OP) species, which, as I show, constitute a large and varied group of garden-worthy plants. If you've grown only the latest Hybrid Tea Rose, a whole world of ancient, antique, and modern classic Roses awaits you. Contrary to accepted wisdom, ours is a tradition rich in plants. If you're interested in edible landscapes, heirloom plants supply plenty of material for making delicious and useful products—from salt substitutes and jellies to homemade detergent. Directions for making such products are sprinkled throughout the book.

In Part 1, the reader will find detailed information and suggestions for growing, preserving or propagating, and landscaping with heirloom flowers based on my own thirty years of gardening experience, and what I have learned from other gardeners and experts. My intention throughout is to encourage people to grow and enjoy the plants that best exemplify our horticultural heritage rather than to confine myself to a strict guide to period plants, although those interested in the subject will find a great deal of useful material here.

At the heart of the book are the ninety-three plant portraits in Part 2. I have tried to balance historical information (to inform rather than overwhelm) with down-to-earth gardening instructions. These practical instructions appear near the end of each portrait under the heading "To Grow." Readers wanting more gardening information are referred to the bibliography, where I have noted especially helpful books.

Latin names throughout are based on common usage, drawn from *Hortus Third,* and supplemented by the more recent RHS Index of Garden Plants. It is most important for gardeners to have a rough familiarity with Latin names because common names, while charming, are unreliable for identification,

and you may want to know the precise name of the plant you admire so you can order it from a plant or seed source. For example, where I live, several different plants are known as "London-pride," but none is the lovely little Saxifrage *(Saxifraga umbrosa)* that most people associate with Gertrude Jekyll's cherished London-pride.

Common names are more than charming, which is why I have included so many of them. They, too, are part of our plant heritage, the stored wisdom and wit of countless generations of ordinary gardeners. They preserve interesting bits of history and often refer to a plant's outstanding physical characteristics in memorable images. Hurt-sickle, for instance, describes the way a mower's sickle was often caught in the wiry stems of *Centaurea cyanus* as it mingled with grain in the fields of Europe. Today we know this plant mainly by its Victorian name—Bachelor's-button—from its use as a boutonniere.

The dates of introduction represent the general period when a plant or group of plants was introduced to American gardens. The dates are drawn mainly from *Landscapes and Gardens for Historic Buildings* by Favretti and Favretti (American Association for State and Local History, 1978) and from the three-volume Leighton work (see Bibliography), supplemented, where necessary, with information from period literature, old plant lists, and assorted reference works. Specific dates of introduction may appear in the text or in the "Collector's Choice" section at the end of each portrait. Sometimes the date range covers several hundred years—for instance, 1600 to 1900 for Old Garden Roses.

Growing zones can be as difficult to ascertain as dates of introduction, since authorities do not always agree. The lower figure represents the coldest growing zone where the plant can be expected to survive the winter without protection; the higher number represents the warmest growing zone where a plant can be expected to perform satisfactorily. Growing zone figures are based on the U.S. Department of Agriculture's (USDA) Hardiness Zone Map (see page 294). As experienced gardeners know, you can push these limits by planting in microclimates (protected sites where extra moisture, protection from the wind, exposure to sun, and so on, are provided) depending on the requirements of the situation.

"Collector's Choice" lists species and the choicest cultivars and strains available (based on the opinions of experienced gardeners and experts), as well as any additional information (such as plant height, bloom season, and hardiness) not discussed in the text. *Strains*, by the way, are plant types resulting from carefully selected seeds from desirable variants *(sports)* in any plant population, the most famous examples of which are Reverend Wilkes's Shirley Poppies and 'Giant Shirley' Foxglove, both created from such variants. "Collector's Choice" is in many instances a much-needed guide for choosing among the wide variety of heirloom plants available in groups such as Tulips, Iris, and Daffodils, as well as a guide to their classification systems. You may need to know, for instance, what is an FD Dahlia, a Division 3 Narcissus, or an IB Iris. Specialty catalogs and plant organizations often assume such knowledge. All of the choices in this section reflect a concern for the varied growing conditions with which gardeners must contend. If, for instance, you're looking for an heirloom Lilac that is drought-resistant or extraordinarily hardy, you will find it here.

I have indicated, where possible, which choices are authentic heirlooms (usually dated) and which are in the spirit of heirlooms (designated *old style*). In the latter category is the list of Russell Hybrid Lupine cultivars, the originals of which wowed the Royal Horticultural Society judges in 1937 when Mr. Russell introduced them. Frankly, I don't know when those I list were introduced, but they certainly are in the spirit of the originals. Clearly, this is not a purist's approach to heirlooms.

Throughout the book I have noted especially fragrant or scented plants (flowers or leaves) with a floral symbol (❀). Fragrance is a characteristic that many heirloom gardeners prize, for it almost guarantees the presence of birds, bees, and butterflies in the garden for pollination and enjoyment.

I have often been asked whether a cottage garden is an heirloom garden. The term *cottage garden* has been used in a variety of contexts, most of which have very little to do with the historic cottage gardens of the English rural poor. Our conception of them has been largely idealized, but the current preoccupation with cottage gardens in America reflects a yearning for freer, more bountiful, and more varied plantings than the suburban ideal of the past fifty years. If you create a garden or a planting, no matter how small, with even a few of the extraordinarily varied plants described in this book, you will also have created an heirloom cottage garden that answers the needs of contemporary North American gardeners.

GROWING HEIRLOOM FLOWERS

❧

The love of flowers brings surely with it
the love of all the green world.

—LOUISA YEOMANS KING
(THE WELL-CONSIDERED GARDEN, 1915)

I F THE IDEAL HEIRLOOM GARDENER is one who grows and preserves heirloom plants to perfection, then the best example I know are old-timers, in town or country, who know every habit, every need of their beloved plants in their allotted ground, and thus know best how to satisfy them and increase them, usually by the simplest means. If you're interested in old plants, then I'm sure you've met them, too—someone in your neighborhood who has a way with plants, who always has roots and slips to share. Such gardeners use their limited repertoire of plants in ingenious, creative ways: as hedges, to frame plantings, in pots, as spectacular accents, or in ways of their own devising that I've never read about in books (much of what they do is original). The theme of the humble yet very successful gardener runs all through garden literature, and although such praise could be dismissed as condescending and romantic idealism, I have seen so many examples myself I know it is a simple truth. What these gardeners share, I think, besides a deep love of growing things, is the virtue of keen observation, one of the most important skills we can bring to garden-making. While they may seem to be the mythical green thumb gardeners, those happy souls who instinctively do the right thing every time, in fact they make mistakes, but they learn to correct them by close observation. Another point in their favor may be their limited resources, for in their thrift and self-reliance, they are pushed to master their craft.

In some ways, old-time cottage gardening mirrors my own experiences on this lonely peninsula, where I've had to improvise, to practice self-reliance as a fine art. This general guide combines what I've absorbed from the sort of gardeners I've described, what I've learned from decades of practice in my own allotted ground, and what I've found helpful from various printed sources (see Bibliography).

Plant Types

It's important to understand plant types so you'll be prepared for the possible disappearance of short-lived perennials after a few seasons or for the non-flowering clumps of foliage produced the first year by biennials. Understanding the growth cycles of your heirlooms will help you to prolong their life in the garden.

Hardy perennials survive for at least three growing seasons. They are of two types: herbaceous and its opposite, shrubby. Herbaceous types, like Bleeding-heart *(Dicentra spectabilis)* and Peony *(Paeonia)*, die down to the ground at the end of their growth cycle, then grow back up from soft aboveground growth at the beginning of the new growing season. Shrubby perennials, like Southernwood *(Artemisia abrotanum)* and Lavender *(Lavandula),* maintain woody growth above ground all year long, then, at the beginning of the new growing season, soft green growth sprouts from their woody stems.

Short-lived perennials don't usually survive more than two seasons, but they are so prolific with their seeds if growing conditions are favorable that the gardener never notices which are the mother plants and which the progeny. In some cases, new plants also sprout from the old. Examples of these types are Golden Marguerite *(Anthemis tinctoria)* and Feverfew *(Tanacetum parthenium).*

Tender perennials are tender to frost in varying degrees. If, for instance, you live in California (Zone 10) where winters are mild, you can grow Scented Geraniums *(Pelargonium)* to shrub size because they stay in the ground all year. Elsewhere, these plants are grown outside in tubs, then wintered-over indoors.

Biennials spend their first growing season putting down roots; their second season they throw up flowering stems, set seed, and then the cycle begins again; sometimes babies grow from the base of the mother plant. The classic biennial is Hollyhock *(Althea rosea).*

Annuals complete their entire growth cycle from seed to flower in one growing season. Sometimes, you will see the mainly European designations H.A. for hardy annual and H.H.A. for half-hardy annual in seed catalogs. A hardy annual can be directly seeded in the ground, like Poppies *(Papaver).* Half-hardy annuals, like Petunias, need to be started indoors, then planted out after the last frost.

Bulbs are the underground food storage warehouses for aboveground plants such as Tulips and Daffodils *(Narcissus).* There are hardy bulbs and tender bulbs. The bulbs of hardy types, like Tulips, remain in the ground over the winter because they require freezing to initiate new top growth the following season; in warm-winter areas, they may be treated as annuals and prechilled. Tender bulbs, on the other hand, cannot tolerate frost, so the "bulbs" or tubers of Dahlias, for instance, are lifted every fall after their tops have been exposed to frost, stored indoors over the winter, and then replanted in the spring. In warm winter areas, tender tubers can remain in the ground.

Vines are of two basic types: twining and tendril. Twiners include Scarlet Runner Beans *(Phaseolus coccinueus),* while those that climb by tendrils or tendril-like leaves include Sweet Pea *(Lathyrus odoratus)* and Clematis; Virginia Creeper *(Parthenocissus quinquefolia)* is a clinging tendril type. Each type requires a different kind of support and it may take some experience to determine how best to accommodate them. The twiners can be trained up strings and wires, the tendril sorts on netting or even chicken-wire, and the clingers, if planted close to a wall or tree trunk, will do fine on their own. If not given any support, vines make good ground covers. Although Roses aren't vines, those with long enough canes (6 feet or over) can be so treated if given some means of support—that is, trained along fences, over arbors, and around poles.

Growing from Seed

Louise Beebe Wilder claimed that gardeners could not experience the full joy of their craft unless they cared for their plants from seedhood to maturity. There are other good reasons, more prosaic, for growing heirlooms from seed. For one thing, for little effort and cost the gardener can raise a virtual army of seedlings for generous landscaping; for another, there may be no other way to obtain the plant if roots or cuttings aren't available.

Before you collect piles of seed packets, though, consider that seed-grown plants are variable in color and form. Some types, like *Achillea* 'The Pearl' don't come true from seed (no matter what the catalogs claim), while others, usually woody types like Lavender, are slow-growing; those that produce bulbous roots, like Chives, may take three years to produce a sizable clump.

That still leaves a lot of plants to grow from seed. Before you sow them, it's vital to understand the mechanics of germination, a subject often scanted in growing guides where the process is taken for granted in the phrase "after seeds germinate. . . ." Wait a minute! They never came up! I know from talking to many gardeners that germination failure is a source of anguish and concern.

Why, they want to know, did the seeds they planted with such great hope just disappear, vanish? Far from experiencing the joy and wonder of initiating the growing process, they feel a sense of loss, even shame.

The key to seed germination success is understanding that all seeds are inhibited from germination until conditions are favorable for their growth. What are those conditions? For most seeds, if they have been properly harvested and stored over the winter, they will germinate when exposed to warmth (about 70°F/21°C) and moisture. Others, like Columbine, require a period of prechilling or freezing (outdoors or in the fridge), exposure to light (Feverfew), darkness (Nasturtium), or presoaking or chipping of their hard seed coats (Lupine); these strategies for unlocking germination are referred to as *conditioning*. Some seeds require more than one kind of conditioning, while others germinate no matter what you do to them, and although more is known about seed germination than ever before, there is still an element of mystery about it all.

OUTDOOR SOWING

Direct-sowing outdoors in the spring is the best method for growing annuals that (1) need to be exposed to frost to germinate and dislike being transplanted, like Bachelor's-button and Poppies; or (2) germinate easily and are fast-growing, like Nigella, Nasturtium, Calendula, and Mallow *(Malva sylvestris)*.

I use outdoor fall-sowing in a cold frame for some perennials, like Lupine, that germinate better from prechilling or freezing outdoors than presoaking indoors. This way, nature does the work of breaking the hard seed coat, then providing the right temperatures of freezing and warming to ensure germination. Other easy-going perennials that bloom the first year from seed, like Mallows and Golden Marguerite, are also fall-sown to germinate the following season when the soil has reached the right degree of warmth. After they become well-established young plants, I move them to their permanent site.

COLD FRAMES

The primary requirement for outdoor sowing is weed-free, pre-dampened, friable, early-warming soil that allows water to penetrate, and, most important, to then drain away. For perennials, this is most easily achieved in a cold frame, a four-sided wooden structure built into a south-facing slope. Cold frames are usually covered with a window, sometimes hinged, of glass or plastic, that can be opened and closed according to conditions of warmth or cold, and filled deeply with the best loose soil enriched with fine compost. My cold frame measures about 4 feet wide and 16 feet long, with the back 9 to 12 inches higher than the front. At some point, I dispensed with windows and now use it rain or shine, in cold or warmth, for outdoor fall seeding (the seeded area can be covered with light mulch to protect seeds from blowing away or being washed out by rain), for temporary storage of extra and mail-order plants that need to be coddled before planting out, for wintered-over Pansies and Rose cuttings, or for any tough plant that needs a temporary home.

INDOOR SOWING AND GROWING

This method is best for slow-growing tender annuals like Petunias and Signet Marigolds, or ones that need a head start in cool climates, like Climbing Nasturtium and a variety of herbs. I prefer this method for per-

ennials, too, because, even though it takes more effort, I have more control over the process, and, I think, greater success.

Before I sow a single seed, I draw up a chart of all the plants I want to grow indoors, then divide them into groups (1, 2, 3) according to the number of weeks they need to be sown before the last frost date—for example, 12, 10, 8, 6, or 4 weeks. Counting back from the last frost-free date (mid-June here), I have a rough idea when to plant each group. In this way, the work is staggered and seedlings are at the best stage of maturity—not too leggy—when it's time to plant them outdoors. The chart is a seasonal record of all the plants I grew indoors, the conditioning method used, and its success or failure, an invaluable record for future reference.

Germination failure can be reduced to the following possibilities:

+ Seeds were planted too deep. The rule of thumb is to cover seeds with twice their thickness of soil; seeds smaller than a pinhead should be just pressed into the soil. If in doubt about depth, always sow shallow. Remember, seeds are small for the tremendous work they have to do.
+ Soil dried out or was soggy. Provide *even* moisture. Seeds must be in contact with moisture to germinate, but if the soil is soggy, they will rot.
+ Temperatures were too cold. The majority of seeds require steady, warm temperatures in the 70°F/21°C range (comfortable room temperature) to germinate.
+ Seeds were old or of poor quality. Some seeds retain their viability for years, like Feverfew, but germination rates decline

SAMPLE INDOOR SEEDING CHART

Name of Plant	Type	Start	Treatment	Germination Time
Anthemis tinctoria	P	8–12	S	8–14 (2)
Calendula	A	4–6	D, C	4–14 (3–5)
Callistephus	A	6–8	JC	8–15 (2–4)
Dianthus	Bi/P	10–12	freeze★ JC	7–21 (2–4)
Lathyrus latifolius	P	10–12	Soak	
Lavandula angustifolia	P	10–12	prechill★ L, S	4–90 (2–6)
Lobularia maritima	A	10–12	S	5–14 (1–2)
Lychnis coronaria	P	8–10	L, S	10–21 (5–7)
Malva sylvestris	A	6–8	JC	5–21 (3)
Nicotiana	A	8–10	L, S	5–20 (3–5)
Petunia	A	10–12	L, S	7–21 (3–6)
Rudbeckia	P	10–12	L, S	5–21 (3–5)
Salvia officinalis	P	10–12	JC	4–12 (5)
Salvia viridis	A	6–8	L–S	10–14 (3)
Saponaria ocymoides	P	10–12	prechill L, S	10–21 (7)
Tagetes tenuifolia	A	4–6	JC	5–15 (1)
Tropaeolum majus	A	4–6	D, C	7–12 (4)
Viola	P	10–12	prechill★ D	14–21 (1–6)

Key:

Type:
  A: annual
  Bi: biennial
  P: perennial

Start: *number of weeks before last expected frost*

Treatment *(same as conditioning):*
  L: *seeds need light to germinate*
  D: *seeds need darkness to germinate*
  S: *sow seeds on pre-moistened soil surface, just pressing them in*
  JC: *just cover seed with soil*
  C: *cover seeds with soil equal to twice their thickness*
  prechill: *spread seeds evenly (don't crowd them) on a moistened, doubled, strong paper towel; fold*

again and place in sandwich bag, loosely closed (seeds need air), in the fridge for two to three weeks. Prechilled seed usually germinates rapidly when sown on the soil surface
★ *prechilling is optional; seeds will germinate without it*

Germination Time: *number of expected days for seeds to germinate; those with a long period indicate irregular germination, i.e., some seeds may germinate very soon, others much later*

( ): *the actual number of days it takes seeds to germinate in my experience*

Note: *all of the above seeds germinate at room temperatures (roughly 70°F/21°C); fridge temperature (40°F/4°C) is sufficient for prechilling seeds*

over time, and it's possible that even commercial seed may be dead on arrival.

Like most gardeners who grow from seed, I've developed my own method:

1. I assemble Styrofoam cups (not more than 2½ inches deep), puncture a few drainage holes in the bottom, then fill cups with pre-moistened sterile Pro-Mix, a commercial seeding formula (this is one area where self-reliance needs a boost). Using warm water, I water in a very small amount of fungicide, just enough to prevent damping-off, a fungal disease that commonly attacks seedlings, causing them to keel over and die. Damping-off is encouraged by unsterilized seeding medium, overwatering, and fluctuating temperatures, especially on the cool side (a problem in an old, drafty farmhouse like mine).

2. I sow seeds according to their needs: just press those that have been prechilled into the soil surface because they need light to germinate; sow others at the recommended depth (if in doubt, I plant shallow). Sow dustlike seeds (such as Petunias) with a bit of sand.

3. I set the cups in washed Styrofoam supermarket meat trays, loosely wrapped in light plastic (dry-cleaning bags work well) to maintain moisture. Place the cups with seeds that need darkness to germinate on separate trays with a newspaper cover on top of the plastic.

4. Set the trays on an old plastic-wrapped heating pad turned to "Me-dium," under a 20-watt fluorescent bulb turned on all day. Bottom heat, the key to rapid germination, is very important. A heating cable would work as well.

5. As soon as seeds sprout, I move each cup in turn under a set of two 4-foot fluorescent growlight tubes mounted in an old bookcase, always with a Styrofoam tray under them for bottom watering (with warm water). I'm not very scientific about it: lights are turned on in the early morning and turned off in the evening before I retire. If the seedlings are very crowded, I thin them by cutting some off at ground level with a small pair of scissors. (Never pull them at this stage; they're too fragile.) With their plastic blanket removed, seeding cups now dry out under the lights and need to be watered frequently.

6. When the seedlings have developed true leaves (not the ones that unfolded from the sprouted seed), they are transplanted to plant cells (2 inches or a little larger, depending on the expected growth of the seedling) or whatever containers are on hand, but I prefer the little cell-packs (used and reused) because, being narrow, they force seedlings to develop roots. Also, because I don't have a lot of space to work with, they take up little room for the plants they hold. I make potting soil from equal parts sifted compost and Pro-Mix, amended for every gallon with several handfuls of vermiculite and perlite (the first retains moisture, the latter promotes

drainage). Seedlings are carefully forked out of their cups by clumps, laid out on a tray, then picked up by their leaves and planted deeply in the plant cells—singly or in clumps, depending on their type and vigor—and the soil is firmed around them.

7. After the transplants are watered with water-soluble fertilizer to overcome transplanting shock, they are placed on Styrofoam trays once more, then placed away from light for 24 hours before being returned to the growlights.

8. Seedlings are gradually introduced to a single-pane, unheated greenhouse, where they thrive in natural light and cool, though not freezing, temperatures, until they are ready to be planted out.

Soil

Heirloom plants are generally easygoing, and although they may persist for years even when neglected, they flourish when given the soil conditions they prefer. Like most garden plants, the majority of heirlooms grow well in what is called "ordinary garden soil," which means loamy, well-drained, moderately enriched ground, slightly acidic (in the pH 6.5 range; 7 is neutral). The pH is important, for if it is too high (alkaline) or too low (acidic), plants won't be able to absorb nutrients in the soil, no matter how rich it is.

There are, of course exceptions. Rhododendrons need acid soil. Lavender prefers a "sweet" (alkaline) soil and dry conditions with "sharp drainage" (water drains quickly

off the roots). Lungwort *(Pulmonaria),* Soapwort *(Saponaria),* and Bee Balm or Bergamot *(Monarda)* are not really happy unless the ground is "evenly moist" (never dries out), while others, like Yellow Flag Iris *(Iris pseudacorus),* actually prefer "wet feet" (having their roots in water). Then there are those plants like annual Mallows that will only produce quantities of bloom, rather than leaves, when they are grown in unimproved, unenriched soil. To sweeten soil (raise the pH level) spread lime (calcium carbonate) on the soil at the recommended rate, then work it in. Calcium sulfate, iron sulfate, and aluminum sulfate all lower the pH level, making it more acidic, but too much can be harmful, so it's best to stick to high-acid but less concentrated organic matter like sawdust, bark, or manure.

Some gardeners, blessed with the porous, naturally fertile soil that most plants require, may only need to add organic matter every season to keep the ground in good tilth (loose and crumbly) and fertility: compost and manure add the basic nutrients of nitrogen, phosphorus, and potassium in varying degrees. Grass clippings add nitrogen; bonemeal is a great source of phosphorus and some nitrogen (look on the bag to make sure it is high in phosphates, for not all bonemeals are created equal); and wood ashes add potassium. All of these materials, except for bonemeal, are called "soil conditioners" because they affect soil structure and tilth. Other organic amendments that condition the soil but do not add much in the way of nutrients are sawdust, straw, and peat moss, among others. All organic matter is vital to the health of the soil because as it breaks down it creates an environment where microorganisms go about their all-important business of converting nitrogen and other nutrients into forms that plants can absorb. Conditioners can be spread on top of the soil to break down over the winter, then worked into the soil, dug into planting holes, or used as a mulch.

Because it is available, we use a great deal of sawdust and wood chips to improve the tilth of the soil. Gardeners are often warned against using fresh or partially aged sawdust on gardens because it robs the soil of nitrogen as it breaks down, but we have not found it to be a problem since the compost we use to replace soil in our raised beds (see below) is already high in nitrogen. Where it is used as a thick mulch, sawdust becomes incorporated into the soil in a single season. It's nice to think of all those trees returning to the earth to grow my heirloom flowers.

If, despite the lavish use of organic matter, germination and general plant growth decline, your soil may need a boost from the more concentrated nutrients found in fertilizers, either organic or inorganic; the latter is often referred to as "chemical," which is misleading, since all plant nutrients are chemical compounds. Whatever their source, these fertilizers list their particular formula on the front of the bag, stating the percentage of nitrogen (N), phosphorus (P) and potassium (K). If you are in doubt as to which nutrients your soil requires, you can purchase a soil-testing kit or inquire about testing from your local agricultural extension service. But you can usually tell what your soil needs by what it grows (and doesn't grow). Excessive soft, leafy growth at the expense of bloom, for instance, indicates abundant nitrogen, but not enough phosphates for good root and bud production, or potassium for general

growth. Never use more fertilizer than is directed and always water it into the soil. Most gardeners I know follow a middle course, using organic matter to build and maintain good soil tilth, and fertilizer to supply nutrients that may be lacking.

Compost is so important to the health of the garden soil that every heirloom gardener should establish a compost heap, but bear this in mind: it takes a lot of waste to produce a small amount of compost. Do not be discouraged, though, for whatever the amount, it is a treasure, like gold, that adds value to your soil. There are many recipes for making the perfect heap, but there is no mystery to it. Basically, organic matter—leaves, plant and animal waste, old hay, shredded or crumpled newspaper—is piled up within an enclosure (it can be made of wood, wire, brick, or any rigid material), and the contents are turned at least once a year, preferably more often, to speed decomposition by providing oxygen. The original heap, when thoroughly decomposed, will be reduced in volume by half, and the finished compost will be dark, moist, and crumbly like the best soil.

My husband, Jigs, made our household compost bin (we have a separate, larger one for barn refuse) from wooden timbers in a partially shaded area to reduce the need to water (dried-out compost rots very slowly). The bin is 10 feet long and 5 feet wide, and it is divided into two bins, each 5 feet by 5 feet, which are open at the far end for shoveling out the finished compost. When the first bin is full it is turned into the second, and a new heap started in the now empty first bin, so there are always two heaps on the go: one ready to use and one decomposing. We always make sure that decomposing fruits, vegetables, or manure are well-covered with plant waste to discourage flies. Odor is never a problem, for a well-regulated heap has a pleasant, earthy aroma.

The length of time it takes to turn organic waste into nutrient-rich compost depends on how frequently you turn the pile; whether you keep the pile moist, not wet; the ratio of "brown" material (leaves, straw, sawdust) to "green" material (grass, vegetable and fruit waste, manure); and whether chunky matter is shredded or reduced before it is composted. With diligence, you can make compost in as little as two to four weeks. Just turning the pile regularly, however, will help ensure finished compost in four to eight months.

Where soil conditions are extreme—either heavy, compacted clay or thin sand—it may be counterproductive to try to improve them. I speak from experience. Even after adding tons of rotted manure and other organic matter to our garden soil over fifteen years, we had little to show for it, not even enough loose soil to cover carrot seeds. Standard advice to remove clay and replace it with better soil, we discovered, created sinkholes that to this day need constant refilling. So we established raised beds enclosed by logs and filled deeply with well-rotted compost amended with sawdust and fertilizer as I have described. The design of the beds varies according to what we want to grow in them: vegetables, fruits, flowers, herbs, or roses. There are several advantages to this growing strategy: beds can be established instantly even on sod ground (see page 19), no digging is ever required, and, since germination is improved, plants shade out the weeds rather than the other way around.

Planting

Hardy perennials of all types are usually planted in the ideal conditions of early spring or fall when the weather is cool and moist. Planting holes need to be prepared beforehand, taking into account the depth and width required to accommodate the roots. Mix in a couple of handfuls of bonemeal, water the hole, then position roots over a mound of soil so they point downwards to ensure good drainage. Fill in the hole, tamp down the soil to firm the plant in place, but leave a little depression for the temporary collection of rainwater which might otherwise be lost. (The depression can be filled in after the plant is well established; sufficient water is vital now.) It's a good idea to mulch around the plants (don't cover the depression) to keep the soil cool and moist and to discourage weeds. Even if weeds grow through the mulch, they'll be easy to pull through the softened soil.

If for some reason (hard ground, weak back), you cannot make your planting hole as large as recommended, do not despair. Instead, simply trim back the plant's roots as needed: a rule of thumb is for the roots and top growth to be about equal in size or mass. After planting, mulch the area more heavily than usual: lay down a double thickness of newspaper about 6 inches from the main stem, cover this with a thick layer of rotted manure or compost, topped by a thick layer of straw, wood chips, or whatever organic material you have available. The mulch will eventually turn into friable soil that will encourage rooting. This method can be used to plant shrubs and roses, too, in sod-covered ground.

Keep a sharp watch out for slugs, who find life underneath mulch very pleasant. My strategy for dealing with them, and with pests and diseases in general, is largely cultural. That is, I look for ways to deter infestations by denying them a habitat (see "Fall Cleanup" on page 20 and under individual plant entries). In the case of slugs, I try to keep garden edges clear of weeds and grass, and I routinely inspect their favorite hiding places—at any time of day, not just in the evening—and not only under mulch but under and between barriers, boards, rocks, and lush plant growth, where I sometimes find whole families taking their ease. All of them go into a small plastic container that I take with me into the garden, then later I dispose of them in the woodstove or by drowning them.

Annuals, on the other hand, often have to be planted out in less than ideal conditions, when the weather is hot, dry, and windy, and when it is hard to follow standard advice about planting on cloudy, windless days (to protect young plants from wilting). I use this method, which works very well even in adversity:

1. Pre-water planting holes; gently pre-water (don't drench) plant containers, so plants slip out without root disturbance after being turned upside down (keep one hand over the top to catch the plant). This is where plant cells prove invaluable for the strong roots they encourage.
2. Plant deep, right up to the bottom leaves, and close together (at the low end of recommended spacing) to make use of available ground moisture and to encourage shading.

3. Fertilize with a dilute solution (by half) of a soluble plant food high in phosphates and potash.

Maintenance

TRIMMING

Heirloom plants growing in rich soil do not usually need extra nutrients during the growing season, but to keep them healthy and blooming it is vital to trim them according to type. Annual Sweet Alyssum *(Lobularia maritima),* for instance, needs shearing after its first flush, so that it can produce a new crop of flowers. Perennials such as Yarrow, Soapwort, Bellflower, and repeat-flowering Roses should be routinely deadheaded or pruned (their spent blooms clipped off with their stems) to promote continued flowering, while others, like Lupines, Sweet Cicely *(Myrrhis odorata),* and Oriental Poppies, should be cut almost to the ground after blooming to encourage a fresh mound of attractive foliage. Trimming and cutting back in a drought, when plants quickly go in and out of bloom, redirects the plant's overtaxed energy into life-sustaining foliage growth, holding out hope for rebloom in more favorable conditions.

To control the growth of tall, weak-stemmed plants like Golden-glow *(Rudbeckia laciniata* 'Hortensia') that might otherwise need staking, cut back by half when the plants are midway through their growth cycle. You may sacrifice flowers to a shorter, bushier plant, but if you detest staking (as I do), this is effective.

WATER CONSERVATION

A prolonged dry spell, exacerbated by drying winds, is a trying time for gardeners,

INSTANT NO-DIG
RAISED BEDS ON SOD GROUND

*I*f you have sufficient time, establish raised beds in the fall to give the soil a chance to settle. The first season, plant all annuals in the perennial bed since, being mostly shallow-rooted, they don't need such deep soil. The following season, the sod beneath the bed will begin breaking down, creating more favorable conditions for deeper-rooted perennials. But since we don't live in a perfect world, you may not be able to arrange this—in which case, follow these directions.

1. Lay down plastic sheets over sod ground for annuals and shallow-rooted perennials, or a thick layer of newspaper for roses and other perennials, except for those with a long taproot (see Note below).

2. Enclose the bed area with barriers: logs, boards, bricks, stone . . . whatever barrier is used, it can be softened by planting trailing plants to hide sharp edges; if plastic is extended beyond the edges of the barrier it will discourage weeds from entering the bed.

3. Cover the edges next to the barrier with wood shavings or other mulch in which shallow-rooted plants like Forget-me-not and Viola will seed themselves, creating a barrier frill.

4. Fill the enclosure with rough compost.

5. Stomp into place and let it settle for a week or two.

6. Top up the bed with soil enriched with finished compost.

7. Let the soil settle before planting.

8. Since the area will be intensively cultivated, it will be necessary to add a thick layer of compost to the soil every season in the spring or fall to maintain a depth of about eight inches.

Raised beds can be established instantly even on sod ground, no digging is ever required, and, since germination is improved, plants shade out the weeds rather than the other way around.

Note: For plants like Lovage that have a long taproot, make a slit in the sod ground with a sharp spade and plant the root in the opening. Close up the opening by pressing the sides together with your heel. Mulch the area heavily with a thick layer of compost topped with rotted sawdust, all of which will eventually become good soil without digging.

but low-tech strategies can make a difference. Wooden or plastic tubs, placed underneath downspouts, are positive landscaping features, as well as a source of stored rainwater. Graywater, reused household water from sinks or showers (not from the toilet), not only keeps plants moist, but adds nutrients, so in this sense it can be regarded as a fertilizer. But it is strong and should be used full strength only on established perennials and shrubs (including Roses); dilute by half with plain water before using it on annuals.

You can also reuse washing-machine water: Direct the drain hose into 6-gallon plastic jugs stored alongside the machine, and stay close to make sure they don't overflow. Use liquid laundry detergent to avoid sodium salts, harmful to roots, that might be in found powdered detergents.

Container-grown plants benefit from a thick mulch (moss works wells), deep, rather than shallow containers, and some shading from the sun. They should be grouped together for easier watering.

It's possible, even in a drought and with limited water resources, to move plants from one place to another when they are in full bloom (true gardeners will understand this need). If the spirit moves you and will not be denied (wrong color, wrong place) try this: Pour a bucket of water over the plant you want to move; dig it up with as much of the root soil as you can; replant; pour another bucket of water over the plant; then mulch and water daily until it has fully recovered (dilute graywater is great for this).

Fall Clean-up

End-of-season maintenance is critical for the continuing health of the heirloom garden. In our love for plants so close to nature, we may develop the attitude of "let nature take its course," but as plants grow, bloom, shed their leaves, go to seed, and decay, the refuse that naturally piles up around them creates very comfortable winter quarters for insects and fungal diseases. After plantings are cleaned of debris and the ground has started to freeze, I spread protective mulch over the area (about 2 inches deep), heaping it up around plants like Lavender and Roses that are especially vulnerable to freezing and wind. I prefer to use a mulch of compost, horse manure, or wood chips, for unlike evergreen boughs that need to be removed in the spring, these other materials eventually break down into soil to become a source of continuing life and health for my heirloom plants.

PRESERVING THE HEIRLOOM GARDEN

IT IS IMPORTANT for heirloom gardeners to understand the principles behind plant propagation—seed saving, root division, and cuttings—because mastery of these methods ensures the survival of rare or choice strains that may not be readily available. With an assured surplus of such plants in whatever form, the heirloom gardener will be helping to preserve our horticultural heritage. This bounty can be shared with others, another strategy in the effort to preserve heirloom ornamentals.

Brother Gilbert Koster, a gardening friend who has taught me a great deal, embodies the ideals of heirloom gardening. He not only knows how to preserve and propagate his treasures (some very old strains), but he achieves results with the utmost simplicity and economy—the kind that underlies conservation in its fundamental sense.

I once asked him how he created his flower gardens more than twenty years ago, carved by hand out of scrub woodland. He said that someone had given him a few Dahlia tubers. He made stem cuttings from them in late winter, thus creating dozens more identical plants (see the Dahlia plant portrait in Part II for directions). He sowed annual and biennial seeds among them and saved the annual seeds at the end of the first season. By the following spring, he had hundreds of robust seedlings growing in an improved cold frame. (He had enclosed a small area on a southern slope with boards and had covered it with a sheet of clear plastic attached to a stick so it could be easily unrolled; on cold nights, he covered the cold frame with an old blanket.)

Seed Saving

Now, years later, inspired by his methods, I too have become an ardent seed saver, not only for my own gardens but to stock my modest seed business under the label "Jo Ann's Kitchen & Garden" (see Sources). Seed collecting for me has become inseparable from gardening itself, a natural part of the whole growing cycle that begins when I sow the first flower seeds in early spring. In late summer and fall, I walk along the garden path with my basket of collecting tools—paper bags, envelopes, marker, clippers—aware of the diversity of fruits and what I must do to harvest them properly: Johnny-jump-ups, I notice, discharge seeds as their pods split apart, so I must not wait too long to pick them; shaker-holders like Poppies, Columbine, and Foxglove spill their seeds if even lightly jostled, so I take care to avoid them unless I am collecting them; others, like Black-eyed-Susan and Mallows hold their seeds in tightly packed heads and rounds that are not always easy to pull apart.

Follow this guide for seed saving.

1. Choose several plants of the same type whose seeds you want to save (insurance in case one of the plants meets with misfortune). You thereby increase the likelihood of discovering worthwhile sports. Don't hesitate to save seeds from hybrids. Brother Gilbert has been doing so for years. These may differ from their parents, but they often do so in interesting and desirable ways.

2. Harvest seeds when the capsules have turned light brown but before they open. Sort out stems, leaves, and debris, then put the seedpods in individually labeled paper bags (I reuse letter envelopes for small amounts of seed). I leave stems on pods that need postharvest ripening or have possible use in floral crafts.

3. Spread out the seeds indoors in a dry, sunny spot like a windowsill. Don't crowd the different groups, since one type can easily mingle with another; if Johnny-jump-ups are left in their capsules, they literally jump all over the place, as do Hollyhocks. Put each kind of seed in separate dishes, trays (I reuse the Styrofoam meat trays from seed germinating), or boxes (deep for jumping seeds); I sometimes leave seeds in their collecting bags and envelopes if they are already partially dry. Seeds in tightly packed heads can be removed now or when dry.

4. Labeling is very important because some seed types look alike (such as the various Mallows); if you are saving a particular color, make note. Even if you think you will remember what's in the bag by the time the seeds are dry, trust me, you won't. I use a felt-tip marker or crayon, which lasts longer than pencil or ballpoint pen.

5. Some seeds like Poppies will be dry in a few days, while others, like Lupines, should be left alone for weeks, after which the ripened seeds will push out of their pods by themselves.

6. Work over spread newspaper when sorting seeds (separating them from their pods, capsules, or heads). Once they are shaken, rubbed, pressed out, or removed in some way from their outer covering, separate them from accumulated chaff by straining them (a kitchen strainer or colander works well), by gently blowing across the seed pile to dislodge chaff, or by carefully lifting off the chaff.

EVERLASTINGS

*P*reserving flowers and pods for winter enjoyment indoors has a long history in our gardening tradition. Pods, flowers, and foliage are easily dried by hanging plants upside down in bunches out of direct light or by laying them out, well spaced, on cookie sheets to dry in a just-warm oven (set no higher than 150°F/65°C).

As you harvest seeds, for instance, you will notice the diverse forms and subtle colorings of their pods. But that is not all, for later you will discover how they may be transformed in appearance after they have completely dried and discharged their seeds. Round Silver Dollar pods change from dirty beige to translucent silver with the removal of the papery disks that cover their seeds. Lupine's pealike pods assume unsuspected grace in their twisted shapes, silvery gray color, and furry texture. In the fall, look for other everlasting pods among wild grasses, flowers, and ferns. Wherever you find them, be sure to cut stems sufficiently long (they can be trimmed later). Most pods will be nearly dry, but if not, place hard-stemmed types upright in a jar, and bunch and hang up soft-stemmed kinds. For best (and quickest) results, don't crowd them.

These are my favorite pods to dry for bouquets and wreaths (I'm sure you will discover others):

Butterfly Weed	Love-in-a-mist *(Nigella)*
Clarkia	Lupine
Clematis	Poppy *(Papaver somniferum)*
Columbine	Rose Hips *(Rosa* spp.)
Garlic Chives *(Allium tuberosum)*	Silver Dollar *(Lunaria annua)*
Iris	

These are some of my favorite flowers and foliage to dry for bouquets, wreaths, and pressed floral crafts. Always pick flowers when they are dry (not wet from rain or dew), either when they are just beginning to open or when they are in fresh bloom.

Bachelor's-button	*Hydrangea paniculata* 'Grandiflora'
Bee Balm	(in pink stage)
Calendula	Lady's Mantle *(Alchemilla mollis)*
Chives	Rose (small flowers and buds)
Costmary (pressed leaves)	Yarrow (especially *Achillea ptarmica*
Dahlia	'The Pearl')
Double Feverfew	'Zebrina' Mallow (pressed flower)

7. Funnel seeds from the newspaper into labeled envelopes or jars placed in a cool, dry place. I use jars for larger amounts, and envelopes, filed alphabetically in a shoebox, for smaller amounts. The temperature of the storage area should never exceed 95°F (34°C).

In my experience, even imperfectly stored and harvested home-saved seeds usually germinate better than store-bought ones. Seeds of Painted Sage *(Salvia viridis),* for instance, have a very high germination rate even when sown inside their capsules.

To test for germination. After storing over the winter, space out a round number of seeds (twenty to fifty) on a moist (not soggy) doubled paper towel laid on a flat dish, then covered with clear plastic. Place the covered dish anywhere there is a source of steady, 70°F (21°C) ambient heat, and check daily to make sure the towel is still moist. After two weeks, or possibly much sooner, count how many seeds of the total amount have sprouted and you will have a good idea of their germination rate, as well as how long it takes them to germinate.

Note: To ensure that heirloom strains are kept pure, some seed savers use handpollination. Brother Gilbert takes a more casual approach, gathering naturally pollinated ripened seeds from the strains he wants to keep, then storing and sowing them separately from other types.

To hand-pollinate. Cover the buds with cheesecloth bags before they open. Do this on different plants of the same strain. When the buds open and the pollen is being re-

leased, remove the bags, and with a small paintbrush rub the pollen from one flower onto another. If the plants being pollinated are close to each other, rub one flower against another. Then bag the blossoms again so that no bee can visit them. Don't remove the bags until the seeds have ripened. Soak the paintbrush in alcohol for five to ten minutes and wash and dry it before reusing.

Wintering Annuals

Another way to preserve annuals is to winter them over indoors and replant them the following season. This works with Petunias, Nasturtiums, Sweet Alyssum, and Nicotiana—plants that are short-lived perennials in their native habitat. Wintering gives you a head start on blooming the following season.

1. Cut back and pot up garden plants four to six weeks before the last frost.
2. Put the potted plants in a shed before bringing them indoors so they can soften up (the reverse of plant hardening). Place them in a cool, sunny window and water them as little as possible without causing wilting. (The point is to conserve energy for the spring push).
3. In late winter, when the plants begin to show signs of new growth, start watering them more regularly and fertilize them weekly with a dilute (half-strength) solution of plant food.
4. Replant them in early spring or when appropriate by tapping on the bottom of the plant container so the whole plant slides out without disturbing its

roots. It will probably be pot-bound and slide out easily, especially if the soil is damp (not wet).

ANNUAL STEM CUTTINGS

An alternative method of wintering annuals is to take *stem cuttings* in late summer (six to eight weeks before the last frost) or anytime when there is sufficient stem growth and steadily increasing temperatures of 70 to 80°F (21 to 28°C) for about ten days. Since the "annuals" become woody after their second season, you will eventually need to preserve them by doing the following:

1. Pick healthy lateral stems. Make a clean, sharp cut at an angle just below a node where the plant's leaves are joined to the stem. The cutting should be 4 to 6 inches long. Remove all the lower leaves, leaving the upper ones to encourage rooting.
2. Dip the stems in water, then in rooting hormone. Shake off excess powder. Plant the stems deeply and firmly in a moistened soilless mix or a sand-vermiculite mixture in a clean cottage cheese container (or something similar) with a slit cut in the bottom for drainage. Stem cuttings root best when crowded together. Those placed on the outer edges also seem to do best.
3. Cover the container with thin, clear plastic to create a moist mini-greenhouse. Check the container daily to make sure excess moisture isn't collecting. If it is, lift the plastic a bit. When the cuttings are growing well, gradually remove the plastic over the period of a couple of days, first untucking it from around the container, then lifting it halfway off, then all the way, so the cuttings gradually become accustomed to normal growing conditions. If they are well-rooted, they should respond favorably to this treatment. Leave the cuttings in the container about two weeks after they have started growing.
4. Repot the well-rooted cuttings in regular potting soil and plant them out as usual with other annuals when all danger of frost has passed.

Plant Division

This is the simplest way to increase perennials (and be assured that your new plants will be identical to the old ones). Some plants need dividing every three years, while others, such as Bleeding-heart, can be left undisturbed indefinitely. A general rule of thumb is that if you find you have to divide a plant every year because of its vigor, plant it in a naturalized setting where it can let go and enjoy itself.

Division is very simple. Cut up (most likely chop) the plants into the desired number of pieces, making sure each piece is vigorous (that is, it has plenty of roots and growing tips). Plants that bloom in the spring should be divided in the fall; those that bloom in the fall should be divided in the spring. Always discard woody pieces.

Any growing medium that encourages root formation can be used for all the propagation methods that follow. You can use sand, a sand and peat mixture, potting soil, or some other medium.

Softwood and Hardwood Stem Cuttings

Use this method to propagate shrubs and vines outdoors in a trench or cold frame. You can use rooting hormone or not, as you choose. Many plants will root well without it.

Softwood stem cuttings (take in summer). Use a sharp knife to cut a 3- to 8-inch length at the node, where the leaves join the stem. Remove the lower leaves and insert the cutting in moist sand up to half its length. Rooted plants can be removed to a cold frame or nursery bed for at least one growing season before being planted in their permanent site. It takes two years from cutting the stem to planting it out permanently in the garden. Exceptions are very vigorous plants.

Hardwood stem cuttings (take in the fall). Take 6- to 10-inch stem cuttings with a sharp knife or clippers. The cut should be ½ inch below the lowest bud and ½ inch or more above the uppermost bud. Tie these stems in bundles (as many as two dozen is okay) and bury them horizontally in moist sand. This is a good way to establish many plants to make a hedge.

In the spring, plant the stems 2 to 4 inches apart in a trench almost covered with soil so that the top bud is at ground level. Water the soil during dry spells. Cuttings should be well established by the end of their second season in the trench. They can then be planted in their permanent site.

A Simple Way to Propagate Old Garden Roses

This method can be used to propagate Old Garden Roses that you find growing neglected in abandoned gardens or other sites.

1. Take 12- to 18-inch side shoots from stems anytime in the summer after they have flowered. Pull, rather than cut, these off the bush, so that each stem has a "heel" from the cane from which it was growing.
2. Remove the bottom leaves and stick the cuttings in rooting hormone, then in soil in your cold frame. Set them 4 inches deep and 6 inches apart, cutting back the tops so that each has at least three leaves. Do not let the soil dry out.
3. In the fall, cover each cutting with a glass canning jar and leave it in place until the following spring, when the cutting should be rooted. Harden it gradually by tipping the jar to let in air. Remove the rooted plants to a nursery bed and plant them out the following season in their permanent site.

Layering

Use this method with shrubs or vines. Some of these will layer themselves, forming roots where branches or vines touch the ground. When the offshoots are rooted, sever them from the mother plant and replant them in a nursery bed for another season unless they are especially vigorous. To layer a branch or vine, follow these directions.

✦ Make a slit on the point of the branch or cane you want to root. Bury it in 3 to 4 inches of soil, pegging it down securely so it will stay in place. During the following growing season, sever the rooted plant from its parent and proceed as described.

◆ To make many plants from one branch, make slits along it, then peg it down and bury the whole branch or cane in 3 to 4 inches of soil, leaving the growing tip exposed. Proceed as described.

Propagating and Preserving Bulbs

Bulbs of various types, hardy or tender, produce offspring in the form of bulblets. These can be replanted in a nursery bed for at least two seasons, then planted our permanently. If you need to dig up bulbs you find growing in neglected gardens or elsewhere, follow this general procedure:

◆ It's very important to wait until the leaves have died down after the plant has flowered (this could take four to six weeks with Daffodils). Carefully loosen the soil in a small area of the planting, using a spading fork so you won't damage the bulbs. Carefully lift out each bulb, put it in a sunny spot to dry, and then replant it in the appropriate season.

◆ Alternatively, dig up the bulb with a good ball of dirt around the roots, then replant it immediately. Water it well.

No-Dig Garden Renovation

You may be lucky enough to buy a house with an overgrown planting that could become the starting point of your heirloom garden, but don't be hasty. Unless you are calling in a professional landscaper, you have the luxury of creating a new garden from the old in a relaxed way, one that evolves naturally from your particular needs, both practical and aesthetic, one that in the long run is more satisfying (but not necessarily perfect). If you dig up the garden prematurely you may unwittingly destroy a desirable heirloom that was less noticeable than its more vigorous neighbors. Be cautious in removing shrubs since they take years to grow to maturity. Those that you know you want to keep should be pruned (if early-blooming like Lilacs, prune them in the late winter or spring; if mid- or late-summer-blooming, prune after they flower). At this point, moderate pruning—removal of one-third of the overgrown branches—is adequate.

Try to envision the restored garden bed and its relation to the house. Is the old site the best place for the new garden? Perhaps you have removed or added on a feature such as a porch and you would prefer a planting closer to or further from the house. If the old garden is now shaded with trees, you can consider removing or thinning them, or you can concentrate on growing shade plants (what seems like a drawback could be an opportunity).

The first season confine your gardening to container plants and hanging baskets while you observe what is growing, beginning in the early spring with bulbs and continuing through the fall with Phlox and other late bloomers. At this stage, it is most important to observe and record: draw a rough diagram of the garden, recording location, bloom time, color, and name, if possible, of all the plants. Then begin your planting campaign in the fall by laying down a thick organic mulch, something rich in nutrients that will both feed the soil and soften it. The following spring, start weeding and dividing. It may not be possible to dig up huge, hardened clumps of Daylilies and Iris all at once, but by softening the soil, digging up plants in early spring, and replacing them with fresh young roots, you will achieve your goal in a few seasons. (I have reclaimed beds wholly overrun with mint in this way with no digging.)

To enlarge an existing planting, spread a black plastic sheet, weighted down with rocks, over the additional ground; old phone books work well as anchors, too, when sodden from rain. In the spring, when you remove the plastic, you will find the ground softened and the weeds sufficiently killed to proceed with planting after adding a thick layer of compost or aged manure. If you decide to establish a planting on sod ground, spread a double thickness of newspaper over the area in the fall, then add heavy mulch, and, the following spring, plant with fresh roots and divisions from the old garden.

The secret of success with any of these methods is to strike a balance between the removal of old plants and a simultaneous planting of new ones. By following the propagation techniques in the previous section, the new heirloom garden will soon look as if it had always been there.

If you cannot decide which plants to save, take care not to dispose of what might in time prove useful. No matter how common, robust survivors like orange Daylilies *(Hemerocallis fulva)* and Hostas should not be discarded wholesale, for they have potential as ground covers or for naturalizing. Variegated Goutweed *(Aegopodium podagraria* 'Variegatum'), often the despair of those who inherit an old garden, can be put to good use as a spectacular background for container plants or as a hedge, confined by mowing. It, like many of the old survivors, is beautiful in the right place.

Discovering and collecting plants from neglected or abandoned gardens, old farm sites, roadsides, or graveyards can be a fascinating and rewarding hobby.

Plant Collector's Guide

Most gardeners buy their heirloom plants from the many established plant and seed sources listed in Part 3. But discovering and collecting plants from neglected or abandoned gardens, old farm sites, roadsides, or graveyards (a great place to find Old Roses, I'm told) can be a fascinating and rewarding hobby: "It's like finding buried treasure," one enthusiast told me. You may find a rare plant hitherto unavailable in commercial trade, and you may be the means of reestablishing it in the plant world. Or you may find an old-time favorite languishing from neglect and feel the need to provide it with a new home where you can care for it and carry on the work of some unknown gardener.

These are praiseworthy goals, but even plant lovers are not immune to greed. Once when I returned to a well-cared-for older garden to take a few roots of a nice old Phlox after receiving permission from the elderly owner to do so, I was taken aback to find that someone had ruthlessly dug in his or her shovel to the hilt and taken away at least half of the planting, along with much of the soil. Other ornamentals nearby had been treated similarly. Hardy types may endure such mishandling, but that's no way to go about saving plants for posterity. Being an heirloom gardener means having a responsibility to both the plants themselves and the world they inhabit. It's very important to offer gardeners sound advice about collecting heirloom plants at the same time we encourage them to grow these plants in their gardens.

The following guide, based on my own experience and that of other collectors, deals wholly with collecting ornamentals. The same principles should be followed in collecting any plants in similar situations.

+ Look for plants in overgrown, neglected gardens, at abandoned farms, along undisturbed byways, in graveyards, and in well-cared-for older gardens in the area. Ask people in the area about old gardens and gardeners interested in growing old ornamentals, and you'll soon have a plant collectors' network. *Always ask permission for exploring an area.* Someone owns that abandoned farm; your graveyard explorations might not be welcome. When you seek permission, ask if it's okay to take a small sample of what you find.

+ Start your search in the spring (earlier in warmer regions) when many plants break their dormancy. This is when you might find very old types of Daffodils, for instance. If you find something on the first trip, be sure to return to the same place at intervals during the growing season. Chances are you will find something else of value.

+ Take several photos of the plant—a few close-ups and some of the general area. These may help in plant identification and shed some light on the plant's history. This is important if you are a researcher interested in creating historical landscapes, for instance. Take brief notes, too, as you're sure to forget some important details.

+ *Unless threatened with destruction, never dig up the whole plant.* If it grows in a clump, take a piece of root from the back of the clump, especially if the plant is growing in an established garden. Carefully dig out a piece of root and put it in a plastic bag moistened with damp moss or a similar substance. Root collecting is the quickest and surest way to establish a clone of the original planting that may be traced back many years. This is important if you are creating a garden of authentic descendant plants of old-time species. Plants established in this way are living links with the past, since they are actually part of the original plant.

+ When dealing with Old Roses, the established procedure is to take a stem cutting. Stem cuttings can also be used for any plant not large enough to divide or for one of hybrid origin that may be difficult to establish from root division (*Lythrum* hybrids, for instance). Seeds of annual and biennial flowers such as Calendula, Hollyhock, Foxglove, and Sweet-William may be gathered after they have ripened on the plant. Take only a small handful of seed capsules, keeping different colors separate. Bulbs should be dug up only after the leaves have turned brown and returned their nutrients to feed the bulb, the source of next year's flowers. *However you take your plant material, the original planting should look undisturbed.*

+ Establish your find in a specially prepared seedbed, nursery bed, or cold frame. Never plant your treasure directly in the garden (unless you have a staff to tend to such matters), or it may be swamped by lush growth in the vicinity.

+ If you are concerned about the plant's

hardiness, grow it in a cold frame for at least three seasons. If, during that time, you manage to divide it, plant the clones in several places in your garden, leaving at least one plant in the cold frame as insurance. Store dried seeds to plant the following season or plant them in a cold frame or specially prepared fine soil. Since some seeds need freezing temperatures to break their dormancy, you may not see growth until the following season. Store dried bulbs in a dry place until it is time to plant them out in your garden. *Label all plants, seeds, and bulbs.* Keep a written account as well; labels have a way of getting lost.

✦ Contact the botany department at your local college or university if you need help with identification. You may need to find a specialist in old plants to help determine the precise variety or cultivar (this is where a clear photograph or slide comes in handy). Contact local plant societies and garden clubs. They may help identify or be interested in heirloom plants. Contact plant nurseries interested in heirloom or choice plants. They may be interested in propagating your treasure, eventually returning it to commercial trade or introducing it for the first time.

✦ Contact seed exchanges (see Part 3). By sending your seeds out to other gardeners, you open the door to a world of unknown plants whose seeds you will receive in exchange.

LANDSCAPING WITH HEIRLOOM FLOWERS

๛

There is no spot of ground, however arid,

bare, or ugly, that cannot be tamed into

. . . an impression of beauty and delight.

—GERTRUDE JEKYLL (*WOOD & GARDEN*, 1899)

EVEN THE WORST growing conditions can be improved, but that is only the first step, and not the most difficult, in creating a pleasing landscape, one that conveys "an impression of beauty and delight." As enthusiastic gardeners we are mainly preoccupied with heirloom plants in their infinite variety of forms, fragrance, and colors, and so we start acquiring them (there is no greed like a flower-lover's). Yet no matter how lovely, plants in themselves do not create an appealing landscape; badly placed, they can actually detract from the overall effect.

The most successful landscapes, however small their scale or humble their conception, inevitably evoke the same reaction. We feel a rightness about them, a sense of harmony. We feel unconsciously as if each separate element, the arrangement of plants and other features—fence, walkway, garden shed, arbor—exists in a natural, logical relationship to the whole picture of house and surrounding area, as if it could be no other way. Professional landscapers express these feelings in

terms of *unity, order, balance,* and *cohesiveness,* what I call an integrated landscape. Conversely, a badly planned landscape, with plantings and other features dotted about in illogical arrangement, is unappealing, even disturbing in its randomness and jarring juxtapositions.

There are two basic ways of going about creating a successful landscape: one is to hire a landscape architect who will deftly map out and install the whole thing for you. The other way is to let the landscape naturally evolve over time from your life as you discover your practical and aesthetic needs, as you learn to know your land through daily, intimate contact. While the installed landscape can be beautiful, flawlessly so, it too often presents a static façade, an architectural solution superimposed upon the land. If, in the living, it proves unsatisfactory, it may be difficult and expensive to correct, especially in the case of hardscaping (permanent features such as driveways, or terraces). While there are obvious advantages to having professional advice where technical problems are beyond ordinary scope, where the architecture of the house and grounds are on a large scale, or where period authenticity is of paramount concern, in most cases successful landscaping can be achieved by the home gardener.

Over the course of three decades, as we have allowed the land and our daily life on a backcountry farm to dictate our plantings, we have created a harmonious landscape that suits our needs, that speaks to our aesthetic vision. It is, moreover, an essential component of our lives, refreshing us each day as we go about our work. We accept the fact that, unlike the installed landscape, it is subject to change, as our tastes and needs change, as the natural and built environment around us changes (buildings are altered, trees grow up, plantings are reduced or enlarged). Creating "an impression of beauty and delight" may be a struggle and we will surely make mistakes along the way, but as a work in progress it is part of and inseparable from the joy of gardening.

First Steps

Site

Until the 1940s, house and grounds were regarded as a single entity, each dependent on the other for practical and aesthetic completion. As people gradually relied less on their own productivity in the home sphere, as their practical needs were met elsewhere, the grounds were no longer thought of as an extension of the home but as a separate, mostly decorative area for display. Too often taken to its extreme in the modern era, the house appears to be a sealed box stranded in a sterile lawn, the house front nearly obscured by overgrown shrubbery (foundation planting), its picture window looking out to nothing especially pictorial. Even the practical function of the front walkway has been superseded by the attached garage with electronic doors, so one can leave and reenter the house without ever touching ground.

One way to rejoin the house to its surroundings is to infuse the outdoor landscape with meaning, to make it a place where you want to be. An interest in heirloom plants is a step in the right direction, for heirlooms are inviting, highly scented, visited by birds and butterflies, and have many uses to explore—all characteristics that literally lead down the garden path.

No matter how confined, tour the ground you call your yard, taking note as you go of any features such as porch, patio, deck, garage, or shed that can serve as connecting links in the landscape and provide a logical place for planting heirloom flowers . . . and don't neglect the dooryard or the path itself. If you live in an up-to-the-minute modern house with established plantings of modern types, bear in mind that old-fashioned flowers and roses can be successfully incorporated into the most austere setting, softening its hard edges and tailored forms, bringing welcome grace and beauty.

Note, I have not used the terms bones or rooms that so often appear in landscaping texts. What do they mean? *Bones* describe the basic structure of a landscape, what can be seen in winter when plant growth is halted and all that is left behind is highly visible: bed or border shapes, paths, perennial hedges and accent plants, garden furnishings—any significant element beyond ephemeral plants that give definition to the landscape. Garden *rooms* refer to areas of the landscape devoted to different types of plantings or functions: the area immediately around a terrace or patio, for instance, is one room, while another is defined by a planting of roses or herbs. It isn't necessary to define either bones or rooms in the beginning of your gardening adventure, since these will naturally grow from your life and needs, as well as the dictates of the land itself. Regardless of what the books say, most gardeners add bones *in the process of creating the garden*. In any case, as you will appreciate over time, rooms inadequately describes outdoor living spaces, which are fluid, always in flux, subject to change.

While the outdoor space is obviously of great importance, so is the view from within, the *sight lines* in landscape parlance. Victorian house plans included a multitude of these dashed lines from every available viewing spot—from doorways, windows, verandah—to show what was seen not only in the immediate landscape but in the middle and far distance. I learned quite by chance about the wisdom of planting for indoor viewing when I noticed one summer that every morning from the breakfast table I could see a hummingbird gathering nectar from a potted Bee Balm plant on the porch. Further away, I saw birds alighting on the feeder, and just beyond, the spreading limbs of the old Lilac—altogether an idyllic, soothing image. Even better than Bee Balm for breakfast, I later discovered, is the cheer of exuberant cottage garden bloom that greets me every morning from my bedroom window from summer through fall.

Before you rush outside to plant your favorite heirlooms, you'd best consider the potential planting site in the more prosaic terms of *exposure* (to sun or shade), *prevailing wind, topography* (the lay of the land), and *soil type,* since these will determine what you plant where.

EXPOSURE

When a plant is described as growing best (reaching its maximum growth and flowering potential) in *full sun,* this means the site receives six hours of direct sun a day. Bear in mind that many plants that do well in full sun will also grow well with only morning or afternoon light, so long as it is direct. *Partial shade* means morning or afternoon sun only, or filtered light from a high tree canopy. *Shade* means varying degrees of dappled light for the whole day, or a few hours of morning or afternoon sun.

PREVAILING WIND

Roses in particular benefit from good air circulation (combined with full sun) to promote growth and resistance to fungal disease, but constantly windy conditions are stressful for most plants, including Roses. You will notice their ill effects in diseased, stunted, and deformed growth, in toppled plants (these should be staked before you think they might fall over), in overwintering damage, and even in death. If wind cannot be avoided, choose dwarf varieties over taller ones and be prepared to offer support in some form. Hedges, walls, fences, and buildings all can ameliorate windy conditions and create a favorable microhabitat. Where extreme wind is a problem, it's best to choose hedging over a wall since hedges slow down wind, whereas a solid barrier can cause the wind to rise upwards and over it, swooping down with force on the other side.

One way to rejoin the house to its surroundings is to infuse the outdoor landscape with meaning, to make it a place where you want to be.

Topography

Land varies in its configurations from flat to sloping with gradients in between. Flat open ground is the easiest to work with, especially for formal, geometric designs. An extensive flat area, which can be boring, benefits from the addition of bushes and vertical accents to vary the scene. Natural slopes and banks (a sharp, prominent rise) are choice sites for plants like Lavender or Roses that need perfect drainage. If the site is difficult to reach, consider turning the area into a semiwild "garden"; many heirloom flowers are close to the wild or actually wildflowers and readily naturalize (see below).

Soil Type

Heirloom plants, like any others, have soil needs, from light and sandy to heavy clay, but most thrive in ordinary (loamy) garden soil. Although you may be able to improve soil conditions (as already discussed in the previous growing section), it's less work to match a plant to its favorite soil type. Check under each individual plant portrait for specific information.

Design

Formal and *informal* are terms often used to describe opposite poles in garden design, yet there are elements of formality in informal design and informal details in a formal layout. Being aware of what each style has to offer will help you create the garden you have in mind. Cottage gardens, for instance, which are supposed to epitomize carefree informality, gain impact when plantings, tightly restrained by formal hedges or rigid material (boards, bricks), spill artlessly (or so it seems)

over their boundaries. In a looser, more open, more informal design, the effect of bounty would be lessened. Hedges, on the other hand, may be loose and informal, and so bring that quality to an otherwise formal planting. The point is, *formal* and *informal* are not mutually exclusive terms, so be open to ways in which you can add a touch of one or the other to your garden.

Raised Beds

Much has already been said about how to establish raised beds when growing conditions on the ground cannot be improved sufficiently, but there are other reasons to use them as well. Just as hedging encloses and frames the planting, raising the level brings it more into focus, as in the traditional formal herb garden of mainly foliage types which benefit from the extra attention. The raised bed design can be carried out as a single free-standing bed, or as a repeated series of squares, circles, rectangles, and triangles in geometric design. Individual beds are edged with low-growing shrubs, then filled with complementary plantings of herbs or flowers. Instead of outlining beds with low shrubs, bricks (especially old ones), stones, or wood (timbers) can be used, each material bringing with it a suggestion of formality or its opposite: low, circular stone walls, for instance, soften the geometric lines of formal design when used on their own or as rounded corners for timber-edged beds. Materials also call forth plant types such as Pinks *(Dianthus)* which especially enjoy association with stone.

Island Beds

When beds are cut into the grass and lack a backdrop such as a wall, fence, or shrubbery, they are called *island beds,* a name well suited to independent, open forms that can be viewed from all sides. Island beds can be any shape, raised or level. In this design, tall plants are featured in the center, with middle and lower forms around them. Victorian style dictated round or oval beds cut into the lawn with the same planting pattern, except the desire was to create a bold, in-your-face effect with a few deft strokes by featuring a tall, striking, upright plant like Canna in the center of the bed, surrounded by low, dwarf bedding plants of contrasting colors and forms, like trailing Sweet Alyssum with mounding Signet Marigolds.

An island bed is cut into the grass and lacks a backdrop such as a wall, fence, or shrubbery.

NATURALIZED PLANTINGS

To naturalize means to grow plants in conditions similar to their native habitat with minimum interference. Also known as "the wild garden," this sort of garden design has been with us for centuries. The desire to experience true nature on home ground as a protest against the "artificiality" of domestic planting is a common urge, one that regularly comes to the fore at the turn of each century, as in the contemporary passion for meadow and naturalistic plantings. Far easier than establishing a meadow (which is difficult and labor-intensive), naturalizing plants involves very little work except picking out the right site, determining plants that thrive there, and then, after planting, roughly mowing around them until they are well established. When you look for the right place—an unmown byway, a piece of damp ground, a dry slope—observe what is already growing there and take advantage: Wild Iris *(Iris versicolor)* grows in wet spots, often with Buttercups, indicating just the spot for Yellow Flag Iris *(I. pseudacorus).* Naturalizing not only creates beauty in otherwise difficult ground, it offers the chance to grow those plants on the wild side, like Yellow Flag, that must be continually trimmed and chopped when they are grown within the confines of more refined plantings.

Follow these steps:

1. In the spring when vegetation is low, locate the habitat, observe what's growing there, then choose your plants.
2. Thrust a sharp spade (or a trowel, if the soil is soft) into the ground to make a slit, push in the roots, then close up the gap all around the plant with your heel. Depending on their height, width, and general impact, plant in groups of five (short), in groups of three (medium-tall), and singly for tall sorts.
3. Roughly mow with a scythe around the plants as the vegetation grows up; encourage some "weeds" (wild grasses,

Block plantings of calendulas in four-foot-wide facing beds can create the illusion of wide drifts of flowers.

daisies, wild asters) to grow where they will improve the picture with their forms, colors, and textures. Meanwhile, discourage other unwanted weeds by keeping them cut down (this is, after all, a planting).

4. Sit back and enjoy the flowers, no weeding allowed. You can either cut back plants after they've bloomed or leave their seedheads for the birds.

BORDERS

This term refers to an oblong or undulating strip with a backdrop, where taller types are planted in the back, medium-tall plants in the middle rank, and shorter ones up front; for best effect plants should not be regimented by type since irregularity gives the border its great appeal. When "herbaceous" is added to the word border, the words evoke lush perennial borders of the type made famous by Gertrude Jekyll, mistress of the painterly garden, who, with William Robinson, transformed gardening style in the late 19th and early 20th centuries. The experts say that the classic herbaceous-dominated border (annuals and bulbs, though even

Roses are not out of place) must be 5 feet wide or more. The famous Jekyllian "drift"— a term she coined to describe a long-shaped rather than block-shaped planting of the same type in the same color or hues—is difficult (some say impossible) to create without a 9-foot wide border and a garden staff. I have never tried, but I have found that one way to create a quasi-drift is to repeat a block planting in two parallel beds, each about 60 feet long and 4 feet wide with a path between. When approached from the front, the path is hidden from view and the two plantings merge into one, as do the blocks from one bed to the other, which appear as a long, uninterrupted line. For this effect, I like to use Calendula, an easygoing annual that blooms all summer through fall and is bright enough to make a statement among perennials.

ACCENTS

A plant accent is a single plant or striking combination used to draw attention to a particular feature in the landscape, or to hide it from view. Accents may also embellish or enliven a dull area, adding distinction to an otherwise uninspired situation. They are especially useful near entranceways, driveways, by a shed, or to draw the eye to a far distance: You'll see what I mean if you let a Rhubarb plant go to seed. The tall, creamy plumes rise above the surrounding area, creating interest for over a month. Single plant accents are, like the Rhubarb, often vertical (Foxglove and Lovage come to mind), but they can also be wide and bushy. Medium-tall shrubs can be used as well as shrublike perennials. I grow Hollyhock Mallow *(Malva alcea* 'Fastigiata') as a corner accent just outside an enclosed flower bed. A vigorous type that would overrun its neighbors within, its wide bushy form smothered in glistening pink bells, it is kept in check by mowing.

Furnishing the Heirloom Garden

When I was growing up in a late-1930s newly made suburb, I remember the well-stocked landscape fore and aft our little Tudor Revival house: a colonial-style picket fence surrounded the front lawn, which was divided into equal halves by a cement walk to the front door. In one half of the tiny lawn, precisely in the middle, there was an early 20th-century example of a gazing globe (a silvered glass sphere on a pedestal); in the other half, a birdbath of the same period design. Behind the house, by the side porch, was a fragrant old-fashioned Lilac, and beyond that a path led to a contemporary patio, entered through a cottage garden Rose-covered arbor.

If it was a landscaper's nightmare, we didn't know it. We lived and worked outdoors in the summer in the tiny "rooms," where the laundry was hung, where the garbage was collected in a removable tub set in the ground (mint was planted at its base), where I learned to catch a baseball, and where, in the early 1940s, a small Victory Garden was added, from which I first tasted radishes straight from the dark earth. With all its disparate elements, it worked for us, and its staying power in my mind after more than fifty years is a tribute to its significance as a living landscape.

Today many gardeners are filling their gardens, large and small, with period furnishings and ornamental tidbits, hungry to infuse meaning into the sterile, bland landscapes we have been living with since the 1950s. However, these items alone cannot give meaning to a piece of ground; they have to be connected in some way with the ongoing life around them. But you don't have to wait for the garden's completion (that may never be) to acquire them, for in themselves, they will suggest desirable, complementary plantings that you might never have thought about. If you can't construct them yourself, mass-produced and handcrafted furnishings and ornaments are now available in every style from colonial to high Victorian, designs popular from the 18th to early 20th centuries. Among them are fences, arbors, trellises, gazebos (a little garden house), benches, pergolas (a series of arches to support climbing plants), Victorian urns, birdhouses, birdbaths, sundials, statuary, even gazing balls (see Sources). Unless you are involved in authentic period restoration, don't be overly concerned about mixing periods. Common

> **These items alone cannot give meaning to a piece of ground; they have to be connected in some way with the ongoing life around them.**

An arbor really should lead some-where.

sense will tell you that an intricately wrought iron fence in the Victorian style, no matter how lovely, will not help to create a rustic atmosphere, so choose materials and design accordingly. The main thing is to try and furnish your outdoor space in logical relation to the overall design, for it will be most satisfying that way, and keep in mind that furniture outside, as in the house, serves a function: an arbor, for instance, really should lead somewhere.

Specialty Plantings

Many heirloom flowers are good sources of nectar, so even if you don't plant with them in mind, hummingbirds and butterflies will visit your garden (bees, too). A sure way to attract them to specific sites is to select flowers they especially like, then plant them in generous groups throughout the landscape for a succession of blooms. Container plantings work well in areas where it's impractical to plant in the ground: by doorways, along paths, near porches, and on decks. There are no hard and fast rules regarding which flowers will be harvested for nectar since conditions vary (an abundance of local wildflowers, one site preferred over another, certain flowers over others). The lists that follow are based on observations in my own garden; scented types are noted with a ❀; all perennials are hardy to Zone 4. Growing directions and bloom periods for all of the plants discussed and listed in the following sections can be found in Part 2 in each portrait entry.

PLANTING FOR HUMMINGBIRDS

Hummingbirds are tiny creatures that require a lot of nectar to keep them going. Lured primarily by red flowers (in fact, by anything red, even a red-handled garden tool), they are also attracted to pink and orange flowers, especially ones that are tubular in form. When they find a flower that they like, hummingbirds push their long beaks and tongues into its depths to extract nectar, then go on to the next until they have explored every bloom on the stem, every floret in a cluster. Darting and hovering at seventy-five wing beats per second is demanding, so once they are in an area, they are game to try almost any bloom of any color. Take care to provide nectar plants for hummingbirds returning in early spring when wildflowers may not be plentiful. Lungwort, the earliest and most reliable spring flower in my landscape, is always in full bloom by early May when they visit each pink and blue little trumpet in a thick azure hedge.

Annuals

Four O'Clock *(Mirabilis)* ❀
Nasturtium (especially *Tropaeolum* 'Empress of India') ❀
Nicotiana (especially *Nicotiana* 'Crimson King') ❀
Petunia *(Petunia × hybrida,* clear red, white, blue) ❀
Policeman's Helmet *(Impatiens glandulifera)* ❀

Perennials

Bee Balm *(Monarda didyma)* ❀
Columbine (especially *Aquilegia canadensis*)
Lily (especially *Lilium* 'Enchantment')
Lungwort *(Pulmonaria officinalis)*
Monkshood *(Aconitum napellus)*

Shrubs

Clove Currant *(Ribes odoratum)* ❀
Golden Currant *(Ribes aureum)* ❀

Lilac *(Syringa vulgaris)* ❀
Tartarian Honeysuckle *(Lonicera tartarica)* ❀
Wiegela *(Wiegela florida)* ❀

Annual Vines

Climbing Nasturtium *(Tropaeolum majus)* ❀
Morning Glory *(Ipomoea tricolor)* ❀
Scarlet Runner Bean *(Phaseolus coccineus)* ❀

Perennial Vines

Honeysuckle *(Lonicera sempervirens)* ❀

PLANTING FOR BUTTERFLIES

Butterflies are attracted to colors, too, although to different ones: yellow, blue, purple, pink, white, and orange in strong tones. Like the succession of blooms in the garden, butterflies of different types come and go, each to its favorite flowers, often those belonging to the Apiaceae, or Celery family—herbs like Dill and Lovage—and the Asteraceae, or Aster family—flowers such as Daisies, Thistles, and Black-eyed-Susan. Keep the following points in mind:

+ Grow a variety of host plants in sunny sites, protected from the wind.
+ Protect flowers from damage and mud splatter (unacceptable) by staking tall types; prune and cut back to encourage more bloom.
+ Butterflies like to gather in damp spots or, even better, puddles, to imbibe moisture and minerals.
+ Paths made of any material that absorbs solar heat—brick, flagstone, gravel, wood chips, close-clipped grass—are favorable sunning sites for drying off and staying warm.
+ Supplement the nectar supply by encouraging the growth of wildflowers in an unmown corner or naturalized area.
+ Remember, before they are the beautiful creatures we love to watch fluttering about alighting on our flowers, butterflies are not-so-pretty larvae and caterpillars; the former incubate over winter in garden refuse (leave some during fall cleanup); the latter dine voraciously on the foliage of trees and shrubs. With a plentiful supply in the wild, you shouldn't notice any damage.

Annuals

Bachelor's-button *(Centaurea cyanus)*
Balsam *(Impatiens balsamita)*
Calendula *(Calendula officinalis)*
Cosmos *(Cosmos bipinnatus)*
Marigold (especially *Tagetes* 'Naughty Marietta')
Nicotiana *(Nicotiana alata,* white flower attracts hummingbird moth) ❀

Biennials & Short-Lived Perennials

Black-eyed-Susan *(Rudbeckia hirta)*
Sweet-William *(Dianthus barbatus)* ❀

Perennials

Blue Flag Iris *(Iris versicolor)*
Butterfly Weed *(Asclepias tuberosa)*
Chives *(Allium schoenoprasum)*
Lemon Lily *(Hemerocallis lilioasphodelus)* ❀
Mountain-bluet *(Centaurea montana)*
Phlox *(Phlox paniculata)* ❀
Wild Bergamot *(Monarda fistulosa)* ❀

Shrubs

Bridal-wreath Spirea *(Spiraea prunifolia)*
Elderberry *(Sambucus canadensis)* ❀
Lilac *(Syringa vulgaris)* ❀
Mock Orange *(Philadelphus coronarius)* ❀

Rhodora *(Rhododendron canadense)* and
  most Rhododendrons
Weigela *(Weigela florida)* ❀

THE EVENING GARDEN

The more time you spend in the garden, the
more you will notice that as evening
approaches, it assumes a new dimension, a
new life. We first became aware of this
phenomenon when, as we walked around
doing evening chores, checking calf tethers,
shutting in poultry, closing pasture gates, we
caught unfamiliar scents, noticed certain
flowers in a different way for their striking
forms and intense hues, became aware of new
visitors. Once, I was surprised by the whir-
ring of a hummingbird moth—startlingly
similar to a hummingbird—as it brushed by
me, seeking nectar from clove-scented white
Nicotiana *N. Alata).* The gardens, so alive with
drifting aromas and glowing flowers, seemed
transformed just for our pleasure at the end
of a busy day in the hot sun.

I purposely plant now for the twilight
hours with flowers such as Four O'Clocks,
which open in the late afternoon (planted
in tubs by the front doorway), and Dame's-
rocket and Bouncing-Bet, whose perfume
floats freely then. Colors are important, too,
always on the light side—pure white, pale
yellows, light pinks—as are strong shapes like
Lupine, Canterbury-bells, and Foxglove. My
evening plants are scattered about, so there
is always something of interest wherever I
walk, but the greatest impact comes from the
two long parallel "Jekyll" borders with a soft,
inviting grass path between them. Plan your
garden paths so they lead you around and
about evening and moonlight plantings.
These are favorites in my garden.

Annuals

Four O'Clock *(Mirabilis)* ❀
Nasturtium (especially *Tropaeolum* 'Gleam
  Series') ❀
Nicotiana (especially *Nicotiana alata,*
  white) ❀
Petunia *(Petunia* X *hybrida,* white) ❀
Sweet Alyssum *(Lobularia maritima,*
  white) ❀

Biennials

Canterbury-bells *(Campanula medium)*
Dame's-rocket *(Hesperis matronalis)* ❀

Perennials

Clustered Bellflower *(Campanula glomerata*
  'Alba'*)*
Foxglove *(Digitalis purpurea* 'Alba')
Hosta *(Hosta* 'Royal Standard') ❀
Lemon Lily *(Hemerocallis lilioasphodelus)* ❀
Lupine *(Lupinus* 'Russell Hybrids')
Oriental Poppy *(Papaver orientale* 'Perry's
  White')
Phlox *(Phlox paniculata,* white, pink) ❀
Soapwort *(Saponaria officinalis* 'Rosea
  Plena')
Sneezewort *(Achillea ptarmica* 'The Pearl')

Bulbs

Acidanthera *(Gladiolus callianthus /
  Acidanthera bicolor)* ❀
Lily-of-the-Valley *(Convallaria majalis)* ❀

Shrubs

Lilac *(Syringa vulgaris* 'Alba') ❀
Mock Orange *(Philadelphus coronarius)* ❀

Annual Vines

Moonflower *(Ipomoea alba)* ❀

PERIOD-INSPIRED GARDEN DESIGNS

❧

THE SUBJECT OF HEIRLOOM PLANTS is broad enough to include the nearly wild, open-pollinated herbs and flowers of old English cottage gardens and early American gardens as well as the relatively new hybrid forms that poured forth in great numbers around the end of the 19th century, especially among Roses, Iris, and Daffodils. If your tastes run to the former category and you think hybrids have no place in the heirloom garden, you can choose from a wide variety of plants introduced from the 17th to the 19th centuries in America, among them many wonderful natives.

I have loosely organized the following groupings historically so that you may choose to plant those types that most satisfy the varied meanings of the word *heirloom*. For the eclectic gardener interested in beautiful and deserving plants from any era (my own preference), I have included a wide-open garden with plants from all periods. The main idea is to enjoy gardening with heirloom flowers, whatever their antiquity.

Colonial Gardens of Use and Delight: 1600–1700

The first American gardens, adaptations of the prevailing medieval raised bed/geometric pattern, were transformed to suit the circumstances of pioneer life. Combining the practical and aesthetic in a characteristically American way, beds might be no more than scraped up soil enclosed by rough plank boards or logs, narrow beaten dirt paths between; the plants, a mixture of Cabbages and Pinks, Onions and Cowslips. This compact arrangement put food for the table close at hand, alongside other plants that provided the raw materials needed to soothe fevers, brew tea or sweeteners, treat wounds, dye fabrics, and a hundred other household uses.

If you're just becoming interested in herbs, a pioneer-inspired herb garden is a good way to start, since these plants are easy to grow and have practical uses that speak to us even today. Many old-world herbs from the colonial period are lovely flowers, too, so even if your garden is confined to useful plants from this period it will also be a visual delight. A surprising number of plants, in any case, seem to have been grown for their ornamental value alone—surprising because we have been told so often about the Puritan gardens of utility. I rather think the early gardens, like most of those planted since the first spade turned earth, were "compounded of dreams and utility." How else can we explain the early appearance of Lily-of-the-Valley, Canterbury-bells, Dame's-rocket, Lilacs, and Mock Orange, whose herbal virtues are almost nonexistent?

A formal raised bed design should be established on flat ground and in full sun for most herbs. It's easy to multiply groups of beds in infinite variety: a series of subdivided squares, circles, or maze of triangles arranged symmetrically with paths between, and a circular bed of old Roses, tall accent plant, or culinary herbs in the middle where the paths intersect. Beds should be enclosed by boards, brick, or stone, then edged with low shrubs amenable to trimming like Box, Lavender,

A rough, slab-board fence gives character to a pioneer-type planting.

or Southernwood. To create a hedge effect, plant shrubs close together (about 2 feet apart) and keep them trimmed to the desired height.

Herbs within the beds can be organized by type—all culinary or all medicinal herbs, for instance. Most of the herbs we grow today, such as Parsley, Thyme, Basil, Chives, Sage, Lovage, and Lavender are colonial plants. For those not featured in the portrait section, see my books on herbs: *Living with Herbs* (Countryman Press, 1997) and *Herbs in Bloom* (Timber Press, 1998) for complete growing information. Don't hesitate to mix vegetables and herbs in the old way; Onions, Garlic, and Lettuce (particularly small, round heirloom butterheads) combine well with other useful plants such as Chives, Sage, and Lovage. For more on heirloom vegetable varieties, see Ben Watson's book, *Taylor's Guide to Heirloom Vegetables* (Houghton Mifflin, 1996).

In a more informal planting, match plants to habitat throughout the landscape: Soapwort and Elecampane, for instance, grow in damp spots, Sweet Cicely, Bee Balm, and

Cowslip prefer shade. Herbs can be grouped by the kitchen door within easy reach: Chives for chopping into salads, Southernwood sprigs for adding to potpourri or sachets, pebbly-leaved Sage for flavoring, Wild Bergamot for tea, Calendula petals for decorating cakes, and at least one Old Garden Rose for rose petal jelly.

Train a Hop, Honeysuckle, or Everlasting Pea vine on an old-fashioned quiggly fence (perhaps the kind the settlers built), and you will also have support for the tall, single-flowered Hollyhock and a variety of settler plants we value primarily for their good looks: Bellflowers, Feverfew, bright red Jerusalem-cross, soft pink Musk Mallow (don't be afraid to pair them), exquisite pearly Florentine Iris, and, rising here and there, flower-laden spikes of the White or Madonna Lily (*Lilium candidum*) and pastel clusters of Dame's-rocket, both to perfume the early evening air. Sow dark blue Bachelor's-buttons among these and add a double-flowered Peony or two on the other side of the doorway. Before you know it, you will have the proverbial cottage garden.

You can carpet the ground beneath nearby Lilacs and Mock Orange with spotted-leaved Lungwort, to be followed by plants that appreciate the partial shade and moist ground they provide: Lily-of-the-Valley, Sweet Cicely, Columbine, Daylilies, Canada Lilies, and little Johnny-jump-ups. All of these plants will thrive with very little attention.

You can choose from the plants listed below to create your own settler's garden. Consult the individual plant portraits in Part II to find those best suited to your area's particular growing conditions.

(❀ indicates fragrant plants)

Herbs

These herbs—medicinal, culinary, and household, are all perennials except where indicated and hardy to Zone 4 unless indicated. Herbs with the species epithet *officinalis* were obtained literally "from the apothecary," signifying their widespread use; plants in other categories were also used as herbs (see under each portrait).

Bee Balm (*Monarda didyma*) ❀
Bouncing-bet (*Saponaria officinalis*) ❀
Calendula, annual (*Calendula officinalis*)
Chives (*Allium schoenoprasum*)
Clary Sage (*Salvia sclarea*) ❀
Clove Pink (*Dianthus caryophyllus*) ❀
Costmary (*Tanacetum balsamita*) ❀
Cottage Pink (*Dianthus plumarius*) ❀
Cowslip (*Primula veris*) ❀
Dyer's Chamomile (*Anthemis tinctoria*)
Elecampane (*Inula helenium*)
Feverfew (*Tanacetum parthenium*)
Lavender (*Lavandula angustifolia*)—
    Zone 4 with protection ❀
Orris (*Iris germanica* 'Florentina') ❀
Poppy (*Papaver somniferum*)
Sage (*Salvia officinalis*)
Southernwood (*Artemisia abrotanum*) ❀
Sweet Cicely (*Myrrhis odorata*) ❀
Valerian (*Valeriana officinalis*) ❀
Woundwort (*Stachys officinalis*)

Biennial & Short-Lived Perennial Flowers

Canterbury-bells (*Campanula medium*)
Dame's-rocket (*Hesperis matronalis*) ❀
Heartsease (*Viola tricolor*)
Hollyhock (*Alcea rosea*)
Honesty (*Lunaria annua*)
Foxglove (*Digitalis purpurea*)

I rather think the early gardens, like most of those planted since the first spade turned earth, were "compounded of dreams and utility."

❀⸱

Perennial Flowers

Grandma's Peony *(Paeonia officinalis)* ✤
Madonna Lily *(Lilium candidum)* ✤
Monkshood *(Aconitum napellus)*
Musk Mallow *(Malva moschata)*
Sneezewort *(Achillea ptarmica)*
Sweet Violet *(Viola odorata)* ✤

Bulbs

Lily-of-the-valley *(Convallaria majalis)* ✤

Shrubs

Box *(Buxus sempervirens)* —Zone 5 with
    protection ✤
Lilac *(Syringa vulgaris)* ✤
Mock Orange *(Philadelphus coronarius)* ✤

Roses

Apothecary *(Rosa gallica* 'Officinalis') ✤
Cabbage *(R. centifolia)* ✤
Damask *(R. damascena)* ✤
Sweet Briar Rose *(R. eglanteria)* ✤

Vines

Everlasting Pea *(Lathyrus latifolius)*
Hop Vine *(Humulus lupulus)* ✤
Scarlet Honeysuckle *(Lonicera
    sempervirens)* ✤

Native Flora in the Natural Garden: 1700–1850

The period from the 18th century through the early to mid-19th century was characterized by a slow but growing awareness of our native plant treasures. Through the efforts of people like John Bartram—farmer, plant collector, and curious gardener extraordinaire—who established his own plant nursery in 1728, Americans for the first time had a commercial source for a variety of native plants, especially shrubs. He, for instance, was responsible for introducing Mountain-laurel and the Catawba Rhododendron (considered to be among our finest native shrubs). In the early 19th century, Bernard M'Mahon introduced some of the plants discovered during the 1803 Lewis and Clark Expedition—flowering Currants (Golden and Clove), for instance. Thomas Jefferson grew many of these native shrubs at his home, Monticello.

If you're interested in practicing the art of naturalizing—growing plants in harmonious association with minimum interference, as already described—find the right spot, make a slit in the ground, push in the plants in groups, and maintain them with high, infrequent mowing or with hand-scything. While some are quite specific in their growth requirements—preferring sun or shade, moist or dry soil—all are easy to grow once these conditions are met. They

A bench, tucked among the wildflowers, invites you to contemplate the beauty of the natural garden.

are especially recommended for low-maintenance natural gardens that blend with more conventional plantings and with the natural surroundings. As a matter of course, the natural garden will be of great interest to wildlife, especially birds and butterflies.

For a garden in partial shade with moist, humus-rich soil, choose among several native Rhododendrons and Azaleas (the former have nearly evergreen leaves, the latter deciduous ones that turn bronze or scarlet in the fall). Underplant them with native wildflowers such as Virginia Bluebells, scarlet Bee Balm (really brilliant in partial shade), and Bleeding-heart *(Dicentra eximia* and *D. formosa),* and among them plant Maidenhair Fern for all-season dainty green foliage.

Shrubs that will grow almost anywhere, resisting both drought and damp conditions, include the flowering Golden and Clove Currants *(Ribes aureum* and *R. odoratum,* respectively), Mountain-laurel, and Highbush Cranberry (this will give you creamy white flower clusters in early summer and bright red berries and foliage in the fall). If planted in full sun, Mountain-laurel will reward you with masses of cup-shaped white flowers in late spring or early summer, but its handsome glossy leaves remain green all season and will provide a background for sun-loving plants such as Eastern Columbine *(Aquilegia canadensis),* Butterfly Weed, Black-eyed-Susan, the yellow-whorled Horsemint *(Monarda punctata),* and the bright orange-red Leopard Lily *(Lilium pardalinum).*

On a dry, rocky slope, plant low-growing Moss Phlox to spill over and between the rocks—a mass of little blue flowers with drought-resistant needlelike green foliage; Rhodora, a diminutive Rhododendron with rose-colored flowers and attractive foliage; and Crested Iris, just 3 to 4 inches high—a mass of violet and gold in the spring. All of these could be accompanied by native wildflowers that love the same conditions: Butterfly Weed, Wild Bergamot, Black-eyed-Susan, for a long and glorious season of bloom and interest.

HOW TO MAKE A QUIGGLY FENCE

*B*uild a three-rail fence by driving treated 6-foot posts 18 inches into the ground as far apart as the length of the fence. If the fence is longer than 12 feet, drive a post in the middle. Nail rails (use treated wood or peeled hardwood saplings) across the posts at 18 inches, 36 inches, and 48 inches above the ground. Weave young, unpeeled, fresh-cut saplings (black spruce or larch are best), no bigger than 2 inches in diameter, vertically through the rails (behind the bottom rail, in front of the middle one, and behind the top rail). Every other sapling should be woven in reverse (in front of the bottom, behind the middle, and in front of the top). Space the saplings an inch or two apart. You may cut them at a uniform height of 7 or 8 feet or vary them for a more natural effect. This type of fence also acts as an effective windbreak.

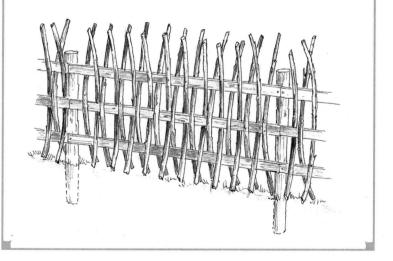

In that damp ground where nothing else will grow, establish Siberian Iris to naturalize with the ancient and native Yellow and Blue Flag Iris. The native Elderberry *(Sambucus canadensis)* is adaptable to damp as well as dry soil, and its thinly branched form won't block out the sun. At its feet you may encourage a colony of the magnificent Turk's-cap Lily *(Lilium superbum),* which is bright orange and heavily spotted. "A plant of so much beauty," Jefferson declared, "will be a valuable addition to our flower gardens."

If you're looking for an easy-to-grow vine for damp conditions, try American Virgin's-bower, a woody twining vine that can be trained over an arbor, where it will produce masses of small white flowers in the spring, followed by unusual fluffy fruits in the fall. You can establish a ground cover at its feet with two fine 18th-century introductions "from away": the azure Blue Lungwort *(Pulmonaria angustifolia)* and variegated Goutweed. If you also let the old-fashioned Bouncing-bet grow in a wide mat as it likes to do, its pink flowers will perfume the air in the early evening. Forget-me-nots should be added to any planting where the soil is moist, either in sun or shade.

A quiet, shaded arbor furnished with a bench, a place to rest and contemplate the beauty of the natural garden (especially satisfying since you allowed nature to do most of the work) calls for a Virginia Creeper Vine *(Parthenocissus quinquefolia).* Usually grown up the side of the house (it's a clinging vine), when grown over an arbor its side shoots trail downward, creating a graceful effect, and in the fall its foliage turns a most brilliant scarlet.

Choose from among these native plants those that are best suited to your area's growing conditions. All plants are hardy to Zone 3 or 4 except as noted. (❀ indicates fragrant plants.)

Annuals

Clarkia *(Clarkia* spp.)
Drummond Phlox *(Phlox drummondii)*
Godetia *(Clarkia amoena)*

Biennial or Short-Lived Perennial

Black-eyed-Susan *(Rudbeckia hirta)*

Perennials

Bee Balm *(Monarda didyma)* ❀
Blue Flag Iris (two species; one, *Iris virginica,* is hardy to Zone 7)
Butterfly Weed *(Asclepias tuberosa)* ❀
Crested Iris *(Iris cristata)*
Eastern Columbine *(Aquilegia canadensis)*
Horsemint *(Monarda punctata,* Zone 6) ❀
Leopard Lily *(Lilium pardalinum)*
Lupine *(Lupinus polyphyllus)*
Maidenhair Fern *(Adiantum pedatum)*
Moss Phlox *(Phlox subulata)*
Turk's-cap Lily *(Lilium superbum,* bulb hardy to Zone 5)
Wild Bergamot *(Monarda fistulosa)* ❀
Wild Bleeding-heart *(Dicentra eximia* and *D. formosa)*

Shrubs

Catawba Rhododendron *(Rhododendron catawbiense* 'Album') ❀
Clove and Golden Currants *(Ribes odoratum* and *R. aureum,* respectively) ❀
Elderberry *(Sambucus canadensis)* ❀
Flame Azalea *(Rhododendron calendulaceum,* Zone 5) ❀
Highbush Cranberry *(Viburnum trilobum)* ❀

Mountain-laurel *(Kalmia latifolia)*

Oregon Holly-grape *(Mahonia aquifolium, Zone 5)*

Pink-shell Azalea *(Rhododendron vaseyi)* ❀

Rosebay Rhododendron *(Rhododendron maximum)* ❀

Swamp Azalea *(Rhododendron viscosum)* ❀

Winter Currant *(Ribes sanguineum, Zone 6)* ❀

Perennial Vines

American Virgin's-bower *(Clematis virginiana)* ❀

Virginia Creeper *(Parthenocissus quinquefolia)*

The Parlor Garden: Late 1700s–1850

The early 19th-century parlor or dooryard garden was one of the most delightful American garden innovations, an unabashedly showy display of favorite flowers by the front of the house, in contrast to the more restricted plantings of the colonial period. The pattern was simple: orderly beds of flowers bordered a central path leading to the front door. Shrubs grew on either side, or by the garden entrance; rambling vines clambered up trellises propped against exterior walls. No wider than the house itself, the parlor garden was usually enclosed by a wooden picket fence to keep out straying livestock. Such a design suited well the spare, clean lines of New England architecture, where parlor gardens were popular.

This garden "room" was, like the parlor itself, a feminine domain, meticulously groomed and set apart from the mundane outdoor activities in the backyard still essential to the time, such as scrubbing clothes, plucking chickens, soapmaking, and chopping wood. Looking back, some saw the parlor garden, so closely attached to the house and marked off from the world at large, as emblematic of the lives of the women who tended them, "restricted and narrowed to a small outlook and monotonous likeness to her neighbor's; but it was a life easily satisfied with small pleasures, and it was comely, sheltered . . . and pleasant to the home household; and these were no mean things . . ." (Alice Morse Earle, "Front Dooryards," *Old-Time Gardens,* 1901). It signified, moreover, a more civilized, relaxed society where such ornamentation was openly acknowledged, proclaimed to every passerby and to the public at large. The American "best room" garden, unlike European front plantings, was framed with a see-through picket fence, rather than hidden from view by tall hedges or brick walls. The mainly old-world jewels within—showy, colorful flowers, often double and fragrant—were meant to be seen and admired.

The establishment of a parlor garden to front the house is still an excellent idea, not only for its authenticity, but for its antique charm, a complement to most architectural styles (the plainer the better). As it was in the past, such an area can be open to the world while at the same time it provides a refuge, a quiet, peaceful oasis from the busy life beyond. Sad to say, the quaint parlor garden described by Alice Morse Earle had all but vanished from the American scene by the late 1800s, mourned by those who saw in it all the virtues of the past, whether real or imagined.

If you'd like to create your own version, here are some pointers:

The early 19th-century parlor or dooryard garden was one of the most delightful American garden innovations.

✦ An attractive and traditional way to plant the border is to have one side mirror the other. This means that the same plants are grown in the same order on both sides of the walkway, but variations are possible (and desirable) by using contrasting colors and forms of the same species.

✦ For formal ambience, a "guard" planting of clipped box or similar shrub on either side of the doorway sets off and unifies borders of brightly colored flowers.

✦ For a more natural style, use low-growing Pinks, Moss Phlox, and Sweet Alyssum to edge the flower border; these are good choices to soften the hard lines of a brick walkway.

✦ However the border is planted, the setting invites antique bulbs such as double-flowered fragrant Daffodils, Tulips like the wild 'Florentine' *(Tulipa sylvestris)* for naturalizing, and the flamed and feathered 17th-century 'Zomerschoon' for bright color.

✦ Carry on the season with a colorful mix of Old World and native showy flowers such as double crimson Grandma's Peony, sweetly fragrant Lemon Lily, white and crimson Phlox, blue, rose, and white Canterbury Bells, bright red London-pride *(Lychnis chalcedonica)*, flaming orange candelabras of Tiger Lilies, and later, Black-eyed-Susan, Butterfly Weed, and scarlet Bee Balm.

✦ Create stunning effects by underplanting shrubs with Snowdrops and other bulbs, then overplant them with a ground cover of native Eastern Columbine (bright yellow and coral) or dusty rose Wild Bleeding-heart; the groundcover will hide the bulbs' ripening foliage.

✦ Grow at least one native vine up a support for vertical effect; Scarlet Honeysuckle is spectacular and attracts hummingbirds, but it's a vigorous spreader. One solution is to plant the tamer version, 'Dropmore Scarlet', a modern introduction with the same appeal. Or grow Climbing Nasturtium on a trellis.

✦ Plant native shrubs for early, fragrant bloom and fall-bearing fruits. Clove or Golden Currant are good choices, not only for their edible fruits but for their masses of clove-scented yellow trumpet flowers, nectar-rich for hummingbirds and deliciously, freely fragrant.

Choose from the plants listed in the *Gardens of Use & Delight* and *The Natural Garden* (see Bibliography), and from the following: (❀ indicates fragrant plants)

Annuals

China Aster *(Callistephus chinensis)*
Climbing Nasturtium *(Tropaeolum majus)* ❀
Cornflower *(Centaurea cyanus)*
Corn Poppy *(Papaver rhoeas)*
Flowering Tobacco *(Nicotiana)* ❀
Four O'Clock *(Mirabilis jalapa)* ❀
Love-in-a-mist *(Nigella damascena)*
Sweet Alyssum *(Lobularia maritima)* ❀

Biennials & Short-Lived Perennials

Rose Campion *(Lychnis coronaria)*
Sweet-William *(Dianthus barbatus)* ❀

Perennials

Lemon Lily *(Hemerocallis lilioasphodelus)* ❀
London-pride *(Lychnis chalcedonica)*
Pinks *(Dianthus plumarius, D. caryophyllus,*
　　double hybrids) ❀
Tiger Lily *(Lilium lancifolium* 'Splendens')

Bulbs

Daffodil *(Narcissus)* ❀
　　Double Yellow, 'Van Sion'
　　Double White *(N. poeticus* 'Albus')
　　Pheasant's Eye *(N. poeticus* var. *recurvus)*
Tulips *(Tulipa)* ❀
　　'Duc Van Thols', early, short
　　'Keizerskroon'
Tulipa sylvestris 'Florentine'
　　'Zomerschoon'
Snowdrops (single and double, *Galanthus nivalis, G. nivalis* 'Flore Pleno')

Perennial Vines

Dutchman's Pipe *(Aristolochia macrophylla)*

Victoriana: 1850 to early 1900s

Rapid development of commerce in the mid–19th century swept away the soft charm of the parlor garden. As commercial goods became readily available, households did not have to set aside outdoor space for the manufacture of basic necessities (soap, for instance), or for raising livestock. Not only the area in front of the house, but the backyard, too, assumed importance as a place for ornamentation and leisure. As fences came down, the front lawn, open to the world, became the hallmark of the new American garden.

New wealth demanded proper recognition in the form of ornate, elaborate architecture with complementary plantings. The simple lines of geometric beds were replaced with intricate flowing shapes in the form of circles, diamonds, crosses, and teardrops cut into the lawn, then raised to show off the latest annuals from the tropics in blazing colors, characteristically planted in intricate designs imitative of a Persian carpet, or in bright waves or ribbons (the origin of "carpet" or "ribbon" plantings). By 1865, such annuals for bedding (temporary plantings) focused on dwarf and double forms that gave consistent and bright color for the growing season. Some native plants, like Drummond's Phlox, discovered in the early 19th century and bred in Europe, now became very fashionable for their "improved" larger flowers in a range of vivid, clear colors. It was a mark of prestige to show off these disposables—good for one season only, unlike the now-neglected old-fashioned perennials—but it entailed constant deadheading to keep the blooms going in carpets and ribbons. Other annuals, like China Asters, were valued for their double, dahlia-like flowers in bouquet-like sprays, the desired effect of the Victorian garden itself being the appearance of a giant, oversize bouquet. Dahlias, too, were in demand, small-flowered pompons like 'Yellow Gem' and the gorgeous peony-flowered 'Bishop of Llandsdorf', with dark burgundy foliage.

Spring bulbs such as Daffodils, Hyacinths, and Tulips were important for early, massed display, the most favored types possessing double or bright flowers and fragrance: Daffodils like 'Laurens Koster' with cluster-flowered, creamy petals and fragrant little yellow-orange cups; the rich amber, sweet-scented 'Generaal De Wet' Tulip; the intoxicatingly sweet double-flowered, showy Hyacinth, 'Chestnut Flower'—all fortunately still available.

Fancy Pansies with blotched faces and fluted petals in a range of colors from creamy white to deep ruby were becoming popular, as were variants of the humble Johnny-jump-up (one of the Pansy's parents), like the darkest blue 'Prince Henry' and the sunny yellow 'Prince John', both lovely companions for Tulips.

Where the parlor garden was primly enclosed by a picket fence, Victorian design dictated sweeping, curved driveways, wide garden paths, and grouped shrubbery (a wealth of introductions from Asia were by then widely available). Unusual plant forms—weeping trees and shrubs—were displayed with pride, but sited so they didn't interfere with the new ideal: uninterrupted lawn from the house front to the property boundary. Foundation plantings, dating from this period, were meant to cover the house foundation

A Victorian-style container planting in a tire, with Dahlias and Sweet Alyssum.

(to about 3 feet), rather than to hide the house front altogether, as happened later.

This was an era, too, for Roses, especially large-flowered, fragrant, repeat-blooming Hybrid Perpetuals, the glory of Victorian gardens (by the end of the 19th century, three thousand cultivars were on the market). The first of the Modern Roses, they were a bridge between old Once-blooming Roses and the everblooming Hybrid Teas to come. Find a place in your landscape for these opulent, richly colored flowers, and don't be afraid to grow them with the old-fashioned perennials that are their natural companions.

Bold, in-your-face Victorian Cannas, with huge leaves, stiff stems, and neon-bright flowers, are the hottest trend in garden design these days, along with anything resembling "tropical." (Garden trends do have an uncanny way of periodically reinventing themselves as "new"!) Victorian heirlooms in this line are striking and it's fun to watch them grow. Taller Cannas show off well against green shrubbery, while shorter ones like 'Firebird' (glowing scarlet flowers, dark green leaves, 2 to 3 feet tall) are stunning in containers. One way to create your own container is to find a really large truck tire and get someone to help you turn it inside out, either leaving the edges as they are or cutting them into scallops. Turned inside-out, the tire resembles an elegant Victorian cast-iron urn, with the rim serving as a stand. Fill the deep bottom with newspaper, rough compost, then fine soil a few inches from the top. Plant Sweet Alyssum or variegated-leaved Nasturtium to trail over the container's edges.

All these plants from Victorian times are well worth growing today for their lasting beauty. Judiciously placed garden furnishings in intricate, elaborate design, whether arches, tubs, fences, benches, or statuary, give coherence to Victorian-inspired plantings, linking them together as an integral part of the landscape. (❀ indicates fragrance)

Annuals

Balsam *(Impatiens balsamina)* ❀
  'Extra Dwarf'
  'Gardenia-Flowered'
China Aster *(Callistephus chinensis)*
Clarkia *(C. pulchella* 'Plena')
Drummond's Phlox *(Phlox drummondii)*
  'Tapestry'
  'Leopoldii'
Godetia *(Clarkia amoena* 'Salmon Princess')
Nasturtium *(Tropaeolum)* ❀
  'Empress of India'
  'Alaska'—modern Victorian style with variegated leaf
Pansy *(Viola* × *wittrockiana)* ❀
  'Adonis'
  'Swiss Giants'
Sweet Alyssum *(Lobularia maritima)* ❀
Johnny-jump-up *(Viola tricolor)*
  'Prince Henry'
  'Prince John'

Hardy Bulbs

Daffodils *(Narcissus)* ❀
  'Barii Conspicuus'
  'Golden Spur'
  'Irene Copeland'
  'Laurens Koster'
  'Little Witch'
  'Mrs. R.O. Backhouse'
Hyacinths *(Hyacinthus orientalis)* ❀
  'Chestnut Flower'
  'Distinction'
  'General Kohler'
  'Grand Monarque'
  'King of the Blues'

  'Lady Derby'
  'La Victoire'
  'L'Innocence'
  'Lord Balfour'
  'Marie'
  'General Kohler'
Tulips *(Tulipa)* ❀
  'Clara Butt'
  'Coleur Cardinal'
  'Diana'
  'Generaal De Wet'
  'Greuze'

Tender Bulbs

Dahlia Hybrids
  'Bishop of Llandsdorf'
  'Stolz von Berlin'
  'Yellow Gem'
Canna Hybrids
  'Florence Vaughn'
  'Firebird'
  'Mme. Paul Caseneuve'
  'Mme Angele Martin'
  'City of Portland'
  'Cleopatra'

Shrubs

Roses: Hybrid Perpetual ❀
  'Baronne Prevost' (Zone 5) ❀
  'Frau Karl Druschki' (Zone 5) ❀
  'Baroness Rothschild' ❀
  'Paul Neyron' ❀
Bridalwreath Spirea *(Spiraea prunifolia)* ❀
Japanese Snowball *(Viburnum plicatum)* ❀
Peegee Hydrangea *(Hydrangea paniculata* 'Grandiflora')
Rhododendrons: Catawba Hybrids ❀
  'Everestianum' (Zone 5)
  'Mrs. Charles S. Sargent' (Zone 5)
  'President Lincoln' (Zone 5)
  'Purpureum Elegans' (Zone 5)

The American Cottage Garden, An Old-Fashioned Mix: late 1800s to early 1900s

In the wake of the country's centennial celebrations, a wave of nostalgia for the past inspired a return to old-fashioned plants in old-fashioned gardens (sometimes called "Grandmother's Garden"). Celia Thaxter's turn-of-the-century garden on the coast of New Hampshire was a brilliant realization of the new ideal, uniting colonial preoccupation—plank-bordered beds filled with old world flowers—with the "artless simplicity" of an idealized cottage garden: a rustic house embowered in vines, abundant flowers in sweet profusion. It is an ideal we continue to admire today, but the question is, how is it achieved?

It is well for anyone hoping to create the proverbial cottage garden to understand, as did Celia, that the genre requires structure and unity of design to succeed. No amount of old-fashioned summer houses and arbors will create a harmonious landscape if it is conceived as "anything you want to do," one of the many non-definitions of a cottage garden that we read about today.

To read Thaxter's classic work, *An Island Garden* (1894), is to recognize at once the affinity all gardeners feel when they read an authentic account of actualities. Beyond her ecstasy over the transcendent beauty of the flowers—Sweet Peas and Poppies were favorites—we hear the voice of a seasoned, hard-headed gardener, one who planted seed, pulled weeds, lugged water, fought bugs and disease, who planned her garden down to the last detail.

Celia's garden was an intimate, extended room of the house; the porch, embowered in twining vines, was at one end, the sea at the other. Only 50 feet long by 15 feet wide, it was small, but every inch of ground was accounted for, the planting methodically arranged for contrast of color and form, achieved through repetition and massed plantings. The area was divided into a series of plank-enclosed beds, six vertical and three horizontal, with access paths between and a path all around surrounded by a board fence; steps and gates led into the garden. Plantings were fit into every space—in front of, in back of, and on the fence, at corners, by gates—with the access paths always clear. No more than four different kinds of plants, a mix of annuals and perennials, were placed in a bed together—usually only two, sometimes one—to allow each type maximum growth and to provide a succession of bloom. Judiciously placed trellises made use of vertical space. Although highly structured, the overall impression was one of artless beauty, *but it was a beauty that was planned every step of the way.*

Whatever design style you choose, plants from this period offer great scope for the

An idealized cottage garden: a rustic house embowered in vines, abundant flowers in sweet profusion.

heirloom gardener, from Bleeding-heart, laden with dangling rosy hearts, to tender annuals (Morning-glories and Nasturtiums), as well as sturdy perennials from the Orient. The untailored forms of lush-flowered Bourbon Roses and fragrant, low-maintenance Rugosa hybrids evoke the past, and as a bonus they bloom almost the entire summer.

Such plants typify an era when art and science were beginning to produce new hybrid forms never seen before, such as the large-flowered Jackman Clematis introduced in 1860 and still popular. Here you can also find the increasingly rare open-pollinated "Essential Petunia," a little sweet-scented pure white or dark purple velvet trumpet. This period offers a fine introduction to the whole concept of *heirloom*, saving the best from the period prior to the modern era.

A child's rustic arbor (see directions on page 55) can be clothed in Morning-glories, Moonflowers, Sweet Pea, and Scarlet Runner Bean vines, all quick-growing plants. Around three sides—leaving room for an entrance path—plant a colorful annual border for all-season bloom from early summer into the fall: Cosmos, double-flowered Balsam, Nicotiana, Shirley or Corn Poppies, Petunias, Marigolds (single French and dwarf Signets). This is certain to be a popular place for children in summer. Even if you have only a little room, several of these can be planted in containers. The heirloom strain Nasturtium 'Empress of India', for instance, is gorgeous in a hanging basket, with its cascading orange-red spurred flowers. The seldom-grown fern-scented Signets, a mound of orange or yellow bloom until frost (and even beyond if sheltered), fit into the landscape almost anywhere. If you plant in containers, remember that the wider the surface area,

the less soil will dry out, especially if the plants are mulched and protected from the glare of the sun at least part of the day where summers are very hot.

If you think Hostas are boring, this is the opportunity to learn more about them. The types here were introduced from the Far East before the end of the 19th century. Try them in filtered shade (a good place for Bleeding-heart, too) and group them for contrast of foliage—broad and glossy, undulating, narrow, or variegated. Most Hostas sport attractive, and sometimes quite fragrant, flowers. These plants, when given the right accommodations—moist and cool—will spread out and look as if they mean to stay a long time (they will), and you won't be sorry you planted them.

The spectacular wild Goldband Lily and the Rubrum Lily from the Orient—fragrant and free-flowering with large, waxy-white, recurved, pendant blooms—will do best among shrubbery, especially Rhododendron, which also enjoy rich, humus-rich soil that is heavily mulched.

Plant Hybrid Roses on a sunny bank and edge them generously with furry gray, drought-resistant mats of Lamb's-ears interplanted with the indispensable Sweet Alyssum, a border that will take care of itself all season.

For a hardy perennial vine to climb up a tree (use chicken wire), Jackman Clematis puts on a good show all summer, but all of the vines below have proven their worth. To cover the side of an old shed, there is no better vine than the Sweet Autumn Clematis.

Following are suggested plants for the old-fashioned mix. To achieve the blazing, shimmering colors and sweet scents of Celia Thaxter's garden, include lots of antique

Sweet Peas (especially the American-bred types Celia may have grown) and Hollyhocks (she sought out the "Black" strain, considered old-fashioned and rare at that time). Make several sowings of annual Poppies of all types, plant more than one variety of Clematis, and don't forget the humble Hop Vine to shade your porch (if you are lucky enough to have one). (❀ indicates fragrant plants)

Annuals

Balsam *(Impatiens balsamina)*
Cosmos *(Cosmos bipinnatus)*
Marigolds *(Tagetes patula* and *T. tenuifolia)* ❀
Moonflower *(Ipomoea alba,* quick-growing twining vine) ❀
Nasturtiums *(Tropaeolum majus,* flower and quick-growing twining vine) ❀
Nicotiana *(Nicotiana alata)* ❀
Peony Poppy *(Papaver somniferum)*
Petunia *(Petunia* X *hybrida)* ❀
   'Alderman' (purple climbing)
   'Old-Fashioned Climbing' (white and lavender) ❀
   'Balcony' (assorted colors for window boxes, containers)
   'Dwarf Mixed'
   'Kentucky Old-Fashioned' (climbing type in assorted colors and designs)
Scarlet Runner Bean and White Runner Bean *(Phaseolus coccineus* and *P. coccineus* 'Albus',* respectively, quick-growing twining vines)
Shirley or Corn Poppy *(Papaver rhoeas)*
Sweet Pea *(Lathyrus odoratus,* twining vine) ❀
   'America' (raspberry sundae stripings)
   'Blanche Ferry' (rose and pink)
   'Flora Norton' (clear blue)
   'Janet Scott' (pearl pink)

Sweet Alyssum *(Lobularia maritima)* ❀
Wild Petunia (small-flowered, purple, and fragrant) ❀

Biennials

Hollyhock *(Alcea rosea,* tall single)
Black Hollyhock *(Alcea rosea* 'Nigra')
Foxglove *(Digitalis* 'Alba')
Rose Campion *(Lychnis coronaria* 'Oculata')

Perennials (hardy to Zone 3 or 4 except as noted)

Bleeding-heart *(Dicentra spectabilis)*
Daffodils (hardy bulbs)
   Angel's-tears *(Narcissus triandus albus;* inquire about zone if nursery-propagated)
   Hoop-petticoat Daffodil *(N. bulbocodium* 'Conspicuous', Zone 6; inquire about zone if nursery-propagated)
Old Pheasant's-eye *(N. poeticus recurvus)* ❀
Hostas
   Blue Plantain Lily *(Hosta ventricosa)*
   Fortune's Plantain Lily *(H. fortunei* 'Hyacinthia')
   Fragrant Plantain Lily (August or Corfu Lily) *(H. plantaginea)* ❀
   Siebold Plantain Lily *(H. sieboldiana* 'Elegans')
Lilies
   Goldband Lily *(Lilium auratum)*
   Rubrum Lily *(L. speciosum* 'Rubrum')
   Oriental Poppy *(Papaver orientale* 'Perry's White')

Shrubs

Roses: Bourbon
   'Louise Odier' (Zone 6) ❀
   'Mme. Isaac Pereire' (Zone 6) ❀
Roses: Hybrid Perpetual
   'Baronne Prevost' (Zone 5) ❀

'Frau Karl Druschki' (Zone 5)
Roses: Rugosa
    'Blanc Double de Coubert' (Zone 3 or
      4) ❀
    'Roseraie de l'Hay' (Zone 3 or 4) ❀

Vines (hardy to Zone 3 or 4; twine like grapes; need horizontal support)

Clematis
    Anemone Clematis *(Clematis montana*
      rubens) ❀
    'Elsa Späth' ❀
    Jackman Clematis *(C. × jackmanii)* ❀
    'Lord Neville' ❀
    'Nelly Moser' ❀
    ' Sweet Autumn Clematis
      (C. paniculata) ❀

The Eclectic Garden: 1600–1950 Plus

This is the place to put it all together—cottage garden herbs and flowers on the wild side with 'New Dawn', the 1930 Hybrid Climbing Rose, which puts forth clusters of blush pink flowers all summer. The eclectic garden is also the place to explore the diverse world of heirloom Glads, Daffodils, Iris, and Lilies (so defined if they were introduced more than thirty years ago). These hardy plants have endured in the marketplace or in the hearts of gardeners because of their superior qualities: adaptability, beauty, and an undefinable essence that elevates them to the status of legend. Did you ever think a Glad could fall into this category? Many enthusiasts feel that way about 'Picardy', a 1931 creation with soft pink blooms that has vanished from the marketplace but is perhaps still growing in a garden somewhere. Some heirloom gardeners feel as strongly about pre-

A CHILD'S ARBOR

*T*o make this charming structure, you need half a dozen freshly cut saplings (alder, willow, or birch are good), 2 inches thick at the butt and 12 feet long. Leave the twigs on. Mark a circle with a 6-foot diameter on the ground. Sharpen the saplings' butts. Thrust two saplings into the ground opposite each other at six and twelve o'clock, and arch them over each other, leaving enough room to walk underneath. Tie the saplings together securely with inconspicuous twine or wire at two or three places where they overlap on both sides. Do the same with two more saplings at two and eight o'clock, then with two more at four and ten o'clock. Plant quick-growing annual vines all around the base of the arbor, except at the low entranceway.

advantage). Among these sow tall white Nicotiana and Cosmos, dark blue Bachelor's-button, and annual Poppies and Calendula. To this generous all-season border, add Bearded Iris (all sizes and colors), vintage large-flowered Glads—grouped together near the middle of the border, where just their blooms will be exposed—and an heirloom Lily or two. The fragrant Regal Lily, with large white trumpets, is a good substitute for the White or Madonna Lily.

The eclectic garden is the place to put it all together—old and new flowers paired with a Classic Rose trained along a rail fence.

serving 'Amigo', a 1938 Bearded Iris with extraordinary pansy coloring and generous form, as others feel about preserving 18th-century laced Pinks. There is room in the eclectic garden for the simple, unadorned beauty of the wild Cowslip *(Primula veris)* and Jan de Graaf's 1947 'Enhancement' Lily, an introduction that set the standard for Hybrid Lilies: reliable, free-flowering, and disease-resistant. Wherever they are planted, ancient, antique, and middle-aged heirlooms enjoy and thrive in each other's company.

In full sun, plant early settlers' flowers and herbs such as Musk Mallow, Bellflower, Sweet-William, Jerusalem-cross, Dame's-rocket, Sweet Cicely, Sage, and Feverfew. Add to these the outrageous but indispensable Oriental Poppy, fortified by the Mountain-bluet to help prop up its sprawling stems. Also add Mr. Russell's late 1930s luscious Hybrid Lupines in every shade you can get, the tall spires of Foxglove, and the sunny daisylike Golden-Marguerite (through which the gray-green Sage foliage will appear to

Did you know that there are wild Glads for naturalizing, some so hardy that you need not dig up their corms in the fall (Hardy Glad)? These can be grown with wild Sweet Flag Iris, which have fragrant lavender-blue flowers and striped foliage. In the rock garden, add 'Little Witch', a 1929 Cyclamineus Daffodil (only 8 inches high) with yellow flared-back petals, and 'Louisa', a lovely variation on the Narrow-leaved Plantain Lily with its narrow, white-edged leaves and white flowers. In partial shade, plant the first pink-apricot trumpeted Daffodil, 'Mrs. R. O. Back-house', with Virginia-bluebells. ('Louisa' will enjoy growing here, too.)

In that damp spot in the sun where nothing else will grow, you can plant the wild Blue Flag Iris (combine it with the European Yellow Flag Iris). Plant the irrepressible Policeman's Helmet here, too, and let it grow in a wide, spectacular swath of speckled bloom in assorted pinks. It would also make a stunning informal, billowy hedge to lead from one area of the garden to another.

Of course, you must have Roses—for making hedges, arbors, adding to the shrubbery, and even planting in containers. Investigate the middle-aged classics such as 'Buff Beauty', a 1939 Hybrid Musk shrub with a strong fragrance and an equable disposition, producing gold-cream flowers all summer long, even in drought conditions. The ever-blooming Polyantha 'The Fairy', with masses of light pink double blossoms that last all summer, will make a low hedge or even a container plant. For a bushy hedge, grow 'Betty Prior', which has bright, single-petaled pink blooms all summer and is spectacular when massed. As for 'Blaze', tie it to a post for full vertical bloom and train it along a fence (pegging down the long, supple canes), or over an arbor, where it will provide a fitting entrance to the eclectic garden. (❀ indicates fragrant plants)

Annual

Policeman's Helmet *(Impatiens gladulifera)*

Perennials

(hardy to Zone 3 or 4 except as noted)

Daffodils
   'Beersheba'
   'Little Witch'
   'Mrs. R.O. Backhouse'
   'Silver Chimes' (Zone 6) ❀
   'Thalia' ❀
Foxglove *(Digitalis purpurea)*
Glads (for naturalizing)
   Colville Glad *(Gladiolus × colvillei* 'Albus', Zone 7) ❀

Hardy Glad *(G. byzantinus,* Zone 4) ❀
Hybrid Glads (treat as annuals) ❀
   'Dawn Glow'
   'Glacier'
   'Peter Pears'
Golden-Marguerite *(Anthemis tinctoria)*
Hostas
   'Louisa'
Iris, Bearded:
   'Amigo'
   'Black Forest'
   'Blue Denim'
   'Honorabile'
   'Wabash'
Iris, Siberian *(Iris sibirica)*
   'Eric the Red'
   'Helen Astor'
   'White Swirl'
Sweet Iris *(Iris pallida,* Zone 5) ❀
Regal Lily *(Lilium regale)* ❀
Lupines (Russell Hybrids)
Mountain-bluet *(Centaurea montana)*
Oriental Poppy *(Papaver orientale)*
Roses (shrubs, ramblers, and climbers used as vines; hardy to Zone 5 except where noted)
   'Betty Prior'
   'Blaze'
   'Buff Beauty' ❀
   'Crimson Glory' ❀
   'Paul's Scarlet Climber'
   'The Fairy' (Zone 4)
   'Therese Bugnet' (Zone 4) ❀

PART II

A Treasury of Heirloom Ornamentals, 1600–1950:
Flowers, Herbs, Shrubs and Vines

"There were Lupines, Sweet Peas, Phlox, Bluebells, Day and Tiger Lilies, Monkshood, Peonies, Columbine, Daffodils, single and double, a Bleeding-heart bush in the front yard, and vines at each corner, which at times nearly covered the house. And always there was Golden-glow by the kitchen door."

—An Old-Time Gardener

PLANT PORTRAIT EXAMPLE

(❀ indicates a fragrance or scent in the flowers or foliage)

Botanical name:

Genus, species 'Cultivar if any'

Botanical name: *Genus, species 'Cultivar if any'*	*Asclepias tuberosa* ❀
FAMILY	ASCLEPIADACEAE
Common name used in portrait Other common names	**Butterfly Weed** Butterfly Flower, Butterfly Milkweed, Chigger Flower, Indian Paintbrush, Pleurisy Root, Swallowwort
DATES OF INTRODUCTION GROWING ZONES NATIVE/NATURALIZED TYPE: Perennial, Biennial, Herb, Bulb, etc. HEIGHT: BLOOM/SEASON OF INTEREST: PREFERRED SITE: Partial Shade; Shade, etc.	INTRODUCED: 1776–1850 ZONES 4–10 NATIVE TYPE: Perennial Wildflower/Herb HEIGHT: 2–3' BLOOM: Summer-Fall SITE: Sun/Partial Shade
Text description	*B*utterfly Weed is a conspicuous wild-flower that grows in dry fields and along woodlands and roadsides from . . . **To Grow:** Butterfly Weed is especially valued where conditions are hot and dry. . .
COLLECTOR'S CHOICE: Recommended plants: species, varieties, cultivars.	COLLECTOR'S CHOICE: *Asclepias tuberosa,* Butterfly Weed (1776– 1850).

Abelia × *grandiflora* ❀

CAPRIFOLIACEAE

Glossy Abelia

INTRODUCED: 1850–1900
ZONES: 6–10
TYPE: Shrub
HEIGHT: 5'
BLOOM: Summer
SITE: Sun/Partial Shade

Glossy Abelia is one of thirty species of shrubs originating in Asia, Mexico, and India. A hybrid of exceptional vigor and beauty, it is widely cultivated in the mid-South, Mid-Atlantic States, and Midwest. It is valued for its season of bloom—intermittently throughout most of the summer—and glossy, almost evergreen leaves. Of medium height and neat habit, it bears showy white, delicately fragrant, bell-shaped flowers tinged with pink. These grow in terminal clusters at the tip of the shrub's branches, creating a mass of bloom. In the fall and winter months where winters are mild, the leaves turn bronze, thus adding another season of interest to this valuable ornamental. The genus is named for Dr. Clark Abel, a doctor and writer who lived in China in the 19th century.

This is a shrub of late 19th-century gardens, bred in Italy *(Abelia chinensis* × *A. uniflora)* sometime before 1880, and like many plants that attained popularity then, it is regarded as old-fashioned. It was well established by the 1930s and highly recommended by Mrs. Francis King, well-known arbiter of horticultural taste of the period, who advised its use as a formal hedge, noting that "its charming bronzy leaves clip well." More than thirty years later, it was selected as a "Rembrandt among shrubs" by a distinguished committee of experts headed by Donald Wyman in *One Hundred Finest Trees and Shrubs for Temperate Climates* (BBG Record Plants & Gardens, 1957). In 1962 it was given the Royal Horticultural Society Award of Garden Merit, "an accolade well deserved by such an admirable plant," according to Will Ingwersen, who considers it a classic.

A shrub of such virtues surely has a place in any garden where conditions permit. It may be used as an all-season hedge, clipped or unclipped; for a mixed foundation planting among evergreens; or as a specimen bush behind early-flowering bulbs. The rub is *where conditions permit,* for, though easy to grow, Glossy Abelia likes heat. Its neat habit recommends its use in small gardens.

To Grow: Plant in well-drained, light, peaty soil—pH 6.0 to 8.0—enriched with leaf mold, in a sunny spot, preferably one that is protected from bright sun and wind. Light shade is especially welcome where summers are very hot. Prune the plant in the spring to maintain its shape (blossoms are formed on new wood, so early pruning is okay) and propagate it by 4-inch softwood cuttings taken in the fall and wintered-over in a cold frame. This Abelia is relatively hardy—to New York City (Zone 6) and possibly farther north to Boston—if it is well protected and planted in a favorable spot (near a building and away from wind). Like all Abelias, though, it thrives in heat, which helps to mature its wood. Mature wood is more resistant to frost, so the secret of maintaining a healthy, frost-resistant shrub is to ensure that it receives steady heat for as long as possible.

Abelia 'Edward Goucher' (before 1911).
    Large lavender-purple flowers, 5' tall.
Abelia × *grandiflora,* Glossy Abelia.

Achillea ptarmica

ASTERACEAE

Sneezewort
Bride's-bouquet, Nosebleed,
Shirtbuttons

A. ptarmica 'The Pearl'

INTRODUCED: 1776–1850
NATURALIZED: 1850–1911
ZONES 3–9
TYPE: Hardy Perennial Flower/Herb
HEIGHT: 2½'
BLOOM: Summer
SITE: Sun

Sneezewort is an old-world weed naturalized in damp fields and roadsides from eastern Canada to Michigan. It grows by creeping roots that send up stems to 2 feet or so with narrow, sawtooth leaves and white-petaled flowers in loose clusters. In the single form, a dull greenish center is apparent, but there is a great deal of variability in the wildflowers; some are semidouble, with more than one layer of petals, while others are almost double, with the center just evident. In the cultivar 'The Pearl', the flowers are fully double, with the center almost entirely hidden.

The uses of Sneezewort are preserved in 16th- and 17th-century herbals. Gerard advised that its juice mixed with vinegar and "holden in the mouth, easeth much of pain of tooth-ache," while Culpeper spoke of using it dried and powdered as snuff (to cause sneezing) against headaches. Its flowers also yield a greenish dye.

Sneezewort's bouquet-like sprays of flowers also suggested its use in bride's bouquets (a common name still used locally) and dried-flower bouquets popular in the 18th century (as they are today). In the 19th century, the seedsman Joseph Breck described Sneezewort as a "desirable border flower, especially the double." The double form, known to Gerard, was listed as *A. ptarmica flore pleno.* (*Flore pleno* and its variants—*flora-plen, flore-pleno, flore-pleno, flo-plen, pleni flora,* and *pleno*—all describe double flowers; the terms turn up on old seed lists. Nowadays such variants are considered cultivars and are usually described with a modern-language name rather than a Latin tag.)

By the late 19th and early 20th centuries, the French nurseryman Lemoine had developed the cultivar known in French as 'Boule de Neige', or 'The Pearl'. It differs significantly from the wild form in that its flowers are of the purest white, fully double, and fluffy, with barely a hint of a central disk. They grow in larger clusters—3 to 6 inches across—and are especially long-lasting cut flowers, for which they were in great demand by florists at the time.

My adventures with Sneezewort began in 1978 when I bought a forty-cent packet of seeds described as 'The Pearl'. The flowers were supposed to be fully double, pure white baby pompoms. This plant and its numerous descendants grew for many years in and out of my garden (I naturalized it along our lane), and I was content until I found the real thing, quite by chance, growing untended in an old abandoned garden in a tangle of weeds. There could be no mistaking the difference between the flowers of my small, semidouble, creamy white wildflower, Sneezewort, and this elegant plant before me, described by Roy Genders as "the whitest of all flowers." Not only were the flowers of 'The Pearl' larger, but the whole plant was taller and more erect than mine (and this after having had no attention for decades). I also compared each as a cut flower and found that 'The Pearl' showed no diminution of its beauty after several weeks in a glass of water, while my interloper passed its peak of freshness after seven to ten days (not bad either). The moral of this story is that when you want a choice cultivar, such as 'The Pearl', buy the plant rather than a packet of seeds, which is more than likely to produce an inferior strain. And, by all means, cut the flowers of either variety for summer bouquets. 'The Pearl' is especially effective when dried for winter bouquets.

To Grow: Plant roots of either common Sneezewort or 'The Pearl' in well-drained, humus-rich soil, in full sun. Both are drought-tolerant, but wind will cause them to sprawl (especially Sneezewort). Both Sneezewort and 'The Pearl' are rambunctious spreaders, so I naturalize the former on a sunny slope and confine the latter to large tubs.

Both plants must be divided every two to four years. 'The Pearl' can be propagated by stem cuttings taken anytime during the summer and wintered-over in a cold frame. Sneezewort seeds can be planted in a cold frame during the summer, and the seedlings can be planted out the following spring, one to two feet apart, as can 'The Pearl'.

COLLECTOR'S CHOICE:

Achillea ptarmica, Sneezewort
    (1776–1850).
A. ptarmica 'The Pearl' (1850–1911).

Aconitum spp.

RANUNCULACEAE

Monkshood
Blue-rocket, Cupid's-ear, Fall Lilac, Friar's-cap, Helmet Flower, Lady's Slipper, Queen-mother-of-poisons, Soldier's-cap, Turk's-cap, Venus's-shell, Wolfsbane

INTRODUCED: 1600–1900
ZONES 2–8
TYPE: Hardy Perennial Flower
HEIGHT: to 6'
BLOOM: Summer–Fall
SITE: Partial Shade/Shade

One hundred or more species of *Aconitum* are native to Europe, Asia, and North America, growing on tall stalks similar in form and flower to Delphinium, except their flowers are quite distinctive upon close examination. Blue, amethyst, violet, purple, and even yellow or pinkish-white in wandlike panicles, each flower has a pronounced "hood," actually a sepal, either fitting closely over the rest of the flower or standing up. The cut-up fernlike foliage, similar to that of the Buttercup, to which family it belongs, is widest nearer the stem and glossy, as if warning passersby of the plant's dangerous properties (strong alkaloids in its roots, a characteristic that has given rise to its many and varied folk names). Wolfsbane was derived from the idea that arrows tipped in the plant's juice were supposed to have killed wolves. The genus name *Aconitum* is Latin, and for centuries has been synonymous with this poisonous herb (the one with which Romeo poisoned himself). *Aconitum,* or Monkshood, turns up so early in gardening lists that it must have been used as a poison against predators, since it appears to have no healing properties for humans. Its flowers are "so beautiful that a man would think they were of some excellent virtue," Gerard wrote.

The steady introduction of new species from Europe and Asia throughout the 18th and 19th centuries, however, is convincing evidence that this beautiful and interesting flower found much favor among American gardeners, who valued it for its ease of culture, hardiness, midsummer to fall bloom, and long-lasting flowers. As far as I know, the plant's poisonous properties have never caused gardeners any trouble, but it is a good idea to wash your hands after handling the roots.

Monkshood, like the Daylily, is a hardy survivor of neglect, and I have often found it on the peninsula in abandoned gardens, growing in great clumps among Daylilies *(Hemerocallis fulva)*. Contrary to most gardening advice, I have found that clumps can be dug up and replanted right away, with no setback, if a good amount of earth is taken with them around their roots. I have seen Monkshood grown as a stunning, low-maintenance hedge—a "room divider" in a garden designed in the 1920s. The hedge was given no special care, just allowed to grow up naturally every year, then die back in the fall, enriched only by its decaying leaves. Some of the most desirable old types here have bright blue flowers; others have distinctive, long-lasting, bicolor blooms—white edged with purplish blue—especially if planted in the shade or partial shade.

In my own garden, I grow violet Monkshood in a partially shaded pastel garden with gray-leaved Lamb's-ears, pure white Nicotiana, mauve-flowered Chives, and pink double Poppies, edged with white Sweet Alyssum. Monkshood would do well in a more shaded site, too, among Hostas and Ferns. I have never had any desire, as an herbalist, to experiment with using Monkshood in any form except as a cut flower, although I have noted that bees are drawn to its nectar in its season of bloom.

To Grow: Plant Monkshood in deeply prepared, well-drained, moist soil on the heavy side, in partial shade or shade. It will grow in moist soil in the sun, but the foliage will spoil and the flowers will fade fast. Space plants 12 to 18 inches apart, with the crowns just below the soil's surface. Where winters are severe, young plants should be protected until they are established. Fresh seeds can be sown in a cold frame to germinate over the winter. Propagation is simple if enough soil is taken with the roots and the reset plants are watered well and protected from the wind and hot sun.

COLLECTOR'S CHOICE:

Aconitum carmichaelii, Azure Monkshood (1850–1900); medium blue blooms; 4'; September to October.

A. lycoctonum, Great Yellow Monkshood (1776–1850); light yellow blooms; 2½'; summer; Zone 3.

A. *napellus,* Monkshood (1600–1699); violet-
    blue or purplish blooms; 4'; summer.
A. × *bicolor* (by 19th century); white, edged
    with purplish blue blooms; 4'; late
    summer.

Adiantum pedatum

POLYPODIACEAE

Maidenhair Fern
American Maidenhair, Five-finger Fern,
Northern Maidenhair

INTRODUCED: 1700–1776
ZONES: 3–9
NATIVE
TYPE: Hardy Fern
HEIGHT: 12–28"
SEASON OF INTEREST: Summer–Fall Foliage
SITE: Partial Shade/Shade

The native Maidenhair Fern, the most
delicate and highly prized of our native
species, grows on shaded slopes and in old
woods wherever the soil is humus-rich and
moist but well drained. Its range extends from
Nova Scotia west to Minnesota and south to
Georgia and Oklahoma. Its emerald green,
deeply divided leaves, or fronds, radiate from
glossy stems—dark reddish to ebony—almost
forming a halo that flutters gracefully in even
a slight breeze. The genus name, from the
Greek *adiantos,* meaning "dry," refers to the
way the fronds shed water in the rain.

The beauty of this native fern became
known to our earliest naturalists and plant
collectors. John Bartram, a farmer and naturalist with a deep interest in native flora, grew
these plants in his gardens on the Schuylkill
River (one of America's first botanical gar-

dens), where people came from all over the
world to see the native plants that would soon
be growing in the gardens of Europe.
Bartram's plant nursery was also one of the
country's first, established in 1728. His listings were eagerly perused by such curious
gardeners as George Washington and Thomas Jefferson. (For more information on Bartram's gardens, see the listing in "Gardens to
Visit" in Part 3.)

Although gardening trends change over
time—with the "wild garden" enjoying great
popularity, then fading into almost total
eclipse—the Maidenhair Fern has remained
popular for its ability to combine well with
many types of flowering plants (bulbs, perennials, and shrubs). It is neither rampant nor
overbearing like other fern species, so it is
far easier to incorporate into a garden setting
(especially a small garden), whether the garden is on the wild side or wholly under the
gardener's control in a semiformal landscape.

Maidenhair Fern is most refined, radiating its lovely grace over the entire growing
season when planted among rocks and clumps
of naturalized Daffodils (so many heirloom
types to choose from), later covering up the
latter's decaying leaves, or at the woodland's
edge, a bridge planting between the garden
proper and the wild, thriving in the dappled
shade among other native plants such as Bee-
balm, Fringed Bleeding-heart, and Columbine *(Aquilegia canadensis).* This fern is even
adaptable to container planting, so you can
move it where needed, as long as its delicate
fronds are protected from the wind. Altogether, Maidenhair Fern is especially recommended to gardeners who think a plant without bright flowers has nothing to offer.

Because Maidenhair Fern is such an admirable plant and grows wild over many parts

of the country, it has long been dug up by both gardeners and commercial collectors. Native populations should be left undisturbed (although spore collection, described below, won't hurt the plant). In areas slated for development, these ferns could be rescued from destruction by following the instructions in the "Plant Collector's Guide" (page 28) and the growing instructions below.

To Grow: The easiest way to establish ferns is by ordering plants from a reputable nursery that propagates native plants. The roots or rhizomes should be planted about 1 foot apart in moist, humus-rich, well-drained soil, in partial or full shade, and protected from the wind. Mulch the plants for a year or so until they are well established. When digging up wild plants to rescue, handle them carefully, since the rhizomes are brittle and break apart easily. Clumps can be divided if at least one bud or frond, 2 inches long, is growing from each section. Plants also can be propagated by collecting the spores that form under the curled-back edges of the leaves. Wait until midsummer or early fall when the spores are dark, then gently shake them into an envelope. Leave the envelope, unsealed, in a warm dry place so the spores can dry. Then sow the spores over moist, well-drained, sterile potting soil. Cover the soil with clear glass and keep it at 65°F (18°C). When a thin green tissue develops on top of the soil, begin misting it twice a week (return the cover each time), to encourage fertilization, the first sign of which is a tiny frond. It is important to keep the frond moist, not wet, in a covered situation (clear plastic or glass) and in a warm place. The little plants should be transplanted, 1 inch apart, to encourage root formation. Leave them indoors (eventually in uncovered pots) until they are well established. Then plant them out as described. The whole process may take eight to twelve months or longer.

COLLECTOR'S CHOICE:

Adiantum pedatum, Maidenhair Fern (1700–1776).

Aegopodium podagraria 'Variegatum'

APIACEAE

Goutweed
Bishop's Weed, Ground-ash, Ground-elder, Youth-before-old-age

INTRODUCED: 1850–1900?
ZONES: 3–9
TYPE: Hardy Perennial Ground Cover
HEIGHT: 6–24"
SEASON OF INTEREST: All-season Foliage
SITE: Sun/Partial Shade/Shade

The wild form, *Aegopodium podagraria,* or Goutweed, is a native of Europe, an ancient medicinal associated with monasteries and church buildings. An invasive plant with shiny green serrated leaves, it grows by creeping roots. The cultivar 'Variegatum' is far less invasive and more attractive, with mounds of soft emerald green leaves irregularly edged with white. Another common name, Youth-before-old-age, doubtless refers to the plant's habit of sending forth all-green leaves that become variegated as they mature.

The green-leaved Goutweed is an herb whose healing properties are associated with sore joints, as the common name suggests.

Culpeper observed that this was not an idle fancy, adding that besides relieving gout, sciatica, and joint aches, it also relieved "cold griefs." It would seem to have been indispensable in any list of settlers' herbs. Its variegated-leaf form, however, is often found thriving around old homesteads, where it was favored as a ground cover because of its ease of culture, lovely leaves, and ability to grow just about anywhere, in any soil and in either sun or shade.

It's true, I think, as has been observed, that in the pursuit of rarity, invaluable garden plants are apt to be overlooked. The ornamental Goutweed is rarely mentioned in garden books, even where ground covers are considered, perhaps because it is so easy to grow that it is taken for granted. Its vigorous, rampant nature is deplored, and gardeners are forewarned about its invasiveness. When it is well handled, however, it is a lovely addition to an heirloom garden, a useful tool that can be used to create different effects, all with great ease.

I first saw 'Variegatum' as a neatly trimmed hedge defining the boundaries of an older backyard planting. It had been part of a rather elaborate scheme devised by a landscape architect around the 1920s that involved shrub-lined "rooms" of Monkshood, Astilbe, and Garden Phlox. The ground cover had been used ingeniously—not like a ground cover at all, but as a stalwart and attractive low wall maintained by mowing both the grass in front of it and the plants themselves, the first time early in the summer when the little umbels of tiny white flowers appear on thin stalks.

A local gardener in the folk tradition added to my knowledge of other ways to grow the accommodating 'Variegatum'. He makes holes in the canopy of leaves, established as a ground cover to light up a shady nook, and in them sinks potted Impatiens or any bright-flowered plant that tolerates shade, such as Nicotiana. The leaves quickly grow back, and the brilliant annuals rise from them—coral, pink, and scarlet amid a sea of emerald and white, as striking a combination as the most discriminating gardener could desire. Potted plants, moreover, need not be sunk in the soil, just placed where you want them.

To Grow: Cultural directions seem superfluous. Just plant the roots in ordinary soil, in sun, partial shade, or shade. Water them and watch them grow. Twelve plants will cover about 10 square feet over two seasons. Be sure to mow down the flowers in early spring or whenever they appear, as well as the area around the planting all season, to contain 'Variegatum's' rambunctious growth.

COLLECTOR'S CHOICE:

Aegopodium podagraria 'Variegatum', Goutweed (1850–1900?).

Alcea rosea

MALVACEAE

Hollyhock
Chinese Hollyhock, Garden Mallow, Holyoke, Outlandish Rose

INTRODUCED: 1600–1699
ZONES: 3–10
TYPE: Biennial Flower/Herb
HEIGHT: 8'
BLOOM: Summer
SITE: Sun

Hollyhocks are native to China and were cultivated in Asia and the Middle East for many centuries before they were introduced to the West, perhaps by returning Crusaders. These are true biennials, the first year producing clumps or mounds of rough, almost heart-shaped lobed foliage close to the ground, and the second year sending up stems—three to six per clump—that can grow as tall as 13 feet, with wide-open, overlapping, five-petaled flowers all along their length in shades of rose and pink. The wider range of colors associated with Hollyhocks is the result of selection as well as crossbreeding with other species.

The Englishman John Josselyn, who left a detailed description of the plants he saw growing in early New England gardens, lists Hollyhocks as garden herbs among "Marygolds" *(Calendula),* "French Mallowes" *(Malva sylvestris),* and "Gillyflowers" *(Dianthus).* This should not be surprising, since Hollyhocks belong to a family of plants renowned for their healing properties, based on the purportedly soothing mucilaginous materials found in them. The Latin name *Malvaceae* is derived from the Greek word *malakos,* meaning "softening."

While the Puritan settlers were, perhaps, drinking brews from dried and powdered Hollyhock flowers to prevent miscarriages and ruptures and to dissolve coagulated blood, early Dutch settlers apparently were growing the double-flowered form—Gerard called them "Outlandish Rose"—for their beauty alone.

Hollyhocks are true biennials. The were valued highly by gardeners in later generations for their long season of bloom from early summer to fall.

Hollyhocks were valued highly by gardeners in later generations for their long season of bloom from early summer to fall—as long as it took each tightly wrapped bud to unfold, starting at the bottom of the stalk and working upward to the tip. In 1845, the Breck catalog listed eight different Hollyhock colors, including a black and a mottled type. Mature plants, with their great clusters of spikes—"buxom in character," one writer noted—were grown at the back of the border or planted against trellises, fences, and stone walls.

Beginning in the 1930s, the tall, stately Hollyhock in the single-flowered classic form gave way to ever-shorter types (no staking required) with fat double blossoms—"like rolled-up Kleenex," a gardening friend complained. However fashion depreciates the value of a plant, "it cannot enhance or depreciate the beauty of a single flower," as 19th-century gardener Shirley Hibberd wisely observed. When we moved to a rented farm in 1962, I saw the tall type for the first time, growing against the stone wall that sheltered our vegetable patch. I vowed that one day I'd have such beauties in my own garden. Even then, seeds of this type were becoming difficult to find from commercial sources.

In 1970 we moved to Cape Breton, and here, on a spit of land isolated from the modern world and its changing tastes, I came across very old strains of Hollyhocks, some quite close to the wild kind, with pale pink single blooms on 13-foot stalks. Inevitably, the color range had narrowed to shades of pink and rose, except for the gorgeous dark purple Black Hollyhock I found growing in one garden in the area. Its flowers were enormous—5 to 6 inches across, with the petals rolled back—on manageable 5- to 6-foot stalks: the flowers of my dreams. I traced their origin back three generations to Elizabeth MacDonald, whom I later saw in a faded photograph, still handsome at age ninety and standing beside a great stand of her favorite flowers.

Although they had been growing on their own in the same site for the past fifty years, their habitat had been disturbed recently by the construction of a deck (a recent phenomenon in the area that has been responsible for the displacement of many heirloom flowers and shrubs), under which seedlings still sought the light of day. I saved seeds from mature plants and passed them along to ensure that Elizabeth's strain would not be lost. Fortunately, tall, single-flowered Hollyhocks, including the Black Hollyhock, are once again in favor, and seeds and plants are both available.

To Grow: In Zones 3 through 8, Hollyhocks may grow as short-lived perennials, with new plants growing up from the base of the mother plant to survive another year or two, while self-sown seedlings grow to maturity in the vicinity. Thus the gardener will regard them as perennials. To establish this desirable condition, Hollyhocks require well-drained, moderately rich soil in a warm location. To start, sow seeds outdoors after the last frost or indoors in peat pots 6 to 8 weeks before the last frost date. Press seeds into moistened soil surface (they need light to germinate) and expect germination in 10 to 14 days at 70°F (21°C). Plant seedlings outdoors after the last frost, spacing plants about 2 feet apart. If you want to move seedlings growing outdoors, do so before the plants develop a long taproot.

To ensure the survival of mature plants, take cuttings in late summer from the bottom of the spent flower stalks (these should be cut back), removing "daughter" plants with their auxiliary roots to a cold frame for the winter. Then plant them out early the next season. Even if tall Hollyhocks are planted in a sheltered spot, they generally need staking, a small price to pay for such beauty. In Zones 9 and 10 Hollyhocks are grown as biennials, with new plants set out every year, usually in the fall, for continuous bloom.

When saving seeds, separate them from the fruit capsule in which they are tightly packed and allow them to dry thoroughly before storing.

The subject of rust, unpleasant though it is, cannot be avoided where the cultivation of Hollyhocks is concerned, because sooner or later if you grow Hollyhocks as well as a variety of Mallows, this fungus may attack. Signs of rust are raised bright orange pus-

HOLLYHOCK DOLLIES

*D*r. Graham Bell Fairchild, in his eighties when I first interviewed him more than a decade ago, remembers summers at Beinn Breagh, his famous grandparents' turn-of-the-century estate about 25 miles from our farm. Alexander Graham Bell's wife was very fond of the tall, single-flowered Hollyhocks, and they were planted along the pergola on the way to the gardener's cottage. The grandchildren, including little Graham, made Hollyhock dollies in the summer from the red, pink, white, and yellow blooms.

To make a dolly, pluck a bud and carefully peel off the sepals that enclose it. Then push the little stem of an opened flower into one of the holes at the base of the bud's folded petals. Voilà: a dolly (the bud) with a lovely billowing skirt (the opened flower).

tules on the backs of leaves, causing them to droop, then fall off the plant. Hollyhock rust is a fungus that may be carried by a host Mallow and finds an encouraging environment in periods of steady moisture (heavy dew, fog, rain, cloud cover) and temperatures between 60 and 70°F (15 to 21°C) for a period of 2 to 4 hours. It makes no distinction between organic and non-organic gardening practices as is sometimes claimed.

I grew Hollyhocks and various mallows for many years before the dreaded fungus appeared, not only on Hollyhocks but on 'Zebrina' Mallow and Hollyhock Mallow (*Malva alcea*) as well. I had been tempting fate with an abundance of suitable host plants. My war on rust begins in early spring when I survey the garden and reduce the general mallow population where it seems excessive. Then I take the following steps:

1. I am careful to grow plants in a sunny site with good air ciculation so their foliage dries quickly after a rain (it's vital to limit the time they are wet).
2. I cut down to the ground any plants (Hollyhocks and Mallows) that were infected the previous season, or, if they have already been cut back, cut off their first new leaves and burn the material. This is essential to destroy fungus spores that have wintered-over in the plant (if not destroyed, they will reproduce every 10 days during the summer).
3. After fresh leaves appear, I start dusting with agricultural sulfur every 10 days unless the weather is exceptionally dry and hot.
4. I monitor plants closely, inspecting leaf undersides, and take action at the slightest sign of pustules forming.
5. In the fall, I cut back plants and clean up all fallen leaves and debris around them.

Once you understand the nature of the disease, rust can be controlled if not entirely eliminated.

COLLECTOR'S CHOICE:

Alcea ficifolia, Antwerp Hollyhock (early 1800s); single yellow, copper, rose, red, and white; 6 to 7'. Less susceptible to rust than *A. rosea.*

A. rosea, Hollyhock (1600–1699); carmine, pink, rose, cream, and white blooms.

A. rosea 'Chater's Doubles' (1888). Fully double flowers in salmon, apricot, red, buff, maroon, white, and the usual pinks; 5 to 6'; comes true from seed. The only Victorian-era cultivar to survive changing fashions.

A. rosea 'Indian Spring' (by 1939); single or semidouble white, or pink blooms; 6'.

A. rosea nigra, Black Hollyhock (1800–1825); same as the cultivar known as "Watchman'.

Alchemilla mollis / A. vulgaris

ROSACEAE

Lady's Mantle
Bear's Foot, Dewcup, Lion's Foot

INTRODUCED: 1800–1850
ZONES: 3–8
TYPE: Hardy Perennial/Herb
HEIGHT: 12–18"
BLOOM: Late Spring/Summer
SITE: Sun/Partial Shade/Shade

Native to Eurasia, Lady's Mantle's most striking asset is its nearly circular leaves, which are toothed, pleated, and cloaklike, as preserved in its common name. Tiny hairs on the leaf's surface catch and hold drops of rain or dew, which sometimes cover the entire leaf, their sparkling roundness magnified as if by magic. Later, the spreading foliage is embellished with numerous loose clusters of very small, starlike flowers, greenish yellow or chartreuse in color. The genus name is derived from the Arabic for alchemy, with which the plant was associated because of a belief in the miraculous nature of the dewdrops.

Described by the 17th-century herbalist Nicholas Culpeper, its virtues are, he said, derived from Venus. These have nothing to do with dewdrops, but owe their effectiveness to the plant's astringency. It was commonly used to treat wounds and women's "disorders" (menstruation and childbirth), which accounts for its dedication to the Virgin.

Lady's Mantle, called "Our Ladies Mantel," was a druggist's plant in England in 1548, and was cultivated in the Chelsea Physic Garden in London in 1731, but despite its high regard as a medicinal its name does not appear on any of the lists of plants brought to the New World by the Pilgrims or planted in later gardens for use or delight. According to the herb authority the late Gertrude Foster, it is listed in the 1845 U.S. edition of the *Ladies Companion to the Flower Garden*. She thought it probably came over with the Pilgrims, and should be planted in colonial garden restorations. (See *Park's Success with Herbs* in Bibliography). Margery Fish regarded it as an old-fashioned cottage garden plant in growing demand among discerning English gardeners in the 1960s.

Whatever its history, Lady's Mantle has been underappreciated in American gardens, for there can be no doubt about its superiority as a garden plant. Its ability to grow in either sun or shade (with moist soil), the beauty of its foliage (especially adorned with dew), and its frilly sprays of long-lasting flowers of a color that combines with virtually any other, make this lovely herb an indispensable asset in any setting.

Although Lady's Mantle is a quiet plant of subtle beauty, it creates a stunning impact when massed. In traditional herb gardens it is used around stone pavings, where its foliage and flowers show to great effect. Grown near box edging, it provides a striking contrast of color and form. I had seen photographs of Lady's Mantle as a thick, luxuriant hedge, outlining paths and walkways. It was very appealing with its loose flower sprays spilling over and softening all hard edges, so when I enlarged my garden of old-world herbs and flowers, I planted it along the the new path that leads from shade, at the back of the garden, to sun in the front. In June it is a long, low, winding counterpoint around the edges of taller plants like white Bleeding-heart, dark pink Dame's-rocket, and deep blue Mountain-bluet. In full sun, I pair it with the purple spikes of *Salvia* 'East Friesland' for weeks of bloom. Lady's Mantle is my fix-it plant, the one I use to spruce up odd, shady corners and to anchor the ends of border plantings. Like basic black, it goes with everything.

To Grow: Plant roots in the fall or spring, spaced 1 to 2½ feet apart in evenly moist soil. In rich soil, the plant may multiply rapidly

Although Lady's Mantle is a quiet plant of subtle beauty, it creates a stunning impact when massed.

and get out of hand, so be forewarned. Yet it is not difficult to control by pulling out extras. In hot, humid conditions, the water that gathers in its leaves may cause fungal disease. Cut back plants after blooming (in cool summer areas, this extends over a long period), and divide by taking separate pieces of the crown with attached roots.

To Use: Flower sprays, fresh or dried, are lovely filler in bouquets, poseys, or tussie-mussies. A posey is a small bunched bouquet; a tussie-mussie is the same thing, but the flowers and foliage are selected to convey a message (Lady's Mantle means "comfort" in the language of flowers). To dry flowers, pick them in fresh bloom, bunch and hang them upside down out of direct light. Their dried color, a soft light green, is unusual and very useful in all floral crafts.

COLLECTOR'S CHOICE:

Alchemilla mollis/A. vulgaris, Lady's Mantle (1800–1850). These may be offered under either name.

Allium schoenoprasum

LILIACEAE

Chives
Chebols, Chibolls

INTRODUCED: 1600–1776
ZONES 3–10

A. tuberosum ❀

Garlic Chives
Chinese Chives, Oriental Garlic, Sweet-scented Garlic

INTRODUCED: 1776–1850
ZONES: 3–10

TYPE: Hardy Herbs/Flowers
HEIGHT: 1–2'
BLOOM: Early Summer–Fall
SITE: Sun

*B*oth Chives and Garlic Chives are herbs that grow from bulbous roots, like onions. Chives, native to Europe and Asia, quickly form tight clusters that sprout grass-like, onion-flavored leaves growing to 1 foot, breaking through even semifrozen ground with the first hint of spring. Later, the flowering stalks produce lovely ball-shaped, lavender-pink heads composed of many small florets that in maturity open to spill out their tiny black seeds, ensuring the prolific production of new generations of bulbs.

Garlic Chives, native to Asia, are more stately plants, growing to 2 feet from stout rhizomes. Their leaves, unlike those of Chives, are flat, grow to ¼ inch wide, and are garlic-flavored. The flowers, produced in late summer, are sweetly scented, growing in round umbels of star-shaped blossoms. They are white with a greenish flush and gradually fall off to reveal distinctive green fruiting knobs.

Chives were universally grown in early American kitchen gardens. They were highly valued as an early spring green or vegetable after a long winter's diet of stored root crops such as carrots, beets, and potatoes. They were probably also eaten as a spring restorative in a salad of bittersweet greens (Dandelions)—a country custom still in practice.

I found one clump, among several examples of Chives used as a pioneer herb on our remote peninsula, where the original plant had been removed to the new farmstead up the road, apparently considered an integral and invaluable part of the household. It had been used in the past to flavor potatoes in the spring, and the old clump, now seldom used for anything but its ornamental flowers, remained in a corner of the herbaceous border that had grown up around it, its outer leaves cut now and then for salad, its girth checked by seasonal digging up of the extra bulblets around it. Treated in this way, it was able to renew itself from its decaying leaves, the source of nutrients for further growth.

Elsewhere on the island, Chives (often called by its older name, Cives) are naturalized in wet meadows near French settlements, where they are used, after being pickled in brine, in Frico, a unique Acadian dish. Among large populations of Chives, as in the wild, there are variations of color and form: rosy globes of flowers, dwarf or taller types, even white-flowered sports (a plant of which was collected from an old garden for the Heritage Garden of the Memorial University Botanical Garden in St. John's, Newfoundland).

You can naturalize Chives if you have the room. They are particularly partial to wet ground—even standing water if it's not too deep—where they will form a beautiful drift of mauve-rose in the spring, followed by Blue and Yellow Flag Iris. They can be massed to edge a bed or grown in clustered clumps among early-blooming flowers such as Columbine, Mountain-bluet, Lupines, and Dame's-rocket, all soft shades of blue, lilac, and rose, and the spreading white umbels of Sweet Cicely. I like to plant a few clumps of Chives by the kitchen door, close at hand for use, where the sprawling mats of Lamb's-ears help to cover the Chives after they have been ravaged by my scissors to flavor salads or cottage cheese. I also use dried bundles of flowering stems in dried bouquets, where they make a splash among the white clusters of 'The Pearl' (Sneezewort), and the felty leaves and stalks of Lamb's-ears.

Garlic Chives, introduced in the 18th or 19th century from Asia, apparently were regarded as an ornamental, as well they might be, for in my opinion the plant's value in the flower border outweighs its use in the herb garden. In my gardens of mixed herbs and flowers, I look forward to its late summer appearance, when fresh blooms are a novelty and very welcome. Then the white-starred Garlic Chives, rising tall, stately, and unexpectedly behind a spreading colony of purple and white annual Clary Sage (*Salvia viridis*) and chartreuse Nicotiana ('Limelight') put on a good show until frost (and even a little while beyond).

To Grow: Chives and Garlic Chives can be grown in Zones 3 to 10, but Chives need to be exposed to freezing temperatures to induce the required period of rest, something that Garlic Chives do not need. Sow the seeds of either indoors six to eight weeks before the last frost, to germinate in about two weeks at 60 to 70°F (16 to 21°C). Set out the seedlings as early as you can: 6 inches apart for Chives, and 1 foot apart for Garlic Chives. The former

Chives were universally grown in early American kitchen gardens.

Garlic Chives are an underrated perennial for late summer bloom.

should be planted in small clusters of bulblets and the latter as individual plants. Enriched soil and a sunny spot will ensure the continued production of leaves and flowers. Harvest mainly the outer leaves of Chives if you want to save the flowers. In any case, cut the plant back after flowering, but not severely, so it will have nutrients to produce fresh leaves and flowers in the fall (make sure the ground is rich). Divide Chives and Garlic Chives as needed, about once every three to five years.

To Use: Pick Chive flowers in fresh bloom to dry for bouquets. Garlic Chive seed heads dry well, too. Put these in a paper bag to dry (don't crowd them or they'll mold), then shake out all the seeds. The pods are prettier with the seeds removed. To use fresh, blend chopped Chive flowers and leaves into cream cheese for a spread on whole wheat or rye bread; garnish cottage cheese and thick slices of ripe tomato with cut-up flowers and leaves. Garlic Chives can be chopped up and added to salad, and with the flower heads can be used to flavor vinegar.

GARLIC CHIVE VINEGAR

Place clean unbroken flower heads and leaves into a sterilized quart jar—the amount depends on the desired strength—and fill to within an inch from the jar top with cider vinegar. Cover with a double layer of plastic wrap or with a nonreactive cover, and set in a cool place for 4 to 6 weeks, or on a sunny windowsill for quicker results. Chive Blossom Vinegar can be made the same way, by infusing clean, rosy blossoms with white vinegar. Use the vinegars in salad dressings (4 tablespoons of vinegar to ½ cup olive oil), or add a dash to stir-fry and meat dishes.

COLLECTOR'S CHOICE:

Allium schoenoprasum, Chives (1600–1776).
A. tuberosum, Garlic Chives (1776–1850).

Anthemis tinctoria

ASTERACEAE

Golden Marguerite
Dyer's Chamomile, Golden Anthemis, Ox-eye Chamomile

INTRODUCED: 1850–1900?
ZONES: 3–10
TYPE: Short-Lived Perennial/Biennial
    FLOWER/HERB
HEIGHT: 2½–3'
BLOOM: Summer–Fall
SITE: Sun/Partial Shade

Golden Marguerite is a bushy and somewhat sprawling short-lived perennial native to central and southern Europe and western Asia. It has profuse golden yellow, daisy-shaped blooms, 2 or more inches across, complemented by distinctive feathery foliage that is dense, aromatic, gray, and downy on the underside. The genus name comes from the Greek *anthemon,* meaning "flower" (used here to describe the plant's free-flowering nature), and the epithet comes from *tinctor,* meaning "dyer." These combine well to sum up Golden Marguerite's outstanding physical characteristic and its use as a dye plant since antiquity. Golden Marguerite was indispensable in any self-respecting medieval household, where it was used to make yellow, gold, or buff dye. Yet it is wholly overshadowed in the literature by its former cousin, *Anthemis nobilis* (now *Chamaemelum nobile)*, of fabled chamomile tea and aromatic lawn carpets.

Golden Marguerite has a strange history as an heirloom ornamental in the New World, seemingly coming from nowhere in the mid-19th century, with no record of prior herb use. Favored for perennial borders, and especially recommended to inexperienced gardeners for its ease of culture, the plant is literally smothered in golden daisies for much of the summer and into the fall, with the lovely almost evergreen foliage an advantage all season long. The flowering plant is both frost-tolerant and disease-resistant.

Garden historians do not come to our aid with tidbits about its culture and lore. Even Margery Fish, usually enamored of any sprawling plant, could work up no enthusiasm for Golden Marguerite. She claimed even the cottage folk would not allow it in their gardens, noting that it grows profusely, especially where chickens have been (as do most plants).

Both cottagers and Mrs. Fish have missed out on a good thing, one that other gardeners in North America have long valued. I suspect that Golden Marguerite is especially appreciated in North America because it thrives in the sunny, dry conditions that often prevail in our summer months. 'Kelwayi' is an improved form, with more finely cut foliage and lovely golden yellow daisies, from the 19th-century British nurseryman and breeder James Kelway.

Cottagers could have grown this obliging plant among their favorite flowers in the sun: Calendula, Feverfew, Elecampane, Rose Campion, Bouncing-Bet, and Daylilies. The golden flowers combine nicely with the brilliant orange Butterfly Weed, the gray-leaved Garden Sage, and the gray-fringed South-

---

DYEING WOOL WITH DYER'S CHAMOMILE

1. Cut the whole plant down near the ground; you can dry the leaves for later use (they yield shades of green) or add them to the compost heap.

2. Cover the flowers with water and boil for 30 to 60 minutes, then strain off the dyebath. It should have a pleasant fragrance. Set aside.

3. To prepare wool for receiving the mordant (the substance that fixes color), it should be clean and wet.

4. Allow at least 1 gallon of water for 4 ounces of wool. Dissolve 1 tablespoon alum and 1 teaspoon cream of tartar in ½ cup boiling water, add to the pot of water, and stir well.

5. Add wet wool, heat slowly to simmer, then simmer for an hour. Remove pot from the heat and let it cool for several hours to lukewarm. Remove wool, and rinse it well.

6. Add mordanted wool to the dyebath. Bring it slowly to simmer and maintain for an hour. Remove yarn or let it cool in the dyebath overnight for a darker color. Wash and rinse the yarn until the color stops bleeding, then squeeze out excess moisture. Spread or hang the yarn to dry.

(Adapted with author's permission from "Getting Started With Dyeing," in *Dyes from Nature*, Brooklyn Botanic Garden Record, 1990; and *A Weaver's Garden*, Interweave Press, 1995, both by Rita Buchanan.)

---

ernwood, for an herby touch to the flower border. Golden Marguerite also can be used as a tall ground cover for a sunny, dry bank. The flowers are excellent for fresh bouquets, a convenient and far less tedious way to deadhead spent blooms in order to prolong the plant's blooming season.

To Grow: Golden Marguerite can be grown in Zones 3 to 10 except in southernmost Florida and along the Gulf Coast. Sow the seed indoors four to six weeks before the last frost to readily germinate at 68 to 78°F (20 to 26°C), or sow them outdoors in early spring in well-drained soil and full sun. Thin the seedlings to 9 inches apart. Poor soil and full sun produce more flowers than enriched soil and shade, but a little shade is appreciated where summers are hot. These are short-lived perennials, so remember to divide the plants about every two years or take stem cuttings, which can be readily rooted in sand to bloom the first summer.

To Use: Golden Marguerite produces masses of flowers all summer for a very good reason. If you want to use them to dye wool yellow in the ancient tradition, you will need about 4 parts flowers to 1 part wool by weight. (So, for instance, if you want to dye 4 ounces of wool you will need a pound of flower heads.) This ratio, according to experienced dyer Rita Buchanan, yields the richest color. Harvesting flowers in midsummer, when the bloom is fading and plants are beginning to flop over, is a good way to encourage fresh flowers on more upright plants.

COLLECTOR'S CHOICE:

Anthemis tinctoria 'Kelwayi', Golden
　　Marguerite (probably 1860s).

Aquilegia canadensis

RANUNCULACEAE

Eastern Columbine
American Columbine, Canadian Columbine, Meetinghouses

INTRODUCED: 1700–1850
ZONES: 3–10
NATIVE

A. vulgaris

European Columbine
Columbine, European-crowfoot, Garden-honeysuckle, Granny's-bonnet

INTRODUCED: 1600–1699
ZONES: 3–10
NATURALIZED

TYPE: PERENNIAL FLOWER
HEIGHT: 1–2½'
BLOOM: Spring–Early Summer
SITE: Sun/Partial Shade

*E*astern Columbine is a native perennial flower of rocky, wooded, or open slopes from Manitoba and Quebec south through New England to Georgia and west to Wisconsin. The genus name comes from the Latin *aquila,* meaning "eagle," a reference to the flowers' talonlike spurs. Wild Columbine flowers are composed of five petal-like, brilliant red sepals alternating with yellow petals and surrounding a column of bright yellow stamens. The backs of the petals are elongated to form a hollow nectar-bearing spur that curves inward and ends in a decisive knob. The fragile-seeming flowers, sitting atop slender stems that grow to almost 3 feet, are firmly anchored to the ground by a long taproot from which grow attractive green rounded and lobed leaves, mostly close to the ground. This species is the parent of many modern hybrids.

Aquilegia vulgaris, a native of Europe growing to 2½ feet, bears less brilliant and more varied flowers, usually in soft shades of blue, purple, rose, or white. These flowers have less pronounced spurs or none at all, as in the fully double types. The European Columbine is naturalized locally in North America as a garden escape.

The showy flowers of the native Eastern Columbine did not long escape the notice of visitors to the New World, and by 1635 Jesuit missionaries in Canada had introduced it to France. In the early 1700s, Eastern Columbine was being grown in American gardens in Pennsylvania and elsewhere with natives such as the Cardinal Flower *(Lobelia cardinalis),* Black-eyed-Susan, and Blue Boneset *(Eupatorium coelestinum).* By the middle of the 19th century, the native Columbine was one of the most popular garden flowers in America, though it later declined significantly with the introduction of hybrids with larger, showier flowers.

The European Columbine was grown in the earliest American gardens, having been a favorite garden flower of variable form (singles and doubles) for centuries in Europe. I traced back a surviving population 120 years. Growing virtually untended, this group produced beautiful double blossoms in a range of colors—purple, blue, pink, and white—a testimony to the plant's endurance. Unlike hybrid forms, these come remarkably true from seed and do not deteriorate in beauty over the years. Though classified as a perennial, Columbine appears to replenish itself by self-seeding, so individual plants are not very old.

A few years ago, friends bought a house in the country built in 1865. They were delighted to find the remnants of an old garden lingering by a stone wall. Among them they discovered Hostas, Cinnamon Fern, and the loveliest semidouble Columbines—pure white and rich pink, one flower set within another, nodding on graceful stems—grow-

ing unaided for at least the past sixty years.

Both Columbines attract hummingbirds, so you should plant them where they can be easily seen—in rock gardens, near the front of a perennial border, in the semishade of a shrubbery, or on a nearby rocky slope. I grow the Eastern Columbine at the edge of a thinly wooded ravine, where they can receive a few hours of direct sun a day—all they need to thrive if soil conditions are right. I grow European Columbine beneath the dappled shade of an old fruit tree underplanted with Daffodils, among Bleeding-heart, Virginia-bluebells, Hostas, and Forget-me-nots.

Columbines are long-lasting cut flowers. 'Nora Barlow' is a favorite with flower arrangers for its striking form and colors: clusters of white-tipped, carmine-pink petal layers, suffused with lime green, and no spurs evident. Apparently this is a renamed ancient strain.

To Grow: Of the two, European Columbine is the easier to establish and the more adaptable. It does well in moist, well-drained soil to which a little bonemeal or rotted manure has been added. The site can be partially shaded or sunny except in hot, dry, windy areas, where some shade is appreciated. Eastern Columbine requires a lighter, sharply drained soil—thin and gravelly is best.

Seeds of both Columbines should be prechilled for three to four weeks and sown in the summer in a cold frame, where germination will take 21 to 25 days (or more) at 70 to 75°F (21 to 24°C.) Set out plants 12 to 28 inches apart in the fall or very early spring before they have developed a long taproot. Both types can be divided if they seem to need it, but letting new seedlings develop or starting a new colony from seed is best.

> Both Columbines attract hummingbirds, so you should plant them where they can be easily seen.

Aristolochia macrophylla / A. durior

ARISTOLOCHIACEAE

Dutchman's Pipe

Pipe Vine, Siphon Flower

INTRODUCED: 1761
ZONES: 4–8
NATIVE
TYPE: Hardy Twining Vine
HEIGHT: 30'
SEASON OF INTEREST: Foliage All Summer
SITE: Sun/Partial Shade

Dutchman's Pipe is a vigorous, deciduous vine that grows wild in rich, moist woodland and along streambanks in the Appalachians, from southwestern Pennsylvania and West Virginia, south to Georgia and Alabama. The odd shape of the flowers in this genus, suggestive of the human fetus, were used as an aid in childbirth, thus the common family name, "Birthwort." Flowers are S-shaped and tubular—1½ inches long and greenish brown—and are often compared to a smoking pipe, a siphon, even a saxophone. Early summer blooms are inconspicuous, hidden beneath the vine's 12-inch-long, glossy, heart-shaped leaves. Perfect in its unique way, it has never been the subject of hybridization.

William Bartram, son of John, discovered Dutchman's Pipe growing along the Ohio River in 1761. His father, who had been sending plants and seeds of native flora to Peter Collinson in England for many years, promptly sent seeds of this new discovery. Collinson was delighted with new-world flora, just as Bartram was overjoyed by Collinson's offerings of English flora. At the same time he sent off Dutchman's Pipe, Bartram senior wrote Collinson about "the glorious appearance of Carnations from thy seed . . . that challenge any garden in America for variety." Plants "from away" have always had more allure for gardeners of every age and country.

It is clear from the Bartrams' plant catalog, and from Prince's on Long Island, that in the early 1790s there was an astonishing variety of native plants (especially shrubs and trees) offered for sale in North America. Admirable in many ways, Dutchman's Pipe did not really catch on as a subject for cultivation until porches, piazzas, arbors, and pergolas came into vogue in the 19th century. It was especially popular in the Northeast, where it was valued for its hardiness, rapid growth, and its thick, dense wall of beautiful foliage, perfect for providing quick shade and covering for various structures. But as styles changed, Dutchman's Pipe was relegated to the status of "old-fashioned." It was widely grown as a green screen into the 1930s and 1940s, but it has never gone out of fashion in the colder regions of the Northeast, where it can still be seen growing on the porches and verandahs of older homes.

Today, Dutchman's Pipe is being called back into service to dress up (or hide) walls, to clamber over arbors, and to provide shady, private bowers. Its ability to adapt to virtually any site and soil conditions and its rapid growth, combined with its striking foliage, recommend this native vine for the contemporary landscape.

To Grow: Dutchman's Pipe grows in full sun or partial shade in most soils, even moist and heavy. Young plants should be protected over the winter and provided with support in the form of a trellis, fence, or strong wire. The main problem, as with any vigorous type, is to keep it within bounds. This is achieved by mowing around the area where the vine is planted. Propagation is by layering.

COLLECTOR'S CHOICE:

Aristolochia macrophylla, Dutchman's Pipe (1761).

Artemisia spp. ❀

ASTERACEAE

A. abrotanum ❀

Southernwood
Lad's-live, Maid's-ruin, Old-man, Old-man's-love, Old-man Wormwood, The Lovers Plant

INTRODUCED: 1600–1900
ZONES: 3–9

A. pontica ❀

Roman Wormwood

A. stelleriana ❀

Beach Wormwood
Dusty Miller, Old Woman

TYPE: Perennial Herb
HEIGHT: 1"–4'
SEASON OF INTEREST: All-Season
SITE: Sun

*A*rtemisias are distributed throughout Asia, the Mediterranean, Europe, and the New World. Mainly subshrubs (wood-based, like lavender) and of varying habits, they are protected from the effects of prolonged drought and drying winds by the multitude of tiny hairs that cover their foliage, a characteristic that gives them their unusual gray to silver-white hues. They have been valued for centuries as aromatic strewing herbs and bitter-tasting medicinals, mainly to treat digestive disorders.

Southernwood is a very hardy herb and subshrub with almost evergreen leaves—threaded or fringed and lemon-scented—growing on slender stems to 3 to 4 feet. It is often clipped to use as a neat border around herb gardens. Its common name, Southernwood, distinguishes this Artemisia, native to southern Europe, from Wormwood (*A. absinthium*), both of which contain the substance absinthe in some degree. Southernwood's Latin epithet, *abrotanum,* meaning "elegance," aptly describes both the form and fragrance of this ancient herb.

Ancient herbals record a wide range of complaints for which Southernwood, in some form, was the answer: inflamed eyes, acne, ulcers, splinters, thorns, even talking in one's sleep. One of the more persistent claims was its ability to relieve baldness in old men and promote beards in young men, hence several of its common names.

Artemisias have been valued for centuries as aromatic strewing herbs and bitter-tasting medicinals, mainly to treat digestive disorders.

Such
enduring
plants
naturally lend
themselves to
becoming
family
heirlooms.

Like any plant that has had a long history of association with people, Southernwood was invested with magical powers. According to country wisdom, a few sprays slipped under a young woman's pillow, down her back, or into her bouquet would cause the first man she met to fall in love with her, leading ultimately to her ruin. Herbal lore of this type probably had little influence on its use in early gardens.

Southernwood was included in the medicinal gardens of early Moravian settlers in North Carolina and in the formal gardens of William Paca, one of the signers of the Declaration of Independence, in Annapolis, Maryland, where it hedged in the kitchen garden. The Plymouth colonists knew Southernwood, too, and most likely used it to scent linens (easier to grow for them than Lavender) and to make a yellow dye. In their informal but neat cottage garden-type plantings, perhaps Southernwood spread out from its usual mounded, clipped form to grow as it liked, a greenish gray foil for the more colorful flowering herbs of a dooryard garden.

Such enduring plants naturally lend themselves to becoming family heirlooms. I found a ninety-year-old specimen that had been grown from a slip taken from Boston around the turn of the century and carefully passed down from great-grandmother to great-granddaughter, who gave me a piece of it. Now "it groweth in my garden" among purple-flowering stalks of Foxglove and pink Mallow. In my experience, Southernwood is the most adaptable of plants. I grow it as an attractive shrubby foil for old roses (a "poor man's Lavender"), and elsewhere it is invaluable for covering the ground where little else will grow—in hard soil, in an exposed, sunny site.

In addition to those Artemisias used for medicine (Wormwood and Mugwort) and flavoring (Tarragon) in the 17th and 18th centuries, several others were grown by the late 19th or early 20th century for their beautiful foliage, as depicted in the stylized plantings of the herb revival movement at the turn of the century and early 1900s. These include the native Western Sage *(A. ludoviciana)*, valued today in the 'Silver King' form for wreaths; European Roman Wormwood, perhaps introduced much earlier for its herbal uses, and Beach Wormwood, naturalized on beaches throughout the Northeast. From a landscaping perspective, the most interesting to me are Roman Wormwood and Beach Wormwood.

Roman Wormwood, Gerard's "ponticke," was used extensively in knot gardens, where its intricately cut leaves could be trimmed to fit designs of alternating green and silver foliage in interlacing squares, circles, and diamonds. It is still used to flavor vermouth. I found a tiny piece surviving in an old Cape Breton city garden and replanted it in my own garden. Of loose, upright, and sprawling habit, to 12 inches, it creates a frothy mound of soft gray, lacy foliage. I grow it as a mounding accent near the base of Roses (especially purplish-flowered Rugosas). In a perennial border it is an effective contrast in color and form to the dark purple spires of *Salvia* 'East Friesland', salmon-rose Russell Lupines, and brassy yellow *Allium moly*. Later, Roman Wormwood provides a frilly background for the rich golden trumpets of 'Stella d'Oro' Daylilies. While it is undeniably a root runner, it is not difficult to pull up where it is not wanted. Once you discover its many garden possibilities, its benefits far outweigh its drawbacks.

When a friend gave me a clump of the plant he called Dusty Miller (a generic term for silvery white foliage plants), I discovered the many virtues of Beach Wormwood. Where it's given light soil and sunny exposure, it keeps grass at bay along paths and at the garden's edge by luxuriantly spreading its thick, white, deeply cut leaves, shaped like those of white oak. In such soil conditions its form is more compact, less sprawling. It is stunning in hanging baskets with spreading old-fashioned single pink, white, and purple balcony-type Petunias. In a border setting, I elevate the plant by growing it in a tall container, then set it deep within the border among 2- to 3-foot-tall perennials such as *Veronica* 'Sunny Border Blue' and red Bee Balm. Gertrude Jekyll praised this type of Dusty Miller and advised growing it as a hardy subsitute for the more frost-tender plant also know as Dusty Miller *(Cineraria maritima)*. Master of the painterly garden, she used its frosty white foliage to great effect among the blues, purples, and pinks of Larkspur, Delphinium, Salvias, and Pinks. Beach Wormwood was once popular in rock gardens, a use I haven't tried, but as H. Lincoln Foster observed about low-growing artemisias in his classic guide to rock gardening, ". . . no species . . . will be out of place in the sunny scree or rocky pasture" *(Rock Gardening)*.

To Grow: All the Artemisias are grown from plants. They thrive in full sun and most soils except damp ones. Beach Wormwood requires sharply drained soil. Clip back Artemisias in early spring to encourage fresh growth, then cut them back in late summer when they begin to flower. To maintain Southernwood as a neat mound, clip it again in early summer. All the Artemisias are easy to propagate by division, cuttings, or by replanting offshoots.

To Use: Southernwood is nice to use fresh in nosegays and tussie-mussies (it means "constancy" in the language of flowers). I cut long sprays to hang in closets (their scent lasts about 6 months). I combine Southernwood with Tansy *(Tanacetum vulgare)* and Wormwood *(Artemisia vulgaris)* in equal amounts as a moth repellent; in fact, an old French name for Southernwood is *garderobe*. For each quart of dried leaves I add 1 teaspoon of clove oil premixed with 3 tablespoons of a plant fixative like orris root. I seal the dried leaves and oil in a container for several weeks, shake it now and then, and use it in sachets among woolens.

COLLECTOR'S CHOICE:

These are most readily obtained from specialty herb sources.

Artemisia abrotanum, Southernwood (1600–1776).

A. lactiflora (1901). Also called White Mugwort, Sweet Mugwort, and Ghost Plant, this is a hardy, underused perennial of shrubby proportions to 6 feet. In late summer its long reddish stems are covered with creamy white, strongly grape-scented flower plumes. Its leaves, unlike those of other Artemisias, are green and deeply toothed. A fine background plant for sun or part shade. Cut it back in midgrowth for shorter, bushier growth. Cut and dry flowering stems for wreaths. In China, White Mugwort has culinary and medicinal uses.

A. pontica, Roman Wormwood (1859–1900 or before?).

A. stelleriana, Beach Wormwood (1859–1900).

Asclepias tuberosa ❀

ASCLEPIADACEAE

Butterfly Weed
Butterfly Flower, Butterfly Milkweed,
Chigger Flower, Indian-paintbrush,
Pleurisy Root, Swallowwort

INTRODUCED: 1776–1850
ZONES: 4–10
NATIVE
TYPE: Perennial Wildflower/Herb
HEIGHT: 2–3'
BLOOM: Summer–Fall
SITE: Sun/Partial Shade

*B*utterfly Weed is a conspicuous wild-flower that grows in dry fields and along woodlands and roadsides from New Hampshire to Florida, as well as on the plains of Minnesota, Colorado, Arizona, and Texas —a reflection of its wide-ranging adaptability. It grows from a deep taproot but, unlike other milkweeds, lacks any juice in its stems. These grow from 1 to 3 feet and have narrow, lance-shaped leaves. At their tops they bear 2-inch clusters of waxy orange, nectar-rich, fragrant flowers and, later, spindle-shaped seedpods that pop open to disperse flat brown seeds with long, silky hairs. The flat-topped clusters present perfect landing pads for the Monarch butterfly in the summer and fall.

This beautiful native flower drew attention to itself very early. It was officially discovered by 1690, but it is quite likely that the settlers learned about its medicinal uses earlier from the Indians, who used it as a remedy for lung and throat troubles and to soothe wounds and sores. The young shoots, boiled in the spring, were eaten as a vegetable, as were the seedpods.

Butterfly Weed is one of the few native plants favored by gardeners from New England to Alabama. To satisfy the great demand, plants were dug up from the wild in great numbers. S.N.F. Sandford, writing for the New England Museum of Natural History in 1937, remarked that "even on Cape Cod, where it was formerly abundant, it is no longer common, and there is not much on Martha's Vineyard, while on Nantucket it is now rare" (*New England Herbs,* New England Museum of Natural History, 1937). Fortunately, Butterfly Weed is difficult to destroy, for a piece of its long taproot ensures renewed life, as do its abundant seeds, blown far and wide.

As a garden plant, it is extraordinarily adaptable, growing in a city garden as well as in a wildflower meadow or border of herbs and flowers. It is especially striking when paired with Wild Bergamot, another active herb that, like Butterfly Weed, loves the sun and is happy in dry soil. Established where it can form a large clump, it is striking against any shrubbery or expanse of lawn. The broad, colorful heads add interest to any garden, and the plant's season of interest is extended by the ornamental seedpods. As a bonus, Butterfly Weed is a long-lasting cut flower, and its dried pods are useful in winter bouquets. The question is, why is this lovely flower called a weed?

To Grow: Butterfly Weed is especially valued where conditions are hot and dry. Seeds (preferably fresh) germinate in about three weeks at 70°F (21°C). They should be sown where you want the plant to bloom because, once it develops its root, it is difficult to move. Space plants 8 to 12 inches apart. Butterfly

Weed requires perfectly drained, sandy soil and tolerates light shade, but it does best in full sun. Take 3- to 4-inch cuttings from the tips of the stems before flowering. The root can be cut into 2-inch sections and rooted in sandy soil if kept moist. To collect the wispy seeds, pull them out from the pod when it begins to split. Sow them at once, or dry them and store them in the refrigerator until needed.

COLLECTOR'S CHOICE:

Asclepias tuberosa, Butterfly Weed (1776–1850).

Buxus sempervirens ❀

BUXACEAE

Box
Common Boxwood, English Box

B. sempervirens 'Suffruticosa' ❀
Dwarf Box
True Edging Box

INTRODUCED: 1600–1750
ZONES: 5 OR 6–9
TYPE: Hardy Shrub
HEIGHT: 3–20'
SEASON OF INTEREST: Evergreen
SITE: Sun/Light Shade

Common Boxwood, native to southern Europe, North Africa, and western Asia, is an evergreen, treelike shrub of billowy form, to 20 feet, with dark green, lustrous, and sharply aromatic leaves. Cultivated in Europe long before it reached the New World, this species gave rise to many cultivars. The best known is true Dwarf Box, with smaller leaves and dense, slow growth. (Some plants that are 150 years old are only 3 feet tall.) Both types of Box are extremely long-lived under favorable conditions.

It's unclear when Box was first planted in the Colonies, but by the 18th century it was well established, especially in Maryland and Virginia. In 1737, John Custis, a prominent Virginia planter and father of Martha Washington, wrote to Peter Collinson—the leading English spirit of his time in transatlantic plant exchange—about his "Dutch Box edgings," and in 1738 Collinson sent him a specimen of variegated Box. George Washington, himself an avid shrub collector, grew tall Tree Box *(B. sempervirens* 'Arborescens') at Mt. Vernon before 1788, and by 1792 John Bartram was offering Box, including the variegated sort, from his Philadelphia nursery.

In its different forms, Box was highly esteemed for its evergreen habit and uses in stylized, formal plantings. It could grow tall and billowy or be trimmed for topiary, for use in mazes, to enclose beds of colorful flowers, or to line walks. Nowhere are its uses better preserved than at Williamsburg, a prime example of the Dutch-English landscape style that wealthier settlers brought to the New World. This form relied on extensive use of hedges, trees, clipped topiary, and ground covers to create a trimmed, green, enclosed universe—symmetrical and balanced. It was just the sort of style that appealed to settlers keen on superimposing their civilization on a wild land. When the Dutch style was superseded in England by a passion for the "natural" look, supposedly imitative of nature—wide, sweeping lawns, carefully sited groups of trees—the Virginians clung to their formal designs. For them, nature was to be kept at bay, not invited

It was just the sort of style that appealed to settlers keen on superimposing their civilization on a wild land.

onto one's home ground. They took comfort in the old form, symbol of the mother country.

It's not surprising that Box was so conspicuous in the self-consciously quaint gardens of the Colonial Revival movement in the early 1900s. Emblematic of what was considered "old-fashioned," Box was heavily invested with nostalgia for the past. Its evocative scent (displeasing to some) has been celebrated by poets as the most stirring of all fragrances, "the heart and soul of memory." From my own sojourn in the South, when we lived for a time near Chesapeake Bay, I recall the sharp scent—stronger after a rain—from overgrown Box-lined walks in a setting of faded Southern elegance.

While I've never planted it, I can imagine the pleasure of setting out Edging Box seedlings in a warm Southern spring when Columbines, Foxgloves, and Canterbury-bells are in bloom. The row must be perfectly straight, the garden cord tightly stretched. The little plants, spaced about 3 inches apart, are placed in a trench half-filled with dirt, a layer of manure is added, finally more soil is packed down, followed by a little worked-in bonemeal.

To Grow: Box grows in most well-drained soils. The method of planting seedlings I have already described should be followed, taking care to avoid deep planting of young roots, which may be smothered. Plants will need protection from strong sun for the first year, or until established, as well as frequent watering. Mulch new plantings with peat or leaf mold to maintain cool, even moisture. If transplanting, preserve a good ball of earth around the roots. In the North, even established plantings of hardier types (see Collector's Choice) should be protected from drying winter winds and very low temperatures with evergreen boughs and burlap (don't tie too tightly). Each spring, clean out dead twigs, branches, and debris, especially in the middle of the plant, to prevent fungal attack. Trim back plants just as they come into growth; cutting back to hardwood will stimulate more branching.

To Use: Box trimmings are nice in flower arrangements and for Christmas decorations.

COLLECTOR'S CHOICE:

Buxus microphylla, Little Leaf Box (circa 1860). From Japan, to 4', with 1" leaves. Zones 5 or 6.

'Compacta' (1940). Dense and green, rounded habit; old plants not bigger than 1' tall by 4' across. Zone 6b.

B. microphylla var. *koreana,* Korean Box (early 1900s?). Looser, open habit, leaves yellow in winter. The hardiest variety; shunned by deer. Zone 4.

'Tide Hill' (before 1954). Retains green leaves in winter; matures to 15" tall by 5' across. Zone 5.

'Wintergreen' (1930s). From Manchuria; green in winter; 2'. Faster-growing than Common Box. Zone 5.

Buxus sempervirens. The aristocrat of hedging plants. Tall, treelike if not pruned. Natural billowy form; good for topiary work. Does not tolerate exposed, windy sites.

'Newport Blue' (before 1949). Short and wide: Wyman reports a 14-year-old plant at Arnold Arboretum that was 18" tall by 3' across. Dense round form with bluish foliage; takes pruning well. Zone 6.

'Suffruticosa', Dwarf Box. The true colonial Edging Box; also the most fragrant variety.

Mature height is 3–5', but with careful pruning it can be kept to a few inches tall. The variety least susceptible to box leaf miner. Zone 6.

'Vardar Valley' (1957). Brought from the Balkans around 1935. Popular for its hardiness; extremely low-growing, compact mound. Zone 6a.

'Variegata'. Leaves margined with creamy yellow; 8–10". Zone 6.

Calendula officinalis

ASTERACEAE

Pot-marigold
Cape-marigold, Marygold, Merrigould, Winking-Mary-budde

INTRODUCED: 1600–1699
TYPE: Hardy Annual Flower/Herb
HEIGHT: 1–2'
BLOOM: Summer–Fall
SITE: Sun/Partial Shade

*P*ot-marigold, an annual flower native to the Mediterranean and southern Europe, grows to 2 feet in the wild. It has single- or double-petaled, daisylike blooms that can be as large as 4 inches across and range in color from pale yellow to deep orange. Some have dark centers. The stems are sturdy yet brittle, and the long, pale green leaves are mostly in evidence near the bottom of the plant. The genus name is derived from the Latin *calendae,* meaning "the first of the month," a reference to the fact that, in its native habitat, the Pot-marigold is almost everblooming. It has long been noted that "the flower goes to bed w' the sun/And with him rises weeping" *(A Winter's Tale),* a habit more precisely defined by Linnaeus as the flower that opens by nine in the morning and closes by three in the afternoon (though very double-flowered types don't quite fit this description).

Calendula officinalis—as its epithet "from the apothecary" indicates—was first considered an herb. As early as the 13th century, its medicinal and culinary uses were described in detail. Its flowers were steeped or dried and used primarily in ointments (still available today); the dried petals were stored in barrels and sold by the ounce to flavor soups and stews. In the New World, the flowers were often used to color cheese and butter (the plant yields a yellow dye).

Jefferson grew Marygolds at Monticello in 1764. (Calendulas were called Marygolds well into the 18th century; later they were referred to as Pot-marigolds to distinguish them from the *Tagetes* species, African and French Marigolds.) These were probably the single-petaled form, but double flowers have been known at least since the 16th century, when Gerard referred to one as "the greatest double Marigold . . . beautiful round, very large and double . . . like pure gold," a description that could fit many modern types. He described an ancient strain known as 'Hens and Chicks' as *prolifera* and called it Jack-an-apes-a-horsebacke: "At the top of the stalke one floure like the other Marigolds; from the which start forth sundry other small flowers, yellow likewise, and of the same fashion." If you grow Pot-marigolds long enough, sports like this sometimes turn up among double-flowered types.

Pot Marigold.

Gradually, the beauty of Calendula flowers, their ease of culture, and their adaptability to extremes of heat and cold (surviving successive frosts to 25°F/-4°C) recommended them as a subject for breeding. Many cultivars that played on the plant's form and size and the color of the flowers were developed. By 1930 'Orange Shaggy' was offered as a "very distinct break in Calendulas," with long and deeply fringed petals resembling some types of Chrysanthemums, but not all gardeners approved of this meddling with the classic design. "'Orange Shaggy'," Louise Beebe Wilder noted scornfully, "is very well described by its name . . . an unsightly and unseemly flower, not fit to consort with such beauties as . . .'Apricot','Chrysantha','Golden Beam','Radio','Campfire' . . .'Ball's Orange', 'Ball's Gold','Ball's Masterpiece', and 'Lemon Queen'."

Two of these older strains have survived. 'Radio', according to Roy Genders in his book *The Cottage Garden* (Viking Penguin, 1987), is "one of the finest cut flower plants ever raised. The habit is ideal, never becoming tall and 'raggedly', whilst the flowers with their attractive quilled petals are of the clearest orange." 'Orange King' is a vigorous plant, almost 2 feet tall, with large flowers whose double rows of deep orange petals do not obscure the central disk, which is sometimes dark but more often pale green. 'Radio' is very useful in the border, with its Cactus Dahlia-shaped blooms as an easy-to-grow Mum stand-in for fall color. I plant 'King' everywhere for late fall color, often alongside dark blue Bachelor's-button. The brightness of bloom of both these plants is astonishing, deepening in cold weather (or so it seems). The unimproved single-petaled type is allowed to self-sow from year to year, especially in the vicinity of spring-flowering Daffodils. In *Plants from the Past* (Viking, 1987), garden historians Stuart and Sutherland note that, in the 18th century, the single-flowered type was the one used as a cooking herb and to flavor butter, while the doubles were kept in the flower garden. In my experience, doubles are more useful, for the simple reason that they have more petals. Both types, particularly those with dark centers, are highly prized cut flowers.

To Grow: You can sow the boat-shaped seeds in the fall or spring. Be sure to cover them with ¼ inch of soil, since they need darkness to germinate. This should occur in four to ten days, or possibly a little longer, if the soil temperature is 70°F (21°C). Sow seeds a second time in early summer for late bloom. The soil should be moderately rich—though the plants will tolerate poor soil if the drainage is good—and the site fairly sunny (partial shade is okay as long as it receives morning sun). In Zones 8 to 10 sow seed in late summer for winter bloom by Christmas. Thin the plants to 8 to 10 inches apart, and if you want to transplant some, do so when they are in the seedling stage, taking care to plant them deeply and water them well. For winter bloom indoors, cut back the most immature plants in the fall and pot them.

COLLECTOR'S CHOICE:

Calendula officinalis, Pot-marigold (1600–1699).

'Cottage Charm' (old style); single orange bloom with dark center.

'Hens and Chicks'.

'Orange King' (late 19th century).

'Radio' (by 1930).

Callistephus chinensis

ASTERACEAE

China Aster
German Aster

INTRODUCED: 1700–1776
TYPE: Tender Annual Flower
HEIGHT: 2½'
BLOOM: Summer–Fall
SITE: Sun/Partial Shade

*I*n the wild, the China Aster (native to China, of course) is an erect, branching annual with stems to 2½ feet. It has showy, daisylike flowers as big as 5 inches across in shades of violet to rose and white. This form has been widely developed to include fully double flowers and dwarf types with an extended color range. "China" distinguishes this flower from the native perennial Asters *(Aster novae-angliae* and *A. novi-belgii).*

The China Aster began its journey to the West when a Jesuit missionary noticed it growing in a field near Peking around 1730. He must have been astonished and delighted to find such a beautiful flower growing in the wild. By 1735 the Englishman Peter Collinson, a leading spirit in transatlantic seed exchange, had sent seeds to John Bartrum, America's first botanist-horticulturalist, to whom we (as well as the British) owe so many plant introductions. Collinson observed that the purple and white flowers were "the noblest and finest plant thee ever saw," a judgement that must have been shared by many Americans, for China Asters were among the most cultivated flowers of the 18th century.

By the early 1800s, Germany had become the center of seed production—especially for the quilled or "hedgehog" type, which has long, curved petals—hence the then-popular name "German Aster." By 1865 the China Aster had been so changed from its original daisy form that James Vick, proprietor of a New York seed firm, observed with approval, "They are now as double as the Chrysanthemum or the Dahlia and almost as large and showy as the Peony," a sentiment not shared by William Robinson, the English gardener and writer (contemporary of Gertrude Jekyll), who especially deplored the stocky, double dwarf form popular in stiff Victorian gardens, which he called "dumpy."

By the late 1800s, fashions in flowers had changed considerably, and the return to "grandmother's garden" required a freer, more classic flower design, as in some of the cultivars developed for the florist trade, such as 'Boston Florists' White', a snowy white, long-stemmed beauty introduced in 1884. As with many plants, I came to the classic shape by the back door, after first growing every other form, from double dwarf pom-poms to frilled and feathery concoctions. Then I discovered 'Heart of France', and I knew at once what I wanted in a China Aster.

'Heart of France' is (or was) a carmine-rose single-petaled flower, 4 inches across, with a yellow center. It grows to about 2½ feet, and is spectacular in the fall among Marigolds and other late bloomers, such as tall white Garden Phlox. It was probably introduced sometime in the late 1920s, for it is described in a 1930 seed catalog as "New! . . . a large full aster with never a trace of hollow center, branching and robust." (But, as anyone familiar with seed-catalog hyper-

China Asters were among the most cultivated flowers of the 18th century.

bole knows, "New!" could mean decades-old.)

I began growing single China Asters in 1973 and 'Heart' by 1975. The last time I saw it offered for sale was in the 1980s. Had I known that someday it would disappear from the market, I could have saved its seed, but I didn't think about plants as heirlooms then. I thought this lovely flower would always be around. Fortunately, the single-flowered type in the classic form and color range, sold as a mix, is still available, and the heirloom gardener can selectively save seeds of ruby-colored flowers similar to my favorite.

To Grow: For July and August bloom, start seeds indoors in March or April; germination takes ten to fourteen days at 70°F (21°C). I have found China Asters easy to raise if temperatures are kept steadily warm. Be sure to transplant the seedlings when the first true leaves appear, because the developed roots don't like being disturbed. For this reason, I usually transplant them into plant cells, which encourage roots to grow as a block that is easy to transplant into the garden. Garden soil should be rich, well drained, and on the sweet side. The site should be sunny, though light shade is acceptable in warmer regions. Plant the seedlings when all danger of frost has passed. Place them about 12 inches apart and mulch the shallow roots with 1 inch of grass clippings. Avoid fresh manure or compost, which might encourage wilt, a dreaded fungus. Resistance to this disease is not always noted in catalogs, so to be on the safe side, plant China Asters in a different location every year to avoid any buildup of the fungus in the soil.

COLLECTOR'S CHOICE:

Callistephus chinensis, China Aster (1700–1776). Single blooms, mixed colors.

'Crego Aster' (old style). Robust plant with 4" flowers like Mums in a range of colors, to 2' tall. Rust-resistant.

'Florett' (old style). Quilled Aster to 2' with 3–4" flowers in violet, white, lavender, salmon-pink, purple, rose, and champagne. Nice with tall Dahlias.

'Single Rainbow Hybrids' (old style).

Campanula spp.

CAMPANULACEAE

Bellflower

INTRODUCED: 1600–1900
ZONES: 3–10
TYPE: Biennial/Perennial Flower
HEIGHT: to 4'
BLOOM: Late Spring–Summer
SITE: Sun/Partial Shade

*B*ellflowers belong to an extraordinarily large genus of more than 1,500 annual, biennial, and perennial species that are widely distributed across the Northern Hemisphere. Several of these are highly regarded as ornamentals for their showy, five-petaled, bell-shaped flowers, which grow in *racemes,* or terminal spikes, on creeping or tall wandlike stems to 4 feet or more. The blue, violet, mauve, pink, or white blooms emerge from a rosette of long basal leaves. The genus name is Latin for "little bell."

Two species of Bellflowers were grown in 17th-century American gardens: the biennial Canterbury- or Coventry-bells and the hardy perennial Peach-leaved Bellflower, both English cottage garden favorites. The former was named for the two English cathedrals near where it grew wild, perhaps a

Roman introduction. The fleshy taproot is reportedly edible, but there is no indication that it was grown on this side of the Atlantic for any reason other than aesthetic appeal and as a living keepsake of the home country. Early strains, closest to the wild, were purplish blue (known since medieval times) and white; their bells were fairly slender rather than inflated (the kind we know today). In the 18th century, Jefferson sowed this Bellflower with African Marigolds (*Tagetes erecta*) and White Poppies (*Papaver somniferum*). Early 19th-century seedsmen and nurserymen offered nine types of Bellflowers, among them Peach-leaved, Creeping (*Campanula rapunculoides*), and Clustered (*C. glomerata*).

The Peach-leaved Bellflower, or Paper Flower (named after the transparency of its petals), was more on the order of an herb in early American gardens. Introduced to England in the 15th century, the plant was used in its entirety, especially the flowers, which, when distilled in water, yielded a medicine to soothe sore throats and cleanse the skin. The roots were boiled and served as a vegetable, as were so many flower roots when other vegetables were scarce. It soon became a valued garden flower, loved for its slightly flaring bells all along its towering stems, as well as its ease of culture. In the 18th century, double forms were widely grown, almost displacing the singles in the public's favor, but by the 19th century, the crisp, elegant singles were back in fashion, heralded as "new."

Also in the 19th century, the harder-to-grow but much-admired Canterbury-bells were offered in the double "cup-and-saucer" and "hose-in-hose" forms. In these types, the flower sits in an enlarged calyx of the same color—cup-and-saucer—or the calyx appears as another row of petals, creating the effect of a double flower with one flower growing inside and from the other—hose-in-hose. Not all gardeners saw these as improvements over the older, daintier form. "A monstrous variety," Mrs. Wilder called the cup-and-saucer. "Who wants a stalk of cups and saucers in his garden!" Apparently many gardeners did and do, as this is the type of Canterbury-bells most widely grown today.

Among popular Bellflowers, two are of special note for their respective histories, both claiming the same titles of "Scottish Bluebell" or "Bluebell of Scotland." The most accepted is *Campanula rotundifolia*, also known as Harebell and Witch's-thimble. Gardeners at Old Sturbridge Village, the reconstructed early 19th-century village in Massachusetts, grow this Bellflower in the Fenno House garden among Phlox, Golden-glow, and Day-lilies (combinations that still speak to us today) and at the Fitch House as part of a low-maintenance garden plan based on a description in Joseph Breck's 1833 garden book for children, *The Young Florist*. This Bellflower is distinguished by its rounded leaves and delicate, drooping pale blue flowers growing in small racemes.

Another Bellflower, *Campanula rapunculoides*, or Creeping Bellflower (offered by M. Mahon, a 19th-century Scotsman), is the undisputed holder of the title "Scottish Bluebell" in New Scotland (Nova Scotia) and on Cape Breton Island, where we live. Who, after all, should know better than the Scots themselves? The plants in my garden came from a friend whose own flowers are descended from the ones that grew in her great-grandmother's garden on our remote peninsula, settled by her forebears from the Scottish Highlands. Although this irrepressible

There should be room in every heirloom garden for a selection of Bellflowers.

black sheep of the Bellflower family is dismissed everywhere in the plant world as a weed to be avoided in the garden *(Hortus Third)*—for if it is admitted, "you will never know peace again" (Reginald Farrer)—it is cherished here for its association with the early settlers and with the old country itself. Its roots can grow between cracks in cement and come up through gravel, bearing delicate light purple bells all along their length—a lovely weed. Around here, it is a sure sign of a former homestead and is still valued as a garden plant despite its vigorous growth.

There should be room in every heirloom garden for a selection of Bellflowers. They say "old-fashioned" in a very appealing way. A most desirable and seldom-grown type, Clustered Bellflower or Danesblood *(Campanula glomerata),* deserves more attention. Its straight spikes, with long-lasting purple or pure white blooms into midsummer, grows on sturdy stems that never need staking, in any soil (dry or moist), and in sun or partial shade, and combines well with clear yellow Sundrops *(Oenothera).* The Peach-leaved Bellflower is a back-of-the-border plant, indispensable in early summer among Lupines and Foxglove, Mallows and Dame's-rocket. Canterbury-bells are most effective when grown in groups of one color in places where their pretty bells won't be lost among other lush growth during the summer: either toward the front of the border or in a small bed by themselves, edged with Sweet Alyssum and Lamb's-ears—an unbeatable, easily maintained combination.

Either contender for the title "Scottish Bluebell" can be left to roam in a wild garden or wherever you want an irrepressible ground cover to shade out *real* weeds—say, around deciduous shrubs. The daintier *Campanula rotundifolia,* or Harebell, deserves a place in a sunny rock garden. As for the Creeping Bellflower, put it where you want it to creep—along a gravel walk or against a cement foundation—and you won't suffer from its vigorous nature. Actually, it is no problem to grow in a border because unwanted growth is easily controlled by pulling it out, just as you would a weed. The stems insinuate themselves among other flowers, creating masses of bells where you did not expect them. All the Bellflowers are exceptional cut flowers.

To Grow: Bellflowers grow well in full sun or light shade in ordinary, well-drained garden soil. The plants should be set 12 to 18 inches apart. Seeds of the perennial type can be sown in late summer in a cold frame to germinate early the following spring. The plants should remain in the cold frame until the following season, then be planted out as early as possible. Biennial Canterbury-bell seeds should be sown in a cold frame in early summer and planted out early the following spring, when they will flower in early summer (unlike the modern strains that may flower the first year from seed). Seeds germinate in six to twelve days at 70°F (21°C); since they need light to germinate, you should barely cover them. If the plants are cut down before they set seed, they may survive to bloom another year, but you should seed annually to be sure of continual bloom. Divide perennials as needed, about every three to five years. The Peach-leaved Bellflower may need staking in a windy, exposed location.

COLLECTOR'S CHOICE:

Campanula glomerata, Clustered Bellflower, Danesblood (1700–1850). Deep purple

---

> Bellflowers
> say
> "old-fashioned"
> in a very
> appealing
> way.

clustered flowers on 2' spikes; early to
midsummer. Zone 2.

'Alba'. White.

C. medium, Canterbury-bells (1600–1699).
   Single, old-style, clear blue, 2–3', late
   spring to midsummer. Available in several
   forms: single rose, single; white, mixed
   singles and doubles, and in the cup-and-
   saucer style, 'Calycanthema'.

C. persicifolia, Peach-leaved Bellflower (1600–
   1699). Blue or white, 3'. Early summer.

'Alba'. Pure white.

'Grandiflora'. Mixed.

'Telham Beauty' (old style). Large single
   blooms, china blue.

C. rapunculoides, Scottish Bluebell, Creeping
   Bellflower (1776–1850). Summer, 3'.

C. rotundifolia, Scottish Bluebell, Harebell,
   Witch's-thimble (1850–1900). Summer,
   1–2', Zone 2.

Canna flaccida
Canna × generalis
Canna indica

CANNACEAE

Canna
Indian Shot, Golden Marsh Canna,
Indian Reed, Swamp Canna, Swamp
Flag

INTRODUCED: 1850–1900

ZONES 7–10

TYPE: Tender Bulb

HEIGHT: 2–7'

BLOOM: Summer–Fall

SITE: Sun

*C*anna is a tropical plant whose exotic
connection is evident in its fantastic
appearance. Growing from a fleshy rhizome,
stiff stems quickly shoot up as high as 10 feet
in the wild (to about 6 or 7 feet in cultivation), bearing broad, stiff leaves that range
from green and bronze to maroon, variegated,
or striped. Iris-shaped flowers are borne in
terminal clusters in a range of bright colors
(the result of hybridization) that include yellow, orange, peach, rose, pink, and deep red.

Like wild Glads, wild Cannas are small-
flowered, more graceful in appearance, their
colors confined to type. For many years, the
only one found in gardens was the native
red-flowered *C. indica,* Indian Shot, so named
because of its hard, round seeds. Cultivated
in Spain and Portugal for making rosary
beeds, *C. indica* was grown as an ornamental
in England by the 16th century. For Louise
Beebe Wilder, writing in the late 1930s, Indian Shot was "an old garden plant," popular
for Victorian bedding because, even though
its flowers were short-lived, the foliage was
long-lasting. Another native species, the yellow-flowered *C. flaccida* or Swamp Canna,
became an important parent in 19th-cen-
tury breeding, mainly in France. Today, there
are so many species in the breeding lines that
all hybrids are now listed under the name *C.*
× *generalis.*

Early hybridizing focused on extending
the bloom season and color range, and by
the late 19th and early 20th centuries, many
new and dazzling cultivars had become available. Victorian style dictated massed planting in the home garden and in public places
(where Cannas were massed on a large scale).
It's no wonder they were so often used in
this way, since their strong, overbearing, even

startling appearance is hard to place in a garden setting . . . what goes with it?

Gertrude Jekyll, the high priestess of garden color and form, saw positive aesthetic possibilities in the plant's appearance. She grew yellow-flowered 'Richard Wallace', an early 20th-century introduction (to 6 feet), in the back of her fall border, "good to see when the sun is behind and the light comes through the leaves" *(Colour Schemes in the Flower Garden),* combining it with claret-red Hollyhock ("a full red . . . blood colour") and, in front, Dahlias—dark red, deep scarlet, and orange—a brilliant garden picture, complementary in color and form, as only she knew how to create.

Despite Canna's general decline after the Victorian era (though in the South, where they over-winter in the ground, Cannas have always been common), some have never lost their popularity because they combine handsome foliage (all green) with contrasting, vivid flowers, making them more versatile as garden flowers: coral-pink 'City of Portland' (1915); tall, red 'King Humbert'/'Roi King Herbert' (1902); and 'President' (1923), with large tomato-red flowers. The most popular Canna among those offered by antique bulb collector and nurseryman, Scott Kunst of Old House Gardens, is the now rare 'Florence Vaughn' (1893). With vibrant blossoms of yellow marked with a large, central orange blotch and leopard spots, offset by green leaves, this classic cultivar is a great asset in Victorian garden design. And with the tropical revolution in full swing, foliage types like 'Striped Beauty' (green, pin-striped yellow ca. 1923) are back in style once again, a hot item in fashion-conscious garden design.

But heirloom gardeners, by definition, don't grow plants because they are fashionable. On the contrary, we grow them because we think they possess enduring qualities that we want to preserve. On this count, too, antique Cannas deserve a place in our landscape, if we have the imagination to use them well. They're fun to grow, surprising, and always entertaining. Tall types show up well against green shrubbery, and, as Gertrude Jekyll demonstrated, they're very effective at the back of the border with tall Hollyhocks and Dahlias. Shorter kinds (to 3 feet), like 'Firebird' (1911), are candidates for containers, paired with soft, graceful open-pollinated Petunias, Sweet Alyssum, or trailing Nasturtiums (or all three together—why not?) for a long season of interest.

To Grow: In Zones 7 through 10, Cannas can be left in the ground over the winter. If you want to discourage their spread, divide them before the new growing season. In other areas, you can lift the tubers to store over the winter, like Dahlias (see page 104), but be forewarned . . . they're large. In the spring (about a month before outdoor temperatures rise to 60°F/16°C), divide tubers with a sharp knife, leaving several eyes on each, then plant them in pots before planting out (this will encourage earlier bloom). Plant them out 15 to 18 inches apart. In the South, plant tubers directly outdoors in the early spring.

Like Dahlias, Cannas need heat and lots of water to grow well and fast. They thrive in rich, moist soil, although they will also grow in dry, poor conditions in warm regions. If insects attack the leaves, try soap spray or, in the South, cut back plants and they will grow up again untroubled.

If you're patient, or if you live in the South where Cannas grow fast, you can try growing them from seed. They'll be variable, but

> Heirloom gardeners don't grow plants because they are fashionable. We grow them because they possess enduring qualities that we want to preserve.

always interesting. Start early (they take 3 to 6 months to bloom); soak seeds overnight in warm water, or chip them to speed germination, then plant them in peat pots, covering them with soil; seeds take 21 to 60 days to germinate.

COLLECTOR'S CHOICE:

Scott Kunst's global search for surviving antique Cannas has resulted in the introduction and reintroduction of some real beauties that are hard, or impossible, to find elsewhere. I've marked these "Rare," and all are available from Old House Gardens/OHG (see Sources).

Canna X *generalis* 'City of Portland' (by 1919). Hailed as "magnificent" in Peter Henderson's 1916 catalog. Green leaves, 4–5' tall.

'Cleopatra' (by 1923?). Common in southern gardens where it is known as the "Harlequin Canna"; blossoms are yellow dotted with red, leaves green, but flowers and leaves are variable; 3–5'.

'En Avant'/Forward (1914). Rare reintroduced antique described by Scott Kunst as "like the feathers of some exotic bird, the broad, rich yellow blossoms . . . are thickly speckled with flowing red dots and lozenges"; green leaves (a good thing). Scott advises planting this beauty where you can enjoy the spectacle up close; 4–6'.

'Firebird' (1911). Rare, a short type for containers. Scott says the "slender, elegant scarlet flowers glowing against dark green leaves remind me of tropical wildflowers"; a French hybrid from the famous firm of Vilmorin-Andrieux; 2–3'.

'Florence Vaughn' (1893). Rare, with large splotched and dotted yellow flowers which Scott says are "very Victorian!"; green leaves, 4–6'.

'Konigen Charlotte'/'Queen Charlotte' (1892). Rare. Described by Scott as "One of our oldest cannas . . . blazingly Victorian"; small bright red blossoms edged bright yellow; green leaves, 3–5'.

'Madame Angele Martin' (1915). Rare, with pewter bronze foliage, apricot-rose flowers; 3–5'.

'Madame Paul Casenueve' (1902). Rare reintroduction with dark-purple foliage and large flesh-pink flowers; 3–5'.

'President' (1923). An enduring classic Canna with big tomato-red flowers and rich green leaves; 3–5'.

'Prince Charmant'/'Prince Charming' (1892). A rare antique with deep strawberry pink flowers and green leaves; 3–5'.

'Richard Wallace' (1902). A popular classic for the Gertrude Jekyll border you've always wanted to make; canary yellow flowers with apple green leaves; 5–6'.

'Roi Humbert'/'Red King Humbert' (1902). Ever-popular for its bold scarlet flowers and bronze foilage; a tall type, 5–8'.

'Semaphore' (1895). Rare French hybrid and Scott's favorite with narrow bronze leaves and slender flowers that he describes as "radiant, golden saffron-orange"; 5–6'.

'Stadt Fellbach' (1934). Unusual for a Canna, this classic from Wilhelm Pfitzer, whom Scott describes as "the greatest canna breeder of the 20th century," has soft apricot flowers; green leaves; 3–5'.

'Striped Beauty' (by 1923). One of the oldest and most reliable striped-leaved types, green with a yellow pinstripe; red buds open to yellow blossoms; 2–4'. Felder

Rushing *(Passalong Plants)* pairs it with a gazing globe for startling effect.

'Wyoming' (1906). More popular than ever since Christopher Lloyd pulled out all his old roses (I don't advise) and replaced them with tropicals. This variety, with dark bronze foliage and glowing orange flowers, is one of his favorites, a classic American heirloom which Scott describes as "the last survivor of the life work of Pennyslvania Canna-master Leon Wintzer."

Canna flaccida, Swamp Canna (1850–1900).
Canna indica, Indian Shot (1850–1900).

Centaurea cyanus

ASTERACEAE

Bachelor's-button

Blew-bottle, Cornflower, Hurt-sickle, Ragged-sailor

INTRODUCED: 1600–1699
ZONES 2–8

C. montana

Mountain-bluet, Mountain-bluebottle, Perennial Bachelor's-button, Perennial Cornflower

TYPE: Hardy Annual/Perennial Flower
HEIGHT: 1–3'
BLOOM: Early Summer–Fall
SITE: Sun

The annual and perennial Bachelor's-buttons belong to the very large knapweed genus, mainly native to the Mediterranean region, Near East, and Europe. The annual Bachelor's-button or Cornflower is a branching plant that grows to 3 feet. Its wiry, silver-leaved stems bear many fringed, brushlike deep blue flowers with prominent white-tipped stamens enclosed in distinctive bracts of tightly overlapping scales. The perennial Mountain-bluet, as the name suggests, is native to mountainous regions of central Europe. Its broader, tapering leaves are also silvery gray in their early growth, while the deep blue feathery flowers—twice the size of the annual at 3 inches across—are thinly rayed and spidery, touched with dark red at the center, and somewhat black at the edges. The flowers are variable in color, from blue to shades of pink and white, as are those of the annual Bachelor's-button.

Once known as the Cornflower and Hurt-sickle because it grew among corn and its wiry stems could blunt a sickle during mowing time, annual Bachelor's-button has been grown in gardens for many centuries. Its herbal use was confined mainly to making a blue ink from the expressed juice of the petals. Long a favorite in English cottage gardens, it was planted in the earliest new-world gardens, perhaps as a source of ink to write letters back home. Under the right conditions, light snow in late fall draws "ink" from the deep blue flower heads, a graphic illustration of its older name, Blew-bottle.

The Bachelor's-button has always been appreciated for its bright, long-lasting, frost-resistant blooms and its ease of culture (a child's first garden flower). Jefferson grew it at Monticello, where it began to flower in late spring, probably from fall-sown seeds, among Marygolds *(Calendula),* Yellow Flag Iris, and Sweet Peas—a lovely enough combination to repeat in any garden today.

Not the least of its charms was its ability

to stay fresh in a boutonniere, a Victorian-era use preserved in the name by which it is now primarily known: Bachelor's-button. Double and single red, violet, pink, and white types, probably taken directly from natural variations, were grown as early as the 17th century in England, but as Stuart and Sutherland point out, "some of the simple but intense blue ones are so handsome that there is rarely any point in using anything else," an opinion well taken in my own garden once I had gone through the color range to my satisfaction. 'Jubilee Gem', a 1937 Silver Medal AAS Winner, is a deep blue dwarf form with double flowers—still popular, I suspect, because of its unequivocal blue, a color "unmatch'd" in any other flower, according to no less a source than the great 1st-century naturalist Pliny the Elder.

"I expect all gardeners have been offered the blue *Centaurea montana,* when they first started making their gardens," Margery Fish observed. "I was given it from a neglected rectory garden and although I have given it away, pulled it up and treated it brutally, I still have it." So do I (after the same treatment), but I have not only become accustomed to it, I have learned to use it to advantage, perhaps in the same way the English cottagers did when they grew it in their overflowing gardens. I find that when three clumps are grown together, they act as support for floppy-stemmed Oriental Poppies and Garden Lupines, whose mixed colors—flaming reds, blues, and various purples—blend together in early summer, highlighted by the white umbels of Sweet Cicely. If Mountain-bluet is cut back after flowering, its fresh mound of silvery gray leaves will provide interest all season, and the plant will bloom again in the fall, when its deep blue is much valued among the tall white globes of Garlic Chives and 'Orange King' Calendula.

Both Bachelor's-buttons make fine cut flowers. The annual also can be used in dried bouquets, where the deep blue is welcome among the usual understated tones. For this purpose, they should be harvested when the flowers are just beginning to open (they'll open up more as they dry).

To Grow: In warm winter regions, sow seeds of annual Bachelor's-button (lightly covered) in late summer for winter or early spring bloom. Elsewhere, sow seeds outside in fall or early spring for continuous bloom through the late fall months. Space plants 10 to 15 inches apart, with the greater distance producing larger flowers. The process of germination may be speeded up by refrigerating the seeds for five days. Sun and any well-drained, not overly rich soil should produce good results, especially if spent flowers are picked off.

Sow seeds of Mountain-bluet in a cold frame during the spring or summer. Set out the seedlings, 12 to 18 inches apart, early the following spring, when growing conditions are cool. Cut plants back after flowering for bushy growth and possible rebloom, and divide them at least every two to four years, as clumps become crowded.

COLLECTOR'S CHOICE:

Centaurea cyanus, Bachelor's-button; deep blue wildflower type; 2–3'.

'Emperor William' (described by J.L. Hudson as "the last of the old, tall, single-flowered varieties in existence . . . the closest to the wild plant . . . Long-blooming, unlike modern types"); deep blue.

'Jubilee Gem' (pre-1937); double deep blue blooms; 12".

The Bachelor's-button has always been appreciated for its bright, long-lasting, frost-resistant blooms and its ease of culture.

C. montana, Mountain-bluet; deep blue
blooms; 2'.
'Alba'; pure white blooms.

Clarkia amoena
(Godetia amoena; G. grandiflora)

ONAGRACEAE

Godetia
Farewell-to-spring, Satin Flower

INTRODUCED: 1800–1850
NATIVE

C. pulchella

Beautiful Clarkia

C. unguiculata (C. elegans)

Rocky Mountain Garland
Clarkia

TYPE: Annual Flower
HEIGHT: 1–3'
BLOOM: Spring–Fall
SITE: Sun/Partial Shade

Clarkias, annual flowers of the American West, grow from the Rocky Mountains to the Pacific coast and were mostly discovered during the Lewis and Clark Expedition; in fact, the genus is named after Captain William Clark. While most gardeners (and seed catalogs) have resisted regarding Godetia as belonging to the Clarkias, it will be so treated here for convenience.

The *true* Clarkia (according to gardeners) is *C. unguiculata (formerly C. elegans),* or Rocky Mountain Garland, aptly named for the plant's habit of producing showy racemes of delicate rose or purple flowers about 1 inch across all along its long stems, which grow to about 3 feet. The Beautiful Clarkia is shorter (12 to 15 inches), with the same triangular petals ranging in color from bright pink to lavender. Cultivated forms of both may be double-flowered, with notched or blotched petals, in an extended color range.

Two Godetias are familiar to gardeners. The taller type (to 3 feet) is Farewell-to-spring, which has rosy purple, satin-petaled, cuplike blooms 3 to 5 inches across clustered along the stems. The shorter form, Satin Flower, grows to about 1 foot and has rose-red, satin-petaled, cuplike flowers that are blotched at the center. Cultivated forms of these two types may have double flowers and come in varying heights and colors.

All of the Clarkias, whatever their vexing nomenclature, are lovely flowers, sharing narrow-pointed foliage and distinctive pointed buds and seedpods (the latter prized for dried arrangements). Clarkias and Godetias complement each other's blooming period: Clarkias bloom in early summer and Godetias from midsummer through fall.

Clarkias dislike the summer weather that prevails over much of the North America, but they continue to be grown and enjoyed because gardeners have been unable to resist their beauty and because late 19th-century cultivars from Europe (where most of the breeding of Clarkias is done due to favorable climatic conditions) provided gorgeous variations on the simple wildflower. In 1861, the French firm Vilmorin introduced Americans to the 'New Double White Clarkia Elegans', which, unlike the sterile-flowered double Petunia, could be reproduced true to form from seed. Between 1890 and 1914, the luscious 'Salmon Queen' was introduced, described in the most glowing terms by Louisa (Mrs. Francis) King, one of the founders of the Garden Club of America, who drew on her own gardening experiences when evaluating various flowers and shrubs for her American audience: "One of the most graceful and remarkably pretty annuals which has ever come beneath my eye" (*The Well-Considered Garden,* 1915).

Until recently, named cultivars enjoyed by gardeners in decades past were unavailable, but the situation is changing with the renewed interest in cut flowers and choice plants from our past. All Clarkias have much to offer on both counts. By growing them carefully with their special needs in mind (protection from very hot summer temperatures), we too can have "fields ablaze" with their beauty all season, a phenomenon observed with envy by American visitors abroad in the 19th century.

Clarkias (the *real* Clarkias) yield sprays and sprays of flowers for cutting. If you are lucky enough to have a cool greenhouse, they will bloom magnificently all winter long. Consider a cutting bed just for them, but also plant them for early summer bloom in the vicinity of spent bulb plants (Daffodils), where they will cover up nicely. Godetias are highly valued in the light shade of shrubbery, a welcome change from the ubiquitous Impatiens one so often sees. In my Zone 4 garden, the shimmering mass of satiny blooms never fails to elicit favorable comment and the inevitable question: "What's the name of those pretty flowers?"

To Grow: Clarkias and Godetias should be sown where they are to bloom because they don't transplant well. Just scatter the seeds on top of the soil (they need light to germinate) in early spring, as soon as the ground can be worked. Germination occurs in about a week at 60°F (16°C). Thin the plants to 6 to 12 inches apart, depending on their height, and give taller species some support with twiggy brush. For larger sprays of flowers, the taller Clarkias need more room to spread out. The soil should be thin (not too rich or high in nitrogen), somewhat sandy, and well drained. Godetias especially enjoy light shade. All Clarkias should be mulched and kept moist during the heat of summer. In Zones 8 to 10, sow both Clarkias and Godetias in the fall for abundant spring bloom.

COLLECTOR'S CHOICE:

Clarkia amoena, Godetia, Farewell-to-spring; single blooms; 1½'. Double blooms; mixed colors; 2½'.

C. amoena, Godetia, Satin Flower; double blooms (old style); 1½'. The following cultivars in single colors are all available as seeds:

'Cattleya'; lilac.

'Maidenblush'; bright rose.

'Ruddigore'; crimson red.

'Sweetheart'; blush pink.

'White Bouquet'; pure white.

'Satin Cups'; semidouble flowers; 16".

'Salmon Princess'; frilled Begonia-like flowers, overlaid with orange; 10–12".

'Single'; close to the wildflower form and beautiful when massed; 12".

C. pulchella, a beautiful Clarkia; double and semidouble blooms; mixed colors; 12–15".

'Plena' (popular in the 19th century).

C. unguiculata / C. elegans (old style), Rocky Mountain Garland; single wildflower; 2'. Double Carnation-like flowers; mixed or separate colors are available.

Clematis spp. and hybrids ❀

RANUNCULACEAE

Clematis

INTRODUCED: 1700–1900
ZONES 3–9
TYPE: Perennial Tendril Vine
HEIGHT: 8–30'
BLOOM: Spring–Fall
SITE: Sun/Partial Shade

About 230 species of Clematis (from the Greek *klematis,* "climbing plant") are distributed throughout the Northern Hemisphere, including some beautiful, extraordinarily hardy natives. Most Clematis, except for a few herbaceous types, are tall climbers, twisting their tendril-like leaf stalks around any support. Unlike twining vines, they do not usually do well on single upright supports but require horizontal support, such as latticework, around which they can fasten their tendrils. The fragrant showy flowers, borne profusely either separately or in clusters, vary in shape from urnlike to starlike. These are actually composed of very small flowers surrounded by larger sepals; their colors include white, rose, purple, and shades in between, sometimes striped, as well as a few yellows. Both the handsome foliage— large, toothed, sometimes brilliant in the fall—and the seed heads (in some species the most attractive feature) are ornamental long after the flowers are spent. *"Klem'-a-tis"* is the favored pronunciation.

One of the first, if not *the* first, Clematis to be grown in North America was the native *C. virginiana,* American Virgin's-bower. It grows wild in thickets, at the wood's edge, and along streambanks from western Canada and Maine southward, bearing long panicles of small white flowers with prominent stamens and fantastic curled seedpods in the fall, punctuated by purple leaves—quite spectacular.

Eighteenth- and 19th-century American gardeners grew wild Clematis until the introduction of hybridized forms. The wild types are similar in that they bear small flowers in profusion, are grow rapidly, and, with few exceptions, are suitable for screening with their dense foliage. They also were used for climbing over fences, arbors, porches, and rocky areas. The very popular Sweet Autumn Clematis from Japan, with fragrant sprays of small white flowers in the fall, and Traveler's-joy or Old-man's-beard (for its fluffy seed heads) from Europe, were both used, we are told repeatedly in period literature, for "covering unsightly roofs." Landscape architects of the day considered vines the "draperies" of a house. They were valued not only for climbing on walls and trellises but also for climbing up and over tree stumps, presumably left from clearing one's plot of land. The vigorous wild types were well suited to this purpose.

The Clematis picture changed dramatically in 1858 when the British firm George Jackman and Sons of Woking introduced the first large-flowered hybrid—*Clematis × jackmanii*—a cross between the Ningpo Clematis from China and the Italian Vine-bower from southern Europe and western Asia. The Jackman Clematis, with its large purple flowers, was an instant success and remains so today. It is synonymous with the word *Clematis,* vigorous, but not so wild as the species, and more manageable for working in small areas. The Jackman was the beginning of the flood of hybrids, choice heirlooms of which many are still available today. More loose and open in habit of growth, shorter, and with fewer masses of foliage than their wild cousins, the hybrids add beauty to any planting with their large, colorful, long-blooming flowers.

My friend Hank, who grows more kinds of Clematis than he can remember in his Zone 6 garden, plants hybrids to cover the stumps of pine trees he has been clearing away on his 2-acre plot—a labor of love extended over thirty years. And, just as the 19th-century garden guides advised, Hank's Clematis scrambles over stumps and up trees on chicken wire wrapped around the trunks. They thrive in these conditions, with their feet in the shade and their heads in the sun.

Which Clematis does Hank grow? He pays no attention to their names, but his eighty-five-year-old mother-in-law knows them all, and she says her favorites are the Jackman hybrid and 'Nelly Moser', an English introduction (1897), that is neat in habit with very showy, twice-blooming flowers—pink outside petal edges with a rose-pink center bar. 'Nelly Moser' is virtually carefree and requires no pruning. Whether or not Hank knows the names of his cultivars, his garden overflows with such heirlooms because they give him the desired results: plenty of flowers with a minimum of trouble. In the case of Clematis, not always the easiest plants to grow, he has met their special requirements with little effort—the way folk gardeners have always met such challenges.

Aside from the various uses of Clematis to screen (wild types) or to climb up trellis supports (hybrids), the latter should be considered for container planting, making them useful in even the smallest garden.

To Grow: Clematis needs to grow in rich, humus-rich, well-drained light loam on the alkaline side, usually in full sun, though some will take a little shade. The advantage of some of the wild types is that they are especially suited to dry or moist conditions (see "Collector's Choice"). Dig a hole 2 to 3 feet wide and deep, fill it with the prepared soil, and leave it to settle over the winter. In early spring, or whenever the plant is dormant, bury the roots 2 to 3 inches into the soil, spreading them out horizontally. If the plant is grafted, it is especially important to bury the graft union well below the soil so it will establish its own roots. During the first season, remove the flower stems so the plant's energy returns to the work at hand: forming heavy roots.

One way to keep the roots of a Clematis moist in the summer (which is essential) is to plant shallow-rooted annuals such as Petunias at its feet; otherwise, a light mulch will do (a heavy mulch is not recommended because it may promote Clematis wilt). Better yet, place a slab of stone at the base of the plant to keep roots moist. A winter mulch of compost or rotted manure will perform the double function of protecting the plant from alternate freezing and thawing, while adding nutrients to the soil. Otherwise, mulch with straw or evergreen boughs, and twice yearly add one handful of balanced garden fertilizer and another of lime around the root area. Plant roots extra deep in containers, burying the bottom two or three buds for more vigorous development.

A good rule of thumb for pruning is to prune early-flowering types lightly to shape *after* blooming. Severely cut back later-blooming vines to within 2 feet when the plant is dormant (this type blooms on new growth). Some gardeners leave the old growth as a support for the new growth.

Hank's Clematis scrambles over stumps and up trees on chicken wire wrapped around the trunks. They thrive in these conditions, with their feet in the shade and their heads in the sun.

Clematis can be left undisturbed indefinitely. To propagate, take cuttings from young wood in May or June and root them in a cold frame. Wild types often layer themselves, but they can also be grown from seed. Freeze the seeds for three weeks, then plant them. Germination takes one to nine months at 70° to 75°F (21 to 24°C). You can also plant the seed directly in a cold frame in the fall.

COLLECTOR'S CHOICE:

Hybrids:

C. x *jackmanii,* Jackman Clematis (1858); dark purple velvet flowers; partial shade okay; summer bloom; 12'.

'Alba' (1878); white flowers.

'Belle of Woking' (1885); large silvery gray flowers; early bloom; 12'.

'Duchess of Edinburgh' (1887); large double white flowers; especially fragrant; early bloom; 9'.

'Elsa Späth' (1891); bright blue flowers 8" across; summer bloom; 9'.

'Lord Neville' (about 1870); dark plum purple striped blooms with wavy edges; blooms almost continuously early to late summer; 8–12'.

'Mme. Edouard André' (1892); medium-sized red velvet flowers; summer bloom; 8–12'.

'Mrs. Chomonderlay' (1870); large light blue flowers 8" across; early and late bloom; 8–12'.

'Nelly Moser' (1897); pale mauve-pink striped blooms; early and late bloom; 8'.

Wild Types:

Clematis montana rubens, Anemone Clematis (1900); one of the best E.H. Wilson introductions from China; masses of small pink flowers in varying shades; spring-early summer bloom; 18–24'; Zone 5.

C. paniculata, Sweet Autumn Clematis (1864); small white very fragrant flowers in masses; vigorous; evergreen in the South, nearly evergreen elsewhere; late summer bloom; 15' or taller when mature (to 30').

C. tangutica, Yellow Lantern Clematis, Golden Clematis (1890); yellow lantern-like flowers and silvery pods; late summer bloom; 9'; Zone 5.

C. texensis, Red-bell Clematis (before 1924); native, small scarlet urn- or tulip-shaped flowers and fuzzy seedpods; a five-year-old plant can produce thousands of blooms, each about an inch long; evergreen for southern regions; withstands dry soil; blooms early and late; 6'; Zones 4 and 5 (to Bar Harbor, Maine).

C. virginiana, American Virgin's-bower (1700-1776); native; small white flowers in masses with fluffy seedpods in the fall; early bloom; withstands wet soil; 18–20'.

C. vitalba, Traveler's-joy (before 1820); greenish white flowers with billowy white fruits; late bloom; 18–20'.

Convallaria majalis ✿

LILIACEAE

Lily-of-the-valley
Convall-lillie, Ephemera, Lily-convally, Liriconfancy, May-lily, Our-Lady's-tears

INTRODUCED: 1600–1699
ZONES: 3–8
TYPE: Hardy Bulb
HEIGHT: 8"
BLOOM: Late Spring–Early Summer
SITE: Partial Shade/Shade

*T*his genus contains either one or three species, as the three are so much alike that botanists do not agree on the distinctions. They all grow in the Northern Hemisphere, including North America *(Convallaria montana)*. Lily-of-the-valley grows from creeping rhizomatous roots and fleshy crowns known as *pips,* which contain the whole flower in embryo. When these are chilled, then exposed to warm temperatures, they grow into the familiar white waxy (and very fragrant) bells that hang down in a graceful line from upright spikes 6 to 8 inches tall. The long green leaves, which also grow from the pip, remain attractive over a long period, making the plant very useful as a ground cover. Variations in the familiar form include pinkish, double, and large-flowered types, as well as variegated-leaf strains.

Lily-of-the-valley has been cultivated since at least 1000 B.C., making it a true ancient heirloom. Its hardiness and ease of culture, not to mention its fabled fragrance, recommended it to early gardeners who were familiar with the plant from the Old World. Its use as an herb was preserved by the indefatigable Gerard, among others, who reported that "the flores . . . distilled in wine and drunke the quantitie of a spoonful restoreth speech unto those that have the dum palsie and that are falne into the Apoplexie," while other authorities have reported that all parts of the plant are poisonous. This apparently does not extend to the perfume of the flowers, which is extracted and still used to scent various products, including soap; essence of Lily-of-the-valley is often used to scent potpourri.

The pinkish type, less well known among gardeners, sparked an interesting controversy beginning in the 16th century when Gerard mentioned having grown both the pink and white forms. He speculated about a red type (like any curious gardener, he would have liked to have grown it in his garden) that was known before 1599 as 'Rubra'. Whether this was indeed red or, as is common in the flower world, a bit of hyperbole, we do not know. Perhaps it was not much different from the pink type with which Gerard was familiar.

Several other gardeners have carried on about the pink form. In the 19th century, English writer Shirley Hibberd extolled its virtues, calling it "exquisitely beautiful . . . running hither and thither, mixed with white." In the 1930s, gardener and writer Louise Beebe Wilder stated her opinion, as usual, without beating around the bush: "I do not think it very pretty." Decades later, Henry Beetle Hough recounted the story of how his wife, Betty, dug up the pink type from her childhood home in Uniontown, Pennsylvania, and planted it in the Hough's new garden on Martha's Vineyard in the 1920s. Neither of them liked the color much, but it was grown, like many plants, for nostalgia's sake. Betty died in 1965, and Henry

FORCING LILY-OF-THE-VALLEY

*Y*ou can force pips indoors during any season by storing them in the refrigerator, then trimming the long roots about halfway back and placing them in a 6-inch bowl (ten to twelve pips per bowl) with their tips just showing over the edge of the bowl. Press a mixture of sand and peat moss around them, fill the bowl with lukewarm water, and place it near light, adding water as necessary. The pips should produce blooms in three to four weeks.

liked to comment that it continued to bloom in her memory, as it may still do in his.

Such variations in flowers are a matter of taste. Mrs. Wilder, ever an opinionated gardener, called the double-flowered form "lumpy," while others thought it exquisite, an example of more being better—more flowers, more perfume. Fortunately, the ancient and antique types are still available, and the heirloom gardener is invited to investigate them and form his or her own opinion.

All types of Lily-of-the-valley make a useful ground cover, creating an attractive leafy carpet most of the season, perhaps beneath the shade of an heirloom shrub or two, while the masses of fragrant bells (in whatever form or color) last for almost a month, from about mid–May to mid–June. Planted along a winding path or near an outdoor seat, their scent (which requires no bruising to be released) can be appreciated to the full. Planted in outdoor tubs, they can be enjoyed anywhere you wish, in sun or shade. The cut flowers should be brought into the house without restraint, where they will fill an entire room with their sweetness.

Any of the types are striking when grown outdoors in a strawberry jar. Plant prechilled pips in light, fibrous soil or peat moss, with one pip emerging from each opening. In three to four weeks, after being exposed to temperatures of about 70°F (21°C), the flowers will begin to bloom. Discard the pips after blooming or replant them in the ground.

To Grow: Outdoors, plant the roots in the fall about 5 inches apart in rich, slightly acid, damp but well-drained soil, in partial or full shade. Cover the pips with 1 inch of soil and leave the planting undisturbed. A yearly application of compost or well-rotted manure (or nothing at all) is all it needs. Propagation is by division after the foliage dies. In growing zones warmer than Zone 8, Lily-of-the-valley can be induced to grow in cool microclimates, or it can be forced by prechilling roots.

COLLECTOR'S CHOICE:

Convallaria majalis, Lily-of-the-valley (1600–1699).

'Flore Pleno' (1770); double white flowers; spreads more slowly than the single-flowered type.

'Rosea' (1830); mauve-pink flowers.

'Variegata' (1870); creamy yellow variegated leaves; needs more sun than green-leaved types.

Cosmos bipinnatus

ASTERACEAE

Cosmos
Mexican Aster

INTRODUCED: 1800–1850
TYPE: Annual Flower
HEIGHT: 4–6'
BLOOM: Summer–Fall
SITE: Sun/Partial Shade

Cosmos is a striking annual native to Mexico and Central America. It bears daisy-like flowers, 4 inches across, with a single row of silky, serrated petals (pink, rosy lilac, deep crimson, or white) overlapping and radiating from a somewhat raised golden center. The flowers grow on tall, branching stems—to 10 feet in the wild—with feathery foliage. Cosmos is a short-day plant, which means that it does not begin to bloom until the days get shorter in the fall.

Cosmos was discovered in Mexico in 1799, and by 1838 the George Thorburn Seed Company of New York was offering seeds of 6-foot 'Late Cosmos' to its customers. More than fifty years later, the late-flowering Cosmos was little changed. In 1891 the Peter Henderson and Company *Manual of Everything for the Garden* offered the same Cosmos, "resembling single Dahlias."

By the early decades of the 20th century, choice cultivars were available: 'Lady Lennox Pink'—"lighting up well at night," we are told—and 'Lady Lennox White'. An 'Early-flowering Mix' (sixty to seventy days) promised earlier blooms, always the subject of discussion in gardening magazines and catalogs, for the long season required to bring Cosmos to flower often meant that it bloomed only a short time before a killing frost. By 1926, double-flowered types were offered: 'Pink Beauty' ("the center is double with many small petals and a rim of larger outer petals") and 'Extra Early Double Crested' or 'Anemone-flowered', a double crimson type.

In 1930 or thereabouts, a new early strain of Cosmos called 'Sensation' appeared on the market, winning an AAS Gold Medal in 1936. Its introduction radically changed the culture of Cosmos and ensured earlier bloom—fifty-six days after sowing. This strain, or one very similar to it, is still the most popular Cosmos today, considered by connoisseurs to be the choicest type: large (4- to 6-inch) single blooms in the classic design, with almost translucent petals; sturdy, somewhat branching (but not rangy) 4- to 5-foot stems decorated with feathery foliage. Two selections from this strain also have

endured: 'Purity', white with a satiny sheen, and 'Radiance', a deep rose with a rich crimson center.

'Sensation' had a huge impact on the cultivation of Cosmos—now considered one of the easiest annuals to grow. Before its introduction, various strategies were recommended to encourage earlier bloom and larger flowers and discourage ranginess, with the inevitable staking that it implied. Gardeners were advised, for instance, to start the plants in the house at the same time as Castor-beans, to sow the seed later in poor soil to dwarf the plants, and to remove some of the buds to encourage fewer and larger flowers. Altogether, 'Sensation' was well named for the gardeners of the day.

Other cultivars have come and gone, but gardeners know what they want in Cosmos—the simple, single-petaled daisy flower with few embellishments. The introduction in the late 1890s of the Yellow Cosmos (*C. sulphureus*) did not diminish the popularity of the taller pink-flowered type—the one that inevitably comes to mind whenever Cosmos is mentioned.

A 1939 Farmer's Bulletin from the U.S. Department of Agriculture advised gardeners to plant Cosmos in broad masses, at the back of the border, against evergreens, or by fences at some distance from the house, "where their special beauty can be appreciated." That is still sound advice. I like to plant 'Purity' with burgundy Dahlias and mixed China Asters in front of a stockade-style fence that is about 6½ feet tall. There they receive sun for half a day and, protected from the wind, never need staking. Cosmos, mixed with Dahlias and Nicotiana ('Limelight'), are indispensable for fall bouquets. Birds are at-

The introduction of 'Sensation' radically changed the culture of Cosmos and ensured earlier bloom

tracted to the conelike seed heads, which are easy to gather.

To Grow: Plant seeds in warm, well-drained soil, barely covering them, since light helps germination, which takes only three to eight days when soil temperatures reach 70 to 85°F (21 to 29°C). Thin the plants to 12 inches apart. Full sun or partial shade and soil that is not overly rich are the primary requirements. If the plants are protected from strong winds by a fence or shrubbery, staking is not usually required; if it is, use twiggy brush. Self-sown seedlings bloom earlier, but eventually these will be mostly light pink. It's a good idea to save seeds, especially of the white flowers, which do not appear to be as vigorous. Keep an eye out for promising sports. I like variations on the daisy theme, with dark-rimmed centers and wavy-edged petals, so I keep seeds from such flowers separate to keep this strain alive.

COLLECTOR'S CHOICE:

Cosmos bipinnatus, Cosmos (1800–1850).
'Purity' (after 1936); white with satiny sheen.
'Radiance' (after 1936); deep rose with
  crimson center.
'Sensation' (around 1930); 4–6" blooms; 4–5'
  stems.

Dahlia hybrids

ASTERACEAE

Dahlia

INTRODUCED: 1850–1900
TYPE: Tender Bulb
HEIGHT: 1–5'
BLOOM: Summer–Fall
SITE: Sun

The modern Dahlia has evolved from several species native to the mountains of Central and South America to Columbia, where they grow as perennial shrubs as high as 20 feet, in volcanic soils that provide them with the long season of moisture necessary for their growth (the Aztec name for Dahlia, *acocohxihuitl,* literally means "water pipe"). Dahlias grow from fleshy roots, not true tubers or bulbs, and the plants in their modern form range from about 1 foot to 5 feet and over. They have stiff stems bearing round flowers in varying colors—shades of yellow, red, purple, white, and bicolors—and forms, divided by the American Dahlia Society into twelve groups. Among these are the following types: Anemone-flowered (**A**), a single outer row of petals, with a central mat (like a pincushion) of short, tube-shaped petals; Cactus (**C**), a profusion of straight or rolled petals, incurved or recurved in varying degrees; Formal Decorative (**FD**), many neatly and regularly arranged petals turning back slightly toward the stem; Informal Decorative (**ID**), a profusion of generally flat petals, sometimes slightly rolled at their tips, irregularly arranged from the center of the flower head; Mignon (**M**), single-flowered to 18 inches tall; Peony (**PE**), open-centered flowers with several rows of outer petals; Pompon (**P**), small ball-shaped flower heads with lush petals produced in masses on freely branching stems. Flower sizes vary from less than 4 inches to more than 8 inches (the "dinner plate" type) across. The genus is named for Anders Dahl, a contemporary of Linnaeus, who had hoped to find in the Dahlia a substitute for the potato.

Although introduced late to American gardens, the Dahlia had probably been grown and refined in Mexico by the Aztecs long before it was discovered by the Spanish in 1519. Many centuries passed before it became the focus of breeding, resulting in the flower we recognize today, which bears very little resemblance to the Mexican wildflower. The early hybrids, much to the disappointment of antique plant collectors, have not survived, at least on this side of the Atlantic, where the earliest surviving types can be traced back only to the 1920s. From what we know, the earliest hybrids were very unattractive and stiff, their colors hard and flat. The more modern hybrids appear to have improved the form for gardeners.

Whatever Dahlias looked like, Americans were wild about them from the beginning because, like Glads, they thrived in the hot summers characteristic of much of North America, providing a succession of bright blooms. Their primary requirements were no more complicated than those of potatoes, which is why they were often paired with them at the end of the vegetable plot. Also, like Glads, they were highly valued as cut flowers.

Joseph Breck, alarmed by this phenomenon, called the Dahlia a "new flower of fancied merit," an opinion that has been proved wrong, thanks in great part to modern breeding. It should be pointed out that in 1845 Breck's own firm carried, as his catalog proclaimed, "upwards of 200 varieties, including the finest new ones to be obtained in England," selling at two dollars for eight dozen tubers.

The star of the summer and fall flower garden became the focus of my search for heirlooms after I'd met several old-time gardeners (interestingly enough, they were all men) who had been growing Dahlias for fifty years or more, often from the same stock, sometimes carefully preserving color strains. The most common types were medium-sized blooms—3 to 4 inches across in the Formal Decorative class—on medium-tall stems—about 3 feet tall—and Informal Decorative types, with larger flowers on taller stems. The oldest strain I found, traced back to the 1920s, came from a gardener, now in his eighties, who had acquired the original roots when he was seventeen from the landlady of a boarding house that catered to railroad workers.

He had long forgotten the individual names of all these Dahlias and instead referred to them as "the big yellow one" or "the small red frilly one." The former was the 1920s strain I dubbed "Old Railroad Yellow," a magnificent primrose yellow Informal Decorative "dinner plate" Dahlia that I planted in my dooryard garden, where, with no particular attention, it grew to 6 feet, bearing in late summer 9-inch-wide flowers, the outer petals quite flared back and the inner ones pointing inward. It was fascinating to observe the unfolding mass of petals, each bloom lasting as long as a month. These large-flowered types set the standard for the modern "dinner plates," whose heads are held on sturdy stems that hold up remarkably well even without staking if they are planted in a protected site. Older types simply could not bear the weight of the massive flower heads, and the weak stems needed much propping.

Making hedges with Dahlias (especially with the smaller-flowered types) is one of the most satisfying ways to grow them. At the end of the vegetable garden, such a hedge provides an effective and colorful windbreak, thereby encouraging the healthy growth of all the other plants. Planted closer together than usually recommended (about 1 foot apart), the roots become jammed together, thus supporting the stiff stems without staking. Gardeners in Nova Scotia plant such hedges with hundreds of Dahlias, sometimes creating long borders that entirely edge their property—a spectacular sight in mid- to late summer and through the first light frosts in fall.

Groups of the same color can be planted among small, immature shrubs, and if their tips are pinched back early in the season, the Dahlias themselves will resemble bushy shrubs covered with blooms by mid- to late summer. Planted in a border, the brilliant flowers, particularly the red and bright yellow types, add a dash of color to a plethora of soft pinks and pastels. The taller types must be planted in the back of the border, perhaps against a fence or stone wall for support, where their large flowers show to advantage. The shorter ones can be grouped together by color in containers. These should be well watered and mulched.

To Grow: Dahlias thrive in sun and well-drained soil rich in organic matter, high in phosphorus and potash, and with a steady supply of moisture. Before planting Dahlias, work up and enrich the soil as necessary with decayed manure or compost and a handful of bonemeal for each plant (or a low-nitrogen fertilizer similar to the kind used for potatoes: 8–16–8 or 6–12–12). When the soil is warm, plant the cut tubers, eyes up, in a hole 7 to 10 inches wide and deep, so that each cut division has one or two eyes and a piece of stem, without which the tuber will not grow. Cover the tubers with 2 inches of soil. Add more soil to the depression as the plant grows, until the hole is filled in. Space tubers according to the height of the Dahlias: 2 to 3 feet apart for tall types; 2 feet apart for medium-sized types; 15 inches apart for short or dwarf types; 12 to 15 inches apart for hedges. Tall types may need staking, which is best accomplished at planting time by placing the stake beside the tuber and driving it into the ground. For bushier plants, pinch off the tip of the main stem as soon as three to four pairs of leaves develop. When plants are well established, scratch in a balanced fertilizer (5–10–10), watering it in well. Then mulch the plants with 2 inches of grass clippings or other material that will help conserve moisture during the growing season. More moisture means more blooms.

To harvest the tubers, wait for several days after a killing frost. (Dahlias will continue to blossom after several light frosts.) Dig them up with a spading fork to avoid puncturing, and place them upside down on slatted trays or boxes, so dirt falls off and air circulates around them. When they are dry, shake off the dirt and store them at a temperature of 40 to 50°F (4° to 10°C). The greatest source of failure in wintering-over tubers comes from storing them at the wrong temperature. The kind of material you use to store them—sand, peat, or vermiculite—is unimportant. Old-time gardeners store tubers in wooden boxes or bags with no packing material at all, but they know just where they will winter well. Wherever you store them, check them once a month to see how they're doing. They should be plump, not moldy or shriveled up.

To increase your Dahlia supply, you can take innumerable cuttings from the sprouts of the tubers if they are planted indoors early in equal parts of peat moss and vermiculite, barely covered, with bottom temperatures from 65° to 70°F (18 to 21°C). When shoots are 3 to 4 inches high, take cuttings from them by slicing them off from the tuber with a sharp knife and rooting them in vermiculite or sand. Repot them once more and let them grow in containers until all danger of frost has passed. Then plant out the cuttings with the tubers as already described. Although plants from cuttings will not have very large, tuberous roots, they will flower in season with the other Dahlias.

In Zone 10, plant the tubers in late summer for winter bloom.

COLLECTOR'S CHOICE:

The following selections and comments come from Arthur Haskins, Dahlia expert and founding member of the Dahlia Society of Nova Scotia. In the Dahlia world, these hybrids are considered "antiques."

'Autumn Blaze' (1947); **ID**; a true giant Dahlia, sometimes with blooms more than 12" across; a blend of red and orange.

'Gerrie Hoek' (1945); **FD**; a personal favorite; a lovely pink Water Lily type; great for cut flowers and basket displays for halls or churches; 4'. Water Lily types are almost saucer-shaped, like a true Water Lily, with fewer rows of petals than FDs.

'Glorie dan Heemstede' (or 'Glory of Heemstede') (1947); **FD**; a personal favorite; another Water Lily type from Holland; a nice yellow for cutting; one of the top Water Lily types for exhibiting.

'Kidd's Climax' (1940); **FD**; perhaps the Dahlia that has best stood the test of time; 10" blooms of pink and yellow; despite all the top competition in recent times, it continues to be ranked as one of the best Dahlias in the world; 3–4'.

'Lavender Perfection' (1941); **FD**; about 8" blooms, a beautiful lavender, similar to early 19th-century types.

'Miss Rose Fletcher' (1948); **C**; a pink Cactus type with 6" blooms; 4'.

The following are not on Arthur's list but are historic and choice:

'Betty Anne' (1928); **P**; rose-pink; still a show winner.

'Bishop of Llandaff' (1927); **PE**. Enjoying a renaissance of interest for its striking dark burgundy foliage and scarlet, nearly single flowers. 3'.

'Bonne Esperance' (1948); **M**; lovely rose-pink single flowers 1–2" across with golden button center; 12–14".

'Honey' (1956); **A**; 3–4" flowers with a primrose yellow center and apricot-pink outer petals; great for cutting and bedding; 30".

'Jersey Beauty' (or 'Jersey's Beauty') (1924); **FD**; a classic of the type, loved for its large 10" pink flowers, as well as its vigor and height, to nearly 5'. A favorite of Louise Beebe Wilder, who thought its rich pink color incomparable, and who liked it for bouquets. Rarely offered now because it is very difficult to find the true type (as is often the case with heirloom bulbs). Worth looking for.

'Mary Munns' (1928); **P**; deep lavender flower 1–2" wide; 3'.

'Master Michael' (1931); **P**; golden-orange flowers 1–2" wide; 3'.

'Mrs. George Le Boutillier' (1934); **ID**; large 6–10" blooms of deep red; 3–4'.

'Sherwood's Peach' (1944); **ID**; peach-amber flower; "dinner-plate" size, to 12" across; 5'.

'Thomas Edison' (1929); **FD**; deep purple flower, 6–8" across; 4'.

'White Fawn' (1942); **FD**; snow-white flowers 3–4" across; a manageable size for hedges or borders and great in bouquets; 3½'.

Dianthus barbatus ❀

CARYOPHYLLACEAE

Sweet-William
Bunch Pink, Poet's Pink, Sweet-John

INTRODUCED: 1750–1800
ZONES: 4–10
TYPE: Short-Lived Perennial/Biennial Flower
HEIGHT: 1–2'
BLOOM: Late Spring
SITE: Sun/Partial Shade

Sweet-William is a short-lived perennial or biennial native to Europe and Asia that has been cultivated at least since the early 16th century. It is distinguished from other Pinks by its stiff, compact mounds of tightly clustered Phlox-like flowers in brilliant shades of crimson, pink, or white, sometimes banded and edged in contrasting colors, with a dark band around the center of the bloom (referred to as *auricula-eyed*). The petals, single or double, are somewhat toothed or fringed. The jointed stems and glossy leaves lie close to the ground in mats before sending up several flowering stalks the second season. Sweet-William may be naturalized in some areas of North America, growing quite well on its own as a wildflower.

"To praise this flower would be like gilding refined gold," a 19th-century writer declared. Single-flowered types were always popular with gardeners, and by the 17th century in England, doubles were considered choice. With very little effort, Sweet-William produced bright flowers on stiff stems, perfect for bouquets. Some of the older strains were sweetly fragrant like their famous cousins in the Pink family, a characteristic that is lacking in the dwarf annuals today.

Some of the best Sweet-William cultivars were associated with the efforts of the Scottish Paisley weavers, who took great interest in creating long-stemmed florist flowers. Among these was 'Pink Beauty', which had large trusses of soft pink, clove-scented flowers flushed with salmon on long stems (no longer available). Among the double-flowered types, often referred to as Sweet-Johns, were the "Mule" Pinks, so called because they were sterile (all the flower's reproductive parts having been turned into petals). One of these, perhaps a cross between Sweet-William and Carnations, is the salmon-pink 'Emile Pare', which heirloom gardeners can still grow today (see "Collector's Choice"). If one looks hard enough among the dwarf annual types offered today, several of these old strains, probably from the Victorian era, can still be found. One of these is 'Harlequin', in which each tiny flower opens white and gradually turns red, so that at any time a single cluster shows many different colors, from white and rose to several shades of red. A Dutch friend told me that in the Netherlands Sweet-William is called "Thousand Colors," a reference to this phenomenon.

Because Sweet-William is a short-lived perennial, I didn't expect to find it among the heirloom flowers still growing on our peninsula. I was astonished to find a thriving colony of fragrant, large-flowered, pure white Sweet-William locally that had been growing and self-seeding for more than fifty years. No one could tell me when the colony was first seeded or whether there were colors other than pure white (most likely), but the woman who lived on the farm where they were growing told me they were there when she arrived in 1940, growing in what had been her mother-in-law's garden. To establish her own turf, as it were, the woman, then a young bride, had created a garden close to the house, and over the years her mother-in-law's garden had been gradually abandoned. The only remnants were the Sweet-William and one Peony under a clump of trees, cast-offs from the local plant peddler, who couldn't sell them and so gave them to the family that put him up for the night.

To ensure the survival of this extraordinarily hardy Sweet-William, dubbed 'Kathleen's White', I harvested a small number of seeds and raised a group of lusty seedlings, whose seeds in time were passed around to individuals and organizations interested in preserving ornamentals.

The availability of 19th-century florist strains in separate and mixed colors suggests a cutting garden just for bouquets, in addition to the lavish use of Sweet-William in the flower border for late spring and early summer bloom among Dame's-rocket, Mountain-bleu, and Sweet Cicely. Jefferson grew a crimson type (you can, too) in a circular bed and an oval bed, both adjoining his house at Monticello, among brilliant flowers such as Scarlet Lychnis, Cardinal Flowers, Double Anemones, and Poppies.

To Grow: Sow seeds in a cold frame in late summer for bloom the following year. Cover the seeds with a little soil to encourage germination. This takes seven to fourteen days when the soil temperature is 70°F (21°C). Older strains will need no coddling over the winter. Once planted out 9 to 12 inches apart in early spring, they may self-sow indefinitely, provided the soil is perfectly drained and moderately rich. If moisture collects around the crowns of the plants in the winter, they will not survive. Mature plants may grow for two or three seasons, but seedlings should always be encouraged. Double-flowered strains can be propagated by "blind shoots," nonflowering stems taken when the plant is in full flower. Root these in a cold frame and plant them out in fall or very early spring, when they will grow best in the cool weather they favor.

COLLECTOR'S CHOICE:

Dianthus barbatus, Sweet-William (17th-century type grown by Jefferson); shades of red, pink, and white; bicolors; 2'.

'Double Sweet-William' (old style). Mostly double flowers; 18–20".

'Harlequin'.

'Holborn's Glory' (by 1926); white with a crimson zone.

'Newport Pink' (before 1928). Salmon pink; 1'. Lily Shohan, old rose expert, loves this flower. "It is fragrant, free blooming, a good cut flower, and almost perennial, surviving for four or five years."

'Ruby Moon' (old style). Deep velvet crimson, fragrant; 18–20".

'White' or 'White Beauty'(old style; in the spirit of 'Kathleen's White'); hard to find, but choice; extra-large flowers; 20".

Hybrid:

'Emile Pare' (1840). Rare, double salmon; 1½'.

Dianthus caryophyllus ✿

CARYOPHYLLACEAE

Clove Pink
Border Carnation, Carnation, Gillyflower, Sops-in-wine

INTRODUCED: 1600–1776
ZONES: 6–10
HEIGHT: 18–24"
BLOOM: Early Summer

Dianthus plumarius ✿

Cottage Pink
Border Pink, Cushion Pink, Gillyflower, Grass Pink, Scotch Pink, Sops-in-wine

INTRODUCED: 1600–1776
ZONES: 3–8
HEIGHT: 4–12"

TYPE: Perennial
BLOOM: Summer
SITE: Sun

The Cottage Pink is native to rocky, limestone areas from central and southern Europe to the Caucasus. Long, silvery green, grasslike leaves grow in wide mats. By late spring or early summer, stems appear bearing a profusion of clove-scented flowers, pink or white. These are relatively small ¾ to 1½ inches—and jagged-petaled or crimped (the meaning of "pink").

Clove Pink, native to rocky limestone areas in the Mediterranean, is instantly recognizable by its longer, stiffer stems with narrow, gray-green leaves attached at swollen intervals. Red, pink, or white flowers—over 1 inch—are broad-petaled, serrated at their edges, usually double, and, in the wild form, flesh-colored. It, too, is strongly clove-scented. Clove Pink is familiar as the hothouse Carnation, bred for long stems and large, long-lasting, almost always unscented flowers. These two species, Cottage and Clove Pink, have been cultivated and bred for so long that their cultivar origins are often unknown, but we can discern their characteristics in flower size, form, color, foliage type, and blooming habit: true Cottage Pinks bloom once in early summer, while Clove Pinks bloom nearly all summer.

Pinks have been grown in England since the Norman Conquest, when both were called gillyflowers, after the French *giroflé*, meaning clove. In time, gillyflower became a generic term to describe similarly scented flowers, all prized for flavoring. Tavern keepers raised pinks as a cheap way to flavor their wines and, from this use, both pinks were also known as Sops-in-wine.

It's difficult to date the arrival of these ancient pinks in the New World. "Red and white" and "pink and white" Gillyflowers are mentioned in 17th-century lists (Leighton), suggesting that Cottage and Clove Pinks were grown in the colonial period. Both were highly regarded for flavoring (something we take for granted when we reach for the vanilla), but for ruggedness and staying power—at least in the earliest New England settlements—I think the Cottage Pink was preferred.

By the mid-1700s both types were grown in American gardens in all their variations—banded, eyed, laced, and edged in contrasting colors. By the 1800s China Pink *(D. chinensis)* and Maiden Pink *(D. deltoides),* both unscented, were added to the gardener's repertoire (these were not flavoring types).

The most significant change in the status of Pinks occurred in the early 1900s when Montague Allwood, an English breeder and nurseryman, crossed the Cottage and Clove Pink by careful selection of varieties to produce *Dianthus X allwoodii.* Known as Border Pinks, these hybrids were hardy (though not as hardy as true Cottage Pinks), with large rounded or fringed everblooming flowers an inch or more in diameter, in a range of colors and forms. Some, like 'Doris'—sweetly scented, Carnation-style, rose-pink flowers—are still popular.

Like many gardeners who have embraced the cottage garden mystique, I craved the scented Pinks I'd read about in the literature, yet I hesitated to grow them because of our harsh climate and heavy, damp soil—anathema to all Pinks. But I couldn't refuse the gift of a nice clump of Cottage Pinks from a departing gardening friend. Planted in a dooryard garden protected from the wind, in a raised bed planting for improved drainage, with Hollyhocks, Foxglove, and Iris as companions, they have been with me many years and require little attention, except for renewing clumps periodically by propagating shoots (very easy). Their season of bloom, in early July here, is crowded with stars—Sweet-William, Apothecary Rose, Rugosa Roses, assorted antique Iris (these are faced with neon-bright Maiden Pink), but none outshine Cottage Pink in charm. I love to pass by them each day to catch their sweet aroma.

I'm not immune, however, to other types, and over the years, I've tried just about every one for hardiness and scent. Among my favorites are the summer-blooming Fringed Pink, *D. superbus,* from the 1700s and its hybrid offspring, 'Rainbow Loveliness', from the 1920s. Their exaggerated fringed flower form is odd, but their aroma—heady, all-embracing, warm like jasmine—is irresistible. I always have a few potted plants near doorways.

I've recently succumbed to a new hybrid form, 'Ballad Blend', derived from 'Spring Beauty'. These are extraordinarily vigorous, with Carnation-like stems and leaves and fringed, scented flowers (not as strongly scented as Cottage Pink) in salmon, rose, red, pink, and bicolors, some with dark eyes. They are nice companions for Old Roses, and their bluish foliage makes a handsome all-season clump (even in winter) in my pseudo "silver garden" with *Artemisia* 'Silver Mound' and the like. They're not really old, in the heirloom sense, but they are Pinks in the best hybrid tradition: long-blooming, large-flowered, and scented.

To Grow: Standard advice to use as a guide: Cottage Pinks and their offspring are perennial in Zones 4 or 5 through Zone 7; Clove Pink (Carnation and its offspring) and the Allwoodii hybrids are perennial in Zones 6 and 7; in Zones 8 to 10 all grow as biennials. In my experience these are short-lived perennials.

By the mid-1700s both types were grown in American gardens in all their variations— banded, eyed, laced, and edged in contrasting colors.

Pinks need a sunny location and sharply drained, gritty soil on the alkaline side. To raise them indoors, sow seed in late winter, just covering them. They germinate quickly in seven to fourteen days at 70°F. Freezing seeds beforehand is sometimes advised, but I've not found it necessary. Space plants outside 12 to 18 inches apart, depending on type. Once established, trim plants carefully in early spring (not ruthlessly, or you'll destroy all possible bloom) to encourage fresh growth. Trim off stems after flowering to keep foliage fresh and to stimulate possible rebloom. Propagate Pinks by cuttings every few years or as needed: pull off, don't cut, side shoots after flowering, taking a bit of the main stem. Trim off lower leaves, dip stem ends in rooting hormone powder (optional), plant them in a potting soil mix amended with extra perlite and vermiculite, then cover loosely with plastic; shoots should root in about six weeks. Remove plastic and, after plants are growing well, transplant them to a cold frame for the winter, to plant out the following spring. Hybrids should always be propagated this way to preserve the strain. Never mulch pinks, since this encourages moisture around the root crown and leads to untimely death. Plants can be protected over the winter with a covering of evergreen boughs.

In warm regions, crickets and sowbugs congregate under wide foliage mats, girdling stems. The leaves eventually turn tan and, by fall, whole sections die off. To discourage this situation, keep plants trim, cultivate around them, and dust with rotenone.

To Use: Pinks are good cut flowers, especially the longer-stemmed hybrids. The larger-flowered types dry well for winter bouquets and wreath decoration (they're pretty with Baby's Breath), but they don't retain their scent. To use for flavoring: infuse two handfuls of washed, trimmed Cottage Pink petals (cut out the bitter white part at their base) in a hot sugar syrup of 1 cup sugar to ½ cup water or white wine. Let the mixture simmer a few minutes. Leave the petals in the syrup until it cools, then strain them out and cool the syrup. Use it to pour over chilled, fresh fruit cup.

COLLECTOR'S CHOICE:

Dianthus caryophyllus 'Clove Pink' (1750). Rose pink flowers over silvery foliage.
D. deltoides (1776–1850). Maiden Pink. Low-growing, sprawling mat covered with a multitude of vivid pink flowers. 3–4".
D. plumarius, Cottage Pink. Single or double, pink and white flowers.
D. superbus (1776–1850). Fringed Pink, Superb Pink, Sweet-John. Deeply fringed lilac flowers; 12–15".

Hybrids:

These are some of the survivors, bred for centuries from *D. caryophyllus* and *D. plumarius,* all well-scented.

'Charles T. Musgrave' (ca. 1730). Large single white flowers with green eyes; lightly fringed petals; 8–10".
'Dad's Favorite' (late 1700s). Famous hybrid with semidouble pearly white flowers laced ruby red with a purple eye.
'Doris' (before 1954). Raised by the Allwood brothers; double rose-pink, 12–15".
'Fair Folly' (mid-1600s). Single white petals laced with maroon edging.
'Helen' (before 1948). Raised by the Allwoods; salmon-pink; 10".

'Her Majesty' (before 1891). Large double white flowers; 10".

'Lady Granville' (ca. 1840). White flower, laced crimson.

'Mrs. Sinkins' (1868). Legendary very double white "cabbage" flower; 10–12".

Old Spice' (1700s). Salmon-pink, fringed double; prolific bloom over long period; 10–12".

'Queen of Sheba' (early 1600s). Fringed petals, feathering of snow white etched with magenta ("painted lady" type).

'Rainbow Loveliness' *(D. × allwoodii × D. superbus;* 1920s). Improved strain of fringed pink that includes carmine, pink, lilac, and white flowers with darker bands; 12–15".

'Rose du Mai' (ca. 1820). Shell-pink, fringed flower; 10".

'White Loveliness' (late 1920s). 10".

Dicentra eximia

FUMARIACEAE

Fringed Bleeding-heart
Fernleaf Bleeding-heart, Plumy Bleeding-heart, Staggerweed, Turkey-corn, Wild Bleeding-heart

INTRODUCED: 1850–1900
ZONES: 2–9
NATIVE

D. formosa

Western Bleeding-heart

NATIVE

D. spectabilis

Bleeding-heart
Lady's-heart, Lady's-locket, Old-fashioned Bleeding-heart, Seal Flower

TYPE: Perennial Flower
HEIGHT: 2–3'
BLOOM: Spring–Summer
SITE: Sun/Partial Shade

Nineteen species of Bleeding-heart are native to North America and Asia, several of which are widely cultivated. Foremost among them is *Dicentra spectabilis* from Japan. This Bleeding-heart, as its Latin epithet suggests, is remarkable. Spreading as wide as it is tall, up to 3 feet, its arching stems bow to the ground in late spring, laden with dangling racemes of perfectly shaped dark pink, white-tipped hearts of fascinating construction. There are two pairs of flower petals: one outer, forming the heart; the other inner, forming the "drop of blood" as the heart spurs open to reveal the inner stamens. The deeply divided blue-green leaves gradually die back with the rest of the plant, whose growing tips poke through the ground the following spring to begin another extravagant cycle of growth. The white types are an elegant variation.

Two other species are native to North America in mountainous areas from New York to Georgia (Fringed Bleeding-heart) and from British Columbia to California (Western Bleeding-heart). These slender plants are valued for their subtle beauty—hearts in racemes dangling over clumps of ferny foliage—and long season of bloom (most of the summer). In the Western Bleeding-heart, the leaves are noticeably grayish, while in both species the hearts are less clearly defined than *D. spectabilis* and rather puffy, in shades of mauve, purplish pink, and white. Both types grow rapidly by rhizomatous roots.

One story surrounding the Asian Bleeding-heart is that it was discovered by Robert Fortune in a mandarin's garden on the Isle of Chusan in China around 1848. It seems, however, that it was first introduced to the West in 1810, then "lost" and reintroduced by Fortune. In any case, it was one of the most successful introductions in the gardening world, for by the turn of the century it was already regarded as "old-fashioned" and is still referred to as Old-fashioned Bleeding-heart by many old-time gardeners.

Under optimum conditions, growing in a moist, partially shaded habitat in enriched soil, undisturbed clumps of Bleeding-heart can attain great size—up to 30 feet wide and 5 feet high (as reported by Stuart and Sutherland). I have never seen a clump even approaching that size, but I did find one that greatly impressed me with its vigor and air of happiness—that look a plant gets when it is growing just as it likes.

This Bleeding-heart was obviously self-sown, perched on the edge of a deep ravine about 30 feet from an old abandoned garden, the outlines of which could be just discerned from a row of Rhubarb and a languishing Bleeding-heart. The magnificent specimen at the ravine's edge spread in an area about 3½ feet wide and almost 3 feet tall, literally dripping with pink-scarlet hearts. The soil was moist and humus-rich from the fallen leaves of nearby trees. There was filtered shade but also morning sun, since the scrubby growth and trees around it had not yet completely leafed out. I learned once

more from nature itself that many heirloom types, closer to wild species than more refined, highly bred modern types, occasionally adjust quite well to neglect if they find their preferred habitat. By the time this Bleeding-heart completed its growth cycle, its spot of ground would be covered by surrounding vegetation, as artful a planting as I would have wished in my own garden, where it is often difficult to achieve such balance.

Both my Fringed and Western Bleeding-hearts came from older gardens, and though I could at first discern little difference between them, the grayish foliage of the latter is special enough to warrant growing both types, especially if the white form of Western Bleeding-heart—with its very distinctive contrast between foliage and flowers—can be found. Although both types are easy to grow, Western Bleeding-heart is especially recommended where summers are cool and moist. Both are invaluable as a long-season flowering ground cover, since many ground covers offer foliage only. Either type can be restrained to grow in shade or semishade, among Primroses, Ferns, and Daylilies, or in the sun wherever long-season bloom and foliage is needed at the front of the border as an edging plant. I grow Fringed and Western Bleeding-heart (pink and white) in partial shade, beneath the arching branches of Golden Currant *(Ribes aureaum)* for a long season of interest.

It's a challenge to find the perfect spot for Old-fashioned Bleeding-heart *(Dicentra spectabilis)*. Although it is often described as "easy to grow," many gardeners are frustrated by their failure with this plant. In truth, scarcely any plant is always, under all circumstances, easy to grow. The term is relative—easy for you, perhaps, but difficult for someone else. As with any planting, care must be taken to provide the minimum growing requirements, which in this case are moisture and partial shade.

Bleeding-heart makes a fine specimen plant, overplanted with annuals or placed in the corner of a border where its dying foliage is soon covered by other perennials. If you are lucky enough to have a ravine on the premises, try naturalizing Bleeding-heart, as described (though any spot that provides similar conditions will do).

In my garden, Bleeding-heart is glorious mulched in a sea of Forget-me-nots in early summer, combined with pale yellow Tulips (just edged with rose) and my middle-aged Bearded Iris, 'Blue Shimmer'. Tall white Nicotiana fills in nicely for the rest of the summer, right into the fall.

To Grow: Plant any of the Bleeding-hearts in moist, well-drained, humus-rich soil, in partial shade (the native species take sun well). Space Old-fashioned Bleeding-heart (*Dicentra spectabilis*) at least 3 feet apart and the other types 15 to 18 inches apart. Bleeding-heart especially thrives where it receives morning sun and afternoon shade. You can sow seeds of any of the Bleeding-hearts in a cold frame in the fall to flower the following season, but propagation is more easily accomplished by simple division of the clumps every three or four years after blooming or when the plants are dormant. *D. spectabilis* can be left undisturbed if it seems happy. I have successfully transplanted it (a chunk from an established clump) in bloom with a good ball of earth around the roots. In Zones 8 to 10, *D. spectabilis* is short-lived and needs to be grown as an annual.

COLLECTOR'S CHOICE:

Dicentra eximia, Fringed Bleeding-heart.
  'Alba'; white. Not as vigorous as the pink sort; provide protection from sun in early growth and mulch well.
D. formosa, Western Bleeding-heart.
  'Alba'; white.
D. spectabilis, Old-fashioned Bleeding-heart.

Digitalis purpurea

SCROPHULARIACEAE

Purple Foxglove
Bloody-fingers, Common Foxglove, Dead-men's-bells, Fairy's-cape, Fairy's-glove, Fairy's-hat, Fairy's-thimbles, Folk's-glove, Foxglove, Gloves-of-Our-Lady, Virgin's-glove, Witches'-gloves

INTRODUCED: 1700–1750
ZONES: 4–10
NATURALIZED
TYPE: Biennial Herb/Flower
HEIGHT: 4–5'
BLOOM: Early Summer
SITE: Sun/Partial Shade

*P*urple Foxglove is one of about nineteen species of *Digitalis* native to Europe and northwest Africa to central Asia. During the first season of growth, it forms a rosette of light green, tapered, somewhat downy leaves that send up, during their second year, tall stalks to 5 feet bearing large, hanging bell-shaped flowers. The flowers are 1½ to 2½ inches long and come in shades of purple and white, usually speckled with maroon at the throat. The spots attract bees and hummingbirds, thus ensuring the fertilization of the flowers and prolific seed production, which explains in part Foxglove's ability to naturalize as a garden escape in North America. A vast literature surrounds the many folk names (only partially listed here), which refers to the glove-shaped flowers (worn by the fox to soften his tread when approaching the chicken pen!). It has also been suggested that the name is derived from the Anglo-Saxon *foxes-gleow,* a musical instrument of arching form hung with bells, like Purple Foxglove in full bloom. The genus name is more straightforward, having been derived from the German word *fingerhut*—literally "finger-hat" or "thimble," a reference to the flower's shape—translated into Latin as *Digitalis,* from *digitus,* which means "finger."

Purple Foxglove is an English wildflower, cultivated in cottage gardens since at least the 15th century. It was not grown in American gardens until the 18th century. Since ancient times, Foxglove has been considered beneficial for healing bruises, but it wasn't until the late 1700s that an English doctor, William Withering, described the powerful alkaloid in its leaves—*digitalin*—and proved its medicinal value as a heart stimulant.

Dr. Withering sent Purple Foxglove seeds to a doctor in New Hampshire, who, in 1789, sent seeds to another doctor in Boston, with the advice "to try of its efficacy" and to grow it "as a beautiful flower in the garden," which is how Americans have been growing it, possibly since the early 1740s. Digitalin in pill form is still manufactured and used as a heart stimulant.

The elegant white form 'Alba' was offered in Joseph Breck's 1838 and 1884 seed catalogs, a testimony to its enduring popularity (especially striking among Old Garden Roses and for bouquets). In the late 1800s, the Reverend Henry Wilkes (of Shirley Poppy fame) produced his large-flowered strain, 'Giant Shirley' (named after his village), the result of selection and reselection and breeding among variants of the common wildflower. How I would love to have had a glimpse of his garden with variant Corn Poppies and Purple Foxglove on their way to becoming the flowers in the classic design—closely packed on sturdy stems up to 5 feet high, facing down at a 60-degree angle to the stem—in an extended color range—white, dark rose, purple, maroon, and crimson, all heavily spotted. A luscious 'Apricot' cultivar, produced in England probably in the early 1900s, adds another color to the repertoire of variations on the classic Foxglove theme, one that was altered in the 'Excelsior' hybrids introduced by 1950. In these, the florets, facing outward rather than downward, are borne all around the stem. As for the wide-open Gloxinia forms *(Digitalis purpurea* 'Gloxiniiflora'), they are so different in appearance from the fabled glove-shaped flowers that it is difficult to consider them as belonging to the same group of plants. They may be beautiful in their own right, but to me they don't say "Foxglove."

Foxglove is another of those "easy-to-grow" plants that many gardeners, including myself, have had difficulty establishing. How frustrating to raise healthy seedlings with all the promise of future bloom, only to have them die over the winter. Until I learned the secret of success, I killed many generations of seedlings, generously supplied by my neighbor, who did nothing at all to encourage their springing up around the basement of her house every year.

One spring I found a large population of Purple Foxglove naturalized at the edge of a road on forested Skye Mountain, unpopulated since the early 1940s. At first they weren't apparent among great sheets of white Bunchberry flowers, brushy Raspberries, Goldenrod, and Ferns, but getting down on my hands and knees, I suddenly saw their healthy, downy leaves everywhere—first- and second-year plants. Here, where they were virtually smothered in weeds in unfertilized ground, they thrived, while in my garden, where I had coddled them, I had known nothing but failure.

Later in the summer I returned to see the Foxglove in full bloom: tall stalks with masses of bells—all variants of purple, pink, and white and heavily spotted—towering over brushy plants and weeds, totally at home in gravelly soil in partial shade or full sun on a slight incline. I gathered ripened seeds, sowed them in my cold frame, and the following year planted the healthy clumps in a slightly raised bed in the sun, the soil lightened with gritty sand. Skye Mountain Foxgloves now self-sow in my garden from year to year, though not as prolifically as those I saw growing *au naturel* (in which case there would be no room for anything else in my garden). There are enough, though, to make a good show in early summer among Bellflowers, Oriental Poppies, Mountain-bluet, and Lupines. The tall stalks, especially the white form, are distinctive among low-growing shrubs, especially when followed by Regal Lilies. Where Foxglove can be grown in light or full shade (where summers are very hot and drainage is perfect), they are lovely companions for Hostas and Ferns, as well as Bleeding-hearts (any type). I have recently succeeded in establishing Foxglove on a steep, partially shady slope where it seems very happy to grow on its own.

Foxglove is a striking and long-lasting cut flower. Even out of flower, the downy leaves are attractive for much of the season.

To Grow: Purple Foxglove and its variants can be grown in Zones 4 to 10, except in Florida and along the Gulf Coast. Where early summer is hot, plant Foxglove in partial or full shade and always in well-drained ordinary garden soil on the light side. The primary cause of winterkill is from moisture gathered around the leafy crowns in late winter or early spring. If you are in doubt about drainage, work in some gritty sand and mound the area where you plant the clumps, about 15 to 18 inches apart. Cut down stalks after they have flowered, unless you want to collect seeds from choice colors. Once established, Foxglove should self-seed. The 'Giant Shirley' strain will need to be reseeded (with purchased seeds) if the range of colors is reduced over the years, a process that can be controlled if you take pains to thin out the more vigorous wild strains (pinks and purples). You can take stem cuttings from the 'Apricot' strain to keep it pure (plant these anytime during the summer in a cold frame).

To grow Foxglove from seeds, sow the seeds in a cold frame in mid to late spring. Very early the following season, plant out the clumps, which should blossom in the summer.

COLLECTOR'S CHOICE:

Digitalis purpurea, Purple Foxglove
    (1700–1750).
'Alba' (1838).
'Apricot' (after 1900).
'Giant Shirley' (late 1800s).

Galanthus elwesii ❀

AMARYLLIDACEAE

Giant Snowdrop
Fair-maid-of-February

INTRODUCED: 1875
ZONES: 6–9
HEIGHT: 8–9"
BLOOM: Late Winter

G. nivalis ❀

Snowdrop
Candlemas Bells, Fair-maid-of-
February, Foolish Maids, Snowbells

INTRODUCED: 1600–1800
ZONES: 4–7
HEIGHT: 4–6"
BLOOM: Fall/Late Winter/Early Spring

TYPE: Hardy Bulb
SITE: Sun/Partial Shade/Shade

Diminutive, white-flowered Snowdrops are native from Western Europe to the Caspian Sea. Deceptively fragile in appearance, they're very tough plants, constructed to push their way through frozen ground in late winter. The leaves, fortified by an outer sheath, are sharply pointed at their tips, giving them the strength they need to shove through hard ground. The nodding flowers of both Snowdrops have six white petals, a set of three long outer ones and three smaller (by half) inner ones touched with green, but in those of the Giant Snowdrop, the petals are larger and the outer segments are rounded. A sweet honey scent is more pronounced in the Giant Snowdrop. The common Snowdrop was called Candlemas Bells in the Middle Ages because its bloom coincided with the February 2 celebration of the Christian Feast of the Purification, marking the end of winter in Europe and the beginning of spring. In the New World, its bloom in early February sometimes coincides with Groundhog Day.

Beloved for its cheerful bloom, even through snow, the common Snowdrop may have been in American gardens quite early, but its history is clouded and confused. In his classic 1914 book, *My Garden in Spring,* the English writer and gardener extraordinaire, E.A. Bowles, takes umbrage at earlier writers like Gerard (1597) and Parkinson (1629), who fail to mention it at all. He points out that it was there, in fact, masquerading as a variant of snowflake *(Leucojum).* A similar problem exists on this side of the Atlantic: Which plant is meant in old garden lists and correspondence, Snowdrop or Snowflake?

The wonderful garden historian Ann Leighton offers the evidence from 18th-century America, then leaves us with the comment, "Your guess . . ." *(American Gardening in the Eighteenth Century).* There's no doubt that by the 19th century the Snowdrop was regarded by all garden authorities as a common, hardy spring flower, one that "defied improvement" (though double-flowered forms and cultivars were also highly esteemed). The Giant Snowdrop, prominently featured in Vaughn's 1897 catalog for its larger-sized nodding bells, was confined to warmer regions. In the South, the common Snowdrop was never much cultivated, not because it can't be grown there, but because, as Elizabeth Lawrence explained, folks say

"Snowdrop" when they mean "Snowflake" (*Leucojum*)—a common southern flower similar in appearance—so they think they're already growing it. An avid collector, Elizabeth Lawrence grew all types of true Snowdrops (*Galanthus* spp.) in her North Carolina garden.

We never fail to be astonished and thrilled by the appearance of drifts of Snowdrop through late winter snow. It seems like a miracle, yet it is one that returns year after year, a triumph of nature over nature. Since we have no spring here, I have learned to wait patiently for early summer, when plant growth actually begins. So I resisted planting the tiny bulbs for years. But one fall, out of curiosity, I bought a few handfuls of the single and double Snowdrop bulbs. I planted the doubles in a small dooryard garden, and the singles beneath the spreading branches of the classic white Rugosa Rose, 'Blanc Double de Coubert' and I forgot all about them. Then one blustery day in March, trudging to the barn, I happened to glance down the slope. I stopped . . . could it be . . . something white on the ground that wasn't snow, but the fabled dainty bells of the common Snowdrop blooming under a cold but warming sun, on frozen ground? I felt the very same astonishment and indescribable pleasure that every gardener since who knows when has felt about this little plant and its extraordinary feat of winter bloom. I have read about Snowdrop plant companions—Crocus, *Iris reticulata*, *Helleborus*—none of which I can grow, but I am quite content to let it have the bare landscape to itself.

To Grow: Snowdrops do well in heavy but well-drained soil, and almost any exposure, ranging from sun and filtered shade to full shade. Always plant the small bulbs in groups for maximum impact—ten bulbs per square foot—spaced 3 inches apart, covered with 2 inches of soil. Divide them immediately after they have flowered, before bulbs have dried out. They also spread slowly by self-seeding. Giant Snowdrop is more heat tolerant, less hardy than the common Snowdrop, but it is grown the same way.

COLLECTOR'S CHOICE:

The rarities are available from Scott Kunst's Old House Gardens.

Galanthus elwesii, Giant Snowdrop (1875).

G. nivalis, Snowdrop (1600–1800).

'Flore-Pleno' (1731). Broad, petal-stuffed cups.

'Magnet' (1880s). Rare; wide-spreading flowers dangle from extra-long stems. Zones 5–7.

'Straffan' (1858). Rare; beautifully proportioned flower, rated by Scott Kunst as "one of the three best . . . established bulbs produce a second, later flowering. . . ."

Galium odoratum (Asperula odorata) ❧

RUBIACEAE

Sweet Woodruff

INTRODUCED: 1850–1900
ZONES: 3–8
TYPE: Perennial/Herb
HEIGHT: 6–8"
BLOOM: Late Spring
SITE: Partial Shade/Shade

Sweet Woodruff is a woodland plant native to Europe and many temperate regions of the world. Lying close to the ground, it spreads by creeping roots, its horizontal stems carrying whorls of dark green, lance-shaped leaves, and above them masses of white starry flowers. When dried, the leaves exude a sweet vanilla aroma from the presence of coumarin, the same substance that gives a sweet smell to freshly dried hay and Meadowsweet *(Filipendula)*. "Wood" accurately describes the plant's favored habitat, while "ruff," derived from the French for "wheel," is a graphic image of the way Sweet Woodruff's leaves grow in a circle around its stems.

The fresh Sweet Woodruff plant, just lightly scented, gives little indication of the power of its perfume in the dried plant.

A plant's usefulness is soon revealed to those who depend on the natural world to fill their daily needs. Who knows who first discovered the magic in Sweet Woodruff's glossy, pointed foliage? The fresh plant, just lightly scented, gives little indication of the power of its perfume in the dried plant. Since the Middle Ages, and probably before, it was highly prized as a strewing herb: when scattered on floors and crushed underfoot, it released a pleasing aroma that filled the household, obscuring less pleasant smells. When Sweet Woodruff's dried leaves were placed in sachets with other dried herbage to discourage must and insects, it not only contributed its characteristically sweet scent, it increased the natural aroma of the other leaves and flowers, like the plant fixative orris root. As a medicinal, it was used inwardly and outwardly (sign of a very useful herb), as a tea for headaches and for digestion, and in a poultice on fresh wounds. Its most famous use was the German custom of infusing the herb in Rhine wine to make "May Wine" in celebration of spring.

There is no indication that the Puritans brought Sweet Woodruff with them. There were other plants for scenting, and the rigors of life, as well as the Puritan outlook, did not encourage the "May Wine" tradition. By 1750, however, the colonists were growing Lady's Bedstraw *(Galium verum),* a weedy cousin with a reputation as a strewing herb. More important, it was a dye plant (red from its root, yellow from the tops) and could also be used like rennet to thicken milk and cheese.

Sweet Woodruff came into its own in the Victorian era as a superior ground cover in "the shrubbery," where newly introduced specimens from Asia were planted in groups along driveways, to set property boundaries, or to create a naturalistic note in a suburban setting. Wherever light woodland and shade conditions prevail, no better plant can be found to cover the ground effectively and beautifully than "our little native woodruff," as the English writer Margery Fish referred to it rather defensively. Some might be shocked, she said, to see it cultivated in the garden, but she thought it "as pretty as many garden plants" *(Gardening in the Shade).* I could understand her feelings when, several years ago, I saw it nearly covering refuse heaps in

TO MAKE MAY WINE

Nearly fill a wide-mouth quart jar with fresh Sweet Woodruff leaves. Add white wine to cover. Put a lid on the jar and let the leaves steep for about 2 weeks on a sunny windowsill. Strain, chill, and serve iced in a wide bowl, decorated with fresh-cut strawberries.

South London. But then, it's in the way we grow them that we show such plants off to advantage. On this same trip I observed Lungwort in a little front garden and, when I remarked on it, the owner confessed he hadn't had time to weed it out.

Nothing has ever been done to alter Sweet Woodruff, yet how beautifully it lights up shady areas, smothering weeds in its wake, carpeting the ground beneath Azaleas in a light woodland setting. I grow it beneath the spreading limbs of an old Lilac of treelike form, where it blooms with the spring whites: Sweet Cicely, Solomon's Seal, white Dame's-rocket, and white-flowered Bugle *(Ajuga)*. Elsewhere, I confine its spread in a fluted steel circle—2½ feet wide, rescued from a tire dump—where it makes a pretty show with dusty pink Wild Bleeding-heart *(Dicentra eximia)* under the shade of an apple tree.

To Grow: Sweet Woodruff is usually grown from roots. Set them 1 foot apart—close to the soil surface—in moist, enriched soil. It will grow in sun if the soil is moist, but the foliage will not be so green or glossy. In early spring, clip out dead stems to encourage fresh growth. Propagate in the spring by digging up small clumps.

To Use: Cut foliage to dry, then add freely to potpourri mixtures.

COLLECTOR'S CHOICE:

Galium odoratum, Sweet Woodruff (1850–1900). May be offered under its old name, *Asperula odorata.*

G. verum, Lady's Bedstraw (1700–1776). Hardy perennial with tiny, frothy, lightly scented yellow flowers in early to midsummer, to 3'. Best grown as an informal ground cover or staked in a theme garden of dye plants.

Gladiolus spp.

IRIDACEAE

Corn-flag
Sword-lily

INTRODUCED: 1600–1900

Gladiolus hybrids

Glad

INTRODUCED: 1900–1958

TYPE: Tender Bulb
HEIGHT: 1–5'
BLOOM: Summer
SITE: Sun

*M*ore than two hundred species of Corn-flag are distributed over South Africa, Europe, and the Mediterranean area. These grow from round, flat, bulbous roots, or corms, that shrivel and die over the course of one growing season, producing offspring to carry on the growth of the plant. The flowering spikes, rising to about 3 feet, bear small, bright, funnel-shaped flowers—often deep red or yellow—opening in succession from two-valved spathes, or bracts. Modern hybrids—large ruffled flowers in many colors produced in great numbers on a single stem—are almost unrecognizable as the simple, graceful wildflower. The Corn-flag's long, narrow, swordlike leaves are preserved in the genus name, derived from the Latin *gladius,* meaning "sword."

We tend to think that Glads are a recent phenomenon, and in a sense they are, having been developed since the early decades of this century. But the wild Corn-flag, from which the modern flowers have been developed, was grown in the earliest American gardens, from the 17th through the 19th centuries. Lady Skipwith of Virginia, a curious and dedicated 18th-century gardener, listed Corn-flag as among these "Flowers for Mrs. Boyd": the Yellow and Tawny Daylily, English Cowslip, and Lily-of-the-valley. She grew *Gladiolus communis* ssp. *byzantinus,* introduced from Europe in the 18th century, with its loose spikes of bright purple flowers curving outward from narrow stems about 2 to 3 feet high.

Several important species and types had been introduced by 1900, and these became important in the breeding of the modern Glad. The first ruffled sort appeared in 1911, by which time the race was on. Thousands of cultivars were produced, bred for bigger flowers, more flowers per stem, and an ever-wider range of colors. Glads, like Iris, are accommodating subjects for plant breeding because they readily hybridize. These Glads were prized for their adaptability throughout North America, blooming in Florida during the winter months and in the Northeast, from wintered-over corms, during the summer. Their ease of culture, bright flowers (especially valued for cutting), and instant popularity encouraged the breeding of new cultivars, each one slightly different to the experienced eye, with the result that "new" became (and becomes) "old" and obsolete in a very short time.

Commenting on this development, Mrs. King remarked, "In looking over the Cornell list of 1916 it is surprising to see how few of the named varieties have survived in the average lists of the day." She goes on to men-

tion their names (long vanished from the marketplace): "'Panama', a lovely tone of warm pink . . . 'Baron Hulot', always conspicuous for its rich violet, 'Alice Tiplady', 'Mary Virginia', 'Maiden Blush', 'Orange Queen', 'Salmon Beauty' . . . the earliness, the grace, and delicate yet glowing colours of this tribe commend it everywhere, and in the South as well as the North they are treasures for gardens."

Like Iris, heirloom Glads are defined as those introduced by or prior to 1960, and considering the speed with which cultivars appear and disappear from the market, this is a reasonable definition. Among the thousands that over the years have been bred and offered for sale, there are good, bad, and indifferent plants, as well as superior ones. Unfortunately, we can no longer evaluate most of them, since most are no longer available, unlike antique Iris, many of which are still carried—true to type—by specialty nurseries. So how do we know which are the choice Glad heirlooms?

As Grant Wilson of the Canadian Gladiolus Society told me, the Society is always evaluating and reevaluating Glads through a comprehensive rating system. A drop in their ratings, he observed, results not so much from the introduction of better varieties, but from the fact that the older varieties have deteriorated. That is, they are no longer the plants they were when they were first introduced, having changed in form or color over many years of propagation.

He also pointed out that many Glad fanciers still consider two cultivars—'Picardy' and 'Violet Charm', long out of the annual rating—to be the greatest of all time. Both were produced in Canada, where breeding has a long tradition (which is why the Society is one of the world's oldest Gladiolus organizations). 'Picardy' was introduced by Milton Jack, son of Canadian garden writer Annie Jack, in 1953. Another of Jack's introductions, the 1945–1946 AAS winner 'Dawn Glow', is now very rare.

"If 'Picardy' and 'Violet Charm' could be grown today as they were for several years after their introduction," Wilson noted, "they would very probably be in the present Top 10 or even right at the top overall . . . Someone, somewhere may still have 'Picardy', 'Violet Charm', or others which they have grown for forty-five years or so and from which they have planted and multiplied only the best." This is, of course, what heirloom gardening is all about, and one only hopes that these antiques can be preserved for future gardeners to enjoy. If you already grow Glads, you may have an older type you cherish for its dependability and special beauty. If not, ask around the gardeners' network and you may find a gem—maybe even the fabled 'Picardy', described in a 1945 catalog as having very large shrimp pink flowers and offered for a dollar a dozen (as corms). Otherwise, check out my list of survivors to compare with the latest introductions.

It has been observed that great breeders such as Childs, Coblentz, Vilmorin, Van Fleet, and Groff took a despised semitropical plant with insignificant flowers and developed it into a magnificent creation with waxy blossoms as wide as a man's hand. I admire the hybrids, but I am one of those who also looks with favor on the old Corn-flag that charmed Lady Skipwith, for it possesses a simple grace that is lacking in the stiff, highly elaborated hybrids. The wild types are lovely if left in the ground to multiply and naturalize (where conditions permit). Similar in habit to wild Iris, they form a bright mass of color and swordlike foliage for most of the season.

A "perennial" question among gardeners is where to plant the modern Glad. The tried-and-true strategy of two end rows in the vegetable garden, perhaps alongside Dahlias, is a straightforward, honest solution and should not be dismissed, for the flowers add color to the garden, make a dramatic border, and are close at hand for cutting (one of the Glad's chief claims to fame).

As Mrs. King maintained, however, "This flower, old yet ever new, is susceptible of the most exquisite treatment in the right hands." So I include her advice for finding the Glad's proper companions in the flower border: "When the gladioli are all in bloom, cut a few spikes, label them, and after rain, when the ground is soft, take these hither and yon throughout the garden, holding now one and another against a flower which may seem to provide for it a lovely foil." Make a note of this match for next season.

Gertrude Jekyll, with whom Mrs. King carried on a lively correspondence, did not hesitate to include bright Hybrid Glads in her famous color-coordinated borders. In the late summer border, for instance, she included dark red Hollyhocks and Dahlias, Phlox, scarlet and orange Nasturtiums, and scarlet Glads, backed by Golden-glow—a planting that is worth repeating. She also planted wild Glads *(G. × colvillei),* set in tubs next to the house. Other suggestions include planting eight to ten of the same color in front of hedges, among low-growing shrubs, or in the perennial border to fill in after early-flowering bulbs. Robert G. Martin, membership secretary of the North American Gladiolus Council, advises growing Glads in the vegetable garden, ". . . so they may be brought into the home for enjoyable bouquets."

To Grow: Glads thrive in enriched, sandy loam that is on the light side. Work compost, leaf mold, or peat moss into the soil in the fall. For a succession of bloom throughout the summer, plant the corms at intervals from the last frost in spring into early summer (during the month of June). Plant them in full sun, 4 to 6 inches apart, and cover them with 4 to 6 inches of soil. When plants are 1 foot high, start hilling up soil around their bases to about 6 inches, to support the stems; otherwise, the large-flowered types will probably need staking. Mulch around plants with a 1-inch layer of grass clippings to conserve moisture throughout the season. To encourage prolific flower production, scratch in some 5–10–5 fertilizer (at a rate of 1 cup per 25-foot row) around the plants when spikes appear, watering the fertilizer into the soil. After foliage yellows or after frost, lift out corms, cutting off the fresh corms close to the old ones, and dry them in the sun for an hour or so before storing them at 40 to 50°F (4 to 10°C) in an old nylon stocking or onion bag to provide good air circulation. Save cormels (little corms) and plant them out the following season if you like. They take two seasons to produce flowers. In Zones 8 to 10, you can leave corms in the ground, but for better flower production of hybrid types, follow the preceding directions.

For cut flowers, cut the flowering stems in the early morning when just one or two flowers have begun to open. Be sure to leave at least four or five leaves per stem to feed the corms. Wild Corn-flag is highly desirable for cutting as well.

COLLECTOR'S CHOICE:

For the non-Glad lover, I recommend the smaller-flowered, more graceful species and Miniature Glads, all great cut flowers for small, informal bouquets, and easier to place in the border.

Gladiolus callianthus / Acidanthera bicolor (by 1930s?). Small-flowered and graceful, this Glad also possesses a wonderful clove fragrance. Its flowers are white with a maroon or chocolate throat, on arching stems 2–3' tall, very desirable for the evening garden. I plant bulbs in tubs by entranceways. Zones 7–10.

G. carneus, 'Painted Lady' (by early 1900?). Creamy white to pinkish with reddish blotch; 12–18"; Zones 6–10.

G. x *colvillei* 'Albus', Colville Glad (by early 1900?). White; to 2'. "Baby Glads" were bred from this group; Zone 7.

G. communis ssp. *byzantinus,* Hardy Glad, Byzantine Glad (1700). Common in the South, where it's also called "Jacob's Ladder," it is coveted in the Northeast where it is marginally hardy to Zone 5 with protection. The white cultivar 'Albus' is especially choice for cutting.

G. dalenii / G. natalensis (early 1900s). Large orange-red and yellow flowers, to 5'. Zone 7.

G. tristis (early 1900s?). Creamy white-yellow flowers, sometimes striped purple, to 2'; lovely fragrance for the evening garden; Zone 7.

Hybrids:

'Atom' (1946). Lovely with small scarlet flowers edged with silver on short stems, to 2½'. One of the most popular of the small-flowered or Miniature Glads since it was introduced, and a favorite of Robert G. Martin, who grows it in his Maine garden. He says that it is extremely healthy and a good parent to use in hybridizing Miniature Glads. "I find it is very popular at the roadside market for those who use it in small home arrangements of flowers. . . . There are many larger Heirloom Glads but I feel that old miniatures have a special place as part of an arrangement to be used in a kitchen."

'Friendship' (1949). Beautifully ruffled fresh pink florets, white throat, 3–4'; valued as a cut flower.

'Green Woodpecker' (1953? 1958?). Flowers slightly larger than 'Atom', lime green with bright wine-red markings; early bloom; fourth in the top-rated Glad antiques at the 1900 symposium of the Canadian Gladiolus Society; 3–3½'.

'Oscar' (1958). Giant dark reddish pink flowers; 4'.

'Peter Pears' (1958). Large, ruffled apricot-red or dark orange flowers; early bloom; 3–4'.

'Spic and Span' (1946). Large salmon-rose flowers; 4'.

'Thomas E. Wilson' (1942). Miniature Glad with salmon upward-facing florets. A Robert Martin favorite.

'Wedding Cake (1950). Miniature Glad with pure white upward-facing florets. Another Robert Martin favorite.

'White Friendship' (1959). Now in the antique class, this is a vigorous sport of 'Friendship' with lightly ruffled, pure white flowers, 3–4'; valued as a cut flower.

Hemerocallis fulva

LILIACEAE

Orange Daylily
Corn Daylily, Daylily, Fulvous Daylily, Tawny Daylily

INTRODUCED: 1600–1699
ZONES: 2–10

H. lilioasphodelus (H. flava) ✿

Lemon Yellow Daylily
Custard Lily, Lemon Daylily, Lemon Lily, Lily Asphodel, Yellow Daylily, Yellow Tuberose

TYPE: Hardy Bulb
HEIGHT: to 3'
BLOOM: Summer
SITE: Sun/Partial Shade

*A*bout fifteen species of Daylilies from Europe and Asia, especially Japan, belong to the large Lily Family, from which come some of our most beautiful garden flowers—Lilies, Tulips, and Hyacinths. Daylilies form clumps of narrow evergreen foliage and spread by tuberous rhizomatous roots, which send up tall, bare stalks—as high as 6 feet in the wild—bearing lilylike trumpets in branched clusters. Although each flower blooms for only one day, continuous color is ensured by the production of many buds. The Orange or Tawny Daylily is a vigorous species with large flowers about 5 inches across—orange with darker zones and stripes in shades of red and mahogany—giving the effect of a tawny color, preserved in the Latin epithet *fulva*. The less vigorous Lemon Yellow Daylily is shorter, growing to 3 feet or less, with smaller flowers and grasslike foliage. It is highly regarded for its more delicate form and lemon yellow, sweetly scented trumpets, about 4 inches across. Its former Latin name, *Hemerocallis flava,* refers to its yellow flowers, while its current name, *H. lilioasphodelus* (actually an older name), describes its asphodel-like roots and lilylike blooms. The wonderfully descriptive genus name, *Hemerocallis,* is derived from the two Greek words *hemeros,* "day," and *kalos,* "beautiful."

In Asia, where Daylilies have been cultivated for thousands of years, they are regarded as a source of food and medicine. The flowers are picked fresh and fried in batter or dried and used to thicken soups. Preparations from the plant are used to relieve jaundice and dropsy and to reduce fever and pain. In Europe and the New World, the Daylily has always been cultivated for its beauty alone. The Lemon Yellow was a special favorite in English cottage gardens. Both the Orange and Yellow Daylily were brought to the New World during the 17th century and widely cultivated across the land. The more vigorous Orange Daylily remains a faithful signpost to many heirloom plant collectors, who know that where it grows, an old garden cannot be far away.

Until the late 19th century, only these two species were grown in America. By 1860 a double form of the Orange—crowded with petals—was introduced from Japan, where it had been noticed by European travelers since about 1712. In 1865 a variegated leaf form (with white-striped foliage) was introduced. Both of these were known as 'Kwanso' types, presumably after their place of origin. In 1897 a new Orange, 'Maculata', was added to the pool of Daylilies, offering later bloom and larger flowers with a deep bronze patch on each petal.

These species liked their new home, where they found growing conditions especially suitable for their cultivation. It was a reciprocal affair: Americans loved Daylilies for their ease of culture, midsummer bloom (at a time when other flowers languish from the heat), and beauty of form.

By the 1920s, America had become the leading center for hybridization, the goal being the creation of ever-new types with larger flowers of diverse forms—wavy, frilled petals, for instance—an expanded color range, and a longer blooming period. The old Orange, naturalized along roadsides across the country, was one of the leading contributors to the breeding process. Although a seed-sterile triploid, its pollen was used to crossbreed with other species. In 1929 the noted hybridizer A.B. Stout attached the cultivar name 'Europa' to it, by which it is sometimes sold today.

By 1970, twelve thousand cultivars had been registered with the American Hemerocallis Society; since then at least eight hundred new types have been added each year, inevitably resulting in the disappearance of old forms. Any that have survived the incredibly tough competition of the marketplace (as is the case with Glads, Iris, and other greatly hybridized types) are especially noteworthy. Among these is 'Hyperion', developed by Franklin B. Mead around 1925. Many consider this Daylily unsurpassable within its type: a majestic 4 feet high with large, very fragrant, wide-open, clean-cut canary yellow blooms with a green-flushed throat and prominent golden stamens. Older plantings of this are often mistaken for the daintier Lemon Yellow, pure strains of which are now increasingly rare.

Having been dug up extensively from naturalized stands that take longer to establish than the Orange, the Lemon Yellow is not seen as often as the Orange, either as an escape or in old gardens. I became aware of its precarious conditions several years ago when Bernard S. Jackson, then curator of the Memorial University Botanical Garden in St. John's, Newfoundland, and the driving force behind the preservation of old ornamentals in Canada, sent me a box of roots of sixteen perennials from his Heritage Garden (where every plant was grown from actual plants found in local gardens planted before 1940). Among these were two carefully labeled bags of *Hemerocallis fulva* and *H. flava,* "120 years plus." Having been delayed in the mail over a week, I did not think either would bloom that season, already well advanced by early June. Nevertheless, I planted the Daylilies in a specially prepared bed and was astonished when the Orange shot up and bloomed on time in early July. I was very curious to see what the blossoms of an Orange Daylily, grown from 120-year-old stock, would look like, so I anxiously peered into a newly opened flower: deep orange flared-back petals with mahogany stripes, exactly like the ones blooming in my sixty-plus-year-old patch. Gorgeous! What I learned is that the Orange or Tawny Daylily, often taken for granted as a weed, is a most beautiful flower.

Lemon Yellow took longer to establish, but eventually produced a mound of foliage and a multitude of its fabled perfumed trumpets (sweet and light). In mid-June they bloom with my modest collection of antique Iris (including the very old 'Honorabile'), lavender-blue Catmint *(Nepeta)* and 'Johnson's Blue' Geranium, its blue flowers climbing through a favorite Explorer Rose, 'Henry Hudson' in first flush of pink-tinged white buds. This is a wonderful season for fresh flowers and new scents, none more welcome than the Lemon Yellow Daylily. No wonder daylily fanciers consider it unmatched for its purity of color, fragrance, and will to survive, but it is often difficult to sort out the different plants that masquerade under its name.

The Orange Daylily is very useful to hold soil on steep slopes or to naturalize in sun or partial shade wherever an all-season ground cover is needed. I have found glorious fields of them by garden remnants, thriving without any care at all. I plant it as a no-care border for one of our rustic log cabins. Planted in semishade, it never fails to put forth plentiful blooms for over a month during the summer. The decaying foliage provides a permanent mulch and source of nourishment. It should be noted that the older, unimproved species are virtually maintenance-free and very hardy. Any of the Daylilies make handsome border plants. The old Lemon Yellow is lovely planted beside blue Bearded Iris, both of which bloom at the same time. I have seen effective plantings of Lemon Yellow with Ribbon Grass as a garden room divider. Grown as accent plants, the Daylily's leaves are attractive all season long, unlike many other flowers that, when their blooms are spent, "seem to lose ambition and more or less go to pieces," as one astute garden writer has observed.

To Grow: Daylilies grow in almost any soil but thrive in well-drained, fertile soil enriched with leaf mold or compost, in sun or partial shade. Set the tubers with their crowns 1 inch below the soil surface, 18 to 24 inches apart. The old Orange and Lemon Yellow can remain undisturbed for years; newer types should be divided and replanted every three to six years, or when they appear to lose their vigor. Propagation is easily accomplished by division of the tubers.

COLLECTOR'S CHOICE:
Hardy to Zone 2; all sold as bulbs or tubers.

Hemerocallis citrina, Citron Lily (early 1900s). Light yellow fragrant flowers on vigorous plants, to 4'. Narrow flowers open in late afternoon and remain open all night. This hard-to-find species is a star in the evening garden (I first learned about it from Peter Loewer's book *The Evening Garden).* Used for breeding hardy, fragrant types, it is not much grown for its own sake because of its night-blooming habit and because its foliage dies back in the fall. But its long arching leaves, to 40 inches, rippled at their edges, are beautiful in all stages, from green to golden, and yellow-brown by autumn. The cultivar 'Lemon Queen' (from the late 1920s or early 1930s) is occasionally offered. ❀

H. fulva, Orange Daylily. Midseason bloom.

H. lilioasphodelus (H. flava), Lemon Yellow Daylily. Early bloom. ❀

H. middendorffii, Amur Daylily (1850–1900). Pale orange flower clusters; early bloom; 1–3'.

H. minor, Grass-leaf Daylily (1840). Valuable rock-garden plant with copper-yellow fragrant flowers; dwarf form; early bloom. ❀

Hybrids:
Hardy to Zone 3; all sold as bulbs or tubers.

'Caballero' (pre-1953). Bicolored rose-yellow; early to midseason bloom; may bloom again in the fall; 3'.

'Goldenii' (1929). Deep golden orange; 3'.

'Hyperion'. Very fragrant; midseason bloom. ❀

'Kindly Light' (1950). Loose, twisted flowers with ruffled edges to 8" long on plants 28" tall. An extended bloomer for the evening garden.

'Kwanso', 'Kwanso Flore Pleno'. Double orange flowers with bluish green foliage; midseason bloom; 40".

'Kwanso Variegated'. A less vigorous form.

'Maculata'. Similar to *H. fulva,* with larger flowers with mahogany blotch at base of each petal; early bloom, recurrent in fall; 3'.

'Melody Lane' (1955). Five-inch-long cream-pink flowers with chartreuse throat, to 4'. An extended bloomer for the evening garden.

'Melon Balls' (1960). Melon with orchid tones and gold throat to 3½" long on plants to 32" tall.

'Neyron Rose' (1950). Deep rose-pink with white midribs to 5" long on stems to 3'.

'Pink Charm' (pre-1953). Coral pink with orange throat and pink stamens; midseason bloom; 4'.

'Tangerine' (1877–1920s). The first recorded *Hemerocallis* cross, by British schoolteacher George Yeld; semidwarf; dark orange flowers with red buds; early bloom.

'Valiant' (1920s). Orange, spider-shaped flowers; midseason bloom.

Hesperis matronalis ❧

BRASSICACEAE

Dame's-rocket
Damask-violet, Dame's-violet,
Evening-rocket, Garden-rocket,
Mother-of-the-evening, Rogue's-
gilliflowers, Queen's-gilliflowers,
Sweet-rocket

INTRODUCED: 1600–1699
ZONES: 4–9
NATURALIZED
TYPE: Short-Lived Perennial/Biennial
    Flower
HEIGHT: 2–3'
BLOOM: Spring–Summer
SITE: Sun/Partial Shade

Dame's-rocket is a sweetly fragrant member of the Mustard Family, long valued as a garden flower. Native from southern and central Europe to Siberia, it is widely naturalized in North America, especially in damp meadowland. It may grow to 3 feet or more and has many branched stems bearing toothed leaves (larger near the bottom of the plant) and loose terminal clusters of four-petaled, Phlox-like flowers. The blooms, ¾ inch across, are purple, dark pink, lilac, and white and have a wonderful clove scent that is evident in the evening air, when they attract moths for pollination. The distinctive cylindrical seed capsules are upright, like long, slender bean pods (similar to those of the other Rocket, *Eruca sativa,* the salad green, to which it is related). The genus name is derived from the Green *hesperos,* "evening

star," an apt reference to the flower's starring role in the night garden.

Although Gerard and other herbalists have recommended using the distilled water from Dame's-rocket flowers to induce sweating, and the young leaves have been eaten to prevent scurvy, this plant has been mostly appreciated for its beauty and evening perfume. The fabled double-flowered white Dame's-rocket familiar to Gerard, with foot-high spikes of sweet double blooms, was commonly grown in 17th-century English cottage gardens and had reached the New World by 1725, when Lady Skipwith grew it with English Cowslips, Columbine, Sweet-William, Hollyhocks, and Monkshood. The single flowers in mixed colors have been grown in America since the 1600s.

Although the double white was still being offered by Joseph Breck in the mid-19th century, by 1884 double whites and double purples had vanished from commerce on this side of the water. An English friend reports having found a double white recently at a plant sale. It was not in the best condition at the end of the day, but she grabbed it up and took it home at once to plant in her garden. "We would all like to grow it," noted Margery Fish, who once having got it from a cottage gardener, could not keep it (it must be reproduced from cuttings). Just in case you should ever find it, follow Gertrude Jekyll's sound advice in such matters: "The massive spikes of double flower necessarily exhaust a good deal of the strength, and the plant remembers that it was originally only a biennial; but at the base of the flowering stem there are always one or two tufts of young green growths; these must

Dame's-rocket is a sweetly fragrant member of the Mustard Family.

be carefully taken off and grown on separately to form flowering plants for the next year *(A Gardener's Testament,* 1937).

Writers of the past recorded double pink Dame's-rockets, as well as double reds and even a striped form. Like any curious gardener, I would like to grow these types (especially the legendary white, a source of mystery and desire), but I am thankful to have the singles in assorted shades of lilac, purple, a nice dark pink, and pure white, so easy to grow in the border or to naturalize in a spot of damp ground with wild Iris (Blue and Yellow Flag) and Bouncing-bet or in partial shade at the edge of the woods, taking care of itself from year to year, quite happy in the cool, humus-rich soil. In the more formal plantings of a proper flower bed, I let Dame's-rocket sow where it will among Lupines, Foxglove, Mallows, Bellflowers, Sweet-William, and Clary Sage. It softens and complements the brilliant blooms of Oriental Poppies. I make a point of strolling by the gardens in the evening, so I can enjoy its delicious clove scent.

Frequent cutting for bouquets helps keep the plants in trim and prolong their bloom. Once they are established, you will have short-lived perennials (two or three years old) growing with one-year-old plants and little seedlings, resulting in almost continuous bloom.

To Grow: Dame's-rocket can be grown in Zone 9, but only on the West Coast. Sow the seeds indoors in late winter or early spring; leave them uncovered, at 70°F (21°C). If planted out early enough, the seedlings may produce flowers the first year. Plants can be started outdoors by sowing seeds in a cold frame and planting out the seedlings early the following spring, 15 to 18 inches apart. Once

established in moist, well-drained soil, in sun or partial shade, Dame's-rocket should replenish itself by self-sowing. The seedlings should be thinned for optimum blooms. Small plants can be lifted and replanted in early spring, though they will wilt at first. Plantlets at the base of older plants can be separated and grown in a cold frame as cuttings or planted out in the garden. Flowering stalks should be cut back after bloom to prolong the life of each plant. Enough seeds will spill out on the ground to ensure a continuous supply of seedlings. Be sure to keep seeds from your favorite colors separate, since mauve may overtake the planting in time. Resow your area with purchased seeds when plants become rangy or when you want to extend the color range.

COLLECTOR'S CHOICE:

Hesperis matronalis, Dame's-rocket (1600–1699).
'Lilac'.
'White'.

Hosta spp. ❀

LILIACEAE

Hosta
Autumn Lily, Corfu Lily, Fragrant Plantain, Funkia, Japan Day-lily, Lilac Funkia, Old White Day-lily, Plantain Lily, Seersucker Plantain Lily

INTRODUCED: 1850–1900
ZONES: 3–8
TYPE: Perennial
HEIGHT: 6"–5'
SEASON OF INTEREST: Summer–Fall Foliage and Flowers
SITE: Sun/Partial Shade/Shade

About forty species of Hostas native to Asia (mostly Japan) are noted for their varied leaves, growing from fairly shallow, fleshy roots from early summer to fall. The size of the plant is often measured not so much by its height as by its spread. Under optimum conditions, for instance, *Hosta sieboldiana* 'Elegans' can grow to 6 feet across, though more usually it is about 30 inches high and 42 inches across. Leaf shape, size, texture, and color all vary considerably from very broad (to 1 foot wide), puckered, ribbed, or glossy to slender and twisted and from shades of pale green and deep greenish blue to gold-edged and variegated white. Leaf colors change with the season and exposure to sun, in most species turning gold in autumn before dying back to the ground over the winter. The flowers, borne in loose clusters, are lily- or funnel-shaped (quite fragrant in the Autumn Lily, *Hosta plantaginea*). In some species, the flowers lie fairly hidden among enormous leaves; in others, they rise well above them in elegant spikes to 5 feet, in shades of lilac, mauve, purple, and white. Formerly classified as *Funkias,* the Hosta genus is named for N.T. Host, who was a physician to the emperor of Austria.

Hostas became part of America's ornamental plant pool by the mid- to late 19th century due to many introductions from Asia, collected by professionals such as Robert Fortune, working for the Royal Horticultural Society in Britain, and amateurs such as Franz von Siebold, who spent six years in Japan with the Dutch East India Company. Siebold is credited with introducing a number of important plants to America (via Europe), including the Flowering Crab *(Malus floribunda),* Japanese Dogwood *(Cornus kousa),* Hydrangea *(Hydrangea paniculata),* and Sie-bold Plantain Lily *(H. sieboldiana),* the Hosta that most frequently comes to mind whenever we hear that name. This species has long, waxy, bluish leaves—10 to 15 inches long and 6 to 10 inches wide—with fragrant pale lilac flowers that are shorter in stem length than the leaves, which largely hide them from view—a foliage plant par excellence. This still-popular species has been described as a classic by Will Ingwersen, who calls it "one of the most handsome of a popular family of garden plants" *(Classic Garden Plants,* Hamlyn, 1975).

Unfortunately, their ease of culture, as well as their tolerance of shade or sun and neglect, has relegated Hostas to dim passageways, shady corners, and undistinguished borders in bright sun along the driveway, a horticultural cliché that in my opinion is not worth repeating. I have seen too many unhappy Hostas in this situation. They deserve a better fate than to be planted in lozenge beds around trees or in a dank shrubbery hidden from view. The situation is not helped by gardening guides that refer to Hostas as "serviceable plants."

Until several years ago, when my husband and I were guests of the late Audrey Harkness O'Connor, retired editor of *Cornell Plantations* and creator of the Plantation's herb garden, I did not even regard Hostas as ornamentals. Who wants "just foliage" for summer gardens when we wait so many months for bright blooms? That opinion, based on ignorance, was altered forever when we saw her Hostas in Pimpernel Gardens at her home in Ithaca, New York. Planted adjacent to the house, they spread out generously, a sea of melting shapes, colors, and heights, yet still distinct in their individuality—green, white, and golden. The sun, filtering through

> Hostas deserve a better fate than to be planted in lozenge beds around trees or in a dank shrubbery hidden from view.

a limbed-up grove of white pines and the spreading branches of a single birch tree, allowed us to view and appreciate the full range of Hostas in a play of light and shadow. At the far edge was one of Mrs. O'Connor's favorites among the small types: 'Louisa', a chance seedling from the garden of Frances Williams (whose name is preserved in a popular Hosta cultivar), featuring dainty green leaves edged with white and pure white flared flowers on 30-inch stalks. To think I had passed up such gorgeous landscaping possibilities—a whole world of interesting forms in foliage and flowers!

Since the late 1960s, hybrids and sports have proliferated at a rapid rate, introduced by hobbyists and professional hybridizers. But for many gardeners, several of the "oldies" are still tops, among them Mrs. O'Connor's favorite large type, Siebold Plantain Lily, and little 'Louisa'.

Hostas are slow-growing, so don't expect to duplicate Audrey O'Connor's mass planting for at least three to five years (she started her collection in 1965 when Hostas were Funkias). Once planted, however, they can be left undisturbed indefinitely, swelling with pride from year to year, which is why they are still found growing on their own in neglected gardens. Mrs. Wilder gave us a poignant description of such a discovery: "My first recollection of it [the Corfu or Old White Day-lily, *Hosta plantaginea*] was in a deserted garden in Delaware persisting in the tangled grass beneath immensely tall high-branched evergreen trees of some sort, a garden that I used to steal into whenever happy chance offered. . . . To smell the old white Day Lily brings back those days and that enchanted old garden to me. . . . Doubtless the garden was long ago reclaimed or is

lost beneath the inexorable march of some development scheme, but for me it will always live, enchantment, youth, high aspirations, and all, so long as the frosted white Day Lilies make their punctual appearance in my garden."

Group Hostas among other shade- or semishade-loving plants, such as Ferns, Bleeding-heart, and the true Daylily. Plant them as a cover to fill in after fading Daffodils under the spreading limbs of an old Lilac tree. I hesitate to advise planting Hostas around or in front of shubberies, as a ground cover, or along walkways. Such plantings do have long-term appeal, but only if executed with flair and imagination. The main thing is to avoid creating big, fat clumps with no raison d'être, stuck in a place where nothing else will grow. Plant no fewer than three of one kind together; plant several different types together for diversity of form and color. Planted on a hillside, Hostas provide spectacular cover all season long. Use the foliage and flowers in bouquets.

To Grow: Hostas are very hardy and will thrive even where winters are mild, except in Zones 9 and 10. They grow well in complete or filtered shade, but prefer several hours of morning sun a day. Plants should be set out in the fall or anytime during the growing season up to mid-September (where winters are severe). They require well-prepared ground: moist, humus-rich, well drained, and enriched with compost. Set the plants with the juncture of roots and leaves at ground level and space them according to their expected full size: 3 feet apart for large-leaved types and 8 to 12 inches for the smaller-leaved types. Propagation is by division from the spring into the fall. Hostas (those that aren't sterile types) also can be grown from seeds gathered from the ripened brown capsules and sown in a cold frame in the fall. This can be an interesting experiment, since seedlings are often variable and you may discover a new type that you like and want to preserve (as well as name).

COLLECTOR'S CHOICE:

Most of these were introduced from the mid-1800s to the early 1900s. ❀ indicates especially fragrant types.

Hosta fortunei 'Hyacinthia', Fortune's Plantain Lily. Large blue-green leaves; violet flowers; July–August bloom; 2–3'; added to Mrs. O'Connor's collection in 1971.

'Aureo-marginata'. Gray-green leaves, waxy underneath, with a narrow gold edge; lavender flowers; July–August bloom, 2'.

H. lancifolia, Narrow-leaved Plantain Lily. Shiny, slender green leaves (6"); low, dense clumps; numerous blue-lavender flowers; late summer-fall bloom; one of three species that formed the basis for Mrs. O'Connor's collection in 1965.

H. plantaginea, August, Autumn, or Corfu Lily; pale green, heart-shaped leaves; large, fragrant white trumpet-shaped flowers with pinkish stamens; August–September bloom; protect over the winter in cold climates until established; 2'; Zone 4. ❀

H. sieboldiana 'Elegans', Siebold Plantain Lily. Large, rounded gray-green leaves; nearly white flowers; 18–24"; nearly 6' across in Mrs. O'Connor's garden in a wet season. ❀

H. undulata 'Albo Marginata'. Large, waxy leaves with a narrow white edge, more pronounced in the shade; lavender flowers; early August bloom; 4'.

H. ventricosa, Blue Plantain Lily. Glossy, dark green, heart-shaped leaves; large, showy purple flowers (plant this with Daylilies); July-August bloom; 3'; another of the originals in Mrs. O'Connor's collection.

Hybrids:

'Louisa'; narrow green leaves with a white margin; August–September bloom; try in the rock garden; 30".

'Royal Standard'. Not very old but a classic. Like its parent, *H. plantaginea,* it bears beautiful, wonderfully fragrant flowers in late summer and is very hardy. ❀

Humulus lupulus ❀

CANNABACEAE

Hop Vine
Old Cluster Hop

INTRODUCED: 1600–1699
ZONES: 3–9
NATIVE/NATURALIZED
TYPE: Perennial Twining Vine/Herb
HEIGHT: TO 20'
BLOOM: Midsummer
SITE: Sun

The perennial Hop Vine, one of a few species native to Europe, western Asia, and North America, is a vigorous twining vine with rough stems and almost heart-shaped, finely toothed leaves (similar to grape leaves) that grows back each season to a height of at least 20 feet. The pleasantly bitter hop flavor used to preserve and flavor beer and once used to raise bread is found deep within the papery leaves of the cone-shaped female flowers in the form of powdery, dark yellow-grained fruits. Over the summer, the loose clusters of flowers, first appearing as tight, light green cones, turn gradually to partially open, light amber-bronze rosettes. This is when they have the greatest flavor. Both native and introduced Hop Vines grow wild in vacant fields and along rivers throughout the United States. The genus name is possibly derived from the Latin *humus,* meaning "ground," an apt description of the vine's sprawling habit when unsupported and its preference for rich, humus-rich soil.

The European Hop Vine, known as Old Cluster Hop, was introduced to North America by the Massachusetts Company in 1629; by 1648 its commercial production had spread to Virginia. The settlers brought seeds with them to grow the vine for their own use. As garden historian Ann Leighton observed, "Hops would seem to rank somewhere with the domestic cat as an indispensable adjunct to any household . . . its functions are as humble and cosy as those of the cat, and as ancient" *(Early American Gardens,* University of Massachusetts Press, 1986). The

colonists must have been relieved to find it growing wild on the banks of Maine rivers—no need to worry about an adequate supply for barm, the name of the mixture used as yeast.

By 1800 hops, used for beer-making, were an important field crop in America, especially in the East. By the 1920s, however, due to an epidemic of downy mildew, their cultivation shifted to the northwestern states, where it remains today.

When the household friend was no longer needed, it lingered on to find a use as an ornamental, providing dense shade for porches and verandas, at home in California as it was in the East. When other perennial vines—climbing Roses and Clematis—were introduced to North American gardens, the Hop Vine declined in favor, but it is still highly regarded in colder regions, where other perennial vines are unreliable, and as an ornamental—a mass of leaves all season and dense clusters of intriguing flowers from midsummer into fall.

I found many old Hop Vines in the local area, often grown neatly up a pole by the side of the house for more than seventy years. Kenneth Roberts has an amusing essay about purchasing a "house in the country" and trying to turn it into the proverbial vine-covered cottage, only to have it strangled by a rampant Hop Vine. It is only fair to say that, while the Hop Vine *is* vigorous, its growth can be brought under control.

The oldest Hop Vine I ever saw was prominently featured in Mr. Jackson's Heritage Garden at the Memorial University Botanical Garden in St. John's, Newfoundland. He found the original (from which this vine was grown) climbing up a tree in a garden abandoned more than 120 years ago. It had been

HOP BARM FOR BREAD STARTER

Boil 2 ounces of hop flowers (as for beer) in 4 quarts of water for 30 minutes. Strain into a large wide bowl, stir in 1 tablespoon of salt and 1 cup sugar. When this mixture has cooled to warm, beat in 4 cups unbleached white flour and 1 tablespoon baking yeast dissolved in ¼ cup warm water. Cover bowl loosely, set it in a warm place, and stir down the mixture once a day for two days. Then bottle and refrigerate. Substitute a generous ½ cup of barm for every package of dry yeast in bread recipes. When the starter has been used down to about ½ cup, use this to start a new barm, substituting it for the 1 tablespoon of baking yeast and ¼ cup of water called for in the original barm.

brought to Newfoundland by an immigrant from the Isle of Skye who originally settled in Cape Breton. When he moved, he took with him one of his most prized possessions, just as Ann Leighton described. Now the old Hop Vine was trained over a quiggly fence (see page 45) of woven softwood saplings. The vine framed a tall stand of Golden-glow (*Rudbeckia laciniata*) in full bloom—a brilliant combination of plant and vine and a clever way to protect both in a windy site.

We became devotees of the Hop Vine when we acquired a piece of root from an old garden and planted it by the doorway of our shop. The second season it shot up, framing the doorway in a "bosky dingle," spreading sideways along the wall, supported by a piece of old nylon parachute line. I was particularly enchanted with the flowers, dry on the vine by late summer in bouquetlike clusters. As an herbalist, I was already planning how I would use them: in dried bouquets, wreaths, perhaps little sleep pillows (the flowers are said to be soporific, supposedly used in pillows by eminent people in need of a good night's rest, such as Abraham Lincoln and King George III)—maybe even to raise bread. The ornamental quality of the vine itself and the decorative uses of the dried flowers have been greatly underestimated. The British have always prized the dried flowers in floral art.

The Hop Vine grows by twining and needs the support of a pole, trellis, rustic arbor, or fence on which to climb and drape itself. As Mr. Jackson proved in his Heritage Garden, it can be a smashing addition to the back of a perennial border if trained along a fence. It was traditionally used to shade porches and verandas, appreciated as a quick-growing vine (6 to 12 inches of growth in a single day have been recorded), but it still can be grown to advantage up a tall pole, just as the settlers probably did.

To Grow: Sow the seeds in late spring in well-drained, rich, humusy soil, in a sunny site. Plant the roots at the same time, 18 inches apart, to grow up a trellis or some support. It will take two seasons for the plants to flower when grown from seed. Propagation is by division of the roots. To keep the vine from spreading on the ground (by the lateral multiplication of its roots), ruthlessly pull up new plants growing alongside the "mother" and keep the grass well mowed around the planting. Make sure the vine has plenty of moisture: mulch or water during a dry spell. Cut the whole plant down to the ground in late fall or clean out the old vine in early spring. You can also leave the old vines for support.

To Use: For floral crafts, pick hop flowers when they are still green (in later stages, they shatter easily). To flavor a 5-gallon batch of beer, cover 2 quarts of flowers—chartreuse-bronze with a hoppy aroma—with water. Cover pot, bring to a boil, and simmer for 10 minutes. Cool to warm, then strain the liquid into the other beer ingredients, tie up the remaining hop flowers in a cheesecloth bag, and float it in the beer until it is ready for bottling. To use hops for barm or bread starter in the old way, follow the directions in the box on page 134.

COLLECTOR'S CHOICE:

Humulus lupulus, Hop Vine (1600–1699).
'Old Early Cluster'; discovered in the late
    1800s at Washington State University;
    produces flowers about two weeks earlier
    than the parent species and is very hardy.

Both native and introduced Hop Vines grow wild in vacant fields and along rivers throughout the United States.

Hyacinthus orientalis ✿

LILIACEAE

Hyacinth
Dutch Hyacinth, Garden Hyacinth

INTRODUCED: 1776–1950
ZONES: 4–8
TYPE: Hardy Bulb
HEIGHT: 8–12"
BLOOM: Mid-Spring

With the fascination for Victorian lavishness in the plant line, antique Hyacinths have returned to the garden.

*A*ll hyacinth garden cultivars are developed from *Hyacinthus orientalis,* one of three species in the genus, and the most fragrant. Native from the Mediterranean area to Asia Minor, the wild ancestor is unrecognizable in garden versions, except for their shared perfume. A bulbous plant, it produces straplike dark green leaves, and three to ten tubular, bell-like flowers of a washed-out lavender hue, loosely arranged at the top of a 12-inch stem. The garden versions—stiff spikes packed with single or double florets in a range of colors that include blue, purple, rose, pink, red, and white—are the result of extensive Dutch hybridizing for more than two hundred years. Roman or Wild Hyacinth, *H. orientalis* var. *albulus,* a variant of the species from southern France, is similar in design, but with bright blue or white flowers.

Hyacinths, like Tulips, were introduced to the West from Turkey in the mid-1500s, but their delicate, modest form evoked little interest until they became the subject of intensive breeding. By 1768, with thousands of named cultivars in circulation, Hyacinth breeding and cultivation formed a very important part of the Dutch bulb industry. They

may have been, as some have claimed, more popular at that time than Tulips, but there is little evidence of that in the New World. Lady Skipwith of Virginia, whose preserved jottings give us a glimpse into late 18th-century gardens, records only two true Hyacinths—a double blue and a blush—in a list that includes the more popular Grape Hyacinths (*Muscari* spp.). Nurseryman Bernard M'Mahon's catalog from the same time lists eleven different "hyacinths," but only one is *Hyacinthus orientalis.* Jefferson, we know, grew them at Monticello, for his garden book records that on March 30, 1776, "Purple Hyacinth begins to bloom" *(Thomas Jefferson's Flower Garden at Monticello).*

By the early 1800s, Hyacinths were becoming popular in a new range of colors, and in single and double forms. Between 1807 and 1812, Jefferson notes receiving four shipments from M'Mahon of "first rate kinds, and nearly . . . as many varieties as roots." He planted four different colors of double Hyacinth in an oval bed in a checkered design, a plan that M'Mahon had sketched in his gardening book, *The American Gardener's Calendar* (1806), the definitive word for the next fifty years on New World gardening.

The public's high regard for Hyacinths soared in the later decades of the 19th century when their stiff, rigid forms, excessively flowered spikes—some too heavy for their stems—and heady aroma appealed to Victorian sensibilities. D.M. Ferry's 1886 catalog lists no fewer than 135 varieties, enough for massing and the popular pastime of indoor winter forcing (Hyacinths are among the easiest bulbs to force).

Many antique varieties have vanished (especially the doubles, which Louise Beebe

Wilder regarded as "fat abominations"), but today, with the fascination for Victorian lavishness in the plant line, antique Hyacinths have returned to the garden. Some of the best, like 'City of Haarlem', retain their popularity, even as stiff Victorian garden design has been rejected in favor of a more natural style. "How can one get along in gardening, or in life," asked gardening authority Mrs. Francis King in 1928 *(From a New Garden),* "without the thought of . . . seeing in bloom . . . such hyacinths as the superb 'King of the Blues' . . . palest yellow 'City of Haarlem', 'Orangjeboven' ['Salmonetta'], dark claret 'Distinction' . . . so beautiful when planted below a coral-pink flowering quince?" Of those named by Mrs. King, all except 'Orangjeboven' (recently vanished) are still available. I think half the fun of growing antique bulbs like Hyacinths are their names, so colorful, so full of kings, queens, lords, and ladies (see Collector's Choice).

Earlier-blooming Roman Hyacinths, introduced around 1850, were grown in southern gardens, and may still be around. A few nurseries are reported to be building up their stock, which is a good thing, for where they are winter-hardy they are choice for naturalizing. Vaughn's 1897 fall catalog lists six colors, describes them as not being hardy north of Washington, D.C., and provides directions for forcing them into winter bloom. He also advertises Dutch Romans, a miniature version for growing in pots that blooms after the Romans.

Wherever you plant the showy hybrids, along a path, for a splash of color in the rock garden, or in a border grouped by color, their mid-spring season of bloom is a glorious one that includes late Daffodils and Tulips, Grape Hyacinth, Pansies, Forget-me-nots, Violas, and the wonderful yellow spring daisy, Leopardsbane *(Doronicum).*

To Grow: Hyacinths grow best in sandy loam. Plant them 6 inches deep in early fall so they have time to grow roots, and space them 5 to 6 inches apart. No matter how fertile the soil, Hyacinths take a lot of food, so be sure to keep the ground well nourished with rotted manure, compost, or fertilizer; otherwise, flowering will decline. On the other hand, some gardeners feel that the more sparse, looser flower spikes that naturally follow the Hyacinth's first season of bloom without a lot of extra food are more graceful and easier to use in border design.

FORCING HYACINTHS

Nothing could be easier than forcing Hyacinth bulbs into winter or early spring bloom, using nothing more than water. Select single-flowered types for forcing. Use a hyacinth glass (attractive Victorian reproductions abound), which holds the bulb in a sort of hour-glass, with the bulb resting on top and the roots growing in water below. Or suspend the bulb with toothpicks over a glass, as you would sprout avocado seeds. Buy prechilled bulbs or prechill them yourself by storing at refrigerator temperature for three months. Place a bulb in the top cup, fill the bottom with enough water so the bulb just touches (add a bit of aquarium-type charcoal to keep the water clear). Store in a cool (above freezing), dark place—a closet will do—then bring into light and room temperature when shoots are about 3 inches tall. Keep up the water level, and in about three to four weeks you should have blooming Hyacinths on your windowsill. After they bloom, dry out bulbs on paper, store until fall, then plant out in the usual way. Depending on type, they may give very good blooms.

The usual way to propagate Hyacinth bulbs is to dig them up in the early summer after their leaves have yellowed, and cut a half-inch-deep criss-cross through the basal plate; replant the bulbs, and by the following fall they should have produced bulblets where the original bulb was cut. Pull these off, replant them in a cold frame for the winter, and leave them there for several seasons before planting them in the garden.

Hyacinths are marginally hardy in zones 3 through 5, where they should be heavily mulched over the winter.

COLLECTOR'S CHOICE:
Scott Kunst's Old House Gardens is a source for the rare Hyacinths listed below.

Hyacinthus orientalis (1776–1950).
'Blue Delft' (1944). Single soft lilac-blue; reliable.
'Blue Giant' (1935). Pale blue, dark veins; extra large; a favorite of bulb experts Brent and Becky Heath (See Brent & Becky's Bulbs under "Sources"), and long-lasting in their Virginia garden.
'Chestnut Flower' (1880). Rare; one of the few doubles still in existence; pale pink, "exquisite," but beware of toppling.
'City of Haarlem' (1893–1898). Ever popular for its soft primrose coloring, maturing to ivory.
'Distinction' (1880). A dainty type, dark maroon, very striking among spring pastels; pair it with pewter-blue 'Perle Brilliante'; good for forcing.
'General Kohler' (1878). A rare double, slightly pyramidal in shape; blue-purple.
'Gipsy Queen' (1927; first sold 1944). Apricot with melon undertones, very fragrant.

'Grand Monarque' (1863). Rare. Light blue, like a spring sky.
'Jan Bos' (1910). Brilliant pinkish red spikes, white blush in center; mixes well with white daffodils; good for forcing.
'King of the Blues' (1863). "Not blue, but lavender as anyone knows" (Mrs. King) "deep, rich, satisfying dark purple . . . reminds me of bittersweet chocolate . . . one of my favorites in the garden and forced . . ." (Scott Kunst).
'Lady Derby' (1875). Soft baby pink, good companion for the blues; strong grower and forcer.
'La Victoire' (1875). Rare. Brilliant rose shading toward magenta; "don't be scared . . . really lovely . . ." (Scott Kunst).
'L'Innocence' (1863). Ivory white, very popular. "It lights up my spring garden and has proven to be one of my most perennial hyacinths; also great for forcing" (Scott Kunst); combine with blues.
'Lord Balfour' (1883). Rare; purplish-rose. Scott suggests pairing it with 'Gipsy Queen'.
'Madame Sophie' (1929). Rare double white, sport of 'L'Innocence'; perfect with pinks and blues.
'Marie' (1860). Rare. One of two existing Hyacinths listed in Vaughn's 1897 catalog; dark purple.
'Menelik' (1911). Rare; elegantly slim spikes; dark purple (for the black garden?).
'Perle Brilliante' (1895). Rare. Pale silvery bluish-purple; combine with 'Distinction', or with 'Lady Derby', 'L'Innocence', 'City of Haarlem'.
'Queen of the Blues' (1870). Similar to above but daintier.
'Queen of the Pinks' (1903). A gold rosy pink; sport of 'King of the Blues'; sturdy.

Hydrangea paniculata 'Grandiflora' ❀

SAXIFRAGACEAE

Peegee Hydrangea
Tree Hydrangea

INTRODUCED: 1862
ZONES: 4–9

H. anomala petiolaris ❀

Climbing Hydrangea

TYPE: Hardy Shrub/Clinging Vine
HEIGHT: 10–75'
BLOOM: Summer-Fall
SITE: Sun/Partial Shade/Shade

The Peegee Hydrangea from Asia is a late-blooming treelike shrub that can grow to 25 feet (usually considerably less, to about 12 feet). It has large, coarsely toothed green leaves and immense (1-foot-long) white pyramidal flower clusters that turn pink, then bronzy green, with age. Its common name (Peegee) is a welcome abbreviation for the mouthful *paniculata* 'Grandiflora'.

The Climbing Hydrangea, also from Asia, clings to brick or stone by means of aerial rootlets on its main and lateral branches. Its fragrant flowers, which bloom in mid-June, are white and showy—flat clusters 6 to 10 inches wide. Its nearly heart-shaped lustrous leaves and vigorous habit make it a very useful vine for covering walls or ground.

These species are part of the treasures from the Orient introduced to American gardeners in the late 19th century. They thrive in growing conditions similar to those in their native habitat.

"The Japan Hydrangea [Peegee] bids fair to be the most valuable of the Hydrangeas," one 19th-century authority asserted. A down-home type of shrub immune to fashion, whose overuse is the despair of landscaping authorities and the delight of those who grow it, it is still a hallmark of rural and small-town North America: dependable, easygoing, and highly decorative, with large, fluffy, oversized blooms of changing color, always anticipated with fresh joy each summer when new blooms, particularly on shrubs, are most wanted in the garden. Even with age, and entirely dried up on the bush, the Peegee's pinkish flower clusters are eagerly sought for use in winter bouquets.

I found an admirable fifty-year-old specimen in full bloom on a hillside farm, where descendants of the original Scottish settlers from the Isle of Barra treated it almost reverently, like an old family friend. It grew in a bower of shrubbery—among Lilacs, Spirea of several sorts, and Weigela—all purchased as rootstock from the traveling plant peddler's last trip to the area in 1939. Several generations of children have played beneath its branches, and countless bouquets, in summer and winter, have been made from its plentiful flowers.

In early fall, I found a Climbing Hydrangea under quite different circumstances, growing untended for at least the past thirty years up the side of "The Lodge," a large turn-of-the-century structure that is the oldest building on the grounds of Beinn Breagh, the summer estate of Alexander Graham Bell and his family. The Lodge eventually became the summer home of the Bells' famous son-in-law, plant collector David Fairchild, who was responsible for the plantings I found there, all now left to their own devices: a once splendid perennial border and rock garden, various Roses, and the Climbing Hydrangea. Keeping company with its old and twisted branches, plastered against the wall like an aged one-dimensional tree, was the native Virginia Creeper (*Parthenocissus quinquefolia*) in all its autumn splendor, a brilliant mass of scarlet leaves.

The Peegee Hydrangea should be planted where its multitude of extravagant blooms can be easily seen and cut for bouquets and dried floral crafts. It is a fine specimen shrub, being somewhat on the order of a small tree, and is striking by itself on the side lawn or behind lower-growing shrubs. (You can remove the lower branches to encourage a cascading form, which is especially beautiful if the bush is planted near the top of a stone wall). The Climbing Hydrangea, one of the most beautiful of all vines, can be used to clothe buildings, climb over doorways, or climb up stone or brick walls—no support needed. It is also useful for covering eyesores (rock-piles and the like) and for climbing up tall, open tree trunks, such as elms. Donald Wyman reported seeing one of the finest specimens of Climbing Hydrangea growing up an American Elm in front of the house where the great plant collector Ernest H. Wilson (of Regal Lily fame) once lived. The tree, Wyman pointed out, was beautiful in its own right, "but with the vine growing up its trunk to the lower branches it was of unusual interest to all who passed under it." This vine is ideal for tree climbing (something I've always read about but not yet practiced), since it tends to grow right up the tree or very slowly around it, not causing any damage (such as constricting translocation in the trunk).

To Grow: Most Hydrangeas do well in moist soil. The Peegee prefers sun or partial shade, while the Climbing Hydrangea can be grown equally well in sun or shade. If the Peegee is grown in fertile soil, it should be severely pruned in early spring. This will produce large flower heads. Mulch the Peegee in the winter with organic matter (rotted manure or compost) and fertilizer scratched into the soil around the shrub. It is easily propagated by softwood cuttings in spring or early summer, which root in two to three weeks when planted in sand and kept moist.

Climbing Hydrangea takes a few seasons to get started, but growth is rapid after that. It grows best on the north or east side of a building, where it is protected from strong sun in early spring. In their early growth, the crowns of the vines should be protected in the winter with a covering of straw or evergreen boughs. The plant is best propagated by layering, though the vines are slow to root.

COLLECTOR'S CHOICE:

Hydrangea paniculata 'Grandiflora', Peegee Hydrangea (1862).

H. anomala petiolaris, Climbing Hydrangea.

Impatiens balsamina ✿

BALSAMINACEAE

Balsam
Bush Balsam, Garden Balsam, Lady's Balsam, Lady's-slipper, Rose Balsam, Touch-me-not

INTRODUCED: 1700–1800
HEIGHT: 8"–2½'
SITE: Sun/Partial Shade

Impatiens glandulifera ❀

Policeman's Helmet
Common Balsam, Himalayan Balsam,
Jumping Jack, Jump Seed,
Red Jewelweed

INTRODUCED: 1850–1900?
NATURALIZED
HEIGHT: 3–6'
SITE: Sun/Partial Shade/Shade

TYPE: Tender Annual
BLOOM: Summer

Two species from Asia are of special interest to heirloom gardeners, both of them known generally as "Touch-me-not" or Impatiens for the eagerness with which they spill their seeds at the slightest touch. In the species form, Balsam is branching and bushy to 2½ feet, with spurred flowers—white, yellow, or dark red and often spotted—growing close to the stem under overhanging, lance-shaped, sawtooth leaves. Cultivated forms are very double and often dwarf. They come in a variety of shades—scarlet, soft rose-pink, deep violet, and pure white—and are often lightly scented. Lady's-slipper, an old-fashioned name for Balsam, is now used almost exclusively in reference to the Wild Orchid, Showy Lady's-slipper *(Cypripedium reginae)*.

Policeman's Helmet, of Himalayan origin, is an extraordinarily robust plant, similar in form and structure to the native spotted Jewelweed *(I. capensis)*, except that it is larger in every way. Shallow-rooted plants are supported by thick, red-tinged, juicy stems (like Jewelweed, their sap has been used to treat poison ivy), with leaves similar to Balsam. The plant's glory is its clusters of numerous flowers—1½ to 1¾ inches long—hooded and spurred in the shape of a London bobby's helmet. Satiny in texture, with a musky perfume, their colors include shades of pink, rose-purple, lavender, and white, speckled yellow inside to lure bees. Policeman's Helmet is a naturalized escape from gardens in the Northeast as far west as Ontario.

Balsam was introduced to Europe in 1596 and grown in the New World by the 17th century, but it was not really well known until the 18th and early 19th centuries. Double Balsam was grown at Shadwell, Jefferson's birthplace, in 1767, and at Monticello in 1812, ordered from Bernard M'Mahon, who regarded it as among a group of "valuable and curious sorts of tender annuals." He gave out detailed instructions on how Balsam could be raised in hotbeds (cold frames heated from below by straw-rotted horse manure). Such a bed is demonstrated at Old Sturbridge Village's early 19th-century Parsonage kitchen garden, where such tender annuals as Balsam, African and French Marigolds *(Tagetes erecta* and *T. patula,* respectively), *Lavatera,* and Snapdragons are germinated and grown for transplanting into the flower borders by late May.

By the 19th century, three cultivated forms of Balsam were widely recognized: Camellia-flowered, in mixed colors and spotted; Rose-flowered, a perfect double; and Carnation-flowered, with stripes. All of these came in dwarf forms as well. In my experience, the differences are academic, as all types resemble little Roses. I have listed the various types available today so you can make up your own mind. All are lovely and worth having in the heirloom garden.

Both species
are known
generally as
"touch-me-not"
or impatiens for
the eagerness
with which they
spill their seeds
at the slightest
touch.

In the Victorian-era passion for double flowers (when didn't gardeners like the showier type?), Balsams reigned supreme, their stiff forms especially suitable for bedding displays. But by the early 1900s, they, along with other old-fashioned flowers, had become passé, though favorites still among those who looked back with nostalgia to "Grandmother's garden" and an idealized past when the world moved at a slower, saner pace.

Despite their ups and downs in popularity, Balsams have been offered continuously to American gardeners since the 18th century, in increasingly improved form, so that the showy flowers aren't hidden by overhanging leaves as in the older types (the soft scent is a recent addition, too). Still, one wonders about reports from 19th-century writers who tell us of having seen Balsam plants of shrublike proportions growing in the Tuileries Garden of Paris with flowers "as large as a moderate rose." Hyperbole or truth? We will never know.

In the wake of the herb renaissance, which we are still enjoying, we are told that the highly ornamental Balsam is an herb. So if you should plant it in your herb garden as a colorful foil for greenery, you can tell the curious that the flowers when mixed with alum may be used to paint fingernails. It is not a use I have ever tried myself. I enjoy the lovely shrubby Balsam at the front of a perennial border to fill in the bare spots left by early-blooming plants such as Sweet-William. Dwarf forms are valued for container planting, moved around wherever colorful, long-season bloom is needed. The taller sorts are fine filler among the evergreens of a foundation planting or to fill in among newly planted shrubs. If well grown, Balsams resemble little shrubs themselves, a mass of double Roses (or Camellias, etc.) from early summer to frost. A mass planting of either taller or dwarf forms is a welcome change from the usual Impatiens (*I. wallerana*). The bouquetlike blossoming stems can be cut for *real* bouquets all season long.

Unlike Balsam, little is known of Policeman's Helmet's history, but if plants could speak, Policeman's Helmet would tell a story something like this:

"I have been grown in English gardens since 1839, loved for my easy going ways and my generous habit of blooming all summer in nearly any situation. Margery Fish regarded me as well-established in the cottage garden genre, calling attention to my country folk names (Jumping Jack and Policeman's Helmet), and the way children never tire of bursting my quaint seedpods. Gertrude Jekyll, mistress of design, rightly saw my possibilities: 'A very handsome plant of rapid growth, useful in the back of the border or among shrubs or at the edge of woodland' (*Annuals and Biennials*).

"The Asian Touch-me-not (*I. noli-tangere*) and the native species, Spotted Jewelweed (*I. capensis*) were grown in New World gardens by 1800. Perhaps I came along by mid-century, but, whenever it was, after my popularity waned I found a compatible home near the edge of the woodland, along roadsides, and in gardens abandoned before 1940.

Actually, Policeman's Helmet is still a favorite among gardeners. I have seen it in older gardens and new ones, even in public display gardens, where it was used imaginatively to lead visitors from one area to another and to provide relief from stiff, stylized plantings in the Victorian mode. I have witnessed the astonishment and unbounded admiration of the most sophisticated, knowledgeable garden people when confronted with a long, informal hedge of Policeman's Helmet, shimmering in the sun, worked over by bees in search of its nectar. "What's the name of that plant?" they want to know. I've also seen it as an eye-riveting, tall central accent in a modest backyard cottage garden among lower growing Daylilies, Hyssop, and *Achillea* 'Moonshine'.

In my own gardens it is happy in the shade of an old apple tree and at the bottom of a steep slope, where it can cast its jumping seeds wherever it likes. A word of caution: when this plant was given to me many years ago, I thought it ugly for its thick, watery stems. Who needs this when space is at a premium? I actually discarded it, and it was not until many years later when a gardening friend brought me a clump in full bloom that I had second thoughts (I successfully transplanted it in midsummer heat by watering and mulching). Other gardeners have experienced the same doubt. My advice is to find a place where it can settle in without interference, then sit back and enjoy the show.

To Grow: In warm regions, Balsams can be seeded directly in the garden, but for earlier bloom elsewhere, start plants indoors four to six weeks before the last frost. Plant seedlings out when the weather has warmed (when you set out tomato plants), allowing ample space (up to 18 inches for the taller types) for them to develop. An old-time gardening trick is to pinch off the side branches and the first flowers to encourage a profusion of blooms near the top of the plant. When in flower, Balsams should resemble a ready-made bouquet. Balsams endear themselves to me by their accommodation to being moved, even when in full bloom, as long

as a ball of soil is attached to the roots. In hot climates, give them a little shade; in cooler areas, plant them in full sun. Always plant them in rich, well-drained soil. Water them well during dry periods.

Sow seeds of Policeman's Helmet in moist, enriched soil after all danger of frost has passed. Thin to about 12 inches apart. There is very little else to do except to confine its growth by mowing around it, as in a hedge or naturalized planting. Wherever it is grown, give it sufficient room to create a wide, striking swathe of bloom.

COLLECTOR'S CHOICE:

Impatiens balsamina, 'Camellia-flowered Mixed'. Lightly scented: 16–28".
'Extra Dwarf'; 8–12".
'Gardenia-flowered'; 14".
I. glandulifera, Policeman's Helmet (1850–1900?). Colors range from palest pink to deep rose-red. It is also offered alone in salmon pink. Occasionally, hybrids (selections from the species) are offered in a wider color range including cream, rose, pink, red, burgundy, and bicolors. These are sometimes referred to as crosses with *I. royleyi,* a synonym for *I. glandulifera.* Gertrude Jekyll admired a white form, perhaps 'Candida'. Check out English seed sources as well as those listed at the back of the book under "Sources."

Inula helenium

ASTERACEAE

Elecampane
Elf-dock, Elfwort, Helen's Flower, Horseheal, Scabwort, Velvet-dock, Wild-sunflower

INTRODUCED: 1600–1776
ZONES: 3–8
NATURALIZED
TYPE: Perennial Herb/Flower
HEIGHT: 4–6'
BLOOM: Midsummer
SITE: Sun

Elecampane originated in the Old World. It is a tall plant, downy in all of its parts, with long, tongue-shaped light green leaves around the base of the stout stem. The flowers, borne at the top of the plant, look like daisies or sunflowers—about 3 inches across, golden yellow, and thinly rayed. Elecampane is naturalized in North America along roadsides and clearings from Ontario and Nova Scotia south to North Carolina and west to Missouri.

This herb, a staple of the well-run medieval household, has been described by all the usual commentators, from the 1st-century Roman naturalist Pliny the Elder to the indefatigable Gerard in 16th-century England. A 14th-century cookbook tells how to make a sweetmeat of its roots (reportedly very bitter no matter how well sugared), whose main use was to treat whooping cough, bronchitis, and asthma. One of Elecampane's common names from the Middle Ages was Horseheal, denoting its use in treating horse complaints, from weak lungs to rough coats.

Elecampane was also highly regarded as an herb in new-world gardens. It was planted at George Washington's birthplace in Wakefield, Virginia, where all the "yarbs" known to the colonists were laid out in square and rectangular beds. There, Elecampane grew

among the tall herbs, such as Tansy, Monkshood, Clary Sage, Bergamot, and Wormwood—a planting worth repeating today in the herb or flower garden. It also turns up on assorted lists of herbs grown as medicinals in America into the 19th century. It would appear that this herb was highly valued for its medicinal properties—one of the most useful being as an antiseptic in surgical dressings. Experiments carried out in Germany in 1885 showed that a preparation of Elecampane root killed bacteria. Before 1914, the United States imported fifty thousand pounds of Elecampane roots annually to use primarily in veterinary products associated with treating horse ailments. With the decline in the use of horses and with the general availability of other medicines, Elecampane fell out of favor (though it may still be used in patent medicines) and was not taken up again until the herb renaissance of the 1930s.

Elecampane was my introduction to the world of flowering herbs and to the idea that plants known primarily for their usefulness could be grown solely for their ornamental virtues. In one of my earliest attempts to establish a flower garden on the old farm, Elecampane, along with Chives and Hyssop, was one of the few perennials to survive the winter. As the summer progressed, I was surprised to see that the clump of homely, oversize Elecampane leaves had changed, like the ugly duckling, into a tall, stately plant bearing cheerful sunflowers, so pretty among purple Monkshood. Though we keep horses, I have never been tempted to use the roots for anything other than establishing a garden on the wild side in a damp, sunny spot, where Elecampane does well on its own among mauve-

Elecampane was my introduction to the world of flowering herbs and to the idea that plants known primarily for their usefulness could be grown solely for their ornamental virtues.

flowered Chives, Blue and Yellow Flag Iris, Purple Loosestrife (noninvasive cultivars), and the double pink Bouncing-bet—a whole season of bloom with virtually no effort, except mowing around the edges. The original plant in my flower garden (now a mixture of herbs and flowers) has not been divided in twenty years. It grows on from year to year with very little attention, faithfully poking its long leaves through the soil in early summer, a reminder of the beauty to come.

To Grow: Elecampane grows best in deep clay loam on the moist side. In lighter soil where summers are hot, grow it in partial shade, which will prolong its bloom period (about two weeks where summers are hot, longer elsewhere). Its natural range suggests that Elecampane accommodates well to various soils and climates. To increase the plant, dig up a piece of root (you may be pleasantly surprised by its sweet aroma) about 2 inches long with a bud or eye and replant it, watering it well until new growth appears. Elecampane can be left indefinitely unless it shows signs of decreased bloom. Though fairly tall, the stout stems usually do not need staking, another thing in its favor.

COLLECTOR'S CHOICE:

Imula helenium, Elecampane (1600–1776).

Ipomoea purpurea

CONVOLVULACEAE

Morning-glory
Bindweed, Blew Bindweed

INTRODUCED: 1600–1699
NATURALIZED

I. alba ⚘

Moonflower
Moonvine, Prickly Ipomoea

INTRODUCED: 1700–1750

I. nil 'Scarlet O'Hara'

Imperial Morning-glory

TYPE: Annual/Tender Perennial Twining Vine
HEIGHT: to 20' or more
BLOOM: Summer–Fall
SITE: Sun/Partial Shade

Ipomoea, from the Greek for "bindweed," is a large genus of more than five hundred species, among which are twining vines such as the prosaic sweet potato and the ornamentals Morning-glory and Moonflower, quick-growing and prized for their lovely trumpet flowers and abundant, attractive foliage.

Morning-glory, as the name suggests, blooms from dawn to early morning, remaining open longer in cloudy weather and when summer temperatures cool down. The trumpet- or funnel-shaped blooms, up to 5 inches across and borne profusely on twining stems that grow to 10 feet or more, may be blue, purple, pink, scarlet, or any shade thereof, as well as white-throated or striped. An annual from tropical America, it is naturalized in North America.

The Moonflower, also native to tropical America, is a tender perennial, usually grown as an annual. Its large, silky white, clove-scented flowers, 6 inches across or more, open at dusk or late afternoon and remain open until noon. They are said to bloom by the moon and close by the sun. The moonflower also grows by twining, bearing a great many 8-inch heart-shaped leaves, attractive in their own right.

Morning-glories were planted in the earliest American gardens and are featured in the dwarf form at Colonial Williamsburg. Eighteenth-century gardener Lady Skipwith grew many colors. By the mid-18th century, the tender perennial climber *Ipomoea tricolor* had been introduced, a somewhat tamer, less vigorous sort (of which the dwarf form is one type) from Mexico, where, we are told, it was used by the Aztecs as a hallucinogen in religious ceremonies. There is no record of this lovely vine being used for the same purposes in American gardens, but it did become important in the breeding of several very popular cultivars, among them the aptly named 'Heavenly Blue', perhaps introduced around the turn of the century (late 1800s), but in any case before 1911. Sky blue, white-throated, and 5 inches across, it has become synonymous with the term "Morning-glory."

By the 19th century, the Imperial or Japanese Morning-glory *(I. nil)* had been introduced from Japan. The ever-popular 'Scarlet O'Hara'—a dark, wine red flower that covers the vine from top to bottom all summer—was derived from it. The pure white 'Pearly Gates', derived from *Ipomoea tricolor,* was introduced by 1940. Both these cultivars have shown marvelous endurance in the form of undiminished popularity since their introduction. 'Scarlet' won an AAS Gold Medal in 1939, 'Pearly' an AAS Silver Medal in 1942.

Moonflower, with its distinctive night-blooming habit and large scented flowers, has never needed improving. Where winters are frost-free and it can be grown as a perennial, it reaches as high as 40 feet in a single season. Even in my Zone 4 garden, it makes a good show along our shop wall or on a trellis by a dooryard garden, where we can enjoy its clove-scented flowers in the late afternoon and evening. If left to their own devices, Moonflower and the rest of the Morning-glories are valuable as a temporary ground cover.

Given support—a trellis, fence, arbor, pole, wires, or twine—these beautiful vines take off, "lifting their heads toward the sky as though they were trying to compete with the sun, moon or stars," as a writer once observed. A cliché (but one that is always welcome) is to plant any of the Morning-glory vines so they twine around the back supports of a rural mailbox. I have seen this neatly done in the most decorous suburbs, where the blue, pink, mauve, or white trumpets are the only bright color in a monotonous sea of green lawns and evergreen shrubs. If planted side by side, Morning-glory and Moonflower complement each other's bloom cycle, one taking up where the other leaves off, providing continuous bloom, night and day. Where these vines are grown as annuals, they can be planted in tubs or raised baskets in even the smallest city garden.

To Grow: Sow Morning-glory seeds in a sunny spot in the spring when the soil is warm. Where the growing season is short, start the seeds indoors. In either case, nick them with a file and soak them overnight in lukewarm water to speed germination, which should occur in a week at 75 to 80°F (24 to 27°C). Since the roots don't like being disturbed, plant seeds in peat pots and set them out in holes in the ground after all danger of frost

If planted side by side, Morning-glory and Moonflower complement each other's bloom cycle, one taking up where the other leaves off, providing continuous bloom, night and day.

has passed, spacing them about 8 to 12 inches apart. Morning-glory is quite drought-tolerant and does not need a rich soil (this will only produce a lot of leaves and few flowers).

In Zones 9 and 10, Moonflower can be grown as a perennial; elsewhere sow seeds as for Morning-glory, spacing plants 9 to 12 inches apart. Moonflowers respond to a weekly feeding of balanced fertilizer (20–20–20) with micronutrients. Use ½ teaspoon per gallon of water at the seedling stage. Plant out the seedlings when all danger of frost has passed and feed them once a month with a rose fertilizer, which promotes flowering. If the vines are growing too tall for your supports or your liking, cut them back and pinch off the tips to slow growth. Be sure to provide sturdy support for either type of vine early in its growth.

COLLECTOR'S CHOICE:

J.L. Hudson says that 5 pounds of seed will plant a mile of bloom, and suggests 'Scarlet O'Hara', 'Pearly Gates', and 'Heavenly Blue' to make a patriotic red, white, and blue display, "a rural American tradition."

Ipomoea alba, Moonflower (1700–1750).
   Choice for the evening garden.
I. nil 'Scarlet O'Hara', Imperial Morning-glory (before 1939).
I. purpurea, Morning-glory. Mixed colors (indigo, maroon, and white).
'Crimson Rambler'. Crimson flowers with a white throat.
'Kniola's Purple-Black'. Deep purple-black velvety flower, 2" wide, with a rosy throat and white eye. Offered by J.L. Hudson, which reports that the plant was discovered by a Mr. Kniola on an abandoned Indiana farm.

I. tricolor 'Heavenly Blue' (before 1911).
'Blue Star'. Sport of 'Heavenly Blue'; its flowers are powder blue with a deep blue star radiating from the center. Becoming rare.
'Grandpa Ott's'. The Whealy family heirloom seeds that inspired the Seed Savers Exchange. Flowers are royal purple with a pink-throated rose star radiating from its center. Possibly the 'Purple Glow' of the 1940s. Two other offered varieties are almost identical if not the same as 'Grandpa Ott's': 'President Tyler' (before 1850), sold by Johnny's Selected Seeds and advertised as early, 45 days; and 'Star of Yalta' from Thompson and Morgan.
'Pearly Gates' (by 1940).

Iris spp. ❀

IRIDACEAE

Iris

INTRODUCED: 1600–1960
ZONES: 3–10
TYPE: Hardy Perennial Bulb/Herb
HEIGHT: 3"–4'
BLOOM: Spring–Early Summer
SITE: Sun/Partial Shade

Two hundred or more species of Iris grow in the Northern Hemisphere, among them the interesting group of garden flowers with rhizomatous, rather than bulbous, roots treated here. These grow horizontally on or underneath the ground, sending up a succession of grassy or swordlike leaves with flower-bearing stalks of six-petaled, often fragrant blooms. The blooms consist of three upright petals *(standards),* three lower hanging or recurved petals *(falls)*, and three strap-shaped divisions *(style branches)*. This distinct form is the pattern for the fleur-de-lis, an ancient symbol of French royalty. In bearded types, raised hairs, sometimes brilliantly colored, grow from the base of the falls, luring insects to the heart of the flower, where they inadvertently fertilize it with pollen carried on their bodies from other blooms. Both the genus and family names are derived from Iris, the Greek goddess of the rainbow, suggestive of the varying colors and shimmering quality of the blooms.

Although several Iris were known in the 17th century, the early settlers brought with them or sent for only one, the Yellow Flag or Flower-de-luce *(Iris pseudacorus)*, apparently for its well-known medicinal properties and ease of culture. It will grow almost anywhere, even (or especially) in swamps and wetlands. Described as "a sovereign remedy for weak eyes" when properly prepared, it was also used to treat ulcers and make a yellow or black dye. Who could ask for anything more from a plant that is also beautiful: bright yellow flowers in the classic fleur-de-lis design (sans beard) and green swordlike leaves.

During the next two hundred years, until the 20th century, Americans were content to grow a variety of wild Iris and their superior strains from many parts of the world. The bearded German Iris *(I. x germanica)* varied from blue to purple and red, and its variety, 'Florentina', the Florentine Iris (almost white) was fabled as a source for violet-scented orris root, used as a fixative in making perfumes and potpourri. As a garden plant, the 'Florentina' has always had its admirers: "In spite of the fact that it is not new or in the least expensive," Helen Fox wrote in the 1930s, "its pearly iridescent color and delicate iris-like fragrance make it one of the most desirable irises" *(Gardening with Herbs for Flavor and Fragrance,* Macmillan, 1933).

Another sweet-scented Iris is Sweet Flag *(Iris pallida)*, a bearded type with lavender-blue to white flowers, and silvery, long-lasting foliage. Nineteenth-century introductions included Japanese Iris *(I. kaempferi)*, with large, graceful, almost flat falls, sometimes veined and mottled, and blue, lavender, and orchid-rose flowers, and Siberian Iris, a wetland type daintier than Yellow Flag but tough, with a crisp fleur-de-lis in shades of purple, blue, or white.

Native Iris were introduced from the late 18th century through the mid-19th century. Among them are the lovely Crested Iris, growing wild from Maryland to Georgia and Missouri, perhaps the finest of all dwarf Iris. It has a distinct fluted yellow-and-white crest on its pale lilac or blue flowers. Blue Flag, native from eastern Canada to Pennsylvania, and Southern Blue Flag, native to the southeastern United States, are wetland types with variable purple and blue flowers, sometimes splashed with yellow.

Whatever their differences, all of the assorted "flags" in grandmother's or great-grandmother's garden were dependable, ironclad Iris with many, though smallish, blooms during their brief season (early spring to early summer). Hybridization of several species (among them *Iris x germanica* and *I. pallida*) began by the 1820s, and by the turn of the century hundreds of new cultivars poured forth, extending the color range, height, and size of flowers—not surprising, considering the Iris is one of the easiest subjects for cross-pollination. The goal was to produce showier

Both the genus and family names are derived from Iris, the Greek goddess of the rainbow, suggestive of the varying colors and shimmering quality of the blooms.

flowers of the bearded type, to which hardiness and ease of culture were sometimes sacrificed. The modern Iris, unlike the wild types, are tetraploid, with two sets of chromosomes, resulting in a doubling of all of the plant parts. But while the flowers are twice as large as older forms, there are fewer on a stalk. There is no doubt, though, that the appearance of these hybrids dazzled the gardening authorities of the day (early 1900s), one of whom likened their beauty to that of the sea: "Everything about it seems mutable and insubstantial as if it had been made by enchantment and might vanish by the same means" (A. Clutton-Brock, *Studies in Gardening*).

In fact, many of these shimmering beauties have vanished, despite their fine qualities, because of the fierce competition among the thousands offered and because what is new instantly supersedes what is "old." Where are the once celebrated Bearded types with the jaunty names: 'Kum-on' (1955), 'Plum Cute' (1963), and 'Sugar Pie' (1965)? Where is 'Patience' (1955), a shade of magenta that, according to aficionados, has yet to be matched by any other Iris? Fortunately the beautiful Siberian Iris 'Perry's Blue' (1921) is still available. "Whenever I see *Iris sibirica* 'Perry's Blue'," Mrs. King wrote in the 1920s, "I bless the name of Perry afresh."

Some of these Iris are known to exist in collector's gardens, but they are no longer in general circulation. This brings up a point that often vexes fans of antique Iris (and Roses as well as other groups of plants); the tendency of hybrids or strains to deteriorate over time, as the *inherent variability* in any genetic structure makes itself apparent in characteristics at odds with the distinctive feature of the named cultivar. Now, instead of,

say, a brilliant red, you begin to see a shade of pink, blossoms are fewer and smaller, and so on. In other words, the plant in question is no longer true to its name.

With seed strains, the process of keeping an old strain up to standard is called *reselection*. The name 'Shirley Reselected Poppies', for instance, indicates that the original Shirley Poppy strain, created by Reverend Wilkes from variants among wild Corn Poppies *(Papaver rhoeas)*, deteriorated over time. Perhaps there were fewer desirable flower types apparent in a group of plants grown from Shirley Poppy seeds; perhaps the wild form

ORRIS ROOT FIXATIVE

*T*o make your own potpourri fixative from the roots of the Florentine Iris is a lesson in patience, for it takes several years of ripening before the prepared roots can be used. But it's not difficult. Dig up rhizomes, separate, wash and dry, then chop them into small pieces. Place these on newspaper near a gentle source of heat to dry (I shove mine under the wood-burning kitchen range). Stir occasionally, and, when the chips snap sharply, store them in a container placed in a cupboard away from light. After a year or two of storage, when you notice a violet sweet fragrance, your orris root is ready to use in potpourri: Pre-scent the orris root with the desired essential oil (lavender or rose, for instance), using about 3 tablespoons of prepared orris root chips to 1 teaspoon of oil for every quart of dried flowers. Combine these in a small jar and let them blend for several days, shaking occasionally, then add the contents to dried petals: the whole mixture must then be seasoned in a sealed container for about 6 weeks, shaken occasionally, before the potpourri is ready. In this way the essential oil is bound to the orris root (absorbed by it then slowly released), so that the potpourri's scent is not dissipated when exposed to air. Prepared orris root lasts indefinitely if properly stored.

was becoming dominant. At some point, a nurseryman or seed company took great care in selecting the seed parents to ensure that the original characteristics that defined Shirley Poppies were reintroduced and preserved. The process of reselection is common among vegetable strains as well.

The problem of plant deterioration was suggested by Grant Wilson in his discussion of antique Glads. If the older Glads could be grown in their true form (as they looked when originally introduced), he felt they might compare very well with the newest introductions, but he did not think such specimens were in circulation, so the question was academic.

The situation with antique Iris is fortunately quite different. Although many old types have probably deteriorated in form as they have been passed from gardener to gardener, a few commercial collectors guarantee the authenticity of a number of historic Iris. I should point out that not every old Iris (or every old plant of any kind) has garden value, although all have value for the garden historian. One of the points made by those who have preserved all the American Dykes Medal winners since 1927 is that such exhibitions provide the opportunity to see the vast improvement in Iris breeding.

I was introduced to Iris through the far less complex ancient types closer to the wild when we moved to our backland farm and I found a sixty-year-old clump of Yellow Flag languishing by the kitchen door, promising much and delivering little—heaps of swordlike Kelly green leaves and, in early summer, small bright yellow flowers on 3-foot stems. I moved them twice before I found the perfect spot, or spots. The original population, having swelled under my tutelage to a horsedrawn wagonful of roots, was flung off by pitchfork into various damp, even boggy, areas in the hope of naturalizing them. I have seldom witnessed such a transformation in the plant world. It was as if each established clump, in sun or dappled shade, was saying "Thank you." Now, in early summer, they bloom, without any aid from me, in lovely yellow drifts among native violet-blue *Iris versicolor* and golden yellow Buttercups, with tiny wild blue Forget-me-nots at their feet.

Any of the Iris species can be naturalized in their favorite habitat—damp or dry ground—and by careful selection among the various hybrids, the Iris blooming season can last three months—April, May, and June, or from early spring through early summer. Plant dwarf or shorter types in rock gardens with Moss Phlox; group the Bearded types according to size and color, among low-growing plants such as Columbine and Lungwort, combined with Oriental Poppies (a favorite and always welcome combination) and the flowers of early summer: Dame's-rocket, Foxglove, and Lupines. If you begin collecting Iris types, you will want to consider separate beds to accommodate them. Consider planting Iris among Peonies and Roses, as well as Daylilies. The old Lemon Yellow Daylily and *Hemerocallis middendorffii* bloom at the same time as the Bearded types. For cut flowers, cut Iris when the first buds begin to unfold.

To Grow: Bearded Iris grow best in full sun and enriched, well-drained soil in Zones 3 to 10, except in Florida and along the Gulf Coast. Plant them from July (in the North) to early fall (in the South) by digging a hole, mounding the soil, and placing the rhizomes on top, 10 to 15 inches apart. Cover them so their tops are even with the soil's surface.

Fertilize the area around the planting in the spring with a low-nitrogen fertilizer and divide the plants when needed (every four or five years). Nonhybrid older types can be left undisturbed for many years.

To divide plants, dig up rhizomes after the flowers fade, shake off soil, and remove two-thirds of the foliage. Select two small rhizomes growing at an angle from the large one, cut them with a sharp knife, and reset them in the soil 6 to 8 inches apart.

Beardless Iris can be divided in late summer or early fall, but you will probably need a bulldozer to dig up established clumps of some types (like Yellow Flag and Siberian Iris). Japanese Iris roots work to the surface about every three or four years; divide the clump at this time. Cut back spent flowering stalks of all types, but let leaves ripen.

To grow wild types from seed, sow seeds when ripe or after six weeks of freezing. Germination should occur in two to four weeks in early summer. Shade seedlings during summer and keep them moist.

COLLECTOR'S CHOICE:
Spring-summer bloom; ❀ indicates especially fragrant types:

Iris cristata, Crested Iris (1850–1900). Useful as a ground cover in partial shade; early bloom; 3–4"; Zone 3.
'Alba'; white.
I. X germanica 'Florentina', Florentine Iris (1600–1699). Early bloom; 2½'; Zone 4. ❀
I. kaempferi, Japanese Iris (1850–1900). Likes lime-free soil and partial shade in warmer regions; needs moisture during growth and blooming but drier conditions later; late bloom; 2–4'; Zone 4.
'Asagira' (1930). Red-violet standards; blue-violet falls.

'Azure' (1919). Vigorous; double violet-blue flowers.
'Goldbound' (1885). Double white flowers with yellow veins.
'Kongo-San' (1900). Double dark purple flowers; extra-late bloom.
'Mahogany' (1893). Double dark wine red flowers.
'Rose Cavalier' (1950). White-rimmed violet-red flowers.
I. pallida 'Dalmatica', Sweet Iris, Sweet Flag Iris (18th century). Early bloom; wide leaves; 2'; Zone 5. ❀
'Variegata'; cream- and green-striped foliage.
I. pseudacorus, Yellow Flag Iris, Flower-de-luce (1600–1699). Sun or partial shade; plant along steams or ponds; late bloom; seedpods attractive; 3–4'; Zone 4.
I. sibirica, Siberian Iris (1850–1900). Bluish violet flowers; adaptable to soil and site but prefers moist soil and sun; very hardy; late spring-early summer bloom; 2–3'; Zone 3.
'Alba'. Elegant, white with yellow at petal's base; lovely among Hostas and Fringed Bleeding-heart in light shade, damp soil.
'Caesar' (1930). Dark purple flowers.
'Eric the Red' (by 1946). Wine red flowers.
'Helen Astor' (by 1942). Rose red flowers.
'Perry's Blue' (before 1920). Light violet-blue.
'White Swirl' (1957). White flowers.
I. versicolor, Blue Flag Iris (1776–1850). For poolside or wetland plantings; seedpods attractive; late spring bloom; Zone 3.
I. virginica, Southern Blue Flag Iris (1776–1850) Similar to *I. versicolor;* Zone 7.

Bearded Iris Hybrids:

TB=Tall Bearded, more than 28" tall, 4–8" flowers

BB=Border Bearded, up to 28" tall, 3–4" flowers

IB=Intermediate Bearded, 15–27" tall, 4–5" flowers

SDB=Standard Dwarf Bearded, 10–14" tall, 3–4" flowers; very free blooming

MDB=Minature Dwarf Bearded, up to 10" tall, 2–3" flowers or a little larger

Earliest to bloom are the MDB Iris, followed by the SDBs, then the IBs and TBs for April to June bloom.

'Amigo' (1934). **BB**; pansy coloring; light violet-blue standards; intense purple velvet falls edged with blue. "The form is much wider than most Iris of this time, very pleasing, and it has always been in my garden" (Verna Laurin, former secretary, Canadian Iris Society).

'Black Forest' (1945). **BB**; black as pitch (ebony/blue-black). "This is an oldie I would like to have' (Verna Laurin).

'Blue Denim' (1959). **SDB**; purplish blue with a bluish white beard.

'Blue Shimmer' (1942); **TB**; fragrant, large white flowers feathered blue. ✤

'Honorabile' (1840); **MDB**. yellow standard and fall; veined maroon red; historic plant.

'Jungle Shadows' (1960). **BB**; used as the standard for the type; slate gray standards flushed purple; grayish brown-tinged lavender falls.

'Ola Kala' (1943). **TB**; golden yellow.

'Wabash' (1937). **TB**; blue-white standards; blue-violet falls. "I have replaced a few older Iris that have disappeared over the years, but only if I felt strongly about them. 'Wabash' is in this group" (Verna Laurin).

'Zua' (1914). **IB**; icy blue; crepe-paper texture.

Several of these Bearded Iris have won medals in their class over the years. Three of them are among the top ten Iris (in popularity) according to Historic Iris Preservation Society surveys. These are #1, 'Honorabile'; #2, 'Wabash'; and #9, 'Ola Kala'.

Kalmia latifolia ✤

ERICACEAE

Mountain-laurel
American-laurel, Calico Bush, Ivybush, Spoonwood

INTRODUCED: 1700–1776
ZONES: 4–9
NATIVE
TYPE: Hardy Shrub
HEIGHT: 10'
BLOOM: Spring–Early Summer
SITE: Sun/Partial Shade/Shade

*M*ountain-laurel is one of North America's loveliest native shrubs, the only one of six *Kalmia* species to be cultivated in the garden. In its perfectly wild state, it needs no elaboration: showy clusters of fragrant, white cup-shaped flowers flushed pink, 6 to 8 inches across, held above handsome, glossy evergreen leaves. Even in bud this shrub has great charm. Buds are deep rose, a striking contrast to the pale flowers, and are composed of ten little pouches into which the stamens fit, held under tension until discharged by the opening of the flower, when the pollen is scattered "as though by a catapult," someone once observed. Mountain-laurel grows wild in the hills and mountains from New Brunswick south to Florida, and west to Ohio and Tennessee.

In 1748 when Peter Kalm, a Finnish pupil of Linnaeus, arrived in the New World looking for interesting flora, he found a genus already named in his honor. In 1786 Jefferson had *Kalmia* seeds or plants sent to France, and during the centuries that followed, it was widely cultivated in America, loved for its beauty, ease of culture, and accommodating, uncomplicated nature. "There is no shrub, foreign or native, that will exceed this in splendor," Joseph Breck wrote in his 19th-century catalog. Not only was Mountain-laurel garden-worthy, but as the common name Spoonwood suggests, its wood was used to make brush and chisel handles, as well as spoons and pipes.

As far as I can tell, Mountain-laurel has only two faults: the time required to propagate it and its inability to be easily transplanted. To transplant it, you must cut the whole bush down to the ground before moving it, and several more growing seasons are required to get it back in shape. At one time, due to its popularity, millions of plants were dug up from their native habitats and shipped by carloads to nurseries, where they were regrown to size, then sold. This practice has been largely replaced by the development of tissue culture, a propagation technique that is fast and requires very little plant material to produce many identical seedlings.

Some friends of mine inherited a planting—at least seventy years old—that continues to delight them every spring with its profuse blooms—a delight increased because they have done virtually nothing to encourage it. "The beauty of the flower," Gertrude Jekyll observed, "was always an unending delight." I can think of no other shrub that is so universally loved by both the experienced gardener and the novice.

When the glorious blooms have faded, Mountain-laurel is striking wherever it grows—as background for a perennial bed, as a specimen planting on the front lawn, by the side of the house, in a mixed shrubbery, or naturalized in a light woodland among Azaleas and Ferns. It can even be used to clothe bare banks or in any place that needs a handsome, long-season cover in bush form.

To Grow: Mountain-laurel prefers light, sandy, moist soil on the acid side (pH 4.5 to 6.0). It will grow, even thrive, in shade, but it produces more flowers in sun or light shade. Work peat moss into the soil when planting and mulch with 1 to 2 inches of pine needles, well-rotted oak leaves, or shredded bark. Pruning is seldom needed except at planting time or when moving the shrub, at which time the bush will have to be cut back to the ground. Propagation by the usual means is easy but slow. The best method (aside from tissue culture) is to take softwood cuttings, plant them in a peat moss and sand mixture, and overwinter them (protected) in a cold frame. Be patient. It will take several seasons before the cuttings can be planted out as shrubs.

COLLECTOR'S CHOICE:

Kalmia latifolia, Mountain-laurel (1700–1776).

Lathyrus latifolius

FABACEAE

Everlasting Pea
Perennial Pea

INTRODUCED: 1600–1699
ZONES: 3–10
NATURALIZED

L. odoratus ❀

Sweet Pea
Lady Pea, Painted Lady Pea

TYPE: Annual Flower/Perennial Tendril
    Vines
HEIGHT: 6–9'
BLOOM: Spring–Summer
SITE: Sun

Both species of *Lathyrus,* native to southern Europe, are climbing plants whose flowers are characteristic of the Bean Family to which they belong: a large upper petal *(standard* or *banner),* two side petals *(wings),* and two smaller bottom petals *(keel),* joined to resemble the prow of a ship. There the similarity ends. Perennial Everlasting Pea bears large rosy or white flowers almost in clusters, climbs to 9 feet, and grows as an escape from Indiana to New England and south to Missouri and Virginia. The species form has been improved by selection, but it has not been greatly altered.

Sweet Pea is a weedy annual that grows to 6 feet, with almost insignificant reddish purple flowers. Its culture is notoriously difficult, and its breeding has been raised to an art form. The Sweet Pea's exquisite perfume, preserved in the Latin epithet *odoratus,* sets this species apart from its scentless cousin and is responsible for the flower's almost mystical hold on generations of gardeners. Both vines climb by tendrils that attach themselves to any support.

Both Washington and Jefferson grew Everlasting Peas; Jefferson planted it (apparently the pink-flowered kind) in the oval bed at Monticello in 1801. Its popularity remained constant through the 19th and early 20th centuries, as long as arbors, fences, porches, and verandas needed clothing. Unsupported, it was valued for covering unsightly odd corners or slopes, where it makes a good show from spring through summer with almost evergreen foliage and faithfully returns each year with little encouragement. When climbing plants fell from fashion, Everlasting Pea found new homes along roads and at the edges of fields, a neglected garden escape. It is a shame, for this plant has much to offer—not only beautiful flowers over a long season and ease of culture but also adaptability, for if it is used with imagination, Everlasting Pea can be grown at the back of a perennial border, supported by stalks of tall perennials such as Elecampane or Globe-thistle. Some of the finest old cultivars are still available: 'White Pearl', with very large pure white flowers on foot-long stems, wonderful for cutting; and 'Pink Beauty', with cascading shell-pink flowers, perhaps the sort that Jefferson grew. The virtues of the Everlasting Pea have been overlooked for too long.

The story of the Sweet Pea, discovered in Italy in 1695 by an amateur botanist and monk named Cupani, is more complex. Although it was grown very early in American gardens, it was not seriously considered as an ornamental until improved by breeding, mainly in England in the 1800s. Hundreds of cultivars poured forth from individual breeders, who focused first on expanding the color range—shades of pink, purple, blue, crimson, violet, rose, orange, and white, as well as marbled and striped types—and then the size and shape of the bloom. The majority of Sweet Pea cultivars available during the late 1800s are attributed to Henry Eckford, a British flower breeder. The shape was changed most notably by the introduction of the wavy, ruffle-petaled Spencer strain introduced in 1901.

By the turn of the century, C.C. Morse Farms of San Francisco began breeding Sweet Peas, mostly scentless, that were better adapted to the North American climate, where summers are hot and dry. Burpee was the first to introduce the all-American 'Cupid', pure white and only 6 inches tall. However much modern cultivars have answered the needs of American gardeners, there remains the yearning to experience "The Essential Sweet Pea"—climbing, sweetly fragrant, and rather small-flowered—as generations of earlier gardeners knew and loved it, when the old hedge of Sweet Peas was the sweetest thing in the garden. "Oh, when the blossoms break ...like heavenly winged angels," wrote Celia Thaxter, "and their pure, cool perfume fills the air, what joy is mine."

If you want to experience this phenomenon, you can still grow Eckford and other old strains, several of which have been reintroduced due to the efforts of plant preservationists. 'Painted Lady' is a truly historic plant, the very first one named (1730): carmine and white bicolor ("Painted Lady" being a generic term to describe such color combinations), intensely fragrant, and climbing in the classic form. It was offered in J.B. Russell's 1827 seed catalog. When cutting the flowers for bouquets, follow Mrs. Wilder's sound advice to pick them "when the dew is still upon them. It is then that they are the sweetest and most refreshing to inhale. . . . If not gathered before 10 o'clock they should be left until evening."

To Grow: Everlasting Pea will grow in almost any well-drained soil, but prefers soil on the sweet side. It also prefers sun but tolerates partial shade. Add some horticultural lime or hardwood ashes if your soil is acid. Plant seeds outside in the late fall; they need freezing and thawing to break their hard seed coats. Give plants some support; their tendrils will cling to almost anything. Try Everlasting Pea as an all-season ground cover or, with a support of twiggy branches, grow it for a stunning effect in the back of the perennial border. However these plants are used, space them 18 to 24 inches apart. Pick spent flowers to encourage continued bloom. Propagate plants by division or by sowing fresh seeds.

To grow old-fashioned climbing Sweet Pea, begin your campaign the season before you want to grow it and remember that it thrives in rich, well-drained soil, in a cool, sunny spot. Scorching winds and blistering sun will kill it. The classic planting method is to dig a trench 1 foot wide by 2 feet deep and fill it to within 4 inches of the top with 40 percent loam, 40 percent manure or compost, and 20 percent sand. It wouldn't hurt to add a handful of bonemeal or high-phosphate fertilizer such as 0–20–20. Sow seeds early, by St. Patrick's Day if possible, a few every 12 inches. Press them down into the soil (they need darkness to germinate). Germination takes about fourteen days at 55 to 65°F (13 to 18°C) and is speeded by soaking seeds in tepid water for a few hours prior to sowing or by cutting off a small piece of the seed coat on the side opposite the growing point. If such seeds are sown ½ inch deep in sand, they will readily absorb water and germinate more rapidly. Keep in mind that red, crimson, and scarlet types bear the hardest seeds, while white, lavender, and mottled types produce softer, light-colored seeds that will decay in the ground unless germinating

The popularity of Everlasting Peas remained constant through the 19th and early 20th centuries, as long as arbors, fences, porches, and verandas needed clothing.

temperatures are optimum. If seeds are sown early, roots will be well established by the time the hot weather hits. In Zones 8 to 10, sow seeds in late summer or early fall for early bloom the following season. If you want to get a head start, sow seeds indoors in peat pots, plant cells, or any container where the roots won't be disturbed when planting out the seedlings.

Outside, when the seedlings are 2 inches tall, start filling in the trench, making sure there is enough soil around the young stems to give them support. Keep filling in the trench with enriched soil with each 2 inches of growth until the trench is almost filled to ground level. Leave a slight depression to gather moisture and mulch around the roots to protect them from hot, dry conditions.

Pinch back the topmost leaves when they reach 4 inches so they will develop side branches. Pinch back the first set of buds to encourage the development of more blooms on each stem. To make a screen of flowers, set 6-foot stakes in the ground 6 feet apart and stretch and secure netting from end to end. Plant Sweet Peas in a double row, on either side of the fence. Or omit the netting and tie strings to top and bottom wires, 1 foot apart, and train the plants on them. Tall, twiggy brush also can be used for support, as can chicken wire. For an interesting effect, sow the seed in a circle and provide support within (netting wrapped around three stakes, set as for tomatoes in a teepee shape). This will produce a mound of blooms in a bush shape. Pick spent blooms, as for Everlasting Peas, to promote long blooming.

COLLECTOR'S CHOICE:
Antique Sweet Pea strains are available from J.L. Hudson, Seed Savers Exchange, and Se-lect Seeds—perhaps elsewhere, too. All are very fragrant and 5 to 6 feet tall, except where noted.

Lathyrus latifolius, Everlasting Pea. Mixed colors.
'Pink Beauty' (before 1924).
'White Pearl' (before 1924).
L. odoratus, Sweet Pea.
'America' (1896). Silvery white striping on cherry red flowers like a raspberry sundae, yummy. First offered in the Morse-Vaughn catalog.
'Annie Gilroy' (1909). Cerise flowers from Eckford.
'Black Knight' (1898). A dark maroon Eckford hybrid.
'Blanche Ferry' (1894). Rose standard, pale pink wings; American-bred.
'Butterfly' (1887). J.L. Hudson offers this historic small-flowered Sweet Pea described as white streaked and flushed purple, very fragrant. Germination may take 1 to 3 weeks.
'Butterfly Hybrids Mixed' (old style). Striped and marbled; red, pink, mauve, and chocolate; lightly scented.
'Captain of the Blues' (1891). Deep mauve Eckford hybrid.
'Countess Cadogan' (1899). Violet standard with light blue wings from Henry Eckford.
'Cupani's Original' (historic). Close to the wildflower discovered by Friar Cupani in 1699; small bicolored flowers of purple and dark blue with intense scent.
'Cupid's' (old style). Similar to the 1897 first dwarf type. Pink and white with a mounding habit; can be grown in containers; 2'.
'Dorothy Eckford' (1903). An elegant pure white Eckford hybrid named for his granddaughter.

'Flora Norton' (1904). Clear blue flowers; a Morse-Vaughn American introduction.

'Henry Eckford'. Named for Eckford, this Sweet Pea is brilliant scarlet orange.

'Indigo King' (1885). Purplish maroon and blue bicolor, an Eckford hybrid.

'Janet Scott' (1903). American bred from Morse and Burpee with pearl pink flowers.

'Kink Edward VII' (1903). A brilliant crimson Eckford hybrid. Select Seeds suggests combining it with the navy blue 'Lord Nelson'.

'Lady Grisel Hamilton' (1899). Lavender and mauve Eckford hybrid, to 6', favored by Louise Beebe Wilder, mistress of scented flowers.

'Lord Nelson' (1907). A navy flower, introduced by House & Son.

'Miss Collier' (1907). Unusual all-cream flowers from Dobbie & Co.

'Nelly Viner' (1901). Wavy pink upper petals, a forerunner of Spencer types. 4'–5'

'Old Spice' (old style). Small, intensely fragrant; rose, red, blue, violet, and white; sometimes sold as 'Antique Fantasy'.

'Painted Lady' (historic 1737 strain). Pink and white bicolor, very scented.

'Prince Edward of York' (1897). A crimson and rose Eckford hybrid.

'Royal Mix'. An old, now rare strain of bright colors—reds, pinks, orange, white, and purples—bred from the Cuthbertson strain, which includes Spencer and an early-flowering American heirloom. Larger-flowered with longer stems than other antiques; drought-tolerant, too.

Spencer Hybrids (old style). Based on the wavy-edged Spencer theme, these are large flowers, to 2" across, on long stems for cutting, in mixed colors of red, purple, pink, mauve, blue, and white. Over 6' tall.

'Quito'. Close to the small-flowered wild Sweet Pea, this has maroon standard and mauve wings; found near Quito, Ecuador. J.L. Hudson advises nicking seed to speed germination, which will take 1 to 2 weeks.

Lavandula angustifolia ❀

LAMIACEAE

Lavender
English Lavender, Hardy Lavender, True Lavender, Spike, Spike Lavender

INTRODUCED: 1600–1776
ZONES: 4–8
TYPE: Perennial Subshrub/Herb
HEIGHT: 18"–3'
BLOOM: Early Summer–Midsummer
SITE: Sun

All the various names associated with hardy lavender—*officinalis, spica,* and *vera*—are synonyms of *L. angustifolia*. This hardiest of Lavender species is native to the western Mediterranean region. Growing from a woody base, its stems are clothed in slender, down-covered leaves—gray-green in their early growth and medium green with a grayish cast in maturity. In early to midsummer, small lavender, purple, or violet flowers (rarely white or pink) are carried in dense whorls of six to ten flowers on straight, broomlike spikes. Lavender belongs to a group of shrubby perennials, like sage, called subshrubs, which each year produce soft, herbaceous top growth from a woody base. Lavender's scent, better known than the plant, encompasses opposing notes of sweetness—like heliotrope and jasmine—and sharpness—like balsam and rosemary—that, when blended together, create a distinctive aroma, both stimulating and tranquilizing.

Lavender has been cultivated for millennia. Its genus name is derived from the Latin *lavare,* to wash, a reference to the Greek and Roman tradition of adding lavender scent to bathwater. Its essential oil was (and is still) used in perfumes, toiletries, and potpourri. According to 15th- and 16th-century English herbalists (Gerard, Culpeper, and Parkinson), Lavender was used outwardly— rather than consumed—for the relief of headaches and for "faintings and swoonings," as in the once-popular remedy known as "palsy drops." Lavender also enjoyed a reputation as an antiseptic, but its greatest use was for scenting stored bedding, especially linen. It was probably for this reason that it was brought to the New World with other "sweet herbs" like Mints, Pennyroyal, and Costmary. Still, Lavender's soothing properties were highly esteemed, for Helen Webster, writing in 1947, remembered being given steaming cups of Lavender tea as a child to treat a cold. "It was sugary and pink," she recalled, "and tasted just the way Lavender flowers smell" *(The American Herb Grower).*

Lavender was traditionally grown as a hedge. The 17th-century garden authority Leonard Meager pointed out a hedge had its practical uses, "to lay small cloaths upon to white and dry"— in other words, a lavender clothesline *(English Gardener,* 1682). Perhaps the pragmatic colonists took this suggestion

Lavender's scent, better known than the plant, encompasses opposing notes of sweetness and sharpness that, when blended together, create a distinctive aroma, both stimulating and tranquilizing.

to heart, but in New England they must have been disappointed by the difficulty of growing Lavender in its new home, where it was subject to winter damage. It continued to be grown for its herbal properties into the 18th century, but by the 19th century it was primarily regarded as a garden plant (no doubt the flowering stalks were often harvested to scent sachets and potpourri).

Lavender enjoyed a renaissance in the wake of the Williamsburg restoration, when all things colonial were of interest to Americans. In the early 1900s, two garden styles emerged from this preoccupation: Grandmother's Garden and the Herb Garden. In the first, everything considered "old-fashioned" was put to work for quaint effect. Lavender was grown to hedge beds of colorful flowers such as Hollyhocks, Canterbury-bells, and Foxglove.

In the Herb Garden, a wholly new genre in America, Lavender was grown with other aromatic herbs like Hyssop, Rosemary, Rue, Mints, and Artemisias in raised beds, geometric in form, with gravel paths between them and a sundial at the central axis. Such stylized plantings, designed to show off the subdued beauty of the plants within, has strongly influenced American herb garden design. On the plus side, many worthy plants that had been neglected after they were no longer of practical use—Rue, Artemisias, and Lavender itself—were rescued from neglect. But such a stylized design limited landscaping possibilities.

Helen Fox, a pioneer of the herb renaissance, was a curious gardener who explored a wide range of useful plants wherever she could get them (in the 1930s it might involve a worldwide search). In the Lavender line she grew many types, but the most successful were dwarf variants of *L. angustifolia*. Although people had been growing such types for centuries (Gerard commented on them), it was not until they were standardized as named cultivars and commercially produced that they became more widely available.

The first dwarf form Mrs. Fox grew was 'Munstead', developed by Gertrude Jekyll at Munstead Wood and introduced in 1916. It is characterized by compact growth, to 18 inches, with early-blooming, closely packed spikes of true lavender-blue over light green leaves. It is valued not only for its dwarf growth and long flowering, but for its hardiness—very important in harsh winter areas. Other types followed: 'Twickel Purple', blooming just after 'Munstead', is not quite as hardy, but it is beautiful, with fanlike spikes of soft purple above a mound of light green leaves; and 'Hidcote', a slow-growing type with lovely deep purple-blue flowers, blackish violet in bud, 18 to 20 inches, with narrow, silvery leaves. (There are now many cultivars of Lavender available, but these mentioned here are enduring classics.)

Such developments spurred the use of Lavender not only for low hedges, but for rockeries (Lavender's natural home), or to outline paths or blend with other perennials in a mixed herbaceous border. Lavender is a natural companion, with Baby's Breath, for soft pink Old Garden Roses like 'Queen of Denmark', a lovely in-the-ground bouquet. I grow the unadorned species in a raised bed of herbs and flowers, among Mallows, Rue, 'Silver King' Artemisia, Black Hollyhock, and sunflowers, where it is glorious in bloom and a lovely cool accent all summer.

To Grow: Many gardeners have difficulty maintaining Lavender even in areas where winters are mild. On the other hand, I've seen old plants that have survived many winters in northern Vermont, where winter temperatures can dip to 40 below. The secret of success is to find just the right spot. The soil must be sharply drained, loose, gritty, and neutral; the site must be sunny, but protected from strong summer winds and burning winter winds; and frost pockets must be avoided. A microclimate can be created when Lavender is planted by a wall. A stone wall in cool summer areas not only gives protection from wind, but absorbs the sun's warmth.

Lavender with hard, seasoned wood has the best chance of surviving harsh winter conditions because it is less susceptible to frost damage. Since it is a slow grower, it makes sense for gardeners in northern regions to buy plants rather than raise them from seed,

LAVENDER POTPOURRI

Collect flowers, a mix of Lavender with blue, pink, and silver flowers and foliage—Bachelor's-button, Mallows, some Rosebuds, 'Silver King' Artemisia—spread them out to dry out of bright light (they must be crispy dry), and when you have 1 quart, put them in a sealed container. Mix together 3 tablespoons fixative (orris root chips; see page 151) with 1 teaspoon lavender oil, place in a small jar, shake occasionally to blend for the next 3 days, then gently stir into the dried flowers. Seal the container, then shake it occasionally for 6 weeks to make sure the fixative blends with the flowers. It's now ready to use. When kept out of bright light, stirred, and sometimes covered, the potpourri should keep its scent for years. Place a small jar by your bedside, take several deep sniffs, and enjoy a good night's rest.

although this is easy to do. Barely cover seeds, supply bottom heat, and germination will be swift (a week or less in my experience). Plant out seedlings only when the ground has warmed, spacing them 24 inches apart all around, or 12 to 18 inches apart for a hedge. Seed-grown Lavender is variable, but usually worthwhile.

In the spring, cut back plants to new growth (wait until you see soft greenish sprouts emerging from the hard wood). Mature plants can be divided if their roots are carefully separated and replanted. Tip cuttings, taken early in the season before blooming, are the fastest way to make new plants. Cut 3 inches from the tips of the most vigorous growth and root cuttings in your favorite medium (I use potting soil amended with perlite and vermiculite). Sometimes Lavender can be left in place for many years, but with age it usually becomes a dense mass of woody stems with few blooms and dead patches.

Fungal disease can be a problem in hot, wet regions. Give plants plenty of air circulation, keep plants trimmed and open to the sun, and avoid dark, heavy mulches. Try Spanish Lavender in these areas (see Collector's Choice).

To Use: What can't you use Lavender for? It is currently enjoying popularity as a flavoring, as in Lavender ice cream, and as a seasoning in the Mediterranean herb mixture Herbes de Provence (lavender, thyme, fennel, basil, and savory). I sprinkle Lavender on cut-up potatoes, lightly brushed with olive oil, then roasted. It is prized above all in potpourri to scent rooms, and in sachets to scent linens.

To Harvest: On a sunny day, cut stems when spikes are just coming into flower (this is when they have the most scent), bunch them—not too thickly—and hang upside down in a cool place out of the light. Use flowers for cooking and scenting, leave stems for bouquets. Flower spikes are usually attached to floral picks when used in wreath work because the dried stems are brittle.

COLLECTOR'S CHOICE:

Lavandula angustifolia, Lavender (1600–1776).
'Hidcote' (before 1950). Medium-tall, to 2', with very dark purple-violet flowers; raised by Major Lawrence Johnston at Hidcote Manor, England; good dried color.
'Munstead' (1916). The ultimate hedge Lavender, to 18", with light purple-violet flowers; raised by Gertrude Jekyll, Munstead Wood, England.
'Nana Alba' (before 1938). Dwarf form, 1–1½', with white flowers and a neat habit of growth.
'Twickel Purple' (before 1922). Medium-tall, to 2', with long flower stems and purple-violet flowers; raised at Kasteel Twickel, Netherlands.
L. stoechas, Spanish Lavender, probably grown in southern regions for some time. This is the Lavender to grow where summers are hot and steamy (Zones 8–10). A beautiful type, to 2', with showy, deep purple top bracts like flags. In its native Mediterranean home, it grows wild between and among large rocks as if planted in a rockery. The oil is more camphorous, not as sweet as English Lavender.

Levisticum officinale ❧

APIACEAE

Lovage
Old English Lovage

INTRODUCED: 1600–1776

ZONES: 3–9

NATURALIZED

TYPE: Perennial Herb

HEIGHT: 5–6'

SEASON OF INTEREST: Nearly Evergreen
 Leaves

SITE: Sun/Partial Shade

Lovage originated in southern Europe and may grow to 6 feet in rich, moist soil, though it usually reaches 5 feet or less. The hollow stem in the center of the plant bears umbels of tiny yellowish flowers in early summer, while the main side branches bear shiny, dark green, deeply divided leaves—like celery on a grand scale—giving the plant a bushy appearance. Lovage has naturalized in the United States from Pennsylvania south to Virginia and west to Missouri and New Mexico. Its long, thick taproot seeks moisture and ensures Lovage an acceptable habitat under diverse conditions, provided there is a period of dormancy (freezing temperatures) in winter. Old English Lovage is a common name once used to distinguish this plant from Scotch Lovage (*Levisticum scoticum*), a plant of similar habitat and use. All parts of the plant are strongly aromatic, reminiscent of a strong celery flavor with a dash of Angelica.

Mrs. M. Grieve (*A Modern Herbal*, Dover, 1971) tells us that Lovage was never an official remedy for anything, but it does carry the epithet *officinale,* meaning, roughly, "from the drugstore." Those tireless English herbalists Gerard and Culpeper noted that the roots are good for "all inward diseases" and that the seed warms the stomach and helps digestion. Distilled Lovage water, they claimed, "cleareth the sight and putteth away all spots and freckles," is good for gargles, and helps break fevers.

The New England colonists were familiar with these uses and grew Lovage in their early gardens. Besides its medicinal properties, the aromatic seeds may be used to flavor confections, and the young stems and leaves can be eaten raw in salads. Even more important for the early settlers, these could be blanched to prolong their sweetness. At a time when fresh vegetables were hard to come by, Lovage provided an acceptable substitute, and it was easy to grow. Perhaps, too, the handsome leaves were admired for their own sake.

Lovage was mentioned in Samuel Stearns' *American Herbal* (1801), then, like so many once useful plants, disappeared from view until its many virtues were rediscovered by pioneering American garden historians and herbalists. Helen Webster observed it in the 1930s in a restored colonial garden in Marlborough, Massachusetts, the old Deacon Goodale farm, where the plantings showed "how the yarbs [herbs] might have been grown in the 18th century. It also reveals how truly beautiful an old yarb patch must have been" (*Herbs,* Ralph T. Hale & Co., 1942). There, Lovage grew in the back of a border along a winding path with Angelica, bordered by Scented Geraniums, Rosemary, and Mignonette. What contemporary gardener would not love to have a similar planting?

OYSTERS CASINO

*W*hen we get fresh oysters, we like to prepare this recipe. Place freshly shucked oysters on the half-shell on a bed of rock salt spread on a cookie sheet. Scatter bread crumbs lightly over the oysters, add a very small piece of bacon to each, then lightly sprinkle oysters with lovage flakes and paprika. Bake in a hot oven (475°F/250°C) until bacon is crisped. Serve with lemon wedges and dark beer.

We first grew Lovage nearly thirty years ago in our vegetable/herb garden. When we moved, we potted a few roots and gave the container to a friend for safekeeping, thinking no more about it. Our friend gave the potted plant to his mother, who shortly afterward won first prize for it in a local *flower* show. Evidently, the uses of Lovage as an ornamental are as versatile as its uses as an herb. I grow Lovage in almost full sun and moist soil as a background for potted brick red bedding Geraniums; in filtered shade it makes a handsome foil for Cowslips, white Bleeding-heart, and Daylilies. In another location, I make a great block planting for harvest. In early spring, as the reddish tips poke through the still-cold ground, I cut them off to flavor an eagerly anticipated spring salad of wild greens, in the best settler tradition.

To Grow: In frost-free climates, Lovage, like most perennials, can be grown as an annual. Elsewhere, plant the roots about 1 foot apart in rich, moist soil, in full sun or partial shade (partial shade is best in hot summer regions; otherwise the foliage will yellow). Seeds sown indoors at 60 to 70°F (16 to 21°C) take ten to fifteen days to germinate.

Seeds also can be sown in a cold frame during the summer and the seedlings planted out the following season. Established clumps can be divided (not a dainty job). Almost any little piece of root will grow into an identical plant as long as it is kept moist, either well watered or mulched. The long roots can be trimmed so they are equal in length to the top part of the plant. To maintain a healthy clump, cut it back when it flowers and make sure the ground is enriched enough to support regrowth later in the season. The second time around, Lovage will be more compact, its leaves remaining green for some time into the fall. The cut foliage and stems make very good mulch.

To Use: Lovage is an indispensable herb in our household as the basic ingredient in my all-purpose Herb Salt (a blend of Lovage with Parsley, Chives, and other herbs and spices), and as a seasoning in its own right, a terrific salt substitute to flavor all foods. You may have tried Lovage and found it too strong. That's because it needs to be dried first, and dried well so it retains its flavor . . . like celery with a hint of Angelica.

To Dry: Cut stems before plants develop a central seed stalk. Remove as many stems as possible, cut up the leaves, and put them to dry on a cookie sheet in a just-warm oven (no higher than 150°F/65°C). When crispy-dry, store them in a jar away from light and heat. For uniform flakes, rub the dried leaves through a strainer or homemade riddle (hardware cloth stretched across a frame). Use Lovage instead of salt on eggs in any form.

COLLECTOR'S CHOICE:
Levisticum officinale, Lovage.

Lilium spp. ❀

LILIACEAE

Lily

INTRODUCED: 1600–1900
ZONES: 3–10
TYPE: Hardy Bulb
HEIGHT: 1–7'
BLOOM: Spring–Fall
SITE: Sun/Partial Shade

*M*ore than eighty species of Lilies are native to Asia, Europe, and North America. Some of them have been very important in breeding the hybrids with which most gardeners are familiar (the Asiatic and Oriental hybrids, for instance).

Lilies grow from underground bulbs made of fleshy scales that lack the papery protective layer associated with Tulips and Daffodils. The showy, often fragrant blooms, whatever their form—trumpet, bowl, bell, or recurved (like a Turk's cap or turban)—or their position—out-facing, down-facing, or up-facing—grow on tough, wiry stems and have six petals and six prominent stamens surrounding a long pistil. To sort out the multiplicity of Lilies, complicated by hybridization, the Royal Horticultural Society has organized them into nine divisions based on flower forms and species derivation. These are discussed under "Collector's Choice" on page 166.

The first Lily grown by the Plymouth settlers in the 1630s was "the fair while lily," or Madonna Lilly *(Lilium candidum),* a cottage garden favorite for centuries and probably the oldest garden plant in the world. It could have been grown for nostalgic reasons or, more probably, for its ancient use in the preparation of an ointment ("stamped with honey"). This Lily's natural characteristics have rarely been combined with such perfection by the breeder's art: the stem rises from a rosette of green leaves close to the ground and bears at its top five to twenty intensely fragrant (like Honeysuckle) pure white trumpets, "within which shyneth the likeness of gold," a reference to the flower's golden-tipped anthers.

Other Lilies, easier to cultivate than the sometimes temperamental Madonna Lily, were soon introduced to American gardens, among them the Martagon or Turk's-cap Lily *(Lilium martagon)* from Europe, with pendulous purplish pink flowers, and the lovely native Canada or Meadow Lily, with drooping, funnel-shaped yellow or red flowers, common in wet meadows and bogs from southeastern Canada to Georgia. The latter was one of the first native plants to be exported to Europe.

By the 18th century, Jefferson was growing the ancient "Fiery Lily" *(Lilium chalcedonicum)* from Greece, described as one of the most thrilling reds in the garden. Jefferson, who seems to have had a penchant for bright red flowers, planted beds of these Lilies at Monticello.

Plant exploration reached a zenith of activity in the 19th century, reflected in the growing number of Lilies at the gardener's disposal, among them several fine native species later important in breeding programs: the Panther or Leopard Lily *(Lilium pardalinum)* from California, vigorous and variable, with down-facing Turk's-cap blossoms, crimson toward the petal's tips and brown-spotted and light-colored toward the center; and the American Turk's-cap Lily *(L. superbum)*, common in moist and acid soils from eastern Massachusetts to northwestern Florida and Alabama. The New World was obviously rich in Lilies.

Several introductions from Asia became very popular: Tiger Lily *(Lilium lancifolium)*, with strongly recurved pinkish orange flowers heavily spotted black and distinctive black bulblets that grow in the axils of the plant's glossy green leaves (by which means it naturalized as a garden escape when it was no long wanted), favored for its dependable beauty and resistance to drought and just about anything else, except as a carrier of a virus (to which it is immune) to other Lilies; the gorgeous Goldband Lily *(L. auratum)*, a striking fall-flowering type with large, fragrant trumpet flowers—ivory with broad yellow bands down the center of each petal and purple blotches on its inner surface; and Regal Lily *(L. regale)*, discovered in China by E. H. Wilson and first grown at the Arnold Arboretum in 1908. Growing to 6 feet, each stem of the Regal Lily bears as many as twenty large, fragrant trumpet flowers—white on the inside and rose-purple on the reverse. A strong competitor to the Madonna Lily in magnificence, it is easier to grow.

Although natural and intentional hybrids existed well before the 20th century, it was not until the 1920s that breeders pursued hybridization in earnest, in an attempt to produce more vigorous, disease-resistant, and easily grown types in a wider range of colors. Jan de Graaf, a great-great-grandson of Cornelis de Graaf, who began hybridizing Lilies in 1790, founded Oregon Bulb Farms in 1934. He was instrumental in taming the wild Lily and devising methods for the mass production of bulbs, making Lilies both attractive and affordable to the ordinary gardener, who no longer had to rely on expensive, sometimes diseased imported bulbs.

While it is probably true that hybrids cannot match the simplicity and elegance of wild forms, crosses between species and cultivars have resulted in generations of robust, beautiful Lilies. De Graaf's 'Enhancement', introduced in 1947, has remained one of the most popular Asiatic Hybrids (the type of Lily most commonly grown today). "It is the best garden lily I grow," observed Will Ingwersen *(Classic Garden Plants,* Hamlyn, 1975). "Its large head of bright red upturned flowers are carried on sturdy two-foot stems."

I first became aware of Lily-mania from my neighbor's daughter, Anne, who grew 'Enchantment' and other hybrids in the unpromising clay sod of northern New Brunswick. Having grown up on a farm barren of all ornamentation, she must have been drawn to the sensuous beauty and brightness of the modern hybrids that de Graaf's work enabled her to enjoy. Her letters were filled with news of her Lily gardens and often with Lily bulblets as well, which she urged me to raise up to maturity. Although she knew she might not live to see them, she had planted wild Lilies in the hope of naturalizing them in a stand of hardwoods, and with a gardener's optimism she wrote, "If they grow or not I'm hoping to try again . . . this spring." She died a few weeks later at thirty-two, as beautiful as any of the Lilies she loved.

Later, I discovered the "Old Red Lily," the same one dismissed by 17th century connoisseurs because it was in every country-woman's garden (Stuart & Sutherland). This is just where I found it, in a fabulous fifty-year-old hillside garden near Mahone Bay,

Nova Scotia. When I commented on its striking beauty—large fire-red, upturned flowers spotted black at their base, in showy clusters on 4- to 5-foot stems—my guide had said, "Oh, that's the "Old Red Lily, " so it wasn't until later, after comparing notes with other gardeners, that I was able to identify it as *Lilium bulbiferum* var. *croceum,* a hardy survivor in the area. In the way of all gardeners, I begged a few bulbs for something in return and now "it groweth in my garden," blooming just before 'Enchantment' in early July, with the first blue stars of Borage and white Bellflowers *(Campanula persicifolia).* What a wonderful thing it is to find the flowers that have outlived fashion still thriving, oblivious of their banishment. I love the "Old Red Lily" not only for its singular beauty, but because I know it can be relied on to return every year without fail. Once planted it is virtually indestructible because of its habit of forming bulb-bearing stolons at the base of its flat bulb, so even when disturbed, these have a good chance of surviving and taking root in the soil.

Native to the European Alps, *Lilium bulbiforum* is the Orange or Saffron Lily of history. A familiar garden plant throughout Northern Ireland because its flowering coincides with the victory of William of Orange in 1691, perhaps it was planted in Nova Scotia gardens for the same reason. Garden historian Ann Leighton described it as an old favorite, like the Tiger Lily, in 18th-century American gardens, noting that both Lilies were still able to take care of themselves. Since the "Old Red Lily" does not seem to be commercially available, look for it in an old garden.

Aside from naturalizing wild Lilies, all types are shown to advantage among shrubs—evergreens such as Mountain-laurel and Rhododendrons or deciduous shrubs like Mock Orange, Hydrangeas, and Azaleas. Classic combinations include Regal or Madonna Lily with Roses (especially the Cabbage Rose); Lilies paired with Climbing Roses; and Lilies mulched with low-growing plants such as Violas, Petunias, Columbine, and Forget-me-nots—a fulfillment of the old adage that "Lilies should grow with their feet in the shade and their heads in the sun."

Lilies are often most striking when planted in groups of one kind and one color to form a colony: Tiger Lilies, for instance, by a doorway; Regal or Madonna Lilies by a stone or brick wall; Canada Lilies along a streambank or at the edge of a woodland; Leopard Lilies rising among Maidenhair Ferns in filtered shade. Madonna, Regal, and Tiger Lilies adapt well to the conditions of an herbaceous border, as do any of the hybrids grown in groups among Lupines, Hostas, and Bellflowers.

To Grow: Lily culture is not difficult if you follow a few basic principles. The first and most important one is that Lilies require perfect drainage. My friend Anne grew hers in raised beds or on a natural slope, adding sharp sand and leaf mulch to improve the soil's tilth and discourage excess moisture. John Moe, an experienced Lily grower on the West Coast (Washington State), adds peat to his sandy loam to retain moisture. Any soil that grows good potatoes, de Graaf claimed, will grow good Lilies (meaning that the soil should be friable to at least a foot).

Lilies do well when planted in partial shade in warmer regions (afternoon shade is best), as long as they receive at least five to six hours of sun each day. Full sun in the North is recommended, or plants will be forever looking for it instead of producing flowers.

Plant Lilies in the fall or spring as soon as you receive them, because, lacking a protective papery coat, the bulbs will soon dry out. Set them 9 to 18 inches apart, depending on their height, and cover them with 4 to 6 inches of soil (1 to 2 inches for the Madonna Lily). A little bonemeal in the planting hole is okay, but no other fertilizer should be applied at this time. For lavish display, plant three to five bulbs per square foot.

When the shoots poke up out of the ground, spread fertilizer around the plants and water it in well. Advice varies as to which kind is best. John Moe uses 9–9–9 formulated for Roses and says "that works just fine for me." Lilies need this annual boost to produce many large flowers throughout their season of bloom. Let the leaves wither naturally, as for Daffodils, to help feed nutrients to the bulb. Remove spent blooms.

A mulch is necessary to keep the soil moist around Lilies. Use whatever you have at hand—wood chips, rotted sawdust, or even rotted manure. When the ground freezes, a mulch of coarse litter or evergreen boughs will protect the plants over the winter.

Do Lilies need staking? That depends on their site (if it's very windy, yes) and type. Most Lilies are sturdy if they are growing in self-supporting clumps. Otherwise, stake them with a circle of bamboo sticks held in place with string, or use individual stakes and tie a loop around the plant's stem in several places before looping and tying it around the stake (so the Lily won't choke to death).

In Zones 9 and 10 where winters are mild (above 40°F, or 5°C), dig up Lilies and refrigerate them for eight weeks to simulate winter rest—unless the plant nursery's instructions indicate otherwise.

Lilies can be left undisturbed for years, but if they lose their vigor, divide them. New plants are easily propagated from roots or stem bulblets. Replant them in a special bed, and don't expect them to bloom for two or three years.

A cutting garden may be a good idea if you want lots of bouquets, because cutting Lily stems is injurious to the plant's vigor (leave more than one-third of the stem when you cut the flowers). And please don't remove the anthers, as florists often do for cosmetic reasons. "Much of the beauty of the flower," wrote the eminent Lily authority George Slate, "is in the richly colored, delicately poised anthers."

The Lily divisions that concern us here are the following:

Division 1 (June bloom): Asiatic Hybrids; 1–6'; usually with upright flowers; easy to grow.

Division 2 (June bloom): Turk's-cap Hybrids, 3–4'; prefer neutral or acid soil and light shade.

Division 4 (late June or early July bloom): American Hybrids, mostly derived from West Coast species; these include the Bellingham Hybrids; 4–8'; good cut flowers.

Division 6 (July or midsummer bloom): Trumpet/Aurelian Hybrids from Asiatic species; 2–6'; very fragrant; trumpet or starburst form; sun or partial shade; hummingbirds love them.

Division 7 (August or late summer bloom): Oriental Hybrids; 2–6'; fragrant, very showy, orchid-like blooms; partial shade in the afternoon and slightly acid soil; disease-resistant; in warmer regions, plant these deeper than usual; in colder regions, mulch for winter protection.

Division 9: Wild types such as *Lilium candidum, L. auratum,* and *L. regale.*

COLLECTORS' CHOICE:

All sold as bulbs unless noted; ❀ indicates fragrant types; Division 9 unless otherwise noted.

Lilium auratum, Goldband Lily (1776–1850). Fall bloom; 4–6'; Zone 4. ❀

L. canadense, Canada or Meadow Lily (1600–1699). Prefers partial shade and leaf mold or humus-rich soil; July bloom; native.

L. candidum, Madonna Lily (by 1630). Prefers dry soil; plant in fall so it can establish its basal leaves; also decorative; June bloom; 3–4'. ❀

'Cascade'. Stockier, more disease-resistant strain; the work of George Slate and Oregon Bulb Farms; heady fragrance. ❀

L. lancifolium (L. tigrinum), Tiger Lily (1800–1850). Cultivated longer than any other Lily except the Madonna Lily; plant deep (7–9"); will grow in almost any lime-free soil; full sun best; August bloom; tolerates both dry and damp soil.

'Splendens' (1870). Larger-flowered than the species type; nodding, rich salmon red flowers with darkly spotted reflexed petals; awarded the Lily Cup for best spike of blooms at the Fifth International Lily Conference in London, 1989.

L. pardalinum, Leopard or Panther Lily (1850–1900). Easy to grow in the Pacific Northwest and northern California, its native habitat; July bloom; 4'; John Moe's favorite among the species.

L. regale, Regal Lily (1908). July bloom; protect shoots from late frosts in the spring; 5'. ❀

L. speciosum 'Rubrum', Rubrum Lily (1850–1900). Fragrant, pendant recurved white and crimson blooms; fall bloom; 5'; Zone 4. ❀

L. superbum, Turk's-cap or Swamp Lily (1776–1850). Magnificent native; 40 or more flowers per stem; likes moist loam; July bloom; 6'; Zone 5.

Hybrids:

Since John Moe made his recommendations, he has kindly shared his wonderful choices with me, and now they "groweth in my garden," too.

'Black Beauty' (1958). **Division 7**; outstanding; this Lily has won so many North American Lily Society popularity polls that it was moved to the Lily Hall of Fame; very dark red recurved flowers with a green star in the center, outlined in white, and white-edged petals; 50 or more flowers per stem; indestructible and vigorous; 5–9'; John Moe selection. ❀

'Citronella' (1958). **Division 1**; down-facing golden flowers covered with small black dots; as many as 30 flowers per stem; July bloom; 4–5'; John Moe selection and one of my favorites.

'Enchantment' (1947). **Division 1**; up-facing nasturtium red flowers; 2–3'; for Anne. Blooms with 'Citronella'.

'Moonlight' (1958). **Division 6**; chartreuse-yellow; 3–5'; John Moe describes the fragrance as "Exquisite, ambrosia."

'Mrs. R.O. Backhouse' (pronounced "Backus") (1921). **Division 2**; best known of the Martagon Hybrids bred by Mrs.

Backhouse, now rare; yellow Turk's-cap flowers flushed magenta-rose with slight spotting; 6'; John Moe selection.

'Shuksan' (1924). **Division 4**; the most famous Bellingham Hybrid; yellow flowers tipped with red and spotted black; needs perfect drainage and moist conditions during active growth; don't water when in flower; protect from winter rains (if there is no snow cover) by placing a flowerpot or tub over the plant; 4'. ❀

'White Henryi' ❀ (1945). **Division 6**; a magnificent Lily bred by Leslie Woodriff ('Black Beauty') with sunburst-type blooms—white with a pale orange throat and cinnamon-colored flecks in the center; hardy and disease-resistant; consistent winner in NALS popularity polls; 4–5'; John Moe selection.

Lobularia maritima ❀

BRASSICACEAE

Sweet Alyssum
Snowdrift, Sweet-Alison

INTRODUCED: 1776–1850
TYPE: Perennial/Hardy Annual Flower
HEIGHT: 3–12"
BLOOM: Late Spring–Fall
SITE: Sun/Partial Shade

Sweet Alyssum (formerly classified as *Alyssum maritimum*) is a perennial of Mediterranean origin, usually grown as an annual. Its honey-scented, tiny white flowers bloom in elongated racemes over small, narrow light green curved leaves for an extended period—all year where conditions permit—creating masses of mounded bloom spreading in a mat wider than the height of the plant (1 foot in the species form). As flowers fade, they leave behind a series of round pods, each containing one seed.

Introduced into late 18th-century American gardens, this profusely blooming little plant of easy and accommodating culture soon became very popular—indispensable for the front of the border and especially favored in the 19th century for massing with the annual Edging Lobelia *(Lobelia erinus)*, a combination first introduced into the gardening world in 1862 at Kew Gardens and one that is still going strong today.

In the 1930s Mrs. Wilder recommended planting Sweet Alyssum to edge broad walks and soften the rawness of the ever-popular Scarlet Sage *(Salvia splendens)*. The colored type she mentioned, 'Violet Queen' (a washed-out lilac), was apparently the only colored form available until the 1950s when two more were introduced: 'Royal Carpet' (1953), a dwarf form with deep purple flowers with a white eye, and 'Rosie O'Day' (1961), a dwarf form with light pink flowers. Both are still popular, and both have been All-American Medal winners (we tend to think they've been around forever). The favored white dwarf form is 'Carpet of Snow', introduced prior to 1926. Also introduced at that time was the now rare 'Little Dorrit', a bush dwarf form especially suited to pot culture.

Of all the types, nothing beats white Sweet Alyssum for fragrance—"drifts of sweetness," it has been called, like new-mown hay. It can be tucked into small pockets here and there between rocks (as it probably grows in its native habitat) or planted to spill out over the border and along walks, to fill in over spring-flowering bulbs, or to cascade from window boxes or planters of any type. The most beautiful and sprawling Sweet Alyssum I ever saw was a self-sown white type in a Zone 4 city garden, frothing over the side of an old dark brown bathtub, blooming away in late November. Sweet Alyssum is among those annuals resistant to frost and to temperatures below 25°F (-4C°), so even in the Northeast it blooms into early winter, a bonus for the northern gardener. In warm winter areas, it is unsurpassed for all-season bloom.

Turn-of-the-century literature mentions double flowers and even variegated leaves— "a variety much used for borders has paler and white-edged leaves" (Asa Gray, *Gray's School & Field Botany,* Ivison, Blakeman & Co., 1887)—both long since vanished from cultivation. But the improved Sweet Alyssum is bounty enough for any heirloom gardener.

To Grow: Sow seeds indoors four to six weeks before the last frost. Leave them uncovered to promote germination in seven to fifteen days at 60 to 70°F (16 to 21°C). (Sow thinly, since the germination rate is usually very high.) As early as possible, plant seedlings outside 4 to 8 inches apart, depending on the type. Or sow seeds outside two to three weeks before the last frost. Just scatter them on the ground; later thin the seedlings to the required distance. Sweet Alyssum thrives in sun but tolerates light shade. It prefers well-drained soil on the light side. If you shear the plants halfway back four weeks after blooming, their season will be extended and the spreading mat will not become too rangy. This is especially important to remember where summers are hot and the plants may bloom themselves out unless cut back. Plants can be moved in small clumps anytime during the season to fill in empty spots in the garden. Be sure to cut them back and water them well. To ensure a continuous sup-

ply of flowers on fresh mats of foliage, make a second sowing in early June. These plants are especially suited for winter bloom indoors if they are cut back and potted in early fall, or for very early bloom the following spring when planted back outside (see directions for wintering-over annuals on page 24).

If you grow cabbages, you can expect cabbage moth larvae to eat away at Sweet Alyssum. When this occurs, cut back plants and dust with rotenone.

In Zones 9 and 10, Sweet Alyssum blooms year-round and grows as a woody shrublet, which may need to be replaced periodically with fresh plants.

COLLECTOR'S CHOICE:

Lobularia maritima, Sweet Alyssum. Close to
    species form; fragrant; 1'.
'Carpet of Snow' (before 1926). Dwarf type;
    to 5"; spreading wide to 12".

Lonicera spp. ❀

CAPRIFOLIACEAE

Honeysuckle

INTRODUCED: 1600–1900
ZONES: 3–10
TYPE: Hardy Shrub/Twining Vine
HEIGHT: 5–50'
BLOOM: Spring–Fall
SITE: Sun/Partial Shade/Shade

Although several other plants are sometimes referred to as "honeysuckle," the term most aptly applies to the *Lonicera* species (named for a German doctor, Lonicer) and in particular to the Scarlet or Coral Honeysuckle *(L. sempervirens),* a beautiful native vine that grows from Connecticut to Florida and Texas. The genus is large—more than 150 species—and includes hardy, vigorous vines and shrubs, several of which are highly regarded for their profuse, usually fragrant blooms beginning in the spring and sometimes lasting all season. The showy trumpet- or funnel-shaped flowers vary from scarlet to yellow or white, grow in pairs or whorls at the ends of branches, and in some species are followed by decorative fruits. All are attractive to hummingbirds. The handsome leaves may be evergreen into the fall (longer in the South) or bronze.

"Honeysuckles," wrote Alfred Hottes, "twine through our memories of delicate fragrances. They typify to our mind the cooling influence of shade during the hot days of summer" (*A Little Book of Climbing Plants*, 1933). This is especially descriptive of the Scarlet Honeysuckle, which was grown by Washington and Jefferson, both of whom would have valued a cool bower in their hot summer climates, just as gardeners do today. Although other *Lonicera* vines were introduced later, the Scarlet Honeysuckle remained one of the most popular, particularly loved for its ease of culture; abundant, nearly evergreen, heart-shaped leaves; and continuous flow of lovely tubular flowers— bright scarlet on the outside, soft yellow on the inside—blooming their hearts out from June through August.

Occasionally, a plant "from away" found conditions in the New World so favorable that it made itself at home, growing where it liked across the land (the Kudzu vine is a cautionary tale). This was the fate of Hall's Honeysuckle (*Lonicera japonica* 'Halliana'), introduced by George Rogers Hall of Rhode Island, who practiced medicine in China in the late 1840s and is credited with the greatest number of 19th-century introductions from the Orient. His Honeysuckle is widely naturalized in the mid Atlantic states and elsewhere, but its commonness should not obscure the fact that it is "one of the aristocrats of the garden," according to the discerning Henry Mitchell. Its white trumpets, mellowing with age to buff yellow (its Chinese name means "gold and silver flowers"), delicate fragrance, and bronze leaves in the fall certainly merit this well-earned reputation.

In the 19th century, Hall's Honeysuckle was virtually synonymous with the vine-covered veranda or porch, as its foliage rapidly makes a dense cover. The Honeysuckle's ability to draw nourishment from the sun to grow abundant leaves that forbid the sun's entry is one of nature's most wonderful designs. My husband remembers when he and the neighborhood kids would gather by his porch to suck the sugary nectar from deep within the flowers of Dr. Hall's Honeysuckle vine.

Several fine species of *Lonicera* shrubs, not to be outdone by the virtues of the hardy, vigorous vines, were introduced during the 18th and 19th centuries. Foremost among them is the Tatarian Honeysuckle or Bush Honeysuckle (*L. tatarica*) first grown by English gardener and writer Philip Miller in 1752, from seeds obtained from Siberia. It is probably the easiest shrub in the world to grow (it grows on dumps, my local wildflower guide reports), but it is no less desirable for the most discriminating shrub authorities. It is "one of the best of all hardy ornamental woody shrubs," Donald Wyman noted, with no further recommendations being required.

I found three bushes of Tatarian Honeysuckle (white, pink, and dark red) growing in a well-kept vintage 1920s shrubbery, among Hawthorns, Spireas, Hydrangeas, and Roses—all soon to be sacrificed to one of the "Big Ds" in our area (a deck—on which no one ever sat, as far as I could tell). I vividly recall the Honeysuckles at their height of bloom: profuse funnel-shaped flowers literally covered with foraging bees, eager to fill up on an early source of nectar during the shrubs' brief blooming period (about two weeks). I found more specimens in a nearby abandoned garden. Although their flowers were spent and they had not been pruned for at least twenty years, they were still handsome, an effective background (I imagined) for the ruined garden in their midst (Daffodils, Bleeding-heart, and Peonies). A 19th-century judgment still rings true today: "Old and common, it still takes the front rank among ornamental shrubs. . . . were we to have but one, we would probably choose the honeysuckle."

Plant shrub types in a mixed border, where their brief bloom will be superseded by later-flowering Roses, Hydrangeas, and Viburnums; as a screen (a single specimen will attain 9 feet or more); or as a focal point for a flower garden, where their green leaves will help show off perennials such as white Lilies. The twining vines need the support of a trellis, arbor, fence, or wires. Hall's Honeysuckle, left to its own devices, will cover steep slopes or banks or wherever it is needed as a dense ground cover.

To Grow: Honeysuckles of all types grow well in open, sunny spots, but all will tolerate partial shade (Hall's Honeysuckle grows well in shade). Make generous planting holes, mound the soil, drape the roots over it, fill in the hole, tamp down the soil, and water well. A seasonal dressing with well-rotted manure or compost is sufficient. For shrubs, prune out the oldest branches to let in light and renew vigor. With the early-blooming Tatarian, it's better to prune after the fruit is shed. Hardwood cuttings root readily at any time. Plant vines 3 feet apart to cover banks or 6 to 8 feet apart to romp over fences, arbors, and porches. Vines readily root where they touch the ground. In early spring, prune out old and hardwood branches.

COLLECTOR'S CHOICE:

Lonicera × *heckrottii,* Everblooming Honeysuckle (before 1895). Of uncertain origin; carmine buds; fragrant rose-pink trumpets with soft yellow inside; a vinelike shrub; scent released in the evening; well suited to the smaller garden; June bloom until frost; fairly resistant to the honeysuckle aphid; to 5'; Zone 4.

L. japonica 'Halliana', Hall's Honeysuckle (before 1860). Twining vine; white to buff trumpets; evergreen or bronze leaves; black berries; 12–15'; Zone 4.

L. sempervirens, Scarlet Honeysuckle (1600–1699). Native twining vine; scarlet-orange trumpets; red berries; mid-June to August bloom; fairly resistant to the honeysuckle aphid; to 50'; Zone 3. 'Dropmore Scarlet', a modern introduction bred in Canada, is a dwarf form, suitable for tighter places, even containers, but it still benefits from support.

L. tatarica, Tatarian Honeysuckle (1752). Pink-white flowers; red berries; spring bloom; resistant to the honeysuckle aphid; 9'; Zone 3.

'Arnold's Red' (1945). Originated at Arnold Arboretum; dark red; very resistant to the honeysuckle aphid.

Lunaria annua/L. biennis

BRASSICACEAE

Honesty
Money Plant, Moneywort, Moonwort, Penny Flower, Satin Flower, Silver Dollar, Silver Penny, Silver Plate

INTRODUCED: 1600–1750
ZONES: 4–10
TYPE: Biennial Herb
HEIGHT: 2–3'
BLOOM: Spring
SITE: Partial Shade/Shade

*A*lthough native to central and southern Europe, Honesty is naturalized throughout the temperate regions of the world. Now described by the epithet *annua,* it is, in fact, a biennial. The first season it produces a basal rosette of heart-shaped, scalloped leaves. The second season, four-petaled flowers in phlox-like clusters of bright purple (rarely white) bloom before the plant has achieved its mature height. Honesty's claim to fame comes later, when the plant has grown up to 3 feet tall and its seed pods have formed on branching sprays. When the dull outer coverings holding the seeds are rubbed off, they leave behind an unbroken, translucent, moon-shaped membrane whose shape and brilliance are reflected in the plant's Latin genus name and many descriptive folk names.

Honesty was already growing wild in England when Gerard described it in the 16th century. Aside from its decorative pods for winter bouquets—always in demand—its white tapered roots could be eaten like a vegetable, boiled or raw (Honesty belongs to the Mustard Family). Ann Leighton passed on an apocryphal story about the Pilgrims, that Honesty was the only plant they brought with them—meaning they were ill-prepared for the rigors they would face in the New World.

There are two schools of thought regarding Honesty as a garden plant: One is that its flowers have no value; the other is that Honesty's early spring bloom is welcome, especially in northern climates. Jefferson belonged to the first group: "Lunaria still in bloom," he recorded in his garden book on April 25, 1767, "an indifferent flower." But then he had many other blooming plants in his warm Virginia garden, including crimson Sweet-William, Virginia-bluebells *(Mertensia),* and the native Eastern Columbine *(Aquilegia canadensis).*

Gertrude Jekyll, responsible for so many choice cultivars, raised white-flowered Honesty and 'Munstead Purple', a good deep color. Margery Fish thought it worthwhile to grow as many types as possible, including those with variegated leaves. Steve Bender reports from the South that "Money Plant" is among the rarities grown for its pods, rather than its flowers *(Passalong Plants).* My own feeling is that Honesty (which I call "Silver Dollar") is a very acceptable spring flower, and I would love to have the white form. Honesty blooms here in May under an old white Lilac, among the ivory bells of Solomon's Seal *(Polygonatum)* and a nearby carpet of Sweet Woodruff. I don't know where it came from, but I know it's here to stay. I let only a few stalks produce ripe seeds; otherwise I would have carpets of Honesty seedlings in the spring. On the steepest part of a slope I let it go its own way. All through the winter months when I pass by on the way to the barn, I am cheered by the transparent moons that appear to be climbing up one side of an old apple tree. And, of course, in late fall I slip off the dried outer coverings of the seedpods I have gathered, and in the traditional way since the time of Gerard and probably before, I arrange clusters of Moon-flowers all about the house to lighten the winter months.

To Grow: Sow the round, dark seeds by midsummer in damp ground (Honesty will grow in full sun if the ground is evenly moist). The following spring space plants 12 to 15 inches apart. Once they have established themselves they will self-sow readily. If this becomes a problem, cut back some of the plants before seedpods mature.

To Use: It's best to separate stems outside when you are gathering them for drying. If you cut back the whole branching plant to dry, stems become difficult to disentangle. Bunch and hang them upside down in a cool, dark place. When they are dry, gently rub off the outer coverings on either side of the pod. You will be amazed by the pod's transformation. The seeds that fall out can be saved and dried. Sprays of Honesty are beautiful alone or mixed with other dried pods and flowers. I like to combine Honesty with dried Poppy pods in dark hues. When I'm done sorting dried sprays, I use short leftovers in dried Artemisia 'Silver King' wreaths, where they glow on its silvery background.

The late herb authority, Gertrude Foster, ate some of the root just to see what it was like . . . "mild, large radishes" *(Park's Success with Herbs).*

COLLECTOR'S CHOICE:

Lunaria annua, Honesty (1600–1750). Purple flowers.

'Alba'. A white-flowered selection. Very choice.

'Variegata'. Cream-edged foliage on second-year plants (perhaps not all of them); the variation might not appear until the plant flowers, so be patient. Variegated types are available with either white or purple flowers.

L. redeviva. A perennial Honesty with fragrant, purple flowers, but the pods are smaller, not as showy as the biennial. Seeds should be sown outdoors in the fall (they need fluctuating temperatures to germinate).

Lupinus polyphyllus

FABACEAE

Wild Lupine
Purple Lupine, Washing Lupine

INTRODUCED: 1827–1900
ZONES: 3–9
NATIVE

Russell Hybrids

Garden Lupine

INTRODUCED: 1937
ZONES: 4–9

TYPE: Hardy Perennial Flower
HEIGHT: 5'
BLOOM: Summer
SITE: Sun/Partial Shade

Wild Lupine is one of ninety species native to western North America (California and British Columbia), but it is widely naturalized along roadsides from Prince Edward Island and Nova Scotia south to New England. The tall, stout 5-foot stalks, with the last 2 feet densely packed with pea-like flowers—shades of bluish purple, red to pink, and white—grow from a rosette of deeply divided leaves, shaped like the palm of a hand, and from a long taproot. Some species are said to be poisonous to cattle, perhaps the source of the genus name, from the Latin *lupus,* meaning "wolf" or "destroyer of the land"—not a pretty description for such an attractive wildflower. In the hybrid form, the color range includes yellow, red, orange, and bicolors, and the plants are shorter, stockier, and more short-lived.

Wild Lupine was discovered in British Columbia in 1825 and offered soon thereafter to the American gardening public in J.B. Russell's 1833 seed catalog, where it was described as "new and rare." It soon became a popular garden plant, highly valued for its relative ease of culture and showy spikes of flowers in early summer. The color range, from selection and crossing of wild strains, included white, rose, purple, and bicolors.

Several other species of Western Lupines were added to the plant pool in the 19th century. Among these were the Tree Lupine *(Lupinus arboreus),* a tall, shrubby plant growing to 5 feet, with many small spikes of pea-like flowers that are often yellow but also white and mauve. In Britain, hybridization to broaden the Lupine's color range probably began by crossing *L. polyphyllus* with *L. arboreus,* culminating in the work of George Russell of York, who by crossing and recrossing desirable color strains over a period of

ten to fifteen years finally began to achieve his goal. His Lupines were greatly admired by all who saw them and were the occasion for lavish words of praise by the Royal Horticultural Society when the flowers were exhibited in 1937, winning the coveted Gold Medal.

"My first impression was indescribable," wrote D.W. Simmons, one of the judges. "Never before have I seen such marvelous colouring, or been thrilled by such exotic blendings . . . self-colours in rich pink, orange-yellow, strawberry-red; bi-colors of royal-purple and gold, apricot and sky blue, rose-pink, and amethysts, and dozens of intermediate shades and combinations on hundreds of massive spikes."

And what became of the native wildflower, once so popular in American gardens? I gained an insight into its history throughout the Northeast, where it is commonly seen along roadsides, on banks, and in fields in early summer. I had always assumed these were garden "escapes," but I observed locally that they are often planted deliberately. On a visit to the Alexander Graham Bell estate to find remnant plantings of old ornamentals, I had the opportunity to discuss Lupines with Dr. Graham "Sandy" Fairchild of Hollyhock dollies fame, and a highly respected medical entomologist. He and his sister confirmed the truth of what had appeared to be an apocryphal story regarding how their famous father, David Fairchild, had planted Wild Lupines along the roadsides, thus introducing them to the area. Sandy described in detail how his father heeled the seeds into the soil (making a depression in the soil by digging in one's heel, then using the whole foot to cover the seed over with soil after it is planted). Mrs. Fairchild also tossed seeds out the car window. They planted not only *Lupinus polyphyllus* but other Western species as well, none of which has survived. But in early July, the roadside areas are spectacular for the great drifts of Wild Lupines in various shades —bluish purple, pink, bicolored, and white.

I had always wondered why the hybrids seem to "run out," or revert to the wild bluish purple color. Sandy Fairchild explained that the hybrids are not as hardy as the wild species; the various strains that produce the incredible color range eventually die out, leaving the field clear for the more vigorous wild type, which is predominantly bluish purple. He also explained why the wild species thrive on roadsides and barren banks (unlike the hybrids, which require richer soil). They prefer disturbed areas where nothing else will grow, so once they find a habitat to their liking, they take it over, much to the delight of those who enjoy seeing the great spikes of bloom, usually from a passing car. Because of their vigorous growth in these circumstances, many people assume that Wild Lupines are very easy to grow and thus are frustrated by their failure when the seeds they plant—as Dr. Fairchild did, simply by heeling them in—fail to germinate. Choice of the Wild Lupine's preferred habitat—barren slopes—is the secret to its success.

If you are content to let them reign supreme, naturalize a colony of Wild Lupines where you know they would like to grow. The seed stalks and the foliage have a long season of interest. And who needs to be told the value of the Russell Lupines in the garden? Their gorgeous stalks rise above early summer flowers. On either side of the pergola at the Bell estate, Lupines still bloom among old Lemon Yellow Daylilies and white Siberian Iris, in borders that have long been neglected. In my own garden, in sun or partial shade, Russell Lupines grow with Oriental Poppies, Sweet Cicely, Dame's-rocket, and Mountain-bluet. The distinctive tall clumps of leaves are attractive all season long, and the long flower spikes make excellent cut flowers.

To Grow: Wild and Garden or Hybrid Lupines thrive where summers are cool and moist: New England, the Canadian Maritime Provinces, and the Pacific Northwest in Zones 8 and 9. Hybrid Lupines are hardy to Zone 4, but they are short-lived relative to Wild Lupine. Wild Lupine, though hardier, is more specific in its growth requirements: dry, light soil, and full sun. For best success with seeds, freeze them for two days, soak them in hot water overnight, then plant them outside, where germination should occur in fourteen to twenty-one days at 55°F (13°C). An easier way to establish Wild Lupine by seed is to nick the seeds with a file, then heel them into the soil in the fall. Germination should occur the following spring. Or sow seeds in a cold frame in the fall—no soaking required—where they will germinate the following spring. They also can be grown by digging up basal rosettes from an established population when the plants are dormant in very early spring. These should bloom the first season after transplanting. An established population growing in a favored habitat can be left undisturbed indefinitely.

Plant roots of the Russell Hybrids about 18 inches apart in well-drained, neutral or slightly acid soil, in sun or light shade. Scratch in bonemeal around the clumps in early spring to ensure the production of many flower spikes. Cut back the spikes after blooming for a second, sparser bloom in the fall. You can propagate these Lupines by seed (as for Wild Lupines), but to retain the most highly prized strains, take 4- to 6-inch stem cuttings in early spring, making sure a bit of the crown (top of the root structure) is attached. These should flower the following season. Clumps should be divided every three or four years in the fall, when the plant is dormant. The taproot is very long, but it can be trimmed before replanting if the top growth is cut back in equal proportion. If you plant these Lupines in an exposed, windy location, staking may be required.

COLLECTOR'S CHOICE:

Lupinus polyphyllus, Wild Lupine. Mixed shades.

'Russell Hybrids Mixed'. Pink, salmon, yellow, red, blue, white, and bicolors.

The following choice cultivars are offered in the spirit of the original Russell Hybrids:

'Chatelaine'. Pink bicolor.
'My Castle'. Red shades.
'Noble Maiden'. Pure white.
'The Chandelier'. Yellow shades.
'The Governor'. Marine blue bicolor.
'The Pages'. Carmine red shades.

Lychnis chalcedonica

CARYOPHYLLACEAE

Jerusalem-cross
London-pride, Maltese-cross, Red Champion, Scarlet-lightning, Scarlet Lychnis

INTRODUCED: 1600–1699
ZONES: 3–10
NATURALIZED

L. coronaria

Rose Campion
Constantinople, Dusty-miller, Flower-of-Bristol, Flower-of-Bristow, Lampflower, Mullein-pink, Nonesuch

ZONES 3–10
NATURALIZED

TYPE: Perennial/Biennial Flower
HEIGHT: 2–3'
BLOOM: Summer
SITE: Sun/Partial Shade

Although both are members of the Pink Family, Jerusalem-cross and Rose Campion are quite different in appearance, at least to the untrained eye. Jerusalem-cross, a perennial native to northern Russia, bears a brilliant head of scarlet or orange-red, 1½-inch flowers—distinctly cross-shaped and very similar in form to the Maltese cross, once a knightly emblem. The plant grows to 2 feet on stout, erect stems with coarse, clasping green leaves. The biennial Rose Campion bears magenta or fuchsia (purplish red) flowers along branched stems with narrow, spear-shaped leaves. Both the stems and leaves are noticeably covered with a whitish wool that gives them a silvery gray appearance similar in their early growth to Lamb's-ears *(Stachys)*. The 1-inch flowers are flat—five broad, slightly overlapping petals, similar in form to those of Phlox—and are borne singly rather than in clusters. Rose Campion is native to southern Europe and, like Jerusalem-cross, is naturalized locally in North America. The genus name is derived from the Greek *lychnos,* "lamp," a reference to the brilliance of the flowers.

Alan Dorey

Brian Oke/Giselle Quesnel

APRIL – JUNE

Alan Dorey

(TOP) Pheasant's
Eye Narcissus,
Narcissus poeticus
var. *recurvus*

(BOTTOM LEFT)
Purple Foxglove,
Digitalis purpurea

(BOTTOM RIGHT)
Cowslip,
Primula veris

APRIL – JUNE

(TOP) Naturalized *Narcissus*

(BOTTOM LEFT) Policeman's-helmet, *Impatiens gladulifera*

(BOTTOM RIGHT) Johnny-jump-ups, *Viola tricolor*

MAY – JUNE

(TOP LEFT) Musk Mallow, *Malva moschata,* and Opium Poppy, *Papaver somniferum*

(TOP RIGHT) Love-in-a-mist, *Nigella damascena*

(BOTTOM) Lavender, *Lavandula angustifolia,* and Creeping Thyme, *Thumus praecox* spp. *articus*

JUNE – JULY

(LEFT) Hollyhock, *Alcea rosea*
(TOP RIGHT) Elecampane, *Inula helenium*
(BOTTOM RIGHT) Elderberry, *Sambucus canadensis*

(TOP) Jackman Clematis,
Clematis jackmanii

(RIGHT) Author with
Climbing Rose 'Excelsa'
and Pink Rambler Rose

(BOTTOM) Rugosa Hybrid
Rose, 'Blanc Double de
Coubert'

JULY – AUGUST

(TOP LEFT) Hollyhock Mallow,
Malva alcea 'Fastigiata'

(TOP RIGHT) Persian Yellow Rose,
Rosa foetida persiana

(BOTTOM) Rugosa Rose, *Rosa rugosa*

Alan Dorey

Alan Dorey

JULY – AUGUST

Alan Dorey

(TOP) Nasturtium, *Tropaeolum majus*

(BOTTOM LEFT) Phlox, *Phlox paniculata*

(BOTTOM RIGHT) Golden-glow, *Rudbeckia laciniata*

AUGUST – SEPTEMBER

(TOP) Bee Balm, *Monarda didyma*

(BOTTOM LEFT) Butterfly Weed, *Asclepias tuberosa*

(BOTTOM RIGHT) Texas sage, *Salvia coccinea* 'Lady in Red', and Signet Marigold, *Tagetes tenuifolia* 'Lemon Gem', growing in an old wheelbarrow.

Jerusalem-cross was common in English gardens by the 16th century. Contrary to the folklore that surrounds it, and which its name suggests, Jerusalem-cross does not grow in the Holy Land and was probably not introduced by returning Crusaders, who were often given credit for plant introductions in lieu of any other evidence. By 1629, a double red or scarlet form was known, as well as white and blush singles. By 1772, a double white form was grown. Virtually nonexistent by the 1920s, it may still grow somewhere. Both it and the double red are high on many heirloom plant collectors' wish lists.

Rose Campion was known as a garden plant by the mid-14th century in Europe. By 1597 the white type was also being grown, but rarely. By 1614 the double magenta Campion was introduced, and by 1615 the double white, which by the 18th century had almost displaced the singles. Today gardeners are offered the single white or magenta, as well as 'Oculata', a rare type with a purplish red eye, perhaps known since the 17th century.

Both Jerusalem-cross and Rose Campion were favorite flowers in early American gardens. Jefferson grew Jerusalem-cross at Monticello, where it was planted in the oval bed in 1807. Rose Campion bloomed in 1767 at Shadwell, his birthplace.

By the end of the 19th century, these plants were regarded as "old-fashioned" types, fondly remembered by Alice Morse Earle in her chapter on New England "Front Door—yards" in *Old-Time Gardens* (Macmillan, 1901). She recalled the sorts of flowers one would find in these simple yet pleasing plantings: "ample glowing London Pride" (*Lychnis chalcedonica*) grew among Daylilies, "Flag" Iris, and Canterbury-bells. She described these enclosures, hard-won from the forest, as emblems of the women's world in earlier days—narrow and monotonous. Yet it was a world easily satisfied by small pleasures, as reflected in those carefully cultivated gardens, pleasant to the home and "no mean things."

Though called "London-pride" in Joseph Breck's catalog, I had never heard Jerusalem-cross referred to by that name until an old-time gardener repeated the name when she gave me a clump of *L. chalcedonica* from her garden, along with some of her cherished beauty, Rose Campion, which she had kept going for fifty years. I soon discovered so many other "London-prides" that I concluded it is a generic term for many older favorites.

I have found folk gardeners less intimidated by Jerusalem-cross's brilliant color than are contemporary gardeners, who are often afraid of offending sensibilities by planting it near the varicolored flowers of early summer and midsummer. But it blends surprisingly well with soft pink Musk Mallow *(Malva moschata),* Lupines of all sorts, Siberian Iris, Bellflowers, Foxglove, the lilac-white plumes of Clary Sage, and the yellow daisy-flowered Golden-Marguerite. One is often advised to banish Jerusalem-cross to the safety of low-growing evergreens, where its glowing color will be reduced or neutralized. Consider that Gertrude Jekyll, the mistress of color in the garden, grouped it among orange Daylilies, Dahlias, Marigolds, and Nasturtiums.

The magenta-fuchsia flowers of Rose Campion also blend well with the flowers of early summer and midsummer, the only caution being not to plant it next to its bright red cousin. Its distinctive gray foliage beautifully offsets its brilliant flowers and remains ornamental all season, providing a dramatic contrast to almost any flower in the vicinity. The white-flowered form, with its pristine blooms, is welcome throughout the border, planted in generous drifts among the dark pinks, blues, and purples of Bellflowers, Lupines, Roses, and, later, Monkshood. Both Jerusalem-cross and Rose Campion (or its white form) are excellent cut flowers. The silvery foliage of Rose Campion is so beautiful in its own right that I am tempted to prevent it from sending up its flowering stems by keeping plants cut back.

To Grow: Jerusalem-cross and Rose Campion can be grown in Zones 3 to 10 except in Florida and along the Gulf Coast. Seeds can be sown indoors in midwinter and planted out in the spring after all danger of frost has passed. Jerusalem-cross may bloom the first year but won't produce many dense clusters until the following year. Seeds of either may also be sown in a cold frame and the seedlings planted out the following spring, 12 to 15 inches apart. Jerusalem-cross prefers rich, moist soil and full sun, although it will grow in partial shade in warmer growing regions. In the Northeast or in colder areas, it is especially important to make sure that the soil is moist but well drained. The established clumps do not need dividing for many years.

Rose Campion (or its white form) needs full sun and light, perfectly well-drained soil. If left to its own devices, it will self-sow with abandon, since it is a short-lived perennial or biennial that must seed prolifically to ensure its survival. In the garden, it's best to control this inclination by cutting down the stalks after flowering, leaving one or two to self-seed. Keep the white and magenta types separate, or the latter will overrun the former. With its woolly leaves, Rose Campion is fairly heat- and drought-tolerant (especially before it has produced flowers).

COLLECTOR'S CHOICE:

Lychnis chalcedonica, Jerusalem-cross. Perennial.
'Alba'. White.
L. coronaria, Rose Campion. Biennial or short-lived perennial.
'Alba'. White
'Oculata'. Flowers have purplish red eye; rare.

Mahonia aquifolium

BERBERIDACEAE

Oregon Holly-grape
Blue Barberry, Holly Barberry, Holly-grape, Holly Mahonia, Mountain-grape, Oregon-grape

INTRODUCED: 1822
ZONES: 5–8
NATIVE
TYPE: Perennial Shrub
HEIGHT: 3–6'
BLOOM: Spring
SITE: Light Shade

Oregon Holly-grape, native to the north western United States and British Columbia, is one of more than one hundred species of evergreen shrubs that also grows in Asia and Central America. It possesses every characteristic a gardener could want in a shrub: medium-short height; spikes of bright yellow flowers in the spring, followed by light blue, then black berries in thick clusters during the summer; glossy hollylike, nearly evergreen leaves changing to bronzy purple in the fall—a plant for all seasons. It is one of the floral treasures brought back from the early 19th-century Lewis and Clark expedition to the Pacific Northwest. (A virtue seldom mentioned is the herbal property of its roots as a laxative, tonic, and to treat skin diseases.) The genus name is a tribute to Bernard M'Mahon, a Philadelphia nurseryman.

A book about American heirloom plants would be incomplete without acknowledging the efforts of M'Mahon, one of the earliest nurserymen to recognize the horticultural value of native flora. His catalogs, the first of which was published in 1806, regularly offered a wide range of plants—no fewer than one thousand in each issue—including the finest plants from abroad and the most garden-worthy from North America. M'Mahon is closely associated with the Lewis and Clark expedition, which is said to have been planned at his house. He was the first to ask President Jefferson for some of the collected seeds so that he could raise the plants himself and then distribute them to American gardeners. Jefferson reportedly gave M'Mahon *all* the seeds that had been given to him from the expedition, apparently recognizing their significance for future gardeners. (How fortunate to have had a gardening president!) Thus, M'Mahon was the first one to cultivate the Oregon Holly-grape, which is now the most widely grown of the western species, popular in the East as well as the West. It is easily grown, and it thrives even under seemingly adverse conditions.

The ornamental virtues of the Oregon Holly-grape were well recognized abroad, especially in England, where it received a series of Royal Horticultural Society awards in 1957, 1959, 1962, and 1969 and is regarded as a classic plant, one of Will Ingwersen's choices. Ingwersen referred to its unelaborated wild form as "this magnificent garden shrub." From its earliest introduction in America, it has been praised as "one of the finest low evergreen shrubs we have."

Oregon Holly-grape is favored for foundation plantings because of its moderate height (it won't block windows), distinctive evergreen leaves (like Christmas Holly), and long season of interest, with its beautiful flowers, clusters of grapelike fruits, and, later, handsome colored foliage. It is the perfect choice for shaded or semishaded spots or for massing with Rhododendrons and Azaleas in light, open woodlands. If kept pruned, it can also be used to cover banks or areas where it is difficult to establish a ground cover. There are dwarf strains available for this purpose as well.

To Grow: Oregon Holly-grape grows in almost any type of soil, even dry and sandy, and prefers light shade and protection from the wind to keep its foliage glossy and healthy. Prune it back in early spring to prevent legginess and maintain a fairly short stature (to 3 feet). A little bonemeal at planting time (in the hole, mixed with the soil) and a dressing of rotted manure will help keep the shrub in good health. Propagation is by suckers, layering, or softwood cuttings taken in the summer and rooted in a cold frame. The foliage and flowers should be considered for use in fresh bouquets.

COLLECTOR'S CHOICE:

Mahonia aquifolium, Oregon Holly-grape
 (1822).

Malva alcea fastigiata

MALVACEAE

Hollyhock Mallow

Garden Mallow

INTRODUCED: 1850–1900
ZONES: 4–10
NATURALIZED

M. moschata ❀

Musk Mallow

INTRODUCED: 1600–1776
ZONES 3–10
NATURALIZED

TYPE: Perennial Flower/Herb
HEIGHT: 2–4'
BLOOM: Summer
SITE: Sun/Partial Shade

Both Hollyhock Mallow and Musk Mallow are native to Europe and quite similar in appearance. The Musk Mallow grows to about 2 feet; its soft green leaves, which exude a musky fragrance when rubbed or brushed, are finely divided into three to seven lobed segments. The five-petaled, wavy-edged flowers, similar in design to those of the Hollyhock, are in shades of light pink or white and are almost transparent, with a hint of veining. The flowers grow mostly at the top of the plant in clusters, with the buds jammed into the axils of the leaves (a Mallow Family trait), which accounts for its tremendous flower and fruit production. The fruits are greenish disks packed with little

black seeds that must be separated to be planted, just like the larger Hollyhock seeds. Musk Mallow is naturalized along roadsides and in old fields all over the northeastern United States and eastern Canada, extending south to Tennessee and Delaware.

Leaves of the Hollyhock Mallow are not so finely divided, and the plant is taller with showier flowers—rosy pink with more noticeable veining. The more upright stems of the variety *fastigiata* (which means "upright") are bristly, whereas the Musk Mallow's stems are smooth. Hollyhock Mallow is naturalized over a smaller area than its cousin, mainly in the eastern United States. Like the Musk Mallow, it produces plentiful blooms and fruits over a long period in the summer. Seeds of both Mallows are almost indistinguishable except for Musk Mallow's down.

Musk Mallow was grown in colonial gardens, probably for its ease of culture and lovely flowers, fondly remembered from the Old Country, where it grew wild in abundance. Perhaps it was also valued as an herb. "Whosoever takes a spoonful of Mallows," proclaimed the 1st-century Roman naturalist Pliny and Elder, "will from the day be cured of all diseases that come to him." For centuries species in the Mallow Family have been used to soothe inflammations and a variety of complaints. All parts of the Musk and Hollyhock Mallows contain a mucilaginous sap suggestive of soothing. The genus name, *Malva,* comes from the Greek *malakos,* meaning "softening."

Unlike other useful plants that were abandoned once they were no longer valued for their healing properties, the Musk Mallow was a favorite ornamental throughout the 18th and 19th centuries. The elegant white form, 'Alba', and Hollyhock Mallow were appreciated in the flower border for their beautiful and plentiful shimmering blooms and accommodating habit.

Musk Mallow is invariably found in older or abandoned gardens in maritime Canada and the northeastern United States, a garden escape growing among old Lilacs and Rhubarb. It is cherished locally, and, according to legend, is one of the plants the Scottish highlanders brought with them to the New World, ranking with the Scottish Bluebell (*Campanula rapunculoides*) for old country nostalgia. There is a subtle variety in the pink shades of the flowers, and enthusiasts are always on the lookout for superior colors (usually darker pink), collecting seeds and passing them around in the best heirloom gardening tradition.

I discovered Musk Mallow as a field weed on our farm, and in the tradition of countless folk gardeners before me, I dug it up to plant in my herb and flower garden, where I value it for its long season of bloom, beautiful and plentiful flowers, and ease of culture. It is one of the few perennials that really *does* bloom a second time, as advertised, if cut back after the first flowering. In fact, it is so accommodating that new blooms open from the base of the plant even before the old flower stalks have been cut. Musk Mallow's soft pink or glistening white flowers complement every other garden plant, toning down, for instance, the hard red of the Jerusalem-cross, a combination I learned about from an old-time local gardener. This partnership works wonders for both plants.

I found a fine specimen of the Hollyhock Mallow growing in a tiny garden literally at the edge of the North Atlantic in a fishing village, braving stiff winds, its stems unbowed. The plant, covered with rosy blooms, had been grown from seeds brought to the site by a young bride more than forty years before. The seeds had been taken from plants originally raised by her mother many years earlier. It was evidently a family favorite, passed down from generation to generation. In rich soil, Hollyhock Mallow grows to shrublike proportions (3 feet by 3 feet), so I confine it to an accent planting just beyond the garden proper.

Both Mallows bloom most of the summer, first among Foxglove, Dame's-rocket, and Sweet-William, and then among Wild-bergamot, Annual Clary Sage, Nicotiana, Feverfew, and, in light shade, Monkshood.

To Grow: Both species of Mallow are easily grown from seeds sown in well-drained garden soil. Seedlings should be thinned to about 1 foot apart. If you sow the seeds in summer, the plants will bloom the following season. If you sow them in spring, when the soil has warmed, they will bloom in late summer and self-seed thereafter for a fresh supply, if needed. Where summers are very hot, plant Mallows in partial shade and cut them back after blooming for a second round. Plants can also be propagated by division or stem cuttings in spring or summer. Neither species grows well in Florida or along the Gulf Coast.

COLLECTOR'S CHOICE:

Malva alcea fastigiata, Hollyhock Mallow (1850–1900).

M. moschata, Musk Mallow (1600–1776).

'Alba'; white.

Musk Mallow was grown in colonial gardens, probably for its ease of culture and lovely flowers, fondly remembered from the Old Country, where it grew wild in abundance.

Malva sylvestris

MALVACEAE

Wild Mallow

Billy-buttons, Blue Mallow, Cheese,
Cheese Mallow, Chinese Hollyhock,
Common Mallow, Flibberty-gibbet,
French Mallow, High Mallow, Pancake
Plant, Rags-and-tatters

INTRODUCED: 1800–1850
ZONES: 4–9
NATURALIZED
TYPE: Annual/Biennial/Short-Lived
    Perennial Herb/Flower
HEIGHT: 3–6'
BLOOM: Spring–Fall
SITE: Sun/Partial Shade

Wild Mallow, native to Eurasia, usually grows to 5 feet from a long taproot. The strong, round stems bear large, very lobed leaves whose axils produce five-petaled mauve flowers in profusion. Each petal is delicately veined with purple. When the flowers fall, round cheeselike fruits are quickly formed—hence the many country names associated with this plant, which grows wild along roadsides throughout the northeastern and north-central United States. The Latin epithet *sylvestris* means "wild" (literally, "of the forest"), to distinguish it from the Garden Mallow.

A common weed of the English countryside, Wild Mallow, like other Mallows, is associated with healing powers because of its mucilaginous flowers and leaves, which are also rich in vitamins. Its leaves have been a source of food for millennia in the Middle East, especially in times of famine. The leaves also are used, like okra, to thicken soups, while the juice of Wild Mallow leaves is said to soothe bee and wasp stings.

There is no evidence that Wild Mallow was used as an herb in the New World, but it is considered an early 19th-century plant and was grown by Jefferson at Monticello. He was, it seems, fond of or curious about Mallows in general, for he grew other flowers in the family, including Hollyhocks, Marsh Mallow *(Alcea officinalis),* and *Lavatera,* besides the Wild Mallow, which he called "French Mallow" because of its mauve flowers (the flower's French name means "mauve").

Elizabeth Lawrence recounted her adventures with *Malva sylvestris* and the cultivar 'Zebrina', describing how she finally learned their identity through correspondence with country gardeners via the market bulletins she made famous: "A little striped mallow that I had been trying to name for some time was in bloom, so I sent a flower and asked whether it was Chinese Hollyhock. It was. It is a biennial but reseeds itself indefinitely. I am always coming on it in old gardens, but no commercial seed companies seem to list it, despite its attractive pink blossoms with lavender stripes and its resistance to heat and drought" *(Gardening for Love).* She eventually found the cultivar 'Zebrina' for sale under the name *Malva alcea* rather than *M. sylvestris.*

Years after she wrote of her adventures with the Mallows, I discovered them both. The origins of 'Zebrina' are unknown, so it is not surprising that it should be listed under both *M. alcea* and *M. sylvestris.* Mallows readily cross-pollinate, so it could be a sport of either, but is most like Wild Mallow. Unlike the wild species, though, it holds its showier flowers above its leaves rather than beneath them.

What is really surprising, considering Elizabeth Lawrence's observation that these Mallows can withstand heat and drought in southern gardens, is that in my northern garden, they really take off as the summer wanes and the temperature begins to drop. 'Zebrina' is an especially beautiful plant, not at all what I had expected from the advertised "striped Hollyhock." It begins to blossom when less than a foot high in early summer, literally covered all along its short stem with shimmering light pink to cream rounded petals that have darker veins radiating out from the center of the bloom, giving the effect of little upturned bells. Later, at about 2½ feet, its side branches also are packed with buds, like so many tightly rolled pink party favors, all crowded in the axils of broad ivy-shaped leaves. By fall, the little Mallow, at 3 feet, is still valiantly pouring forth its buds, flowers, and fruits (our resident rooster really enjoys these), seemingly impervious to freezing nighttime temperatures and surviving hard frosts into November. I photographed it once still blooming under a light blanket of snow. Like other hardy plants, its flowers seem to take on a more intense color under cold conditions.

Malva sylvestris mauritiana is a variant Mallow type. Taller than the usual form (growing to 6 feet), it has spectacular flowers—rosy mauve, loosely doubled, and deeply veined. It was introduced to American gardeners with great fanfare in 1987 as "new," but it was commonly grown long before that, for it is listed in Liberty Hyde Bailey's 1942 *Gardener's Handbook* (Macmillan).

All these Mallows look best when massed against a stone wall, fence, or building, especially against weathered or white boards, where the beautiful blooms show themselves to advantage. The shorter 'Zebrina' is stunning when planted in groups in a mixed flower border, where it always elicits favorable comment. Jefferson's Mallow *(Malva sylvestris)* can be planted in a sunny wild garden where it can self-sow as it likes from year to year.

To Grow: Wild Mallow and 'Zebrina' can be grown from seeds sown outside in spring when the soil has warmed (when you plant beans). They like light, spare soil (richer soil

---

DRORA'S MALLOW PIE

Dough (makes enough for two pies, both thinly covered):
1 cup yogurt
¾ cup margarine
3 cups flour
dash of salt

Mix all the ingredients together, and roll out the dough as for a pie.

Filling:
1 cup cooked Mallow leaves
5 ounces cheese cut in small pieces (a mixture of hard and soft cheeses, one of them salted)
2–3 eggs
½ cup flour
2–3 tablespoons powdered mushroom soup mix
garlic powder and black pepper to taste

Mix all the ingredients together. Spread the bottom crust in a greased and floured baking dish, add filling, and cover with another thin layer of dough. Brush top of dough with an egg yolk before baking, then sprinkle thickly with sesame seeds. Bake at 350°F (175°C) for about 45 minutes.

The Latin epithet sylvestris means "wild" (literally, "of the forest"), to distinguish it from the Garden Mallow.

produces many leaves and fewer flowers). Seedlings should be thinned to 1 foot apart. Once established, plants should self-seed. In warmer regions, where the plants are almost evergreen, they may be perennials or short-lived perennials, always leaving progeny behind from season to season. The more compact 'Zebrina' can be cut back in the fall and potted to grow and bloom profusely in a cool greenhouse, then cut back and replanted in the spring. Since 'Zebrina' may revert to type or cross-pollinate with Wild Mallow, it is best propagated from stem cuttings or plantlets that grow at its base. Never plant these two Mallows near each other if you want to keep 'Zebrina' pure.

Malva sylvestris mauritiana needs a longer growing season than the other two Mallows. Except in southern gardens, it should be grown from seeds started indoors in late winter or early spring. Seeds germinate in fifteen to twenty-one days at 70°F (21°C). Plants grow in full sun or partial shade and light soil, and need some protection from the wind (otherwise they may need staking). The other two Mallows also grow well in sun or filtered shade.

To Use: Mallow flowers are pretty embellishments for puddings, gelatin desserts, ice cream, and sorbet (especially black currant). My favorite way to use the leaves is in my friend's elegant quiche (see page 183).

COLLECTOR'S CHOICE:

Malva sylvestris, Wild Mallow (1800–1850).
  Mauve flowers veined in purple; to 5'.
M. sylvestris mauritiana (before 1942). Rosy
  mauve, loosely doubled flowers; to 6'.
M. sylvestris 'Zebrina', Zebrina Mallow. Light
  pink to cream rounded petals striped with
  darker veins; to 3'.

Mertensia virginica

BORAGINACEAE

Virginia-bluebells
Blue Funnel Flower, Mountain-cowslip,
Roanoke-bells, Virginia-cowslip

INTRODUCED: 1700–1776
ZONES: 3–8
NATIVE
TYPE: Perennial Flower
HEIGHT: 2'
BLOOM: Spring
SITE: Partial Shade

Virginia-bluebells, one of our most beautiful wildflowers, has long been cultivated as a garden plant. Native to Virginia, it also grows in moist woodlands and along streams from New York south to Tennessee and Alabama and west to Kansas, which suggests that it adapts well to different climatic conditions. It is among the earliest flowers to break through the ground in early spring, rising to about 2 feet and bearing trumpetlike blooms—pink in bud and light blue in flower—most attractive to bees (like Lungwort, *Pulmonaria officinalis,* to which it is closely related). Virginia-bluebells' smooth oval leaves are strongly veined, emerging first as pink shoots, then turning silvery green. After the flowers have bloomed, the whole plant gradually dies back to earth.

The early settlers compared Virginia-bluebells to the Lungwort they remembered from cottage gardens—a cure-all for lung ailments. By the 18th century, Virginia-bluebells was grown as an ornamental, as in the gardens of Lady Skipwith of Virginia. She called it "blue funnel flower" and probably got it from the wild to plant among her Monkshood, Florentine Iris, Cowslips, and Sweet-William. She and her husband, Sir Peyton, left detailed records of their gardening activities, which were discovered in 1946 when their estate was being auctioned. These were sometimes written on the backs of old bills and scraps of paper, in the tradition of gardeners since time immemorial (or at least since the invention of the alphabet and paper). Pieced together, they give us a good idea of what was grown in 18th-century American gardens and the sorts of native plants—like Virginia-bluebells—that were considered choice. These records also tell us that while nursery stock could be ordered from commercial sources (some came from William Prince Nurseries on Long Island—a source for Washington and Jefferson as well), many other came from various other sources, including neighbors and the wild: "Shrubs to be got where I can," Lady Skipwith noted. "Bulbous roots to get when in my power." Only a determined and curious gardener like Lady Skipwith (with the means at her disposal) could have assembled the wide variety of plants grown at Prestwould, the family estate.

I first saw Virginia-bluebells growing in a sprawling garden on a remote hillside farm among bright yellow Leopard's-bane *(Doronicum)*—a striking combination. I should add that these were planted in full sun, in contradiction to the usual advice to plant Virginia-bluebells in partial shade. Like most plants that usually require partial shade, Virginia-bluebells will grow well in a sunny spot the farther north it is planted, provided soil conditions are suitable. Since plants are dormant by late spring or early summer, consider grouping them among other plants that will fill in after them—Wild Bleeding-heart, Maidenhair Fern, Bergamot, and Nicotiana, all of which grow well in light shade or in sun in the North. Hostas of different sorts also work well.

To Grow: Where springs are warm, plant Virginia-bluebells in partial shade; elsewhere full sun is okay if the soil is moderately moist, cool, and humus-rich. Plant roots 1 foot deep and about 6 inches apart. The plant increases rapidly under optimum conditions and can be divided anytime after blooming. Replant young roots (not old black ones) or collect seeds and sow them in a cold frame anytime during the summer (preferably when the seeds are fresh) to produce blooming plants the third year.

COLLECTOR'S CHOICE:

Mertensia virginica, Virginia-bluebells (1700–1776).

Mirabilis jalapa ❀

NYCTAGINACEAE

Four O'Clock
False Jalap, Marvel of Peru

INTRODUCED: 1776–1800
ZONES: 8–9
TYPE: Annual/Tender Perennial
HEIGHT: 2–3'
BLOOM: Summer
SITE: Sun/Partial Shade

The tropical Four O'Clock tells its story in its genus name, *Mirabilis,* "marvellous". A dense, bushy plant with deep green, heart-shaped leaves grows up from an underground tuber. A mass of flowers, slender and tubular in form, in colors of clear yellow, red, rose, pink, and white—often striped, mottled, and splashed in various combinations—sometimes appear together on a single plant. Further marvels are in store when the tightly closed flowers open precisely at four o'clock in the afternoon, closing the following day before noon; on cloudy days flowers stay open all day. Their fragrance is hard to define: like oranges or Cowslips with a hint of spice. Hummingbirds visit the flowers in the late afternoon, and moths come in the evening. The roots of Four O'Clock, which can weigh up to 40 pounds, were once used with other plants in a strong laxative called *jalap,* named after the city in Mexico (Jalapa) where the flower may have originated.

Seeds of Four O'Clock were brought from Peru to Spain, and from there to England in the 16th century, but they do not seem to have been widely grown in America until the 19th century. Jefferson, always ahead of his time, imported Four O'Clock seed from France, and in July 1767 expressed delight in their afternoon bloom in an oval bed near the house: "...just opened ... very clever." Later, in 1812, he got seeds of Showy Four O'Clock *(M. longiflora)* from M'Mahon. Native to the American Southwest, this species bears larger, sweet-scented white flowers, tinged with violet.

By mid-century, Four O'Clocks were popular in Victorian theme plantings, where a single bed would be devoted to the working out of a particular idea. Intricate patterns simulated maps, fountains, and floral "clocks"—plants that open and close at set times of the day. Linnaeus, the father of modern botany, had observed this phenomenon in the wild with two weeds, Hawk's Beard *(Crepis)* and Hawkbit *(Leontodon).* This was so interesting to him that in 1770 he arranged a floral clock garden in the Botanical Gardens of Uppsala, Sweden, to show typical opening and closing times of various flowers. With the introduction of colorful annuals from the tropics during the 19th century, Victorians had much to choose from in this line. Besides Four O'Clocks there were Nicotiana, Portulaca, Morning-glory, and Moonflower.

Four O'Clocks declined with the passing of the Victorian era, and by the 1930s the plant was regarded as passé, old-fashioned, and out of tune with contemporary sensibilities, which found no charm in its quirky habits and unpredictable colors. "It is a plant which will take you back to your country-spent childhood," wrote Louise Beebe Wilder *(The Fragrant Path).* The archetypal Grandmother's Garden flower, it evokes memories of a time past, when—or so it is remembered—children picked what they pleased, since nothing was rare or choice, all was carefree and artless. Felder Rushing describes Four O'Clock plantings in the South (where they're tough perennials) that have survived forty years of "hard neglect" *(Passalong Plants).*

I discovered the pleasures of growing Four O'Clocks late in my gardening life, but I quickly became a convert. I plant them in tubs by the farmhouse door, and sit on the front steps in the early July evening to breathe in their sweet, almost clovelike perfume. Like Linnaeus, I have closely observed their opening and closing. My notebook records that fuschia-colored flowers opened at 5 P.M. (Daylight Saving Time), and that they were fully open by 5:15. By 5:25, insects covered with pollen were busy at work deep within the blossoms, their feet covered with pollen. Still open by 10 o'clock the fol-

Marvels are in store when the tightly closed flowers open precisely at four o'clock in the afternoon, closing the following day before noon; on cloudy days flowers stay open all day.

lowing morning, they closed before noon.

Even out of bloom, the plants are attractive, like miniature shrubs. I place tubs of Four O'Clocks in a small container garden of various herbs and flowers placed on and around the foot of a large wooden flatbed wheelbarrow. As plants pass in and out of bloom, I move them around for best effect, except for Four O'Clocks, which are permanently paired with 'Purple Ruffles' Basil. I have also seen Four O'Clocks grown as a low hedge near the front door of a local inn, judiciously placed so guests can benefit from their colorful blooms and wonderful aroma. Elizabeth Lawrence remembered making "flower people" from the blossoms of Four O'Clocks, Rose of Sharon *(Althea),* and Petunias, all prime candidates for the Child's Garden.

To Grow: Four O'Clock seeds are round and dark, almost black, and easy to germinate. Sow seeds 6 weeks before the last frost in peat pots, and cover the seeds well with soil. They germinate in six to twelve days at 70°F (21°C) or warmer. I start seeds in May in our leaky greenhouse (temperatures are still higher than outdoors) to get a head start, since every day counts when it takes two months from germination for plants to produce flowers. It's true that Four O'Clocks grow rapidly, but, like Basil, only where temperatures are steadily warm. In hot-climate areas, plant seeds outside in well-drained soil as soon as the ground warms, or purchase tubers. This may be more practical, since tubers produce flowers earlier than seed, but it's fun to watch Four O'Clock seeds sprout and produce their heart-shaped leaves tinged with purple. Outdoors, space plants 1 to 2 feet apart (space tubers according to size), or two to three plants in a half whisky barrel. Water plants well, especially in a dry period

(they are not, as sometimes reported, drought-tolerant, at least in the North). Tubers can be dug up after frost and stored over winter like Dahlias (Gerard reportedly stored his in a butter firkin), but their size is daunting. Recently I stored them in containers, well covered, in a cool place above freezing, and, if they survive, I should have earlier bloom next season. I'll raise a new crop of plants, though, as insurance. In frost-free areas Four O'Clocks are robust, long-lasting perennials.

COLLECTOR'S CHOICE:

Mirabilis jalapa, Four O'Clock (1776–1800). Mixed colors; not always streaked.

'Broken Colors'. These guarantee streaking on hot pink, white, clear yellow, and magenta flowers.

M. longiflora, Showy Four O'Clock (1776–1850). Longer flowers, more upright plant habit, white flowers tinged with violet.

Monarda didyma ❀

LAMIACEAE

Bee-balm
Bergamot, Fragrant-balm, Oswego-tea, Red Bee-balm, Red-bergamot, Red-mint, Scarlet-bergamot, Sweet-bergamot

INTRODUCED: 1700–1776
ZONES: 4–10
NATIVE

M. fistulosa ❀

Wild-bergamot
Blue Monarda, Purple-bergamot

M. punctata ❀

Horsemint
Dotted Monarda

TYPE: Perennial Flower/Herb
HEIGHT: 2–5'
BLOOM: Summer–Fall
SITE: Sun/Partial Shade/Shade

Native Bergamots grow by vigorous stolons or runners that develop a dense mat of basal foliage—tapering, toothed, and aromatic. Bee-balm can grow to 6 feet, though cultivars and hybrids are shorter (3 to 4 feet). It favors moist woodlands and bottomlands from New England to Georgia and Tennessee. Whorled flowers sit atop square stems—typical of the Mint Family, to which Bergamots belong. These are borne in clusters, sometimes two-tiered, from red-tinged bracts. The scarlet petals are long and tubular, giving the flower head a ragged or fringed appearance. Hummingbirds, rather than bees (as the common name would suggest), visit the blooms to sip the sweet nectar with their long beaks.

Bee-balm favors moist woodlands and bottomlands from New England to Georgia and Tennessee.

Wild-bergamot grows in a quite different habitat—the dry soil of abandoned fields and mountainous areas from New England south. Its flowers, growing from lilac-tinged bracts, are pale lilac in color. The petals are shorter than those of Bee-balm, thus allowing fertilization by visiting bees and large moths.

Both species have a sweet, citrusy aroma (evident when weeding or even just walking in their vicinity) similar to that of bergamot oil, which is actually extracted from the tropical tree *Citrus aurantium*. The genus is named for Nicholas Monardes, a Spanish physician and 16th-century author of *Joyful News of the New Founde World*, wherein the useful properties of such native herbs as the Bergamots are described.

The herbal uses of both Bergamots were well known to the Indians, from whom the early settlers learned to use the leaves to make a soothing tea, flavor meat dishes, relieve bronchial congestion, and dry up pimples, as well as in pomade to oil hair.

Bee-balm has earned a permanent place in American history because of its widespread use as Oswego tea by American patriots during their struggles with the British over import duties on Chinese teas. Oswego tea was first associated with the Oswego Indians, who lived by the shores of Lake Ontario, where Bee-balm was gathered for tea and other purposes. By 1656 the British were enjoying Wild-bergamot as an herb and garden flower, and after 1744, when Bartram sent seeds of Bee-balm to Peter Collinson, it, too, was cultivated and enjoyed as an American exotic.

By the 19th century, a number of other species were introduced to American gardeners. Two of these were Dotted Monarda or Horsemint (*Monarda punctata*), with whorls of yellow, purple-spotted flowers and showy white or lilac bracts, and Red and White Monarda (*M. russeliana*), named for Dr. Russell, who aided the English botanist Thomas Nutall in his 1819 explorations in Arkansas. Both these Bergamots prefer the same habitat as the Wild-bergamots (dry, sandy soil), though both are less hardy. Hybrids and cultivars, mostly from *M. didyma* and *M. fistulosa*, followed; the most popular and enduring one was 'Cambridge Scarlet', developed in the early 1900s.

My experience many years ago with the Bergamots is a cautionary tale for the novice who admires a plant in bloom and wants it without ever considering its proper Latin name. I thought I was raising up the bright scarlet Bee-balm, from seeds listed simply as "Bergamot" under the heading "Herbs" in a seed catalog. In fact, the flower that eventually bloomed was the pale lavender Wild-bergamot, a fine plant too, and one I learned to appreciate in the wild garden, but not what I had had in mind. One need not be a botanist to order plants and seeds, but a good working knowledge of botanical nomenclature is helpful.

Bergamots are treasured in the garden for their fresh flowers—flamboyant in the case of Bee-balm—in midsummer, when their long-lasting blooms bring new life to any planting. All species can be naturalized in their favored habitats. Bee-balm does best along streams and ponds and in light woodland settings with Hostas and Maidenhair Ferns, or in the shade of a perennial border. In filtered shade, its glorious scarlet flowers are brighter and longer-lasting than in sun. The other species favor dry, sunny growing conditions and can be naturalized with such natives as Butterfly Weed and Black-eyed-Susans on an exposed slope or grown in a more formal flower border. All Bergamots are surprisingly adaptable as long as their basic requirements are met. I like to use them as easy-care plantings wherever possible.

One summer a young guest was given the task of pulling the petals off the bright flower heads of Bee-balm to scatter over a large bowl of colorful lettuces. She really enjoyed the job, which was new to her, but the next day we were puzzled when she asked whether it was "Okay to eat a whole big bowl of petals," nodding toward our 12-inch wooden bowl. After the guests left and we'd tidied up the little cabin—bordered generously with Bee-balm—we understood the significance of her question: She had plucked and eaten every petal (apparently none the worse for it), but there would be no more humming-birds that season to entertain guests.

To Grow: Bergamots can be grown to Zone 10 except in Florida and along the Gulf Coast. Plant roots 1½ to 2 feet apart and 1 inch deep. Bee-balm will grow in full sun if the soil is moist, but its flowers are not as brilliant or as long-lasting as in dappled shade. Rich soil is best. Clumps should be divided every three or four years because the center loses vigor and becomes hard. Use side shoots with their roots to establish new plantings, discarding the hard center mat. Seeds can be sown indoors in January for bloom the first season. Germination takes one to two weeks at 70°F (21°C). Or sow seeds in a cold frame during the summer and plant out the seedlings the following spring.

Wild-bergamot and Horsemint can be grown in light shade where summers are hot; elsewhere they prefer full sun and light, or even poor soil for best blooming. They bloom earlier then Bee-balm, so if you cut their stalks back after flowering, a new mound of fresh leaves will be of interest the rest of the season.

COLLECTOR'S CHOICE:

Monarda didyma 'Cambridge Scarlet', Bee-balm (early 1900s).

Wild-bergamot can be grown in light shade where summers are hot; elsewhere they prefer full sun and light, even poor soil for best blooming.

M. fistulosa, Wild-bergamot. Pale lilac flowers.

M. punctata, Horsemint. Thyme-scented; yellow, purple-spotted flowers; showy white or lilac bracts; Zone 6.

Myosotis spp.

BORAGINACEAE

Forget-me-not

Garden Forget-me-not, Scorpion Grass, True Forget-me-not, Woodland Forget-me-not

INTRODUCED: 1776–1900

ZONES 3–10

NATURALIZED

TYPE: Annual/Biennial/Short-Lived Perennial Flower

HEIGHT: 4"–2'

BLOOM: Spring–Summer

SITE: Sun/Partial Shade/Shade

Forget-me-nots, members of the Borage Family, are widely distributed throughout the temperate zone. Both native and introduced types (from Europe and Asia) grow across North America, mainly in damp or wet areas. Plants are easily recognized by their small sky blue or bright blue five-petaled flowers, usually with a bright yellow center, growing on erect and trailing stems with angled, lance-shaped downy leaves. A profusion of flowers is borne in false racemes or rolled-up spikes that uncoil over the course of the season as the flowers open, leaving behind seedpods along the length of the stem that spill out over the ground to ensure a new generation of plants. The genus name, *Myosotis,* from the Greek *mys,* "mouse," and *otis,* "ear," refers to the plant's leaves.

The Forget-me-not of romance and legend is the perennial bright blue True Forget-me-not *(Myosotis scorpioides/M. palustris)* from Europe and Asia, so named, the story goes, because a knight who drowned while fetching the pretty flowers for his lover called out, "Forget-me-not!" Ever since it has been a symbol of loving remembrance. Less well known (and far less romantic) is the legend that Henry Bolingbroke, banished from England by his cousin King Richard II, adopted the flower as a badge of revenge, an association based on the curled-up flower spikes, in the shape of a scorpion. This characteristic led to the belief among ancient herbalists that the Forget-me-not was an antidote for venomous bites. The scorpion association is preserved in the Latin epithet *scorpioides,* while the romantic legend is preserved in the plant's common name.

Although known since antiquity and introduced to American gardeners by the 18th century or earlier, Forget-me-nots were not widely grown until the 19th century. Like other plants that were introduced relatively late but enjoyed great popularity, Forget-me-nots are considered old-fashioned in the best sense—"the heart's darlings of the garden," one early 20th-century writer observed.

There are two types of Forget-me-nots for heirloom gardeners to consider: the short-lived perennial True Forget-me-not of romance and legend and the Garden or Woodland Forget-me-not *(Myosotis sylvatica).* The latter is an annual or biennial that has been the source of most of the cultivars that remain popular today and is most commonly found around old homesites and graveyards, growing as a garden escape. The advantage of the perennial type is that it has flowers all season long, not just in the spring. The advantage of the annual/biennial is that, except for pulling out excessive growth, virtually no attention is required after its initial establishment. In fact, one tends to forget the bright blue perennial, and after several seasons it may disappear unless care is taken to replenish the planting by division or reseeding. This habit of growth is always a sure test of the gardener's observance.

I like both types: the perennial for its ever-blooming nature and the annual/biennial for its froth of bloom, which is inextricably associated with the flowers of spring—foamy clouds of blue, rose, or white (natural variations) that look particularly at home among Daffodils, Bleeding-heart, Columbine, Sweet Cicely, and Cowslips. The perennial provides bright blue mats of color in shady and damp spots, often so difficult to embellish with flowers. There it can grow with Bee-balm and Monkshood, as well as with the stunning Japanese Primrose *(Primula japonica)*. Both types of Forget-me-not can be cut for bouquets, especially little nosegays and tussie-mussies.

To Grow: Sow seeds of either type indoors six to eight weeks before the last frost. Keep them at 55 to 60°F (13 to 16°C) and cover them well, since they need darkness to germinate. This should occur in five to twelve days. Plant out seedlings 9 to 12 inches apart, keeping in mind that they may spread in an area as wide as their height. The annual/biennial may bloom the first season, self-seeding thereafter. Don't worry about ruthlessly thinning it out after its bloom has passed; enough seeds will be left to sprout plenty of new plants. Untended, this Forget-me-not will form mats that can smother other plants or take up needed room. Choice cultivars may need to be reseeded or watched closely to keep the strains pure.

You can also sow seeds of either type in a cold frame or directly in the ground anytime over the summer for bloom the following spring (or winter where conditions permit). The perennial type needs dividing every three or four years or reseeding if necessary. Both types of Forget-me-nots will grow in sun or shade if the soil is moist; wild forms will grow in very wet conditions.

COLLECTOR'S CHOICE:

Myosotis scorpioides/M. palustris, True Forget-me-not. Perennial; bright blue with yellow, pink, or white eye, 1½'.

M. sylvatica, Garden Forget-me-not. Annual/biennial; sky blue; 1–2'.

'Blue Bird' (by 1934). Large bright blue flowers; 1'.

'King Henry' (rare old strain; close to wild form).

'Rose'. Pale rose; 16".

'Royal Blue' (by 1928). Early, free-flowering type; deep blue; 12".

'Victoria' (by 1929). Large flowers; sky blue or mixed; dwarf form; good for pot culture.

Myrrhis odorata ✽

APIACEAE

Sweet Cicely
British Myrrh, Giant-chervil, Shepherd's-needle, Sweet-bracken, Sweet-chervil, Sweet-fern, Sweets

INTRODUCED: 1600–1776
ZONES 3–10
TYPE: Perennial Herb/Flower
HEIGHT: 2–3'
BLOOM: Spring
SITE: Partial Shade/Shade

Sweet Cicely's Latin name *(Myrrhis odorata)* comes form the Greek word for perfume, a reference to this plant's sweetly fragrant flowers, leaves, and seeds (similar to anise or licorice). A native of Europe, it has naturalized in Great Britain along riverbanks and in wet, shady areas. In spring the stalks rise to 3 feet from ferny mounds of soft green leaves with whitish flecks, bearing saucer-sized umbels of sweet white florets. The roots are thick (about 2 inches around) and grow down about a foot into the ground, making it difficult to dig up a plant once it's established. Sweet Cicely spreads its long, flat, oily seeds generously, however, ensuring new seedlings every year.

This plant has been cultivated since at least the 6th century for culinary and medicinal purposes. All its parts—leaves, seeds, and roots—can be eaten. The pressed oil was once prized for scenting and polishing oak floors and furniture; stalks and leaves are said to yield a beautiful green dye. Medicinally, Sweet Cicely was used to treat coughs, flatulence, consumption, and other complaints.

Sweet Cicely was cultivated in the earliest American gardens, probably by the Plymouth settlers—a hardy, unpretentious lot, who would hardly have had the time or the need to scent their furniture. Most likely Sweet Cicely was regarded as very useful because all its parts were edible and it was easy to grow. In lieu of other fresh vegetables, a salad of boiled roots dressed with oil and vinegar would have been quite acceptable. And it was said to be "very good for old people that are dull and without courage; it rejoiceth and comforteth the heart and increaseth their lust and strength"—altogether a most useful settler herb.

Once it was no longer needed, Sweet Cicely disappeared from the American garden scene. "It had a certain vogue in the 16th and 17th centuries," observed American herbalist Helen Fox, "but now is rarely cultivated in gardens" *(Gardening with Herbs for Flavor and Fragrance,* 1933). The herb renaissance that Mrs. Fox pioneered helped to bring this lovely plant back in fashion among herb gardeners and, increasingly, among all discerning gardeners partial to beautiful and hardy perennials.

Sweet Cicely has a most pleasing habit, whether in leaf, bloom, or seed. It is essential in the early spring border—its graceful umbels rising from a ferny mound of leaves, growing among old-time favorites such as Fringed Bleeding-heart *(Dicentra eximia),* Cowslips, and early Iris. The long, shiny black seeds that quickly follow the flowers make a spectacular backdrop for later-blooming plants such as Mountain-bluet and Poppies. After it is cut back, the leaves quickly return as an attractive evergreen mound until the snow flies.

To Grow: Sweet Cicely is usually grown in shade or partial shade, but it can be grown in sun if the soil is moist and the roots are well covered and shaded by nearby plants such as Forget-me-nots. The soil, in any case, should be enriched and humusy. Plants are most easily propagated by self-sown seedlings that turn up in the vicinity of the mother plant in early spring. At this stage, they are easy to pull up and replant where you want them. If you are lulled by the beauty of the plant covered with its distinctive seedpods, you can expect a little forest of seed-

Sweet Cicely has been cultivated since at least the 6th century for culinary and medicinal purposes.

lings the following season. The fresh seeds fall to the ground and germinate after freezing during the winter. To grow Sweet Cicely from seed, freeze the seeds for one to three months before sowing them outside in early spring. Thin the seedlings to about 1 foot apart.

To Use: Pressed Sweet Cicely leaves are lovely in floral designs. The mature black seeds can be eaten like candy, and the fresh leaves reduce the need for sugar in stewed fruits, especially rhubarb. Or use fresh leaves to flavor this coffee cake from Louise Hyde of Well-Sweep Herb Farm in Port Murray, New Jersey.

COLLECTOR'S CHOICE:
Myrrhis odorata, Sweet Cicely (1600–1776).

LOUISE HYDE'S SWEET CICELY COFFEE CAKE

2 cups biscuit mix (such as Bisquick)
2 tablespoons margarine
½ cup milk
3 tablespoons sugar plus ¾ cup sugar
one 12-ounce can almond paste
4 large Sweet Cicely leaves, chopped fine
one 20-ounce can crushed pineapple,
    unsweetened
3 tablespoons flour

Make a dough using the biscuit mix, margarine, milk, and 3 tablespoons of sugar. Spread out the dough on a greased 11 x 7-inch jelly-roll pan. Spread almond paste over the dough, then sprinkle it with the chopped Sweet Cicely leaves. Mix the drained pineapple with the flour and ¾ cup sugar, and spoon this mixture over the leaves. Sprinkle extra sugar on top if desired. Bake at 400°F (around 200°C) for 30 to 40 minutes. Cut into squares.

Narcissus spp. ❀

AMARYLLIDACEAE

Daffodil
Daffadowndilly, Jonquil

INTRODUCED: 1600–1950
ZONES: 3–10
TYPE: Hardy Bulb
HEIGHT 6–18"
BLOOM: Spring
SITE: Sun/Partial Shade

There are about twenty-six species of *Narcissus* native to Asia, the Mediterranean region, and Europe, where they have been highly regarded for centuries, if not millennia, for their beauty. For instance, the "lily among thorns," from the Old Testament's *Song of Songs,* alludes to the dainty bunches of *N. tazetta* that grow wild in the fertile valleys of the Holy Land among the spent stalks of wild thorns.

Daffodils grow from underground bulbs that send up strong stems with straplike or rushlike foliage in early spring, sometimes breaking through snow or frozen ground in colder regions. The beautiful six-petaled flowers, fragrant in varying degrees, are usually white, yellow, or a combination of both and are composed of a *perianth* (the petals) and a *corona* (the central cup or trumpet). This structure has been of great interest to breeders, who have created hundreds, probably thousands, of variants since the early 19th century, when botanical knowledge was greatly expanded. In nature, Daffodils also cross-pollinate readily, giving rise to natural hybrids.

Although Jonquil is frequently used as a generic term to describe *Narcissus,* this word actually refers to only one species, *N. jonquilla,* an especially fragrant type with rushlike foliage. Daffodil, however, correctly refers to all the many species, hybrids, and cultivars.

The colonists in New England and the Dutch settlers grew Daffodils (Daffadown-dillies) as early as the 1600s—"trumpets, poets, doubles, and multiplex" types. Since these have no medicinal value worth noting (though the poisonous bulbs have been used in the preparation of ointments), they were obviously grown for the same reason they are today. "No other flower in the world," Rockwell and Grayson noted, "is quite so universally and definitely associated with any one season, or so completely embodies in its characteristics the atmosphere and essence of a season. Nature has made the daffodil the perfect symbol of that time of year . . . that not all the hybridizers in the world have been able to change" *(The Complete Book of Bulbs,* 1977). Daffodils bloom brightly and bravely in the face of stiff winds and cold temperatures, heralds of the new growing season ahead. How that must have cheered the early settlers!

Old Daffodils of various types still mark the remnant gardens of abandoned homesteads throughout North America, proof of their tremendous vigor. Finding and collecting them, thus saving them from extinction,

is one of the most pleasurable pursuits of the heirloom gardener. And where they bloom, other treasures may not be far away.

When we moved to the old farm in 1970, I noticed a Daffodil I'd never seen before: late-blooming (often a sign of an old type), with smallish white double flowers, faintly tinged, with yellow centers, growing on tall stalks (to 18 inches) with long, narrow leaves. Just a few of these in a vase fill our farm kitchen with their sweet, though not cloying, fragrance after the hundreds of Daffodils naturalized along our lane have spent their beauty. Locally, this type is known as the "French Lily" or "White Lily," rather common in old gardens and now commercially available (see *N. albus plenus odoratus* under "Collector's Choice").

Another old type that now grows in my garden (a gift from a neighboring farm) is the very early golden yellow "Double English Daffodil," described by Parkinson as "Pseudonarcissus Anglicus flore pleno," with very doubled trumpets. When it first bloomed, it had the appearance of a "Ragged Robin" type, with both double corona and perianth, often described as "sloppy." This is the Telemoneus Plenus or 'Van Sion' also described by Parkinson in 1629, common here in older gardens. It could be that the blooms have actually been transformed in my garden, reacting to soil or climatic conditions. A.E. Bowles, an authority on the genus and its variants, observed that "the origin of the common double daffodil is as much a mystery as that of domestic animals" *(Double Flowers,* 1983), so I no longer worry about its identity but enjoy its hardiness, very early bloom, and extraordinary vigor, flowering in drifts among the multicolored little pink and blue bells of my old Lungwort *(Pulmonaria officinalis)* beneath the dappled shade of an old Lilac tree. A favorite later in the season is Old Pheasant's-eye, strongly perfumed with flared-back white petals and a flat, disk-shaped cup rimmed in red with a large green eye. This was probably an early 19th-century introduction and a variant form of the older Poet *(Narcissus poeticus)* that was grown in America between 1700 and 1776. In my opinion, there has never been an improvement in the form of my Old Pheasant's-eye, but connoisseurs might disagree. Both 'Van Sion' and Old Pheasant's-eye are also available from commercial sources.

Modern Daffodil forms, today regarded as old-fashioned classics, also survive in local gardens, doing very well on their own. One day in late spring my husband and I were exploring the remnants of an old garden recently demolished by one of the island's "3 Ds" (in this case a 'dozer; the other two being the deck and the satellite dish). We were startled by a great expanse of bright yellow carpeting the ground beneath a stand of poplars. All around were piles of brush from a recent logging operation, but the poplars, of no commercial value, had been left untouched. The bright yellow came from a large population of the splendid 'King Alfred' Daffodil, a feature of North American gardens since it was bred by English clergyman John Kendall and introduced to the gardening world in 1899, the eve of the modern era. 'King' has been described as the "single greatest advance ever made in the progress of daffodils." It is certainly one of the best loved, with its clean lines and large, bold yellow trumpets—the essence of Daffodil for many gardeners. Unfortunately, bulbs offered as 'King Alfred' do not always conform to the original hybrids, as I've learned from experience.

The uses of Daffodils in the landscape are varied, but foremost among them, if you have the space, is to plant them generously beneath old fruit trees (plum, cherry, or apple) or any deciduous tree or shrub (Lilac or Mock Orange), where they will receive sufficient sun before the trees leaf out and sufficient shade later in the season to allow the foliage and bulbs to ripen without drying out. The diminutive types, such as Angel's-tears *(Narcissus triandrus),* are well suited to rock gardens or pot culture (as is almost any Daffodil) for the terrace or patio. Choice cultivars such as 'Mrs. R.O. Backhouse', the first pink Daffodil (it's really a light apricot), are seen best in a flower bed among a cloud of blue Forget-me-nots and Virginia-bluebells *(Mertensia virginica).* Annuals such as Poppies, Marigolds, Balsam, and Nicotiana fill in nicely when the Daffodils' blooms are spent. By planting early, midseason, and late-blooming types, you can have eight weeks or more of bloom.

To naturalize Daffodils, use this simple method: Throw a handful of bulbs in the area where you want them to grow, then plant them where they fall by plunging in your trowel to its handle; planting the bulb, growing tip up, at the bottom of the opened slit of earth; and covering the slit well with your foot. Dust the area with bonemeal once a season and remove spent flower stalks (not everyone thinks this is necessary, but I do it). Gardeners are usually advised to plant one of a kind—one hundred to each drift—but I prefer a mixed planting (I have the deservedly famous collection known as "The Works") where the bloom period is extended by a range of beauties, from early-flowering singles to later, very fragrant doubles and multiple-flower types. Such a planting provides great scope for bouquets, which brings me to the cutting bed.

After you become familiar with the possibilities within the range of heirloom Daffodils (far more than I have listed), you will know which ones you like best for cutting. Dig these up after they have flowered (see the directions for propagating bulbs in Part I, page 27), either setting aside the bulbs to dry and replanting them in the fall in a specially prepared cutting garden with plants arranged in rows for easy access, or replanting the bulbs at once with a good ball of dirt still around their roots. In either case, mulch the area several inches deep so the ground will retain moisture all summer. Plant extra-early varieties to prolong the "golden and glorious" Daffodil season indoors. When cutting stems for bouquets, choose flowers that are well budded out and just barely opened. After cutting, plunge the long stems into deep, cold water for several hours before making your arrangements.

To Grow: Daffodils grow best in well-drained clay or sandy loam with a pH of 6.0 to 7.0. In Zones 3 to 5, plant the bulbs in September or early October; in Zones 6 and 7, in October or early November; and in Zones 8 to 10, in November or December. (Most of the Daffodils discussed here are hardy from Zone 3 to 8 and require freezing temperatures to break their dormancy. Tender types are listed under "Collector's Choice"; these do not require freezing temperatures to bloom.) Daffodils planted during the optimum period have the best chance of developing roots in the fall and plentiful flowers the following spring.

The rule of thumb for planting depth is two to three times the height of the bulb;

large bulbs need 5 to 6 inches of soil on top of them, while smaller species need only 3 inches. Put a teaspoon of bonemeal in the bottom of each hole, cover it with a little loamy soil or sand, and plant the bulb on top, firming it in place and covering it with the required amount of soil. Allow five large bulbs, or seven to ten smaller ones, per square foot.

Daffodils, especially the wild kinds, are perfectly designed to supply their own nutrients through their decaying leaves, which in turn feed the underground bulb. The secret of success, in my experience, is not to interfere in this process, which takes up to six weeks, after which the leaves may be cut back or removed. Dust the plant with bonemeal annually; a good time is after flowering, while the leaves still mark the spot. Dig up and replant bulbs only when they lose vigor, apparent in reduced blooms. The small bulbs that develop around the larger ones can be replanted; it will take a few years before they reach the blooming stage.

Narcissus are organized into Divisions according to the American Daffodil Society:

Division 1: Trumpet Narcissus. The most popular type, with one flower per stem and the trumpet as long or longer than the perianth ('King Alfred'). Zones 3–8.

Division 2: Large-cupped Narcissus. One flower per stem, with the cup or trumpet more than one-third but less than the total length of the perianth ('Mrs. R.O. Backhouse'). Zones 3–8.

Division 3: Small-cupped Narcissus. One flower per stem, with the cup not more than one-third the length of the perianth ('Barrett Browning'). Zones 3–8.

Division 4: Double Narcissus. All with more than one layer of petals ('Cheerfulness'). Zones vary.

Division 5: Triandus Narcissus. Hybrids or cultivars derived from *Narcissus triandus.* Characterized by slender foliage and one to six flowers (often fragrant) per stem, with the petals turned back and slightly twisted ('Thalia'). Zones 4–9.

Division 6: Cyclamineus Narcissus. Hybrid descendants of *Narcissus tazetta.* One of the most widely distributed and oldest known forms of Narcissus, characterized by clusters of many small white flowers per stem with prominent golden crowns or cups; usually quite fragrant and tender ('Silver Chimes'). Zones 4–9.

Division 8: Tazetta Narcissus or Poetaz Narcissus, descended from *Narcissus tazetta.* One of the most widely distributed and oldest known forms of Narcissus, characterized by clusters of many small white flowers per stem with prominent golden crowns or cups; usually quite fragrant and tender ('Silver Chimes').

Division 9: Poeticus Narcissus, also called Poet's Narcissus or Old Pheasant's-eye, derived from *Narcissus poeticus.* Usually one flower per stem; pure white petals with a small, almost flat, red-rimmed and red-eyed cup ('Actaea'). Zones 3–7.

Division 10: Bulbocodium. The species and offspring of *N. bulbocodium conspicuus,* called the "Hoop-petticoat" daffodil because of the peculiar shape of its flowers. Zones 6–9.

Division 11: Split Corona. Cup is split into segments and spreads back against the petals, sometimes frilly, sometimes smooth in appearance.

Division 13: Cultivated forms of wild Narcissus, wild variants and natural hybrids. Zones vary.

COLLECTOR'S CHOICE:

Division 13:

Narcissus albus plenus odoratus (1601/1861?). The "Old Double White" found in old gardens in the Northeast. Late-blooming, long-stemmed, very fragrant double white flowers with a hint of a double center, this is the "French Lily" that has grown on our farm since the 1920s or before. A good cut flower. Because it blooms so late (June here), buds are sometimes afflicted with a fungus that prevents them from opening. Flowers can still be cut for bouquets by carefully removing the papery covering on the outside of swelled buds. Naturalizing in a light woodland helps to protect plants from heat; 12–14"; Zones 3–7. ❀

N. bulbocodium 'Conspicuous', Hoop-petticoat Daffodil (1776–1850). Dainty golden yellow, almost funnel-shaped flowers that resemble an old-fashioned hoop petticoat; Zones 6–9. Purchase these species, said to be overcollected from the wild, from nursery-grown sources.

N. jonquilla, Single Jonquil, Early Louisiana, Sweeties (1700–1776). Two or three deep yellow flowers per stem; late bloom; 10–12" (or shorter); Zones 6–9. Favorite Daffodil of Celia Anne Jones of Sisters' Bulb Farm: "The aroma is heavenly. Here in Louisiana at least one blooms before anything else." ❀

N. x *odorus,* Single Campernelle (1776–1850). Golden yellow, bell-shaped corona with rounded petals; midseason bloom; 12"; Zones 6–9. ❀

N. × *odorus plenus,* Double Campernelle. Same as previous entry but double. ❀

N. poeticus var. *recurvus,* Old Pheasant's-eye (1600–1699/1831?). A dainty, very fragrant, late-blooming type with glistening flared-back petals surrounding a flat, red-rimmed and green-eyed cup; it blooms late, just before "Double White," and shows to best advantage when massed in a naturalized planting; 10–12"; Zones 4–7. ❀

N. triandus albus, Angel's-tears, Silver-bells. Midseason bloom; two to five bell-shaped cream flowers per stem; good for rock gardens and containers; likes some shade and rich soil; 6"; Zones 4–9. Purchase these species, said to be overcollected from the wild, from nursery-grown sources.

'Van Sion' (1620). The "Double English Daffodil" or "Old Yellow" of many old gardens in the Northeast (my "Telemonius plenus"), valued for its very early bloom. Variable doubling of trumpet and perianth, bright yellow; 12"; Zones 4–8.

Other Types:

'Actaea' (1927). **Division 9**; supposed to be the largest Poet flower ever raised; yellow eye; red-rimmed cup; midseason bloom; 16". ❀

'Avalanche' (1700). **Division 8**; the old "Seventeen Sisters," so named because of its mass of petals (15 to 20) and cupped form; 16–18"; Zones 6–9. ❀

'Barrett Browning' (1945). **Division 3**; circular white perianth with large, slightly frilled orange cup; early bloom; 18".

'Beersheba' (1923). **Division 1**; pure white perianth and trumpet; midseason bloom;

14". "Still to me the most beautiful of all white trumpets" (Elizabeth Lawrence). ❀

'Carlton' (1927). **Division 2**; giant, frilled golden yellow cup with soft yellow perianth; early bloom; 18". ❀

'Cheerfulness' (1923). **Division 4**; double white flowers in clusters with creamy yellow centers; late bloom; a sport of 'Elvira', another *N. tazetta* hybrid, from which later came 'Yellow Cheerfulness'; both now classics; 15". ❀

'Conspicuus'/Barri Conspicuus' (1869). **Division 3**; a charming old favorite, cherished for its delicate yellow petals with short yellow cup just edged with red. A vigorous type found in old gardens, midseason bloom; 16–18"; Zones 4–7.

'Fortune' (1923). **Division 2**; large bright orange cup with bright yellow perianth; midsummer bloom; 17".

'King Alfred' (1899). **Division 1**; so well known it hardly needs description; early bloom; 18". It has been called "the most loved Daffodil of all time." Old House Gardens offers the real thing.

'Laurens Koster' (1906). **Division 8**; one of the earliest crosses between *N. poeticus* and *N. tazetta.* Very similar in appearance to the biblical "Lily of the Valley" (*N. tazetta*) from Solomon's *Song of Songs,* a conspicuous wild flower in Israel in early winter. This variety is the one to grow in a Bible Garden where *N. tazetta* is not hardy. Cluster-flowered, creamy petals with little yellow-orange cups; strong fragrance; 16–18". Zones 6–8. ❀

'Little Witch' (1929). **Division 6**; yellow perianth with yellow trumpet; midseason bloom; 8"

'Mary Copeland' (1914). **Division 4**; double

white flowers with small tufts of orange between petals; midseason to late bloom; 16".

'Milan' (1932). **Division 9**; slightly reflexed white petals, yellow cup with green eye and thin red rim; late blooming; 16–18". ❀

'Mount Hood' (1937). **Division 1**; a beautiful large-flowered striking white, 15–17"; midseason bloom; does best in Zones 3–6.

'Mrs R.O. Backhouse', Pink Daffodil (1923). **Division 2**; named for the famous English breeder; the first pink daffodil; white perianth with shell-pink or apricot trumpet; midseason bloom; 15".

'Orange Queen' (1908). **Division 7**; unusual for its bronzy golden color and grasslike foliage; 10–12"; early to midseason bloom.

'Papillon Blanc'/'White Butterfly' (1940). **Division 11**; white overlapping petals with touches of green and yellow maturing to white; 17–18"; mid to late bloom; Zones 4–8?

'Silver Chimes' (1916). **Division 8**; a fairly hardy *tazetta* with silver-white petals and a pale yellow cup; blooms in clusters; late bloom; 12"; Zones 6–10. ❀

'Thalia' (1916); **Division 5**; several pendant white blooms (two or more), with the petals reflexed "like the wings of an angel"; late bloom; 16". ❀

'W.P. Wilmer' (1884). **Division 1**; a tiny version of the large trumpet form in sulfur-white; early to midseason bloom; pot culture or rock garden.

Note: Gardeners in Zones 9 and 10 can grow hardy varieties by prechilling bulbs for eight to ten weeks at 40 to 45°F (4 to 7°C) before planting in December.

Nicotiana alata ❀

SOLANACEAE

Nicotiana
Flowering Tobacco, Jasmine Tobacco, Winged Tobacco

INTRODUCED: 1850–1900
ZONES: 3–10
TYPE: Hardy Annual/Short-Lived Perennial
HEIGHT: 1½–4'
BLOOM: Summer–Fall
SITE: Sun/Partial Shade

Nicotiana alata, native to tropical South America, is one of several species of ornamental Tobaccos of the Nightshade Family. It is a branching plant, growing to 4 feet, with long, soft green felty leaves mainly clustered at its base and five-petaled, long-tubed flowers growing in graceful sprays all along its stems. These flowers open wide in the evening and release a sweet, jasmine-like scent. They close by noon the following day, drooping their heads as if from exhaustion. The species flower is creamy white tinged with green on the outside of the petals and pure white inside. The genus takes its name from the Frenchman Nicot, who in 1560 obtained *Nicotiana tabacum* (smoking tobacco) from a Belgian merchant and presented it to the queen of France.

Ornamental Tobaccos were among the tender annuals and short-lived perennials whose discovery in the tropics and Mexico during the 19th century caused a sensation in American gardening circles. The Breck catalog carried *Nicotiana longiflora*, Long-flowered Tobacco or Star-petunia. Nicotiana flowers do resemble those of Petunias (both belong to the Nightshade Family): rounded petals somewhat pointed at the tip, the flowers releasing their scent in the evening. But Nicotiana blooms close up by noon, having spent all their energy on the debauchery of the night before. This habit was considered very unfortunate, and by 1916, hybrids, the result of crossing *N. alata* with other species, resulted in shorter, virtually unscented, day-blooming plants with a wider range of colors. By the 1930s, 'Crimson King', still scented, a velvety crimson red and only 15 inches tall, was introduced (a fine plant, still available), and by the late 1940s or 1950s, 'Sensation' hybrids in mixed colors and two white cultivars—'Daylight' and 'Snowstorm'— were available to American gardeners.

Louise Beebe Wilder observed that the old "Dumb white nicotine," celebrated in Edna St. Vincent Millay's poem, ("which wakes and utters her fragrance/In a garden sleeping"), "makes a poor figure by day, and we are apt to feel that it takes up a good deal of room. But with the coming of the night the long creamy tubes freshen and expand and give forth their rich perfume and we are then glad we have so much of it. . . . There are varieties with rose and crimson blossoms but they are not as sweet as the old white kind."

I discovered the old white after having grown all the latest hybrids. I liked their bright colors, ease of culture, accommodation to heat and cold, and long blooming season (from early summer to late fall). I was tantalized by a whiff of sweet scent in the evening air. I wanted more of that, and I was not satisfied until I grew *N. alata* in its unimproved form. Contrary to my expectation of an old-fashioned (in the passé sense),

gawky plant whose only redeeming feature was its celebrated perfume, I found that it makes a great splash in the garden, lighting up shady places in the rear of the border (stately among Monkshood and Bee-balm), equally striking in the sun (featured among annuals such as Poppies), and useful in covering up holes left by early-flowering perennials (Bleeding-heart and Oriental Poppies) or spring bulbs. Cut back in the fall and potted, it makes a decorative windowsill plant—a mound of tapering velvet leaves and rising (to 15 inches) stalks of bloom by midwinter.

I still favor a few older strains, such as the incomparable nonhybrid, 30-inch 'Lime Green'. Its exquisite color has never been rivaled, as its chartreuse blooms complement every other color in the garden and are beautiful in fall bouquets with scarlet Dahlias and white Cosmos. I plant 'Crimson King' in containers with white Sweet Alyssum for reliable all-season color in the sun or shade. I plant the old white in large tubs (at least three plants per tub) or mass them near doorways, along paths, and beside the porch, where we can enjoy their fragrance and beauty. In my experience, the flowers open by midafternoon, well before evening. I suspect that flower opening has a lot to do with climatic conditions, day length, and whether any shade is provided. And when the flowers do open, Nicotiana shows off another of its many attributes—its attractiveness to hummingbirds.

To Grow: In warm winter regions, if you sow the seeds outdoors, Nicotiana will grow as a short-lived perennial. Elsewhere, sow the seeds indoors four to eight weeks before the last frost, sprinkling them with a little sand for even distribution. (There is no need to

Nicotiana blooms close up by noon, having spent all their energy on the debauchery of the night before.

cover them, since light speeds germination.) This should occur in five to twenty days at 70 to 85°F (21 to 29°C). The seedlings resemble Petunias at first but soon develop their characteristic long, tapering leaves. Plant seedlings out after all danger of frost has passed, in fertile, well-drained, light soil, 9 to 12 inches apart, in full sun or partial shade. In many regions, even in my Zone 4 garden, Nicotiana will self-seed for many years. It may be wintered over and propagated by stem cuttings (see "Wintering Annuals," page 24).

COLLECTOR'S CHOICE:

Nicotiana alata, Nicotiana (1850–1900).

'Crimson King' (by 1930s).

'Lime Green' (before 1950).

N. langsdorfii (1900). Very desirable lime-green flowers on tall branching plant to 4'. Same color as 'Lime Green', but a more robust plant.

N. longifolia, Star-petunia (1900). Rare.

Nigella spp.

RANUNCULACEAE

INTRODUCED: 1600–1850

Nigella damascena

Love-in-a-mist
Love-in-a-puzzle

N. hispanica

Spanish Fennel Flower
Devil-in-a-bush

N. sativa

Nutmeg Flower
Bitter Fitch, Black Caraway, Black Cumin, Fennel Flower, Roman Coriander, Wild Fennel

TYPE: Annual/Herb
HEIGHT: 8–24"
BLOOM: Summer
SITE: Sun

Three species of *Nigella* are of historical and horticultural interest, all of them with similar characteristics. Each five-petaled flower with a multitude of protruding stamens is surrounded by a "mist" of bright green, threadlike bracts, and, as the petals fall, a striped, balloon-like pod quickly takes shape; lacy foliage, similar in design to fennel, to which it is often compared, swirls around wiry stems. The most familiar type is Love-in-a-mist—with white, rose-pink, or pale purple-blue flowers—hailing from southern Europe, North Africa, and, as its species name suggests, Damascus. Spanish Fennel Flower, from Spain and southern France, is an arresting plant with larger, purple-blue flowers and maroon stamens. Nutmeg Flower, the "Bitter Fitch" of the Bible (Isaiah 28:27), is native to the Middle East and Asia. The most modest species, it bears violet to white flowers, followed by prominently horned pods that are filled with small, black peppery seeds (a characteristic preserved in the genus name, which is derived from the Latin for "black"). These seeds are important in the cuisines of southern Europe, the Middle East, and India.

The first *Nigella* to reach England was Nutmeg Flower, recorded in *The Grete Herball* of 1526, where it was prized for its aromatic seeds used for flavoring cakes. They were also put into muslin bags for scenting linen and clothes in the same way as Lavender and Costmary leaves were used (natural fragrance was very important in the household economy). Gerard advised heating seeds over hot ashes to scent a musty room or clear the head. Love-in-a-mist followed, introduced from Damascus in 1570. Gerard advised mixing these non-aromatic seeds with vinegar to take away freckles. Of greater interest were its pretty flowers, single blue or double white. In 1640, Parkinson recorded double blue flowers. Spanish Fennel Flower arrived in England by 1620, and by 1693 a double form was grown.

The first *Nigella* in the New World colonies was Nutmeg Flower cultivated for its general usefulness. By the early 1800s all three *Nigellas* were offered in American seed catalogs: Love-in-a-mist and Spanish Fennel Flower as ornamentals, and Nutmeg Flower for its culinary uses. The only one to survive as a garden flower was Love-in-a-mist, valued for its ease of culture and grace at every stage, from flower to seedpod. It was a favorite of Gertrude Jekyll, a discerning gardener with an artist's eye who could see possibilities in the most common, unpretentious flowers. Through careful selection over many years, she bred the ever-popular seed strain 'Miss Jekyll'—semidouble, soft blue—a classic of the type.

I grow Love-in-a-mist as a solid block of blue at the front of a border with Calendulas, yellow and orange. For several years, I have been sowing its seeds to form a colorful Oriental carpet on a steep bank among soft orange California Poppies, single red Poppies *(Papaver rhoeas),* California Bluebells *(Phacelia campanularia),* purple Heliotrope *(Phacelia*

tanacetifolia), Purple-top Sage *(Salvia viridis),* and annual white Baby's-breath *(Gypsophila elegans).* In a perennial border, Love-in-a-mist's lacy haze of soft blue shows up well against silver foliage, especially the nearly white, felty leaves of Beach Wormwood *(Artemisia stelleriana).* With successive sowings, I always have flowers in bloom and the decorative pods that follow. I've grown Spanish Fennel Flower as an exotic, since it doesn't reseed in my garden. It should be grown in small groups as an accent near the front of the border, where individual plants can be appreciated.

To Grow: In cool climates, sow seeds of Love-in-a-mist directly in the ground after the soil warms in early spring (before it gets hot). In warm climates, sow seeds in the fall for spring bloom. Space plants 12 inches apart; they dislike transplanting, but you can succeed by replanting young seedlings in clumps and watering them well (some will survive). Make successive sowings to prolong blooming. Given sun and well-drained soil, Love-in-a-mist will self-sow indefinitely, but to keep special colors and forms, resow occasionally with commercial seed. Spanish Fennel Flower needs more heat, so sow seeds in peat pots indoors in early spring, then plant seedlings outside when all danger of frost has passed. Seeds of Nutmeg Flower can be sown outside like Love-in-a-mist.

To Use: Nigellas are good cut flowers. There are two things to remember when harvesting *Nigella* seedpods for floral crafts or dried bouquets: pick stems before the narrow slits at the top of the pod have opened to release quantities of seed, and harvest stems individually rather than in sprays. Bunch stems and hang them upside down to dry in a cool, dark place, then lay them down in a box lined with tissue paper until ready to use, or place them upright, wrapped in newspaper, in a bucket. Blue flowers dry well and should be picked when they are in fresh bloom.

COLLECTOR'S CHOICE:

Nigella damascena, Love-in-a-mist. Single flowers; white, rose, pale purple-blue; 1½" wide; plant to 18".

N. hispanica, Spanish Fennel Flower. Purple-blue flowers, slightly scented, to 24" tall.

'Miss Jekyll' (before 1916). Semidouble soft blue flowers, larger than the species, to 2" across on 12" stems. Miss Jekyll comments, "the colour is a pure, soft blue of a quality distinctively its own" *(Annuals and Biennials).*

'Miss Jekyll Alba'. Semidouble white flowers; 12" tall.

'Miss Jekyll Deep Blue'. Semidouble deep blue flowers.

'Miss Jekyll Rose'. Semidouble rose flowers; 18" tall.

N. sativa, Nutmeg flower. White or violet flowers; 8–12" tall.

Paeonia spp. ❀

RANUNCULACEAE

Peony
Piony

INTRODUCED: 1600–1950
ZONES: 2–9
TYPE: Perennial Flower
HEIGHT: 1½–4'
BLOOM: Spring–Early Summer
SITE: Sun/Partial Shade

*P*eonies are very hardy shrublike perennials native to Europe and Asia, where they have long been cultivated. By 1086 A.D., for instance, the Chinese were growing superior strains of *Paeonia lactiflora,* from which has come the most popular type grown today. Its large double blooms are synonymous with the word "Peony."

Peonies grow from fleshy rhizomatous roots whose crowns sprout red buds in early spring after a period of dormancy, usually brought on by freezing temperatures. Plants are unusually long-lived, with fifty-year-old specimens being common. The often fragrant flowers grow out of round, tightly wrapped buds on sturdy stems. The stems vary in height from the dainty, very early-blooming Fern-leaved Peony *(Paeonia tenuifolia)*—1½ feet tall with 3-inch single or double crimson or white flowers; to the old-fashioned Grandma's or Memorial Day Peony *(P. officinalis)*—2 to 3 feet tall with 5-inch double crimson or white blooms; to the later-blooming Asiatic hybrids, mostly developed from *P. lactiflora*—up to 4 feet tall and varying in flower form from elegant single-petaled types with numerous golden stamens to enormous fully double globular blooms as wide as 10 inches across. Fern-leaved Peony dies back after flowering, but the other types retain their glossy foliage all season.

The genus name is derived from the Greek *paeon,* a word associated with healing. In the well-regulated medieval household, the European *Paeonia officinalis* was a sovereign remedy for a variety of complaints and a food item, too. The Alewife in *Piers Plowman* declares, "I have pepper and peony seed and a pound of garlic . . . for fasting days." The root was used as a cure for palsy and, according to Gerard and Culpeper, as an an-

The genus name is derived from the Greek paeon, a word associated with healing.

❧

tidote, in some form, for "nightmares" and "melancholie." This was the so-called "Female Peionie" *(P. mascula* was known as the "Male Peionie")—single-petaled and crimson, commonly grown in England by the 16th century, when Gerard also knew the "double red with flowers like the great double rose of Provence." The latter was the form grown in early American gardens (whether for use or pleasure is not recorded).

Chinese Peony *(Paeonia lactiflora),* whose roots were used as a source of food in China as early as 536 A.D., was introduced to American gardeners by the early 19th century, when it was greatly prized for its enormous blooms. By 1820, breeding Peonies began in Europe using *P. officinalis* and *P. lactiflora,* resulting in popular strains that are still with us today. Foremost among these is the classic 'Festiva Maxima' (1851), regarded as the greatest of white Peonies: large, fragrant white blooms flecked with crimson, vigorous and early blooming, 3 to 4 feet high, and always loaded with flowers, their centers hidden in a mass of petals. In 1866, Joseph Breck offered one hundred Peonies, "all desirable," including the newest cultivars from Europe and the indestructible, ever-popular *P. officinalis* 'Rubra Plena', a household friend since earliest settler days.

Peonies, like Roses, epitomize the heirloom quality inherent in certain plants that seem to embody cherished family ties and associations. I have discovered many venerable clumps, lovingly planted by young brides more than fifty years ago from a few pieces of roots carefully brought from the home farm. Peonies, also like Roses, often endure neglect, living on long after the people who planted them, surviving among weeds, even

unblooming in light woods, a mute testimony to former human activity. One reason for Peonies' longevity is that they have no natural enemies. They are cherished for their beauty of form, color—pink, rose, crimson, and white—and fragrance.

In older gardens, Peonies are often found growing in grand spreading clumps by themselves in a bed cut into the grass. After the flowers bloom in late spring and early summer (the late-blooming types), the foliage is still attractive. Another device is to plant them near early-flowering bulbs as an all-season cover. Borders of Peonies planted as a hedge along driveways or to define garden "rooms" also provide gorgeous blooms and handsome all-season foliage. The shorter, less vigorous types can be combined with Wild Bleeding-hearts *(Dicentra eximia* or *D. formosa),* early-flowering perennials such as Dame's-rocket and Lupines, and later-blooming Daylilies. The Bleeding-hearts will carry on with flowers all season, a low-growing ground cover among the handsome Peony shrubs. Fern-leaved Peony, a mass of small blooms in very early spring, is a perfect rock garden plant. By carefully choosing from among the varied forms of heirloom types (many bred in the United States), you can extend the Peony's period of bloom over six weeks, from early spring to early summer.

Generous bouquets of Peonies are certainly part of the pleasure of growing these plants. If cut when some of the flower buds are just beginning to open, bouquets will keep a week in water. Never cut more than two-thirds of the buds from a four-year-old plant, or more than 10 percent from a younger one, and leave two or three leaves on each stem to nourish the plant in the ground.

To Grow: Plant roots with three to five buds in the fall, in rich, slightly acid, well-drained soil well supplemented with organic matter. Choose a sunny spot (slightly shaded in warmer regions) protected from high winds—near an established shrubbery, for instance. Dig a hole about 2 feet wide and 1½ feet deep and throw in a couple of handfuls of bonemeal mixed with soil; fill in the hole with a compost-soil mixture. The tops of the buds should be no more than 2 inches below the soil's surface. Planting too deep is the most common cause of unblooming Peonies, an unfortunate state of affairs. Remember that patience is required, for Peonies do not attain perfection for three to five years. In heavy clay and in warmer growing regions, plant the buds only 1 inch deep. Shallow planting actually encourages flower production. Space plants 3 feet apart, and for the first winter mulch the area when the ground freezes with a blanket of straw or evergreen boughs. Once the plants are established, no winter protection is required. Peonies do best in cold climates but can be grown in the West Coast areas of Zone 9, where nights are cool. There, withhold water in the early fall, from September through mid-October, and cut the plant to the ground. This will induce dormancy, which is needed for another season of bloom.

Heavy-headed types will probably need some support, such as circular rings set around each plant before it begins to grow. Divide the plant if you wish (you don't have to) in the fall, cutting large, fleshy roots into smaller pieces with three eyes each.

If you're familiar with only the commonly grown large double-flowered type, explore this rich world of heirloom Peonies, classified below according to flower form:

S=Single, with one row of five or more petals and showy golden stamens.

SD=Semidouble, with more than one row of petals and stamens still apparent.

D=Double, with stamens entirely hidden in petals.

J=Japanese, with two or more rows of petals, usually flattish, and feathery petaloid stamens (staminodes).

COLLECTOR'S CHOICE:

❀ indicates especially fragrant types.

Paeonia officinalis 'Alba Plena' (1600–1800).
   Double white; early bloom; 2–3'. ❀
'Rosa Superba'. Double pink. ❀
'Rubra Plena', Grandma's Peony. Double
   crimson. ❀
'*P. tenuifolia* 'Flora Plena', Fern-leaved Peony,
   Adonis Peony ❀ (1776–1800). Small,
   erect double flowers with ferny foliage;
   very early bloom; 1½'. This is supposed to
   be one of the plants the settlers took
   westward from the East. ❀

Hybrids:

'Chestine Gowdy' (1913). **D**; silvery pink
   with a creamy collar of petals; late bloom;
   2–4'. ❀
'Duchesse de Nemours' (1856). **D**; white
   with a yellow center just apparent;
   midseason bloom; 2–4'. ❀
'Elsa Sass' (1930). **D**; creamy white; late
   bloom; 2–4'.
'Felix Crouse' (1881). **D**; deep rosy red; late
   bloom; 2–4'.
'Festiva Maxima' (1851); **D**; white-flecked

crimson; especially fine cut flower; early
bloom; 3–4'. ❀

'Firelight' (1950). **S**; rosy pink with red
stigmas; early bloom; 2–4'.

'Gypsy Rose' (1939). **J**; rosy pink with mass
of curled staminodes; midseason bloom;
2–4'.

'Harriet Olney' (1920). **S**; rose; midseason
bloom; 3'.

'Martha Bullock' (1907). **D**; large pink and
ivory flowers (8–10"); midseason bloom;
4'.

'Mikado' (1893). **J**; crimson red with yellow
staminodes; late bloom; 2–4'.

'Minnie Shaylor' (1919). **SD**; a lovely flower,
pale pink to white petals surrounding
golden anthers; midseason; 3'.

'Miss America' (1936). **SD**; large, white
bowl-shaped blooms; early bloom;
recommended for warmer regions; 2–4'.

'Mons. Jules Elie' (1888). **D**; Enormous
flower heads, silver-pink; (yes, this does
need strong staking); wonderfully long-
lasting cut flower; early; 34".

'Nippon Beauty' (1927). **J**; deep red; late
bloom; 2–4'.

'Philippe Revoire' (1911). **D**; Dark crimson
satiny flowers (small to medium) with a
rose scent; late; 30".❀

'Red Charm' (1944). **D**; very striking for its
full deep red flower head against dark
green foliage; American Peony Society
Gold Medal selection; early; 3'.

'Rosedale' (1936). **SD**; dark red; roselike in
form; early bloom; 2–3'.

'Walter Faxon' (1904). **D**; bright pink;
midseason bloom; 2–4'. ❀

'White Cap' (1956). **J**; raspberry flower with
ivory and pale pink center; midseason;
32".

Papaver spp.

PAPAVERACEAE

Poppy

INTRODUCED: 1600–1930
ZONES: 3–9
TYPE: Hardy Annual/Perennial Flower
HEIGHT: 1½–4'
BLOOM: Spring–Fall
SITE: Sun

*A*bout fifty species of Poppies, annuals
and perennials, are native to Europe; a
few are also native to western North America.
The types discussed here share silky, crinkled
single or double flowers with four or five
petals—from 2 inches wide in the annual
Corn Poppy *(Papaver rhoeas)* to as big as 12
inches wide in the perennial Oriental Poppy
(P. orientale)—in colors ranging from brilliant
vermilion to pastels, sometimes delicately
bordered white or blotched black, with
showy black stamens and anthers in the center of the bloom. Leaves vary from deeply
lobed, almost ferny in the Oriental Poppy to
grayish, jagged (like lettuce), and clasping in
the annual Lettuce Poppy *(P. somniferum)*. Two
subspecies of this Poppy have been cultivated
since time immemorial as a source of medicine and food.

The garden form—Peony Poppy—is
grown for its beautiful double flowers and
distinctive seed heads, which are often used
in indoor arrangements. An ancient symbol
of fertility, a single plump Peony Poppy pod
can hold as many as thirty-two thousand seeds
(Linnaeus is supposed to have counted them).

The Lettuce or Opium Poppy was the first

type to be grown in America, perhaps for medicinal and culinary purposes, but soon ornamental types, appreciated for their diverse forms—fringed, delicately veined and splotched, and peony-flowered (very double) —and colors—white, red, purple, and pink— were favored for late spring and summer bloom. They cause a sensation when massed, as there are usually a wide variety of flowers and seed heads in any planting. The various colors and forms readily crossbreed, creating new designs. Collecting and swapping seeds of these crosses was a regular feature of old-time gardening and is still practiced in some areas. I have found old peony-flowered strains kept alive by an eighty-year-old gardener who called them "Champagne Poppies"— very elegant on 3-foot stems with bluish green pinked and clasping leaves and fully double flower heads of numerous translucent peach-pink petals, lightly veined a darker pink. As with many naturally occurring double-flowered forms that have been selected and cultivated over the years, there is always some variation in form—some flowers with fewer petals, some with a grayish blotch. This gardener rogues out the undesirable types to keep his strain pure, a practice I follow.

Jefferson grew both the single white Poppy *(Papaver somniferum),* which he called the "Larger Poppy," and the Corn Poppy *(P. rhoeas),* which he referred to as the "Lesser Poppy." This is the humble weed of European grain fields, grown for centuries as a medicinal and ornamental plant. In England, where the red petals were gathered from the fields to use in the preparation of a syrup (to soothe various ailments), children employed to gather them in vast amounts were advised to wear small muslin bags suspended from their necks so both hands would be free to pick the petals.

Double garden forms were known as early as 1629, and by the 18th century there were many variants, one of which was described by Philip Miller, curator of the Chelsea Physic Garden, as "very double firy flowers, which are beautifully edged with white." It wasn't until the 1880s that the Reverend Wilkes, continuing the same process of selection and breeding, produced a similar type from a wild sport—one flower in a mass of wild Corn Poppies, the margins of its petals lined with white—the descendants of which bear the name Shirley Poppy in honor of the village where Wilkes lived. He worked diligently and methodically to achieve his results. Every growing season he selected seedlings that showed marked variation, carefully collecting their seeds and sowing them again. Eventually, he created a well-defined strain characterized by an infinite range of colors from crimson and orange-scarlet through tints of rose and salmon pink. These silky-petaled, waved flowers were edged with white and still had all the airy grace of the wild type— an achievement that remains a lasting tribute to his breeding skills. Although the single form was reported to be Wilkes's favorite type, many gardeners prefer the doubles out of sheer greed—the blooms last longer, as do most double types in general. Both the Peony and Corn Poppy types are hardy annuals, surviving into the fall and self-seeding from year to year.

The flamboyant Oriental Poppy, a long-lasting perennial, was introduced around 1744 from Armenia. The extraordinary size of the flowers—at least 6 inches across and

An ancient symbol of fertility, a single plump Peony Poppy pod can hold as many as thirty-two thousand seeds.

often bigger—and their incredible color made them an immediate success with gardeners. As Mrs. Wilder complained, however, after the first thrill had subsided, its very brilliance became the reason for its fall from grace, as if "a scarlet flower was only less terrible than a scarlet sin." Added to this, its vigorous, sprawling habit of growth and early bloom tended to cause an undeniable hole in even the best-planned border. Gertrude Jekyll offered a solution that has been standard advice for decades: overplant with Baby's-breath (*Gypsophila paniculata*). In fact, Baby's-breath is not so easy to establish for all gardeners, and other devices must be sought.

In my own gardens, I have a running battle with my husband, Jigs, who adores the sinful scarlet flowers—the more the merrier. No matter how they flop, smothering everything in their midst in a 3-foot-wide circle, and how they propagate, we must have them all. In defense, I have resorted to ruthlessly pulling out extras in the spring (not to worry, they come right back from their roots), ringing them with slender stakes, and against them planting lower-growing bushy perennials such as Mountain-bluet, whose silvery gray leaves are decorative all season. Then the gorgeous Oriental Poppies complement the flowers of early summer—blue Lupines, Iris, and Foxglove. With a few seedlings of Hollyhock Mallow growing in their vicinity, and Nicotiana on hand as well, I know I can carry on without shame for the rest of the summer.

My favorite Oriental Poppy is a self-seeded soft salmon pink variety that never spreads and grows conveniently under the low branches of an old plum tree along our lane, blooming just after the Daffodils are finished for the season. I have found surviving Oriental Poppies doing very well on their own in abandoned gardens after more than thirty years, blooming in spring shade. From these observations I have concluded that naturalizing them, if you have the room, may be the ultimate answer to their tendency to sprawl.

Superior strains, some of the best developed by the English nurseryman Amos Perry (of 'Perry's Blue' Siberian Iris fame), are still available, all developed in the early 1900s. "Earth tones!" Jigs complains, but they are undeniably beautiful and far easier to accommodate to planting schemes. The best are 'Mrs. Perry', a handsome apricot pink, and 'Queen Alexandra', a lovely pink, which gave rise to 'Silver Queen', the first white, no

VERA'S POPPY SEED CAKE

1 stick (8 tablespoons or ¼ pound) butter
¾ cup sugar
2 eggs
1 tablespoon vanilla
Juice of one orange (⅓ cup)
¾ cup poppy seeds
½ cup sour cream
1½ cup unbleached white flour
1 teaspoon baking powder
½ teaspoon baking soda

Beat together the butter and sugar, then beat in eggs, add vanilla, and mix until fluffy. Add juice from one fresh orange (or ⅓ cup orange juice), the poppy seeds, sour cream, and dry ingredients. Mix thoroughly. Pour batter into greased standard-size angel food cake form, and bake at 350° F (175°C) for 30 to 40 minutes. The top of the cake should turn light brown. Dense and delicious, this is the real thing. Serve in thin slices.

longer available. 'Mrs. Perry', though, threw up some chance white-flowering seedlings in the garden of one of Mr. Perry's customers. He went to see them and eventually brought the new variety to market as 'Perrys' White' (1914), a satiny white Oriental Poppy with a conspicuous eye or blotch, a favorite since it was introduced. All of these are hybrids arising from initial crosses with *Papaver bracteatum* and introduced sometime in the 19th century. The true species form of the Oriental Poppy is the only one to come true from seed—an unmistakable, unregenerate, brilliant vermilion. "Its immense flame-colored blossoms . . . will astonish the novice," 19th-century Canadian writer Annie Jack observed. And, she could have added, it will thrill even the most hardened gardeners.

Annual Poppies are elegant additions to any planting, either of perennials or annuals, and two sowings, early and late, will ensure a long season of bloom. Corn Poppies, especially the form known as 'Lady Bird' (derived form *Papaver commutatum,* introduced in the 19th century), are dramatic if planted in a large group bordered by single white Petunias. Annual Poppies are especially beautiful in summer bouquets. One is advised to singe their stems to prolong their bloom indoors, but this has never worked for me. The ephemeral flowers last well in bouquets if picked when the drooping buds are just beginning to look up but before they have opened at all. Peony Poppy seed heads, on their long stems, are used to great effect in winter bouquets.

To Grow: While annual Poppies are easy to grow, their growth requirements are quite specific. The three most common reasons for failure are as follows:

1. Too deep planting of the seeds. Sow seeds sparingly with a small amount of sand, then lightly press them on top of the soil with a board (they need light to germinate).

2. Too late planting. Seeds must be sown outdoors, since Poppies don't transplant well, and they need cool temperatures to germinate. The best plants are produced from seeds sown in late fall, which germinate the following spring; in Zones 8 to 10, such a sowing produces blooms by late winter or very early spring. For almost continuous bloom from late spring to fall, you can sow twice—once in the fall and once in early spring—to establish a cycle of early- and late-blooming plants.

3. Too close planting. Poppies should be thinned way back in their early growth, to 9 to 12 inches apart. This will encourage vigorous, healthy plants with large, beautiful flowers. The soil should be well drained and moderately enriched, and the site should be sunny, preferably protected from the wind, though the thin, wiry stems are tougher than they look.

Oriental Poppies, if grown from seeds in moderately enriched, well-drained soil, need full sun and a 55°F (13° C) soil temperature to germinate in about ten to fifteen days. Young plants should be set out when dormant, at least 15 to 18 inches apart, with the top of the roots 3 inches below the soil surface. I have never found them difficult to divide and replant in late fall (they can be left undisturbed for years), but a bit of root is inevitably left behind. Mature plants die back after blooming in early summer, but fresh leaves, and even a few flowers, reappear by fall. Oriental Poppies are perennial to Zone 9 where nights are cool. Elsewhere, they can be grown as annuals, from plants rather than seeds, in a cool, protected spot.

To Use: When seedpods of *P. somniferum* begin to mature, cut stems with pods for drying. Place stems in a paper bag (don't crowd them or they'll mold) and leave in a sunny spot indoors until they are perfectly dry. The seeds will shake out and these can be used for baking. My Czech friend Vera comes by in the summer to harvest Lettuce Poppy seeds by the gallon, then she sends us an authentic European Poppy Seed Cake.

COLLECTOR'S CHOICE:

Papaver commutatum 'Lady Bird' (1876). Vigorous, showier type of Corn Poppy; bright red with black blotch; 20".

P. orientale, Oriental Poppy (around 1744). Late spring bloom; 3'.

'Beauty of Livermore'. Close to species form.

'Mrs. Perry' (1914). White with maroon blotches.

'Princess Victoria Louise' (by 1930s). Salmon pink.

'Queen Alexandra' (before 1912). Soft rose.

P. rhoeas, African-rose, Corn Poppy, Corn Rose, Flanders Field Poppy, Redweed (1700–1776).

'Single Shirley' (late 19th century). sometimes offered as 'Rev. Wilkes Mixed', semidoubles and singles, 18–24".

'Double Shirley' or 'Shirley Reselected Double Mixed'.

P. somniferum, Lettuce Poppy, Peony Poppy (1600–1699). Peony-flowered hybrids— very double flowers—may be offered as *Papaver paeoniflorum.* These are indispen-sable for a Celia Thaxter–style cottage garden. All are wonderful in bouquets. Look for singles. They're beautiful, too, perhaps even more so because of their wide, translucent petals (their flowers are more fleeting, of course). After you have grown these a while you will have many variants.

'Black'. Gorgeous deep purple flowers; 2'.

'Creamy Yellow'. Double flowers; 3–4'.

'Flemish Antique Shades'. Shades of red striped white, apricot-cream brushed with burgundy, white striped dusty rose; 3–4'.

'Frosted Salmon'. Soft salmon-rose; 3–4'.

'Oase'. Deep scarlet with white blotch; 3–4'.

'Rose'. Double rose flowers; 3–4'.

'White Cloud'. Pure white; 2½'.

Other Types:

'Rose Feathers'. Doubled-flowered with laciniated or fringed petals; 2½'.

'Red Ruby'; tulip-shaped single flower with plum blotch; 2½' tall.

Parthenocissus quinquefolia

VITACEAE

Virginia Creeper

American-ivy, Five-leaved-ivy, Woodbine

INTRODUCED: 1600–1699
ZONES: 3–10
NATIVE
TYPE: High-Climbing Perennial Clinging Vine
SEASON OF INTEREST: All-Season Foliage
SITE: Sun/Partial Shade

Virginia Creeper is one of about fifteen species of *Parthencissus* native to North American and the West Indies. It grows wild from Quebec west to Minnesota and south to Florida, Texas, and Mexico in woods and on rocks. Rapid-growing, of loose, open habit, it is highly valued for its ability to grow in damp or dry conditions and cling to walls by means of tendrils, like the grapevine and Clematis. Its much-admired foliage—long and coarsely toothed with five leaflets—turns a brilliant scarlet in early fall when few other leaves have colored. The bluish black berries are handsome, too—a contrast to the foliage and especially attractive to birds. When the leaves eventually fall, they reveal a delicate tracery of woody stems.

The ornamental value of this easily grown native vine must have been apparent to early American gardeners, who could not help noticing its brilliant autumn foliage and loosely branching habit, for which it became prized for covering arbors, the side shoots gracefully dropping downward. The bark is reported to have medicinal use, but if the settlers used the vine for this purpose, they have left no record of it. Virginia Creeper maintained its popularity throughout the 19th century, when it was described as "the most ornamental plant of its genus." Joseph Breck was lavish in his praise, pointing out that it could be found growing on the best houses on Beacon Street in Boston. Elsewhere, its uses were more humble, but highly regarded nevertheless, when, for instance, it was planted on railroad embankments to help prevent erosion. Discerning gardeners such as Mrs. Wilder valued Virginia Creeper for clinging to trees "up which it clambers, twining free here and there, and in the autumn making the tree appear as if on fire."

And, as she pointed out, the scarlet leaves can be added to indoor bouquets for a dramatic effect.

I found Virginia Creeper in two quite different circumstances: the first was growing up the side of a tumbling-down farmstead built in the 1870s by descendants of settlers from the Isle of Skye; the second was growing up the side of the elegant lodge, built around the same time, on the Bell estate. Both vines had been growing untended for decades and were none the worse for it, as far as I could tell. David Fairchild had planted the Virginia Creeper at the lodge as a climbing companion for Climbing Hydrangea, and they made a handsome pair—one a mass of green leaves, the other brilliant red—almost side by side against the wooden wall soaring to the top of the roof. Evidently, Virginia Creeper has always had a wide appeal, at home in the country as well as in the city, on all types of buildings, and in a variety of situations.

Fairchild, despite his fame and fortune as a plant collector and author, never forgot that he was a country boy who, until the age of eighteen, lived where streets were made of dirt and mud holes were a matter of course. His taste in flora was shaped by his travels to exotic places, but he valued native plants too, as reflected in the surviving plantings at the lodge, particularly in the high-climbing Virginia Creeper, a lasting tribute to this American who worked all his life to enlarge our collective pool of useful and ornamental plants. "Fragrant and charming . . . vines and trees," he noted, "enrich our lives with a beauty far more lasting than casual visits to any museum of art" (*The World Grows Round My Door*, 1947).

Although the species form is a splendid

Virginia Creeper's much-admired foliage turns a brilliant scarlet in early fall when few other leaves have colored.

plant, Engelmann's-ivy *(Parthenocissus quinquefolia* 'Engelmannii'), introduced in the late 19th century, is denser in habit, with smaller, leathery leaves. A more refined type, it also makes a good ground cover and screen, as well as a climber on stone walls or trellises. The wild form, used to cover steep banks, makes a foot-high carpet. Boston-ivy or Japanese Creeper *(P. tricuspidata),* introduced from Japan in 1862, is considered by some to be the best for clinging to stonework, which it does by means of small, rootlike holdfasts. It is very well suited to city conditions, immune to dirt and pollution, with overlapping leaves like shingles that also turn color with the season. "In sheer splendor," a New Jersey Experiment Station Bulletin proclaimed (circa 1900), "there is no climbing plant that equals the Japanese Ivy when it assumes its October garb. . . . it seems as if the artist had dipped the giant brush in a harmonious mixture of crimson and gold and touched the walls as an earnest of Infinite purpose and perfection."

To Grow: All of these vines are rapid growers, attaining 6 to 10 feet during their first season and much more thereafter, growing as high as 60 feet. They tolerate dry or wet conditions, sun or partial shade. For best growth, plant them in moist but well-drained, loamy soil. Set plants 3 to 4 feet apart near the wall, arbor, or support you want them to climb. Prune them early in the spring to restrain unwanted growth, redirect growth, or induce side branching for use as a groundcover. Propagate by spring cuttings or from self-rooted layered stems.

COLLECTOR'S CHOICE (all sold as plants):

Parthenocissus quinquefolia, Virginia Creeper (1600–1699).

'Engelmannii' (late 19th century).

P. tricuspidata, Boston-ivy, Japanese Creeper (1862).

Pelargonium spp. ❀

GERANIACEAE

Scented Geranium
Storksbill

INTRODUCED: 1760–1948
ZONE: 10
TYPE: Tender Shrubby Perennial Herb/ Flower
HEIGHT: Trailing, to 5'
BLOOM: Summer
SEASON OF INTEREST: All-Season Foliage
SITE: Sun

Scented Geraniums belong to the large and interesting *Pelargonium* genus of about 280 species, mostly native to South Africa, which also includes the familiar Garden Geranium *(P. X hortorum),* Ivy Geranium *(P. peltatum),* and Martha Washington Geranium *(P. X domesticum).* These tender perennials should not be confused with the hardy perennials from Europe of the genus *Geranium* that are commonly known as Cranesbill. All of these plants belong to the same family and share distinctive fruits shaped like a bird's beak, as preserved in their common names.

Scented Geraniums are extraordinarily varied in leaf form and habit, ranging from low, bushy trailing types to medium-sized shrubs. The leaves, gray to deep green and usually velvety in texture, are curled and crimped, deeply lobed, large and small, undulating, variegated, and even fringed. Fragrance (the plants' main claim to fame) matches leaf form in diversity: light to heavy rose, mint, lemon, musk, fruit, pine, and pungent, as well as combinations of these. In areas where they enjoy the same climate as in their native habitat (hot, dry summers with cool evenings and frost-free winters), they may attain their maximum size—4 to 5 feet—and become truly shrubby. Elsewhere they are grown as annuals in the summer and as houseplants in the winter.

Fragrant oils, distilled from their leaves, have been used to scent perfumes, soaps, and cosmetics, often as a cheap substitute for the more expensive attar of roses. Scented Geraniums have been grown in England since the reign of Charles I, when they were used as a strewing and potpourri herb by cottagers and gentry alike. Although useful as a flavoring, in much the same way as vanilla, for cakes and puddings, it seems unlikely that the early settlers regarded Geraniums as a household necessity. The earliest record of any *Pelargonium* in America is 1760, when John Bartram received seeds from abroad. By 1791 Jefferson was growing potted Geraniums in the White House (the familiar Garden Geranium), but after the 1840s, all types marched westward with the pioneers, one of a group of treasured plants that was gradually introduced across the land.

In time, scented types were regarded as passé, of interest only to those who like to have a pot or two around the kitchen to flavor jellies, add to potpourri, or slip into nosegays. Of greater interest were the brightly flowered bedding Geraniums that filled Victorian flower gardens with solid blocks of dazzling color—scarlet, red, bright pink, and white. But the wheel of horticultural fashion keeps going around, and today's gardeners are beginning once more to appreciate the more subdued beauty of Scented Geraniums, with their infinite variety and appealing fragrances. Scented Geraniums can be grown all winter indoors on the windowsill, then planted out to enhance any garden, especially an herb garden. Where conditions permit, they can be grown as perennial shrubs of varied habit—upright, stocky, and branching, or low and trailing—often with beautiful flowers.

Perhaps the best way to show off a group of choice cultivars is in containers set in a sunny spot, "standing on the terrace or porch where we drink tea or after-dinner coffee to give off their pleasant perfume as we walk past them and our clothes and hands touch their leaves" (Helen Fox, *Gardening with Herbs for Flavor and Fragrance,* 1933). "Dampness is said to bring out their scent," Fox observed, "so they are placed along the margins of our garden pool as in Spain, where the fragrance in flowers or leaves is as much valued as their form or color."

To Grow: Indoors, pot Scented Geraniums in humusy soil, slightly on the heavy side to retain moisture (three parts loam to one part sand plus a little peat moss) and somewhat acid. Place the pots where conditions are cool and sunny. They thrive in 70°F (21°C) daytime and 55 to 65°F (13 to 18°C) nighttime temperatures. Turn the pot occasionally for even growth and water it thoroughly when the soil is dry below the surface. All Geraniums are remarkably drought-tolerant and can do with very little water. Fertilize the soil about every three weeks with a dilute solution of indoor plant food.

Outdoors, space plants 1 foot or more apart, depending on the type, in humusy, friable soil, prepared to a depth of 10 to 12

Today's gardeners are beginning once more to appreciate the more subdued beauty of Scented Geraniums, with their infinite variety and appealing fragrances.

inches. Prune the plants regularly to maintain their shape, cutting out woody and weak branches. Frequent cutting of branches for use is probably all that is needed, especially for plants grown in containers. For potting Geraniums outdoors, use the same soil mix as for indoors. Depending on the size of the container and the site, these will need more frequent watering than in the garden proper. Both indoors and out, Geraniums appreciate good air circulation to discourage disease, so don't crowd them.

When you pot outdoor plants before frost, prune back the roots and top in equal proportions, or take midsummer stem cuttings from tender, not woody, tips of branches, sliced cleanly with a sharp knife just below a node or joint (short joints make the best plants). I have increased plants of my hand-me-down Rose Geranium by rooting a branch in soil, but more care should be taken to ensure success. The goal of every gardener is to grow bushy plants of whatever type. To encourage this, pinch back growing tips when the plant is 4 to 5 feet tall, repeating the process until you achieve the desired shape. Move the plant to a larger container (only one size larger) when it has entirely filled its pot and has lost its vigor. Scented Geraniums like to be pot-bound, up to a point.

COLLECTOR'S CHOICE (all sold as plants): Though scented Geraniums are famed for their fragrance, the beauty of their flowers should not be overlooked, as represented in this collection of heirloom types.

Pelargonium capitatum 'Attar of Roses', Rose-scented Geranium (1923). Descended from the species form introduced into English gardens circa 1690; rose scent; rosy pink flowers in dense clusters; useful wherever a strong musky rose scent is wanted; to 3'.

P. × citrosum 'Prince of Orange', Orange Geranium (before 1850). Orange scent; large form with broad leaves and lavender pink flowers feathered red.

P. crispum 'French Lace', Lemon Geranium (1948). Lemon scent; bush, with white-margined leaves; also known as 'Prince Rupert Variegated'; to 3'.

P. denticulatum 'Filicifolium', Fern-leaf Geranium (1879). Pungent scent; shrubby and branched with finely cut feathery leaves; purple-veined pink flowers.

P. fulgidum 'Scarlet Unique' (before 1855). Mild scent; large, brilliant scarlet flowers feathered deep purple; deeply cut grayish green leaves; very tall, to 5'.

P. logeei 'Old Spice' (Ernest Logee, 1948, now a classic). Nutmeg/old spice scent; grayish, deeply lobed ruffled leaves with whitish flowers veined pink; fine basket plant.

P. quercifolium 'Pretty Polly', Oak-leaved Geranium (1850). Almond scent; deeply lobed heart-shaped leaves blotched brown or purple; rarely flowers; short and shrubby.

'Skeleton's Unique' (1861). Pungent; vigorous habit; branching, with dense light pink flower clusters and waxy leaves; prostrate when potted; fine for baskets.

P. tomentosum 'Joy Lucille' (Ernest Logee, 1940s). Herb-scented; tall habit with large leaves and small carmine-pink flowers; to 3'.

Petunia × hybrida ❀

SOLANACEAE

Petunia

INTRODUCED: 1850–1900
TYPE: Tender Perennial/Annual
HEIGHT: ½'–1½'
BLOOM: Summer–Fall
SITE: Sun/Partial Shade

The parents of the modern Petunia are two wild, short-lived perennials of the Nightshade Family discovered in South America by a French botanist named Petun, for whom the genus is named. *Petunia axillaris* was discovered in Brazil in 1923. Its small, white funnel- or trumpet-shaped fragrant flowers are about 2 inches across. *P. integrifolia*, discovered in Argentina in 1830, grows to 10 inches, has violet to rose flowers 1½ inches across, and is naturalized locally in the warmer regions of the United States. Hybrid forms, commonly grown as annuals, bear little resemblance to the originals and are generally sold as single or double Multifloras, with 2- to 3-inch-wide flowers, or single and double Grandifloras, with 5-inch-wide frilled, ringed, veined, striped, or starred flowers in any shades, including red, blue, yellow, and everything in between. Breeders are forever inventing new types.

Although a relative newcomer to American gardens, Petunias were enormously popular by the mid-19th century, favored for their accommodating habit (they can be grown in the varying soil and climatic conditions that exist across North America), and for giving themselves over so completely to flowering nonstop from early summer to well into the fall (and beyond in warmer regions). By the mid-1840s, deeply fringed and semi-double flowers were described, and, not long after, double bicolored types were introduced from France, causing a sensation with their carnation-like, vigorous, long-lasting blooms. These types were (and are) expensive to reproduce because they are female-sterile (the flowers have anthers but not pistils); pollen must be laboriously collected from the blossoms and emasculated single flowers fertilized. While initially popular as something out of the ordinary, double-flowered forms were not considered as useful as the single varieties, especially the smaller-flowered Multiflora kinds, with their long season of hundreds of flowers from a few plants that could be grown in the flower border, window boxes, hanging baskets, and containers of all kinds. Louise Beebe Wilder, an American Gertrude Jekyll when it came to refined gardening taste, recommended planting the small, single-flowered 'Rose Morn'—rosy carmine trumpets with a creamy yellow throat—with gentian blue *Salvia patens*.

Not everyone celebrated the phenomenal rise of the Petunia. It has always had its detractors, who consider it common and vulgar. European visitors to America in the 1860s, for instance, deplored widespread planting of Petunias, referring to them as "worthless and weedy with no shading in color, no luring perfume."

One wonders what these visitors to America actually saw, for the 1865 Breck catalog gloried in the ever-new and colorful strains from this "worthless weed": white, rose, or light purple, beautifully veined, striped, or shaded crimson or purple, with dark throats.

As for scent, Mrs. Wilder, our unfailing guide in such matters, observed that "the deep purple single kinds enrich the borders with both colour and fragrance, but the old single white is best for sweetness, particularly after sunset," when the scent is a "refined and delicious perfume."

Since the early introductions, hundreds of cultivars have appeared and disappeared with great frequency. Mrs. Wilder's 'Rosy Morn' held out for decades because of its unusually beautiful color (for which there is no modern substitute). It was probably introduced well before the 1930s because it was offered in a 1930 catalog as a "Reselected Strain." It was last seen around 1945. 'Black Prince' (a pendulous or balcony type, deep velvety mahogany with a black throat, unlike any contemporary Petunia among the hundreds now offered) also disappeared after 1945. Until a few years ago the heavily veined *superbissima* type 'Giants of California' introduced by Mrs. Theodosia Burr around 1800 was still available. The original was reported to have been up to 7 inches wide, had a wide-open throat, and came in various pastel colors.

As for the small-flowered, open-pollinated Petunias that Mrs. Wilder preferred—the purple velvet and sweet white forms close to the wild type—they are now rare, as are the pendulous, small-flowered balcony types. The question is, are they worth finding and growing with so many improved types on the market, particularly the F_1 hybrids developed in the mid-1950s? The seeds from these F_1 hybrids are obtained by cross-pollinating two inbred hybrids whose characteristics—large flowers and vigorous growth—are not usually passed on to the second generation of seedlings. Old-style open-pollinated Petunias (often referred to as OP Pe-

tunias), were established from hybrid strains, inbred and standardized. They retain the same general characteristics as the variety, except for small variations in color and form.

I don't condemn this development out of hand as some critics have done ("just mutant blobs"), for I recognize it as an achievement in plant breeding. For many years, I bought these expensive seeds and raised generations of seedlings, wintering-over choice types by making cuttings in the early spring. Then, on impulse, I bought a packet of very cheap (by Petunia standards) seeds, advertised as balcony types. That summer, when the flowers from the plants I'd raised opened their trumpets, I discovered something I'd never seen before and that I now recognize as the "Essential Petunia": that unassuming but delightfully graceful little flower with waved petals, sweetly scented in the evening, ranging in color from deep purple velvet to pure white, as well as shades in between, variously striped and starred. The flowers of even one plant differ among themselves, but all have the same classic design. I was so enchanted with my discovery that I kept close watch on the opening blossoms, to see anew a flower that was basically unknown to me before. I soon began to grow all the OP Petunias I could find, either balcony types for container planting or dwarf bedding types such as 'Snowball', introduced in the early 1900s. Surviving strains of the fabled 'Giants of California', a modest 4 inches across, brought me beautifully striped, veined, and blotched Petunias in a style, like blowsy Old Roses, seldom seen in newer types.

In the late 1980s when I was looking into the subject, the old strains were increasingly hard to find. I asked J.L. Hudson's, a repository of many hard-to-find seeds, why it had

The old-fashioned Essential Petunia has fewer trumpets, a more open habitat, and a powerful evening aroma.

discontinued selling the wild purple type *(Petunia integrifolia),* and I was told that it is almost impossible to find commercial seed growers for OP Petunias because the demand does not justify growing them on a wide scale. Perhaps increased awareness of the heirloom value of OP Petunias—their irreplaceable charm, ease of culture, and value in the garden—would initiate small-scale seed production, I thought, so that future generations could discover the "Essential Petunia" as I had done. Maybe an enterprising breeder like the Reverend Wilkes would recreate 'Rosy Morn' and 'Black Prince', introducing them as "New!" in the best seed catalog tradition. Heirloom gardeners could, perhaps, create their own heirloom types by back-breeding—that is, collecting and sowing seeds of successive generations of F_1 Petunias to produce the simple single type or (who knows?) 'Rosy Morn' or 'Black Prince'.

Postscript: A decade after I speculated on the state of the "Essential Petunia," seeds of open-pollinated types had virtually disappeared from commercial sources. In that time, numerous seed strains came and went (each hailed as "New!" and better than the last). The most recent entries are trailing, ever-blooming Petunias like 'Wave', bred to produce vigorous trailing plants with relatively small flowers for hanging baskets, window boxes, and containers, no deadheading or pinching required. While this may be a breakthrough in plant breeding, there is something mechanical and synthetic about these hanging balls of bloom, and one does not see in them the more graceful "Essential Petunia" of the past ... fewer, less crowded trumpets, a more open habit, and, what is most important, a powerful evening aroma, sweet with a hint of spice.

Now something new is occurring on the Petunia front, a quiet revolution to bring back the Essential Petunia, as gardeners have taken matters into their own hands by passing on saved seed from Petunias they have been growing for decades. Described as "Vining" or "Heirloom", they are Essential Petunias in their habit, 2 to 4 feet tall, relatively small-flowered, vigorous, most often purple, pink, and white-flowered, the latter with the strongest evening fragrance. You'll find them offered by a few specialty seed sources (see Sources), seed exchanges, and organizations like the North American Cottage Garden Society. Sometimes these seeds are reversions from commercial seed saved over several seasons or from self-sown plants in warm areas like Kentucky, Maryland, and New Mexico. This gardener-to-gardener movement represents a welcome antidote to the commercial plant industry, reflecting a desire to return to simpler, more satisying forms . . . tough, beautiful, and fragrant. My advice is to get these seeds while they are offered.

The uses of Petunias in the garden hardly need elaboration. Containers of all types can be planted with Petunias, including hanging baskets for the balcony strains. The dwarf bedding type can be used to edge or define a bed of annuals or perennials—a foil for annual Poppies (especially the old red Corn Poppies)—or to fill in the front of the border to complement soft, furry Lamb's-ears spilling over the rocks of a raised bed. They create a season-long blooming ground cover in my raised bed planting of assorted hardy roses. I grow my own balcony strain (saved seed from the Milliflora 'Fantasy' series) in containers with silvery False Licorice *(Helichrysum petiolatum)* or nearly white Beach Wormwood *(Artemisia stellerana).*

To Grow: Eight to ten weeks before the last frost, sow the tiny Petunia seeds, mixed with a small amount of fine sand, on top of pulverized soil-vermiculite mix and gently firm them down. Don't cover the seeds, as they need light to germinate. Germination should occur in seven days if the soil temperature is kept at 80°F (27°C). I set an old heating pad wrapped in a plastic bag (over a heating pad cover) under the seeding tray for bottom heat; this works as well as a heating cable. After germination, move the seedlings to light and try to maintain a soil temperature of 60°F (16°C). When the little plants have three or four sets of leaves, transplant them to individual pots or plant cells 2½ to 3 inches wide. Harden them off in a cold frame (buds develop best at 55°F (13°C), then plant out seedlings, spaced 8 to 12 inches apart, when all danger of frost has passed, pinching back the tips of the plants to encourage stockiness. The soil should be rich and well drained, and the site should receive at least half a day of sun. Remove spent flowers to encourage constant bloom (cut for fresh bouquets when flowers are almost open). Save seeds of desirable types and/or winter-over and propagate plants by stem cuttings (see the directions under "Wintering Annuals," page 24).

COLLECTOR'S CHOICE:

All of these open-pollinated Petunias should be deadheaded and pinched for fuller form. Purple or white flowers are the most fragrant.

Petunia X *hybrida*, Petunia (old style). Single-flowered bedding type; cream, red, silver-blue, rosy pink, salmon, and bicolors; 12–14".

'Alderman'. A very satisfying Essential Petunia with deep velvety purple trumpets 2½" across, with maroon tracery threads in its violet throat; a climbing type, to 18". Select Seed suggests combining this with lime green Jasmine Tobacco *(Nicotiana langsdorfii).*

'Balcony Petunia'. Old, hard-to-find, very desirable pendulous strain with small, fragrant flowers of white, pale lavender, pink, and purple; for window boxes, and containers. Popular in the 1920s and 1930s. 3'.

'Blue Bedder' (old style). Medium blue flowers; 12–14".

'Chiffon Morn'. An All-America Selection that looks very much like an old favorite, 'Apple Blossom', with 2½"-wide frilly flowers of soft pink with white throat, 9–12".

'Dwarf Mixed'. Small-flowered and short, in a range of colors.

P. integrifolia, Wild Petunia. Vivid rosy purple, 1½"-wide blooms with dark throat; to 8" tall, spreading to 18" wide. One of the parents of all hybrid Petunias. Gorgeous in a hanging basket by itself or paired with False Licorice *(Helichrysum petiolatum).*

'Kentucky Old Fashioned'. An old, small-flowered, self-seeding strain in rose-pink, fuschia, burgundy, purple, dark purple, deep royal purple, light and dark lavender, some whites, red; in solid colors, with white throat, white edges, stars; 2–3'.

'Old-Fashioned Climbing'. Small-flowered; white, lavender, violet; to 3'.

'Snowball' (1903–1914). Pure white dwarf form, 6–8".

'Vining Petunias' (from seed exchanges and organizations like the North American Cottage Garden Society). Pinks, purple, white; with a vining habit, to 4'. Flowers are 2" wide. The white ones do best with a little protection from full sun. They take on a new life at dusk when they perk up and pour forth a pleasant sweet aroma. Very desirable and striking in a planter by itself.

Phalaris arundinacea picta

POACEAE

Ribbon Grass
Dodder, French Grass, Gardener's-garters, Lady's-garters, Lady's-laces, Lady's-ribands

INTRODUCED: 1850–1900
ZONES: 3–9
TYPE: Perennial Grass
HEIGHT: 1½–3'
SEASON OF INTEREST: All-Season Foliage
SITE: Sun/Partial Shade

Ribbon Grass is a cultivated form of Canary Grass that has been grown in Europe for centuries. Plants form tight mats of growth by means of spreading underground stolons, while the flowering stems (which grow to 3 feet) bear colorless panicles of flowers typical of grasses. Interest is centered almost wholly on the plant's attractive leaves—green with white or cream stripes—which are about 6½ inches long and ¾ inch wide.

This ornamental grass belongs in the category of truly antique plants. Judging from its many folk names, it has been around a long time. The French called it "Aiguillette d'Armes," because the striped leaves were said to resemble the pennants used by knights at war. Gerard knew it as "Ladies' Laces," yet another variant of the names associated with the Virgin's dress. Commenting on this phenomenon, folklorist Hilderic Friend remarked, "Having adjusted her hose, the Virgin stoops to tie her laces; for the plant Dodder, whilst it is associated by some with the Evil One, is by others dedicated to Mary, and called Lady's Laces" (*Flowers and Flower Lore,* 1883).

Despite its long history of cultivation, Ribbon Grass was not widely grown in America until the Victorian era, when grasses in general were called upon to make a grand statement in the garden. Other types, such as the Giant Reed *(Arundo donax)* as well as huge clumps of Plume Grass *(Miscanthus),* and Pampas Grass *(Cortaderia Selloana),* were better suited for this purpose than the old cottage garden favorite. An unsophisticated and undemanding plant, easily tamed by repeated mowing, Ribbon Grass was more suited to humble, easy-care gardens from Maine to Alabama, where it was used to light up shady corners behind the house, appreciated by those who paid less attention to style than to what grew easily.

Some of the best and longest-lasting plantings I have seen were in small, unpretentious rural gardens. In one it was used to edge a thick bed of Lemon Yellow Daylilies in full sun by the front porch. In the other it was used as a "room" divider in a partially shaded garden bordered by a 1920s-vintage shrubbery. In these cases, Ribbon Grass gave a sense of form, like a little wall, continually refreshed by mowing and never (miraculously enough) overstepping its assigned role. Sometimes a creative planting brings out a new dimension of the plant, as in a shrubbery where it is left to flower—its long leaves distinctive

An unsophisticated and undemanding plant, Ribbon Grass is easily tamed by repeated mowing.

against the greenery, the foliage turning from variegated to ivory to cream by winter. My Ribbon Grass, rescued from a weedy, overgrown garden, now keeps weeds at bay in damp ground with Siberian Iris and Meadowsweet *(Filipendula ulmaria)*.

Margery Fish had the right idea about Ribbon Grass: "The handsome striped grass that we know as Gardener's Garters spreads . . . but it does it in an . . . honest, straightforward way, and one deals with it firmly by planting it in an old bucket, without a bottom, and enjoys it without worry" (*Cottage Garden Flowers*, 1961). Elsewhere she describes planting it in a large drainpipe sunk in the ground and as an accent plant wherever needed. The leaves should not be forgotten for fresh bouquets, especially striking with the purple-flowered stalks of Monkshood.

To Grow: Ribbon Grass is grown from roots in ordinary soil (not too rich), in sun or in varying degrees of shade. Space plants 6 to 12 inches apart to establish them as a ground cover. You need only three plants for accent or bucket planting, as described. Mow them back several times during the summer to control their spread if they are used as an edging, at the front of a border, or as a divider. Propagation is by division, which can be done almost anytime during the season.

COLLECTORS' CHOICE

Phalaris arundinacea picta, Ribbon Grass (1850–1900).

Phaseolus coccineus

FABACEAE

Scarlet Runner Bean
Fire Bean, Scarlet Flowering Bean

INTRODUCED: 1700–1825

P. c. 'Albus'

White Runner Bean
White Dutch Runner Bean

TYPE: Annual Twining Vine
HEIGHT: 6'–8'
BLOOM: Summer
SITE: Sun

Scarlet and White Runner Beans are one of four groups of garden beans native to tropical America. These two beans, referred to as pole beans, grow by twining themselves around any support, climbing to 8 feet. They bear bright scarlet or pure white flowers that mature over the summer to form 4- to 12-inch pods filled with large, edible black beans mottled purplish pink (Scarlet Runner) or pure white beans (White Runner).

One of nature's greatest gifts must be a plant that can be enjoyed both as a delicious food and as a beautiful ornament. The Scarlet Runner Bean was the first to be introduced to American gardens, sometime before 1750, followed by the White Runner Bean before 1825. How they must have been valued for their ease of culture, decorative flowers, and very useful beans, harvested over the whole summer to use at their different stages of development in a variety of ways. Before frost the long pods, almost dry on the vine, could be picked and shelled, the beans stored for winter use and for replanting the following season. As a quick-growing screen to divide the vegetable garden, shade the porch, or cover an arbor, these vines had many garden and landscape uses. Both vines are planted at Old Sturbridge Village to climb the rustic little arbor in the children's garden at the Fenno House. It is clear that by the early 19th century, Scarlet Runner Bean, at least, was highly regarded as an ornamental, for it is listed under flowers in the catalog of the D. & C. Landreth Company of Philadelphia.

One hundred years later, Runner Beans were still in vogue with even the most discerning gardeners. Gertrude Jekyll reminded her readers in the early 1900s that "where the space devoted to flowers requires a screen from the vegetable ground, it may be well to remember that a hedge of Scarlet Runner Beans, trained in the usual way, is beautiful as well as useful." It may not be what she had in mind, but many gardeners today train them up chicken wire in the vegetable garden, often on the pea fence, where they can be easily harvested yet still contribute to the overall beauty of the planting.

The White Runner Bean is seldom grown now, and commercial sources are hard to find. But since bean seeds are the most widely collected heirloom seeds, because of their size and individual beauty, it is likely that gardeners may find old strains through seed exchanges (see the resources section in Part 3). The type known as 'Painted Lady', once classified as *Phaseolus multiflorus,* which has large flowers with white wings and salmon standards, has reappeared, kept alive by plant preservationists. In my experience, white-flowered beans are a little harder to grow in cold climates and not as vigorous as the scarlet-flowered type under these conditions, but they are still worth growing as a twining vine. I train both, as well as 'Painted Lady', up bal-

ing twine supports on the stockade fence that divides my harvest bed of herbs and flowers from the poultry yard, and in the fall I reap a generous bounty of large-podded beans for winter soups and baking.

You can run either type of bean up a pole, as the name *pole bean* suggests, or let them twine around strings or wires trained over fences, gates, arbors, trellises, porches, or doorways. You can make a simple trellis by setting two fence posts in the ground, then running a wire along the top and bottom between them. Loop strings, baling twine, stout string, or wire up and down between the top and bottom wires to form a trellis.

To Grow: Both Runner Beans require heat and moisture to make them happy, but moisture without heat will cause an early death. The White Runner Bean especially requires heat. Sow beans outside when the soil is warm (when you plant other garden beans or corn). Plant five or six seeds 1½ to 2 inches deep in a little hill (this provides the drainage). Make sure they are no more than 3 inches away from the support they are meant to climb. Space hills 6 inches apart. If the soil is moderately rich, no further fertilization will be needed. Sow seeds successively for a week to prolong bloom.

COLLECTOR'S CHOICE:

Note: Select Seeds is one source for all three Runner Beans.

Phaseolus coccineus, Scarlet Runner Bean
   (before 1750).
'Albus', White Runner Bean (before 1825).
'Painted Lady' (1855).

Philadelphus coronarius ✤

SAXIFRAGACEAE

Mock Orange

Orange-blossom, Sweet Mock Orange,
Syringa, White-pipe

INTRODUCED: 1600–1699
ZONES: 3–8
TYPE: Hardy Shrub
HEIGHT: to 9'
BLOOM: Early to Late Summer
SITE: Sun

More than forty species of Mock Orange are native to the Northern Hemisphere, nearly half of them to North America, though the type most often found growing on old homesteads *(Philadelphus coronarius)* is from the rocky hills of southern Austria and Italy. The most widely cultivated Mock Orange types vary in their height and form from low and moundlike to leggy and upright, some with great arching branches. The four-petaled white flowers—single or double—are loosely formed and slightly cupped with prominent golden stamens. They grow in racemes to the tips of each stem, so that a bush in full flower is covered with blossoms. Mock Orange's claim to fame rests on its beautiful flowers and their fabled fragrance (sweetly orange-scented), though a few types, such as the native Lewis Mock Orange *(P. lewisii),* have no scent at all. The genus name is derived from Ptolemy Philadelphus, who ruled Egypt around 280 B.C. The epithet *coronarius,* meaning "used for garlands," suggests that the supple flower-covered branches were used to make coronets in ancient times. At one time Syringa, the

genus name for Lilacs, was the common name for what is now known as Mock Orange.

Mock Orange bushes were cultivated in England by at least 1560. Gerard, who seems to have grown anything worth growing at all, had many in his garden. It is not surprising that it was one of the earliest shrubs grown in the colonial gardens, rivaling Lilacs in popularity. Both are easy to grow and accommodating to a wide range of soils and growing conditions; Mock Orange is even tolerant of drought. Both shrubs also have a long history of use: White-pipe, a common name formerly used to distinguish Mock Orange from Lilac (Blue-pipe), refers to the shrub's wood, once used to make pipe stems. The dried blossoms and the young, scented shoots were reportedly used to make tea, while the leaves, supposedly cucumbery in flavor, may have been used as a food in Elizabethan times.

The subsequent history of Mock Orange also closely parallels that of Lilac, both of which were taken up as the subjects of intensive hybridization by the brilliant French nurseryman and breeder Victor Lemoine. But unlike the heirloom cultivars of Lilacs now available in modest numbers (compared to the hundreds that are known to have been created), there is a paucity of antique Mock Oranges, now the stuff of legend.

Alfred Hottes, the noted shrub authority writing in the 1950s, extolled the virtues of Lemoine hybrids, the products of an initial cross between the old Mock Orange of Gerard's garden *(Philadelphus coronarius)*—indestructible, beautifully flowered, and fragrant—and the frost-tender native Littleleaf Mock Orange *(P. microphyllus)* of exquisite fragrance (pineapple-scented) and indifferent blooms: "For beauty of arching shrubs loaded with bloom such varieties as 'Avalanche', 'Bouquet Blanc', 'Glacier', 'Candelabra', and 'Manteau d'Hermine' should be chosen. . . . Those with a purple or rose center . . . include 'Étoile Rose', 'Fantasie', 'Oeil d'Pourpre', and 'Sirène'. Other desirable Lemoine hybrids, noted for their fragrance, beauty of form, and flowers, include 'Belle Étoile', 'Boule d'Argent', 'Erectus', 'Fleur de Neige', 'Girandole', 'Innocence', and 'Mont Blanc'."

Of all of these, the ones still available are 'Bouquet Blanc' (1894), a single-flowered rather late-blooming type of moundlike habit with arching sprays in ready-made bouquets, and 'Belle Étoile' (1925), another single-flowered, late-blooming type with a purple blotch in the center of each blossom. According to some connoisseurs, the latter is the best of all Mock Oranges—"its chalice-shaped flowers of purest white having a refreshing pineapple scent" (Roy Genders, *The Cottage Garden and the Old-Fashioned Flowers,* 1984).

One of the most popular of the French hybrids today is the double-flowered Virginal Mock Orange *(Philadelphus × lemoinei),* which originated in the Lemoine nurseries, probably from a cross between *P.* × *lemoinei,* Lemoine Mock Orange, and *P.* × *nivalis* 'Plena', developed before 1910. The cultivars originating from this cross, of which 'Bouquet Blanc' is one, are characterized by intensely fragrant flowers—single, semi-double, and double—on bushes of varying heights and habits, all less hardy than the old-fashioned, unadorned White-pipe of ancient times. American breeders have worked hard to correct this deficiency (most noticeable in the famous 'Virginal', with very fragrant double flowers). One of the first American cultivars was 'Minnesota Snowflake'. Just as

the older French cultivar names reflect the genteel world from which they came, the American types reflect their origin and pre-occupation with the American landscape. 'Minnesota Snowflake', created by Guy D. Bush and introduced in 1935, bears very double, almost gardenia-like blossoms. These sweetly fragrant flowers, 1½ inches across and three to seven blooms per cluster, cover the bush from head to toe in early June. This cultivar, hardy to -35°F (-37°C), is now the most popular of all, and is a good choice for colder climates, as is the Lewis Mock Orange, native to Alberta, Idaho, Montana, Washington, and Oregon, most likely named after the Lewis and Clark Expedition. While the flowers of the Lewis Mock Orange are unscented, they bloom in dense racemes for a good part of the summer.

Alfred Hottes was right when he remarked that such a lovely flowering shrub as Mock Orange should not bear a name inferring that it mocks anything. And, as Mrs. King observed, "There is no other such bush of white flowers . . . every bud a pearl; and from all this lovely whiteness a fragrance thrillingly sweet."

Plant Mock Orange where you can enjoy its wonderful fragrance. We dug up the old one we found on our farm and moved it close to one of our guest log cabins, where its arching sprays curve over the shower curtain of an outdoor shower stall, giving guests an especially fragrant bathing experience. If this is not part of your landscaping scene, consider a border of Mock Orange with Roses. The latter will cover the leggy stems of the former. The general upright habit of Mock Orange makes it a good screen or green barrier wherever it is needed. The individual lawn specimen is striking when the

Mock Orange's claim to fame rests on its beautiful flowers and their fabled fragrance. . .

bush is in bloom, and the foliage is attractive most of the season. Mock Orange can be planted at the back of a flower border as a focal point or among other shrubs that bloom at various times during the season, from Lilacs in the spring to Peegee Hydrangea in late summer and fall.

To Grow: The old Mock Orange, increasingly difficult to find from commercial sources, is the hardiest and most tolerant of soil conditions. All types thrive in enriched, well-drained soil and a sunny site. Mulch in the winter with organic matter and fertilize in the spring with a balanced fertilizer or with rotted manure or compost mixed with wood ashes—this is to counteract the acid nature of compost and manure, since Mock Orange prefers a little sweetness in the soil. To keep bushes blossoming freely, prune out old wood right after flowering (they flower on wood of the previous season) and remove dead wood as the bush ages. Propagate by digging up suckers (in very early spring when the plant is dormant or in the fall), or take softwood cuttings during the spring or summer. These usually root readily when planted in fine soil.

COLLECTOR'S CHOICE (all sold as plants):

Philadelphus coronarius, Mock Orange (1600–1699).

P. x *lemoinei,* 'Belle Étoile' (1925). 6'; Zone 5. Rare.

P. x *virginalis,* Virginal Mock Orange; 9'. Zone 5.

'Bouquet Blanc' (1894). Moundlike habit; flowers well distributed over whole plant; 6'; Zone 5.

'Minnesota Snowflake' (1935). Somewhat leggy, so plant behind lower-growing shrubs or plants; 8'; Zone 3.

'Virginal' (1905). Vigorous, but lacking in branches at its base, so overplant with Roses; best for cut sprays of flowers; 9'; Zone 5.

P. lewisii, Lewis Mock Orange (1823). 6'; Zone 4.

Phlox spp. ❀

POLEMONIACEAE

Phlox

INTRODUCED: 1776–1900
ZONES: 2–8
TYPE: Annual/Perennial Flower
HEIGHT: 4"–4'
BLOOM: Spring–Fall
SITE: Sun

Annual and perennial Phlox, among our most popular and beautiful garden flowers, are derived from native species that grow from New York to Texas. Their habits vary considerably, from mat-forming in the very hardy perennial Moss Phlox *(Phlox subulata),* densely moundlike in the annual Drummond Phlox *(P. drummondii),* to upright and almost shrubby in the perennial Border Phlox *(P. paniculata, P. carolina).* Phlox flowers are wheel-like—with narrow, notched petals in Moss Phlox and broad to at least 1 inch across in the other types—and grow in clusters up and down the stem or in great pyramidal heads that reach 6 to 10 inches in Border Phlox. They come in varying shades of rose, scarlet, lilac, pink, and white, often with contrasting eyes, and are sweetly scented. The genus name is derived from the Greek work for "flame" and aptly describes the vivid scarlet and magenta of the wild types, preserved in the common name Flame Flower.

Our native Phlox did not become popular in American gardens until the mid-19th century, after they had spent some time in Europe becoming prettified by breeding and selection, although they were grown earlier. The familiar spring-blooming Moss Phlox was exported to Europe by 1745, when John Bartram sent seeds to Peter Collinson in England. The latter remarked, "It is wonderful to see the fertility of your country in Phlox." It was grown on this side of the water sometime between 1776 and 1850, gaining in popularity with the rise of planting schemes that involved combining spring-flowering bulbs such as Tulips and Daffodils, as well as early-blooming Iris, with low-growing mats of color, for which Moss Phlox was well suited. It also fit in well with the increasing interest in rock gardens, where it flows over and between rocks, creating a lovely effect when in bloom, while the evergreen needlelike leaves remain a foil for later-blooming plants. It became so popular by the late 19th and early 20th centuries that it was regarded then as old-fashioned. Mrs. Jack could write, without a trace of irony, that it belonged to that group of "dear old-fashioned flowers of English gardens, to which we look back with tender longing." Some of the superior strains, developed by the early 20th century, are still available, among them 'Blue Hills', with pale lavender-blue flowers; 'Brilliant', a distinctive carmine red, bright without being flashy; 'Apple Blossom', blush pink with dark pink eyes; and 'May Snow' ('Maischnee'), a pure sheet of white. For a change, try planting these in a dry wall—one that is laid up without cement, with earth between the cracks, and slanted slightly backward so that rain will drain into the little crevices to nourish the plants' roots.

Annual Phlox was discovered in Texas by Thomas Drummond, a British naturalist, on his second exploration of North America during the 1820s and early 1830s. He suffered great hardships on his journey through Texas and elsewhere and never returned home, but the seeds of the beautiful wildflower Texas-pride—in varying shades of scarlet, rose, purple, and buff—were sent back home, where the flowers became very popular, favored for carpet bedding—a specialized form of planting popular in the Victorian era for which one needs bright-flowered plants, usually tender annuals. These are grouped for mass display, literally covering the ground in a carpet of bloom, as in the dwarf forms. By 1860 a wide range of colors was available, creating quite a show when massed—a sea of crimson, purple, rose, and lilac. "The Annual Phlox alone has produced distinct varieties enough to furnish a garden, with almost every shade of color," wrote William Robinson in *The English Flower Garden* (1883)—high praise for a Texas weed whose great popularity stemmed primarily from its use in the carpet bedding style that Robinson admired and Gertrude Jekyll so deplored. Still, the variety of forms—dwarf, large-flowered, fringed, eyed, compact, and bushlike—and their beautiful clear colors must have been irresistible to such a keen gardener.

By the 1870s, the native Drummond Phlox had at last conquered its own country, well established across the land into Canada. In *The Canadian Fruit, Flower, and Kitchen Gardener* of 1872, author D. W. Beadle describes it in glowing terms as "one of the loveliest flowers in the garden," and so it is today. Though the range of types available to the 19th-century gardener (seven in all) are not in circulation today, we have the two basic types: 'Grandiflora', growing to 18 inches, with flattened flower clusters in mixed colors of pink, lilac blue, salmon, crimson, and scarlet (among them the magnificent 'Brilliant', introduced by 1901, with dense heads of white blending to rose, choice for cutting, as are all the 'Grandiflora' types); and dwarf or 'Nana Compacta' types, growing to 8 inches, with large flowers in the usual range of rich colors, useful in rock gardens, window boxes, containers of all types, or at the front of the flower border, a brilliant splash of color that lasts until fall.

The sweetly scented "queen of garden flowers," Border Phlox, was the last Phlox to return home—between 1850 and 1900—though it was the first to be introduced to England, in 1730. By the time it was being grown in American gardens, the straggly magenta wildflower had been greatly improved by the efforts of Victor Lemoine and others. Few of these heirloom strains have survived commercially (though many still grow in older gardens), but a notable exception is 'Miss Lingard', a slender plant with blooms—white with pale pink centers—all along its stems and thick, glossy leaves, a hybrid form of *Phlox carolina*. 'Miss Lingard' appeared on the scene by the early 1900s, the creation of a British amateur named, not surprisingly, Mr. Lingard.

Elizabeth Lawrence favored white-flowering Phlox in her legendary gardens (in Raleigh and Charlotte, North Carolina) because she found they best withstood the summer heat. Neither of the whites from this group *(Phlox paniculata)* that Elizabeth grew—'Mrs. Jenkins' and the sparkling white 'Mary

Louise'—is available today. Another favorite, the choice old strain 'Graf Zeppelin'—large white flower heads with a cherry-colored eye—is rare. 'Miss Lingard' remains popular for its bloom in late spring or early summer, before the other types have flowered.

We are told that modern Phlox types are vastly improved over older kinds, and there is no quarreling with the beautiful flowers now offered. But if you look around in older gardens, you will find an astonishing range of flowers doing very well, some growing on their own for sixty years or more, all beautiful and disease-resistant. I have found them growing all over the peninsula and beyond, often in a tangle of weeds: short types with fluffy clusters of lilac flowers; taller bright pinks; soft pinks with a red eye; tall late-blooming whites; a medium-height white with a delicate rose-lilac eye; a tall type with light purple, very fragrant flower clusters. I've also heard about an "old red" planted in the 1920s or earlier, but it has vanished.

One of the drawbacks of growing Border Phlox is the dread of powdery mildew. Gardeners are advised to give the plants plenty of air circulation and regular division. This is sound advice, but the older types I saw were crowded and often growing against a building—yet they were all vigorous. The ones I have included under "Collector's Choice," below, have survived in a tough marketplace for thirty years or more and have proved their value to the gardener, so they may be as tough as the old strains.

Border Phlox is the backbone of a sound perennial border, for it carries on with blooms over a long season when many other perennials are past their prime. The glory of the colors and the size of the clusters make this plant indispensable. A mixed planting could include Glads, Dahlias, Marigolds, China Asters, and Black-eyed-Susans or Golden-glow (*Rudbeckia laciniata* 'Hortensia')—a gorgeous way to conclude the flowering season. In my garden I have devoted an entire island to old Phlox. The early bloom of antique Tulips is succeeded by Peony, Bleeding-heart, Lilies, and then Phlox, among them a very strong-scented red-eyed pink. I don't know about newer sorts, but my collection from this remote peninsula is well perfumed, vigorous, and resistant (though not immune) to powdery mildew.

To Grow: Annual Phlox likes hot summers and grows best in full sun or very light shade. Sow seeds outside in ordinary well-drained soil after the danger of frost has passed. Or plant seeds indoors six weeks before the last frost if you want earlier bloom. Space seedlings 6 inches apart. When plants have bloomed themselves out, cut them back 2 inches from the ground, and they will rebloom.

Moss Phlox prefers well-drained sandy soil and full sun. It is quite drought-tolerant. Space the plants 8 to 12 inches apart and shear them back after blooming to refresh foliage and encourage repeat bloom in the fall. Propagate by division as needed. If grass grows up between the roots, carefully lift out the whole plant in early spring by shoving a trowel under it (without disturbing the roots) then pull out the grass and carefully reset the plant.

Border Phlox requires deep, rich, moist soil and full sun (dry, windy conditions spell disaster). Space plants 18 inches apart and divide them at least every four or five years. Thin out old shoots every spring, as well as half the new shoots on newly purchased plants, to encourage stronger blooming. Be sure to remove spent flower heads before they set seeds. The "running out" about which gardeners often complain is due to the overpopulation of the wild strain of vigorous magenta flowers that crowd out the superior strains, thus reducing the planting to one undesirable color. Border Phlox is splendid for cut flowers.

COLLECTOR'S CHOICE:

Phlox carolina 'Miss Lingard'.

P. drummondii, Drummond Phlox (old-style 'Grandiflora' type).

'Brilliant' (by 1901).

'Roseo alba-oculata' (old style).

P. drummondii (old-style dwarf or 'Nana Compacta' type).

P. paniculata, Border Phlox (1850–1900). 2–4'.

'Dresden China'. A popular Symons-Jeune strain, bred for disease resistance; shell-pink with deeper pink eye; 48".

'Graf Zeppelin'. Rare.

'Leo Schlageter'. Red. Rare.

'Mia Ruys'. White; increasingly rare; 20".

'Progress'. Lavender with blue-purple eye; especially scented; 30". Rare. ❀

'Sir John Falstaff'. Salmon pink; 30".

'White Admiral'. Huge white clusters; 36". Very popular.

P. subulata, Awl-shaped Phlox, Ground Phlox, Moss Phlox; Moss Pink (1776–1850).

The following cultivars of *P. paniculata* and *P. carolina* were all introduced by the early 20th century.

'Apple Blossom'.

'Blue Hills'.

'Brilliant'.

'May Snow' ('Maischnee').

Primula veris (P. officinalis) ❀

PRIMULACEAE

Cowslip
Fairy-cups, Herb Peter, Key Flower, Key-of-heaven, Mayflower, Palsywort, Password

INTRODUCED: 1776–1850
ZONES: 4–8

P. japonica

Japanese Primrose
Candelabra Primrose

INTRODUCED: 1870–1900
ZONES: 5–8

TYPE: Perennial Flower/Herb
HEIGHT: 1–2½'
BLOOM: Spring–Early Summer
SITE: Sun/Partial Shade

The large *Primula* genus of more than four hundred species, native to the North Temperate Zone, includes many garden types of exquisite beauty, but none lovelier than the humble Cowslip *(P. veris)* of damp English meadows. An unpretentious and appealing plant, it grows from crinkled basal leaves to no more than 1 foot (usually less), and bears ½-inch bright yellow, sweetly scented flowers that seem to be held at the end of a pale green tube (an inflated calyx that is longer than the flower). At the base of each petal is an orange dot, said to be responsible for the flower's fabled fragrance "of balmy breath." The buds stand erect in um-

bels, but when the flowers open, they hang down like a bunch of golden keys, then become erect again after fertilization so their seeds are not lost.

Japanese Primrose grows to 2½ feet, also from a basal clump of leaves—in this case, long and tapering. Its flowers bloom in circular tiers as the stem elongates over a period of three weeks, at the end of which the candelabra is wholly lit with several tiers of showy purplish pink flowers about 1 inch across, some of which have darker eyes. The genus name, *Primula,* is a contraction from the Italian *fiore de primavera,* "flower of spring," a fitting reference to Cowslip's early bloom.

Since ancient times, Cowslips have been used by the bushel to make wine, conserves, tea, and ointments to cure everything from insomnia and palsy to freckles. Considering this tradition, as well as the plant's ease of culture, it is surprising that it does not seem to have been planted generally in America until the 18th century. Earlier references to "Cowslips" may have alluded to several plants known by this name, including yellow Marsh-marigold *(Caltha palustris)* of swamps and brooks, whose young leaves were eaten as greens. By the 18th century, though, the familiar wildflower of the English countryside was a common ingredient in American cookery. Old recipes refer to "gathering 7 pecks of cowslip" to make wine, said to be a very pleasant cure-all similar in flavor to a rich muscatel made from muscat grapes or raisins.

By the early 19th century, Cowslip had been hybridized with its cousin English Primrose *(Primula vulgaris),* resulting in choice types known as Polyanthas, which were grown by Jefferson at Monticello. Gradually,

Polyanthas became synonymous with laced types in which each flower lobe, usually very dark red, is outlined with a narrow band of yellow or white (gold or silver), regularly dividing up the whole flower into ten portions. When these passed from favor, other types were developed in various colors and forms, both single and double, but the original Cowslip remained a favorite in country gardens for its undemanding ways and cheerful, nodding clusters of bright yellow flowers in early to mid spring. Though rare now, the double form known as "hose-in-hose" (one flower appearing as if slipped inside another) was so common in Gerard's time that "it needeth no description." The reddish orange type, not quite as hardy as the familiar yellow, and used in the earliest Primrose crosses, also is hard to find. As the result of intensive efforts by plant preservationists, the 'Gold-lace' strain is available (see "Collector's Choice").

Japanese Primrose was discovered by Robert Fortune on his fourth and last trip to Japan in 1860. It was one of several candelabra types discovered in the late 19th century in various parts of Asia. All of these were especially valued for their hardiness, showiness, and ability to grow in wet conditions—near streams and pools and even in bogs, where they make a grand show of bloom in late spring and early summer. Gardeners are sometimes advised to grow them in great drifts, which is just how I saw them at Audrey O'Connor's gardens, where they were naturalized in an area of open woodland—growing beneath and among slender hardwood trees, rising above a carpet of green growth in a dramatic and striking mass of tiered blooms in shades of pink and rose.

In my own garden, these lovely Primroses grow very well in unadulterated soggy ground (shaded to boot) near plantings of Siberian Iris. Ferns, Hostas, Bergamot, and Bouncing-Bet keep the damp garden in continuous bloom well into the fall.

Cowslips belong in dappled shade in moist, not soggy, ground, blooming among Wild Bleeding-heart and Johnny-jump-ups at the base of a Lilac bush or old apple tree. They show themselves to advantage in a rock garden, where their relative height and conspicuous flowers are distinctive among lower ground-hugging plants such as Moss Phlox. I grow enough in my herb garden (where Cowslips are right at home) to pick as many flowers as I want to add to salads, to decorate cakes (when crystallized, without their

COWSLIP WINE

1 gallon Cowslip flower heads
2 1/2 pounds of white sugar
Juice of 2 lemons
1 tablespoon baker's yeast (or wine yeast for white wine)
1 teaspoon malt extract or 1 vitamin B tablet (yeast nutrient)

Put the flower heads in a crock or clean plastic bucket and cover with 1 gallon boiling water. Stir often to keep the flowers submerged. After two to three days, strain off the flower juice, squeezing the flowers dry. Discard the flowers. Add the sugar, lemon juice, yeast, and nutrient to the flower juice. Cover and ferment the mixture. Siphon it into a gallon jug once the foam has died down. Fit the jug with an airlock or stuff the opening with cotton. When all bubbling has ceased and the wine has cleared, *carefully* siphon it into bottles. The wine is potable right away but much better if aged for a few months.

long calyx, like rose petals), or for an occasional modest batch of Cowslip wine.

I also treasure a Polyantha that I call "Antigonish" after the town in Nova Scotia, where a gardening friend raised it from a packet of seeds. It was the only one to survive year after year and has proved indestructible in my garden. Earlier-blooming than Cowslips, this low-growing Primrose with rose flowers and a yellow eye has reverted to its *P. vulgaris* ancestry. If you cannot keep the fancy Polyanthas in your garden, try raising them from seed for an "Antigonish" reversion.

To Grow: Japanese Primroses require moisture and do not take kindly to very exposed, hot, sunny, and windy conditions. So if spring is very hot in your area, plant them in a shaded, protected spot. They can be grown quite well to Zone 4, though they are only reliably hardy to Zone 5.

Sow Japanese Primrose or Cowslip seeds in early spring (prechill Cowslip seeds for several weeks) in a cold frame, or sow them outside in the fall to germinate early the following growing season. Do not cover seeds, as they require light to germinate (from two to ten weeks at 65°F ≠18°C). When planting out the seedlings—6 to 12 inches apart for Cowslips, 1 foot apart for Japanese Primroses—be sure the soil (for Cowslips in particular) is well prepared: deep, humusy, somewhat acid, and moist. Cowslips should be divided every year just after blooming to maintain prolific flowers. Japanese Primroses can be grown quite well in somewhat acid, dampish, heavy soil. In mild winter climates where they may grow as biennials, it's best to sow seeds every year (fresh seeds germinate readily) to ensure a continuous supply of flowering plants. Japanese Primroses, like Cowslips, are easily propagated by division, either after blooming or in the fall. They can be grown indoors in a cool but sunny window. Pinch back the first flush of buds for a bushier plant.

COLLECTOR'S CHOICE:

Primula japonica, Japanese Primrose (1870–1900).

P. × *polyantha* 'Gold-laced' (18th and 19th centuries). A very old strain that was developed by English weavers, lost, rescued, then rebred over thirty years to reproduce the original: deep velvety red petals outlined with a narrow band of yellow which neatly divides them into ten equal parts looped around a golden center. Grow like Cowslips; 6-9".

P. veris, Cowslip (1776–1850).

'Ruby Red' ✿

P. vulgaris (1750). The delightful unadorned English wildflower with fragrant pale yellow flowers to 6". Early-blooming, like "Antigonish"; prefers sunnier, drier conditions than Cowslips.✿

Pulmonaria spp.

BORAGINACEAE

Lungwort

Adam-and Eve, Bethlehem-sage, Bloody-butcher, Blue-cowslip, Blue Lungwort, Boys-and-girls, Children-of-Israel, Christmas-cowslip, Cowslip Lungwort, Hundreds-and-thousands, Jacob-and-Rachel, Jerusalem-cowslip, Jerusalem-sage, Joseph-and-Mary, Mary-and-Martha, Mary's-milk-drops, Spotted-comfrey, Spoted-cowslip, Spotted-dog, Spotted-Mary, Spotted-Virgin

INTRODUCED: 1600–1960

ZONES: 3–8

TYPE: Perennial Flower/Herb

HEIGHT: 6"–1½'

BLOOM: Early Spring

SEASON OF INTEREST: All-Season Foliage

SITE: Sun/Partial Shade/Shade

*D*espite their biblical names, all Lung-worts are native to Europe. They grow by creeping rhizomatous roots that spread in moist, cool soil, establishing large colonies unless checked. All are characterized by clusters of nodding trumpet-shaped flowers, usually changing from pink to blue as they mature, with heart-shaped, rather downy leaves that in some types are "as rough as a calf's tongue." Blue or Cowslip Lungwort *(P. officinalis),* growing to 1 foot, has rough, spotted leaves and pink and violet-blue flowers. Christmas-cowslip *(P. montana / P. rubra),* growing to one foot, has lightly spotted leaves and coral red flowers. Bethlehem-sage *(P. saccharata)* is the tallest type, growing to 18 inches, and has heavily spotted, almost silver leaves and pink and violet-blue flowers. The genus name is based on the shape of the leaves, thought to resemble lungs, and their supposed curative powers. "Cowslip" refers to the early-blooming nature of all the Lung-worts, which begin to flower with the first hint of spring, even breaking through semifrozen ground in the North. In warmer regions, the aptly named Christmas-cowslip blooms by Christmas. The flowers of all types are well designed to receive hungry bees in search of an early source of nectar or pollen.

According to ancient tradition, Lungwort exemplifies the "Doctrine of Signatures" whereby a plant advertises its uses. Thus, splotched or lung-shaped leaves suggested an antidote for lung or bronchial ailments. All *Pulmonaria* species do contain a mucilaginous substance suggestive of healing properties, and it may be for this reason that the common Lungwort was grown in early American gardens. In this connection, Audrey O'Connor passed along one of her favorite stories about a Belgian nun who lived among the Sioux at the time of an outbreak of tuberculosis. She is credited with having sent to Europe for seeds of *P. saccharata,* thereby saving so many lives that the Sioux named the plant "Sweet Ann" in her memory.

When Lungwort had outlived its usefulness as a healing plant, it found a welcome place in the garden, appreciated for its ease of culture, early bloom, and attractive, long-lasting foliage. Various types were introduced from the 17th through the 19th centuries, the last one being Christmas-cowslip. The one most often found in older gardens is the easy-to-grow but increasingly rare common Lungwort *(P. officinalis).* Today one looks in vain between *Perilla* and *Pyrethrum* for this cottage garden favorite.

I inherited a large mat of common Lungwort when we moved to the old farm. Every spring its flowers bring us joy as a herald of the new growing season, never failing to show their deep pink buds through last season's decayed vegetation even as the winds still blow hard from the north and temperatures remain low. Gradually the little flowers open—first pink, then violet-blue, then white, a family habit preserved in the many two-part folk names, such as Soldiers-and-sailors. Barely discernible in the budding plants, the small, pointed light green

The flowers of all types of lungwort are well designed to receive hungry bees in search of an early source of nectar or pollen.

leaves grow in importance during the blooming period, to be covered eventually with lighter spots—little moons of varying size that, descending in a rush toward the tips of the foliage, seem to have dropped from heaven.

In full bloom on a warm spring day, these splendid plants are a shimmering mass of violet-blue, their small trumpets nodding in the breeze, calling forth our resident honeybees who come by the dozens, methodically visiting each opened flower and then returning to the hive with the first harvest of the season. We aren't the only ones to appreciate the common Lungwort. All Lungworts are variable in the coloration of their flowers and the spotting of their leaves. They hybridize readily in nature and under the breeder's hand, but in my many years of growing Lungworts, I have never found any sports. Fortunately, superior strains are available for the heirloom gardener (though not as many as one would wish). These have been grown for at least thirty years and include the ever-popular 'Mrs. Moon', a well-named cultivar of *Pulmonaria saccharata* with heavily spotted, almost silver foliage. "I have never found out who Mrs. Moon was or where she lived," wrote Margery Fish. She was, in fact, the wife of illustrator H.G. Moon, a friend of William Robinson, and not a fanciful allusion to Lungwort's moon-spotted leaves.

I have found Lungworts to be an effective edging plant for my herb garden—a thick, attractive, and impenetrable barrier to weeds and grass, kept in check by annual mowing (I use a sickle). These plants aren't called Hundreds-and-thousands for nothing! Lungworts also accompany a host of Daffodils in their season of bloom and cover up

for them when their foliage withers. They serve as an effective ground cover beneath the dappled shade of trees and shrubs, where their spotted leaves have the best color. If the plant is cut down to the ground after it blooms, its leaves return quickly, refreshed and soft, lasting until the snow flies.

To Grow: While Lungworts grow easily from a piece of root, they do not tolerate dry, windy conditions, so be sure to protect young plants and water them well until they are established. You can plant them in full sun as long as the soil is moist, but the leaves look best in partial shade. Propagation is easily accomplished by division in the fall.

COLLECTOR'S CHOICE:

Pulmonaria angustifolia 'Azurea', Blue Lungwort (between 1700 and 1776).
P. montana/P. rubra, Christmas-cowslip (early 20th century).
P. officinalis, Lungwort (1600–1699).
'Sissinghurst White' (before 1960). Pearly bells.
P. saccharata 'Mrs. Moon' (by late 19th century). Pink flowers.

Rhododendron spp. ❀

ERICACEAE

Azalea
Rhododendron

INTRODUCED: 1731–1930
ZONE: 3–9
TYPE: Perennial Shrub
HEIGHT: 2½–33'
BLOOM: Early Spring–Summer
SITE: Sun/Partial Shade/Shade

> With their multitude of creeping roots, these plants aren't called Hundreds-and-thousands for nothing!

Rhododendrons (from the Greek for "rose tree") are the aristocrats of the plant world, considered by some to be the most gorgeous of all flowering plants in the North Temperate Zone (they appear to grow everywhere in the world except Africa and South America). Azaleas are included in this enormous genus of more than eight hundred species with thousands of named cultivars. Some types are as short as 2½ to 3 feet, such as the slender, diminutive Rhodora *(Rhododendron canadense),* while others, such as the grand Rosebay Rhododendron *(R. maximum),* are as tall as trees.

The differences between Rhododendrons and Azaleas are as follows: the former generally have long, leathery evergreen leaves and bear their bell-shaped flowers in clusters, with each bloom containing ten or more prominent stamens; the latter are usually deciduous (lose their leaves in the fall) and have funnel-shaped or tubular flowers with five prominent stamens. Colors of both range from delicate pastels—blush, mauve, and lilac—to brilliant orange, scarlet, and crimson. Many of the blooms are noticeably scented. Although most of the popular hybrids today are of Oriental origin (from China, the Himalayas, Japan, and Korea), quite a few choice species are native, growing in the mountains and forests of the Appalachians. Among the native species are Flame Azalea *(Rhododendron calendulaceum),* with large brilliant yellow, orange, or scarlet flowers and flared-back petals, and Catawba Rhododendron *(R. catawbiense),* whose white form is regarded as one of the best garden Rhododendrons.

One can imagine the astonishment and delight of the early plant explorers when they discovered the first wild Rhododendron in the New World to bring back to enthusiastic Europeans, eager to grow American "exotics." Reverend John Banister, an Oxford-trained naturalist of the 17th century, is credited with discovering the beautiful Swamp Azalea *(Rhododendron viscosum)*—fragrant, white tubular blossoms—found in wet soils and swamps from Maine to South Carolina. During the 18th century, the French government sent André Michaux to search for likely ornamentals. In 1796, after several years of exploring, he discovered Catawba Rhododendron, growing in Kentucky and Tennessee, at the westernmost point of settlement. This species became very important in the breeding of Rhododendrons after it was introduced in England in 1809 and crossed with other species. These hybrid forms are among the most popular types grown today.

Although Europeans were excited about the plants brought back from the wilds of America, gardeners on this side of the Atlantic were generally slow to acknowledge their native wealth, at least in the form of Rhododendrons. It is true that Jefferson grew the treelike Rosebay Rhododendron, but it was his French friends who demanded seeds of the elegant Rhodora or False Honeysuckle to grace their gardens. Rhodora was described by Joseph Breck as "magnificent in appearance with flowers of a fine purple." Another nurseryman observed, "Choice but not very often grown."

"The most entrancing pictures may be made in gardens," Louise Beebe Wilder commented, "by means of the free use of these lovely shrubs . . . massed against evergreens, where their vibrant colors are thrown into relief, or clustered in thickets in light woods

One can imagine the astonishment and delight of the early plant explorers when they discovered the first wild Rhododendron.

or difficult corners." Gertrude Jekyll gave her readers the same advice—to use Rhododendrons and Azaleas for background plantings, taking advantage of their strong foliage to enhance Lilies (she favored the elegant Goldband Lily), white Foxglove, and white Columbine planted in groups, the ground beneath them carpeted with Daffodils and Lily-of-the-valley.

A few chance seedlings along our lane introduced me to the garden possibilities of wild Rhodora, which I later saw as a focal point of spring bloom in a striking rock garden planting: colorful splashes of rose-purple rising among bright yellow Cowslips, cascading Moss Phlox in matching rose, and foamy drifts of bright blue Forget-me-nots. When I returned later in the season after the Rhodora blooms were spent, I noted how its handsome evergreen foliage (mostly evident after the flowers have unfurled) was still a striking asset to the garden as an all-season background for later-blooming plants.

Tall types of Rhododendrons and Azaleas can be naturalized on slopes or planted in the filtered shade of oaks or pines and other evergreens. In the shrubbery they are often paired with Mountain-laurel, another fine native. As for the proverbial "difficult corner," they can provide a long season of interest there with their burst of spring or summer bloom and glossy evergreen foliage (light red or bronze on some types by fall), but it is important to protect such plantings from driving winds or blistering sun, their worst enemies.

Native species provide the gardener with beautiful shrubs for some difficult places aside from corners. Rhodora, for instance, will grow in heavy soil, even at the edge of bogs, while Rosebay Rhododendron grows very well in shade, where it makes a fine screen. Swamp Azalea, as the name suggests, tolerates damp conditions that would be the death of fancy hybrids. The early Catawba hybrids, developed by the first few decades of this century, are ironclad (superhardy), with large, beautiful flower clusters in a variety of colors—some with frilled petals, all with handsome foliage. These heirloom types continue to be grown in spite of the many newer introductions because they have proved their worth. 'Roseum Elegans', with huge clusters of fuchsia-purple flowers, is nearly indestructible and very hardy.

To Grow: Rhododendrons and Azaleas have shallow roots and require humusy, well-drained, evenly moist soil with a pH of 4.5 to 5.2 (blueberry soil) and a generous amount of peat moss or ground bark to retain moisture. If necessary, build up the bed to ensure good drainage. Plant out rootstock in early spring or early autumn. Plant it slightly deeper than it was grown in the nursery, and leave a shallow depression around the stem after tamping down the soil. Fill the depression with a mulch of leaves, pine needles, rotted sawdust, or compost, built up as much as 6 to 8 inches over the season. Add new mulch every fall, and if drought or wind is a problem, be sure to water the plants frequently. You can apply an acid-forming balanced fertilizer sparingly in the spring. In the North, Rhododendrons and Azaleas can be grown in full sun if protected from the wind, but elsewhere filtered shade is best. Some species may be easily propagated by tip cuttings taken in the summer or by layering. If plants become leggy, cut them back hard (to 1 foot) to induce bushiness. Otherwise, pruning is unnecessary, other than to remove dead or damaged branches.

To plant from seed (nonhybrid types), sow seeds as soon as they are ripe in a cold frame or a cool greenhouse on top of a damp mixture of loam, sand, and leaf mold or peat moss. Shade them from bright light. Germination takes two to four weeks. Transplant seedlings 4 inches apart in sandy soil. Water well and allow them to grow one year before transplanting them to a nursery bed.

COLLECTOR'S CHOICE:

Rhododendron calendulaceum, Flame Azalea (1800). Large yellow, orange, or scarlet flowers; the most showy native species; unlike fancier hybrids, it holds flowers well in full sun for nearly two weeks; early June bloom; 9–15' (usually shorter); Zone 4.

R. canadense, False Honeysuckle, Rhodora (1756). Slender, rose-purple, two-lipped bells; small leaves; low, branching habit; mid-May bloom; very hardy and soil-tolerant; grows well in sun; 2½–3'; Zone 3.
'Album', very elegant white form.

R. carolinianum, Carolina Rhododendron (1815). Very pretty rose pink to white flowers; mid-May bloom; very hardy, 6'; Zone 4.

R. catawbiense, Catawba Rhododendron (1809).
'Album'. Perhaps of hybrid origin, with huge flower clusters of pure white with gold-patched throat; late June bloom after other types have faded; very hardy; low, dense habit to 6'; Zone 4.

Catawba Hybrids (late 19th century):

'Everestianum'. Rose-lilac with frilled petals and beautiful dark green foliage; mid-May to early June; Zone 5.
'Mrs. Charles S. Sargent'. Deep rose with yellow-green markings; an old Catawba hybrid favorite; Zone 5.
'President Lincoln' (also listed as 'Abraham Lincoln'). Rose with reddish markings, fading to pink; May bloom; very hardy for a hybrid; Zone 5.
'Purpureum Elegans'. Purple-violet with orange-brown markings; Zone 5.
'Roseum Elegans'. The easiest Catawba hybrid to grow; withstands neglect; huge clusters of fuchsia-purple flowers with greenish markings; May–June bloom; Zone 5.

R. maximum, Rosebay Rhododendron (1736). Rose to purple-pink flowers; a large and vigorous shrub growing to 36' in optimum conditions but usually less (15–20'); dark evergreen leaves 5–10" long; the hardiest of evergreen Rhododendrons; late June bloom; Zone 4 with winter shade.

R. roseum/R. prinophyllum, Rose-shell Azalea (1790). Deep pink, very fragrant flowers; late May bloom; 9'; Zone 4. ✿

R. vaseyi, Pink-shell Azalea (1891). Light pink to rose flowers and light red foliage in the fall; mid-May bloom; 5–9'; Zone 4.

R. viscosum, Swamp Azalea (1731). Blush pink tubular flowers; very fragrant; bronze foliage in the fall; grows well in partial shade; early July bloom, the last of the group to flower; excellent for naturalizing in lightly wooded areas; 6–9' or taller; Zone 4. ✿

Ribes aureum ❀

SAXIFRAGACEAE

Golden Currant
Buffalo Currant, Missouri Currant,
Slender Golden Currant

INTRODUCED: 1830–1850
ZONES: 2–9
NATIVE

R. odoratum ❀

Clove Currant
Buffalo Currant, Missouri Currant

R. sanguineum ❀

Winter Currant
Redflower Currant

ZONES 6–10

TYPE: Perennial Shrub
HEIGHT: 6–9'
BLOOM: Spring
SITE: Sun/Partial Shade

Several species of *Ribes* native to North America are desirable ornamentals and hummingbird flowers. The very hardy Golden Currant grows from Washington State east to Montana and south to California, bearing a profusion of bright yellow, spice-scented, small, narrow trumpet-shaped flowers tinged with red in racemes of five to fifteen blossoms on arching stems growing to 6 feet. Clusters of yellow-orange to red-black berries form by midsummer, followed by burnished purplish gold foliage in the fall,

thus extending the shrub's season of interest. Clove Currant, growing from South Dakota and Minnesota south to Texas and Arizona, is quite similar in appearance, except that the flowers grow in smaller racemes of five to ten blossoms and are larger and more heavily scented, while the fruit is purple-black (fully black when ripe). Its handsome lobed, almost heart-shaped foliage also colors attractively in the fall. Since both types of shrubs are variable, it is sometimes difficult to tell them apart. *The New Britton & Brown Illustrated Flora* (1952) considers these two species to be synonymous. My own experience does not bear this out; I believe Clove and Golden Currant are two separate species, the former with larger flowers than the latter, as described in the *RHS Index of Plants*. One sure way to distinguish them is to examine a flower from each shrub: Clove Currant flower has a longer calyx tube. Golden Currant is preferred where growing conditions are drier, while Clove Currant does better in wet spring and humid summer weather. The Golden Currant's fruit can be used for preserves, but its quality is variable. The large fruited 'Crandall' cultivar from the Clove Currant has been around for decades and is the type from which most Clove Currant stock is grown, making it highly desirable for landscape and kitchen use.

Winter Currant grows from northern California to British Columbia and is hardy to −5°F (−21°C). An erect shrub growing to 9 feet or more in its wild form, it has attractive lobed evergreen foliage and dense racemes of clove-scented pink to carmine red flowers beginning in April, followed by inedible but attractive bluish black berries with a waxy or grayish bloom.

All the Currants are associated with western exploration from 1790 to 1879, when plant collectors accompanied expeditions into an unknown and unmapped wilderness. The Golden and Clove Currants were literal fruits of the 1803 Lewis and Clark expedition, while Winter Currant was discovered by Archibald Menzie, a British physician with the Royal Navy, in the late 1700s.

Golden and Clove Currants were grown in America by 1812. Jefferson, who commissioned the Lewis and Clark Expedition, grew both shrubs at Monticello. When he died in 1826, his granddaughter sent a box of plants to her sister in Boston as a remembrance of their grandfather; among them was the Golden Currant, with its "beautiful yellow flowers."

These shrubs, smothered in golden bloom by mid-May, remained very popular into the late 19th and early 20th centuries, when they could be found gracing doorways, verandas, or shrubberies of modest gardens across America, highly regarded for their numerous flowers, ease of culture, and (not least of all) powerful aroma "perfuming the whole region in their neighborhood," according to Breck's catalog. With their graceful, rather spreading habit (especially in the Clove Currant), they could be planted to good effect as an accent plant where needed, underplanted with spring bulbs, or placed in front of larger trees. Flowering Currants became synonymous with the American garden style—informal and homey.

With the outbreak of the white pine blister rust disease in the early 1900s (from white pine seedlings imported from Europe, infected with a fungus carried by the European Black Currant, *Ribes nigrum),* all Currants, including natives and ornamentals, were looked upon as a threat to the large white pine industry, and throughout the country thousands of plants were uprooted and destroyed. With the decline of the white pine industry in many states and the development of rust-resistant pine trees, Currants of all types have lost their pariah status and can now be grown in most states. (Consult your local Department of Agriculture office.)

Golden and Clove Currants are enjoying a revival of interest as quintessential cottage garden plants—fragrant, beautiful, useful, and well suited to contemporary ideas about low maintenance—and as edible landscape plants that are attractive to birds, bees, and butterflies. Both shrubs withstand city conditions well and can be used as informal hedges or lower-story windbreaks.

The more frost-tender Winter Currant enjoyed relative popularity in the 19th century, when double-flowered forms such as the Double Crimson Currant were offered. The handsome Winter Currant, "with dangling racemes of rich deep red," became a popular garden subject in Britain in the early

> Flowering Currants became synonymous with the American garden style—informal and homey.

CURRANT JAM

4 cups dead-ripe berries (either Clove, Golden, or Black Currants or a mixture) mixed with just-ripe berries, all without stems

1/4 cup grape juice

3 cups sugar

Cook the berries and grape juice in a covered, wide-mouth stainless steel pot (1- to 2-gallon size). When the berries are simmering, stir in the sugar. Bring the mixture to a boil and simmer, uncovered, for 10 minutes, or until it thickens and just begins to cling to the bottom of the pot. Pour the jam into sterilized jars and seal. (Adapted from my book *The Old-Fashioned Fruit Garden*, Nimbus Publishing, 1989).

19th century after David Douglas (of fir tree fame) rediscovered it in 1822. "Though entering England as an alien," one writer observed of the phenomenon, "it has since found its way there into the gardens of every rank, while here in America, its native country, it is still scarcely known and seldom grown."

In the late 1930s, Louise Beebe Wilder urged her readers to consider the Winter Currant, "a very old shrub in gardens, so old that in the superabundance of new introductions it is often overlooked. . . . At present it is known and loved in cottage gardens but ignored elsewhere." She advised grouping several shrubs together and carpeting the ground beneath them with early Daffodils and other spring-flowering bulbs. A hybrid cross between the Winter Currant and the Clove Currant, known as the Gordon Currant, also was recommended, created by Donald Beaton of Hertfordshire around 1837 and named after his employer, William Gordon. A robust shrub of free-flowering habit with beautiful pinkish orange blooms, it is about as frost-tender as the Winter Currant, although Mrs. Wilder claimed it could be grown in colder localities. The question is academic today, however, since this lovely shrub is not available to American gardeners through mail-order sources. It is worth hunting for in specialty nurseries, though.

In my gardens, richly clove-scented Golden Currant bushes grace a corner dooryard garden underplanted with white Bleeding-heart *(Dicentra eximia);* and provide a handsome accent at one end of an island bed, underplanted with *Lamium* 'Beacon Silver'. Over the fall months these shrubs provide new color to the landscape with their reddish bronze foliage.

To Grow: All of the flowering Currants will grow in sun or partial shade and in any soil, even dry, though they thrive in well-drained loam with a pH of 6.0 to 8.0. In very hot, humid weather, the Clove and Golden Currants can lose their leaves, so provide them with partial shade under these conditions. Space Currants 5 to 6 feet apart, since they can spread almost as wide as their height. The wild form of the Winter Currant is more upright, so it requires a little less space. All of them benefit from a thick, yearly mulch of organic material—compost covered by a layer of old sawdust, for instance —and a yearly pruning of unwanted suckers and old woody stems from the base of the plants when they're dormant. After flowering, extra growth can be pruned out as desired to maintain the plant's shape. Propagation is by suckers or softwood or hardwood cuttings taken in the spring or summer. Some authorities claim Clove Currant is dioecious, so you are advised to plant a male and female plant to produce fruit. Consult the nursery where you purchase the shrub.

To grow from seed, sow seeds in the fall and lightly cover them with a mulch of straw. Or sow them in the spring after stratifying (prechilling in a moistened medium) seeds for three months at 40°F (4°C).

Standard advice for all *Ribes* species is to plant them 1,000 feet from stands of white pine.

Collector's Choice:

Ribes aureum, Golden Currant; Zone 3.
'Idaho Buffalo'. Superior fruit flavor; useful for preserving; very hardy; Zone 2.
R. odoratum, Clove Currant. 'Crandall' type or from 'Crandall' stock; all with large flowers and superior fruit; Zone 3.

'Aureum'. Very hardy, Zone 2.

R. sanguineum, Winter Currant. Zone 6.

'King Edward VII' (pre-1904). Choice cultivar with bright red flowers and more spreading habit than wild type; 6'.

Rosa spp. and groups ✿

ROSACEAE

Roses

INTRODUCED: 1600–1901

ZONES 3–10

TYPE: Hardy/Tender Shrub/Vine/Herb/ Flower

HEIGHT: 3–12'

BLOOM: Spring/Summer/Fall

SITE: Sun/Partial Shade

Look into the face of a wild rose, and you will find the face of the "Queen of Flowers" in its most simple yet beautiful form: five green sepals, five petals (shades of rose, yellow, or white) loosely arranged around numerous golden stamens, and, in the center, a cluster of pistils. Not all wild roses are single-petaled; some are semidouble or double. Most have varying degrees of fragrance though some have none at all. All grow on canes of differing lengths and thorniness, with their foliage divided into three to nine leaflets, and after flowering all bear distinctive plump, rosy, urn-shaped fruits (hips)—in some species considered as ornamental as the flowers.

Old Garden Roses (OGRs) are variously defined as those varieties or types introduced to American gardens before 1867 (the advent of the Hybrid Tea Rose) or 1900 (the natural beginning of the modern era). OGRs can be divided into two groups: hardy, often blowsy shrublike plants, relaxed in flower and habit, intensely fragrant, cultivated in Europe and Asia Minor since Classical times, and, for the most part, blooming only once a season—the Alba, Cabbage (Centifolia), Damask, Moss, and French (Gallica) Roses, as well as various cultivated wild kinds; and the tender, more refined types (in both form and scent) from China, introduced to Europe after 1790—the China and Tea Roses. The most significant characteristic of these lightly tea-scented types is that they bloom non-stop all season long.

The exact lineage of all of these Roses is impossible to discern, as they have been cultivated for thousands of years. Some of them may be the result of the Rose's natural tendency to cross-pollinate from one species to another, creating a new rose, while others are probably the result of early attempts at hybridization. OGRs are not wild Roses, but wild Roses can be OGRs.

The early settlers regarded the Rose as a basic necessity of life in the New World, primarily to treat a thousand ailments and flavor food. The tannin-rich petals with soothing properties (especially in dark red- or pink-flowered Roses) provided a pharmacopoeia of syrups and infusions to soothe sore throats, heal mouth sores, and when infused in vinegar, lessen the pain of headaches. In the kitchen, all sorts of wines, teas, waters, lotions, jellies, jam, conserves, and potpourris were created from the Rose's petals and fruits to nourish the body and cheer the soul. Roses were planted just outside the kitchen door among Lilies, Hollyhocks, Peonies, Pinks, Calendula, Iris, Poppies, and other useful plants, within easy reach to harvest when needed. Wild Roses of the countryside were pressed into service, too, so great

Rosa virginiana is an undeveloped native landscape shrub.

was the need for Rose blossoms and their fruits. The best Roses for household use were old-world types: the Apothecary Rose (*Rosa gallica officinalis*), and a semidouble form of the Damask Rose (*R. damascena* 'Trigintapetala').

As Roses took their place in the pleasure garden, more types were added, favored for their ease of culture, fragrance, hardiness, and exquisite beauty. Most of them bloomed only once a season, but what a glorious display, with hundreds, even thousands, of blooms smothering a single bush or vine.

Important things happened in the Rose world in the early 19th century, when several important crosses were made between hardy old-world once-blooming Roses and tender everblooming Chinas. John Champneys, a rice planter from South Carolina, crossed an Old Musk Rose (*Rosa moschata*) with a pink China Rose, from which came a new race called Noisettes, everblooming but tender. Then in 1819 an Autumn Damask, the only repeat-blooming European Rose, was accidentally crossed with a China Rose on the Isle of Bourbon (now Réunion, in the Indian Ocean), creating the Bourbon Rose, the first hardy repeat bloomer.

These developments inevitably led to a decline in popularity of the older Roses. The emphasis was on repeat-blooming types with ever-bigger flowers, most of them fragrant. The acme of success in this line was the creation of the Hybrid Perpetual, the glory of Victorian gardens. It was the product of complicated crossings of Damasks, Chinas, and Bourbons, and it promised better winter hardiness and recurrent blooming, though it did not always deliver "perpetually." Profuse bloom in June was followed by moderate rebloom in the fall, with occasional bloom in between. Hybrid Perpetuals, with their

Rosa officiallis, the Apothecary Rose, was one of the best Roses for household use in early colonial times.

large, fragrant flowers, were hugely popular, and by the end of the 19th century three thousand cultivars were being offered to gardeners. These were really the first of the modern Roses, actually a bridge between old and new. They eventually declined in popularity when they were superseded by hardy, even more everblooming types.

The first Hybrid Tea Rose, introduced in 1867 (a complicated cross combining the virtues of Chinas with the vigor and hardiness of Hybrid Perpetuals), marked the beginning of a relentless stylistic movement toward developing everblooming, long-budded, strong-stemmed tailored Roses (to which fragrance was often sacrificed), setting the standard by which all later Roses were judged. Hybrid Teas and their descendants—Polyanthas, Floribundas, Grandifloras, and the Ramblers and Climbers bred from them—offered gardeners nonstop bloom, relative hardiness, and crisp, neat flowers in an astonishing range of bright colors—the sort lacking in the mainly pastel shades of Old Roses and wild Roses.

So why would anyone today want to grow OGRs? Enthusiasts may vary in their answers, but among them will be found the following:

1. OGRs grow well, even thrive, with a minimum of attention (with very little or no pruning, for instance).
2. OGRs lend themselves readily to the kind of informal, low-maintenance gardening that is popular today.
3. OGRs, especially those closest to the wild, are able to withstand and survive the stresses of disease and insect infestation when they occur.
4. OGRs *smell* like Roses—an immensely satisfying sweet perfume

associated with the fragrance of the Damask Rose and usually absent in modern Roses.

5. OGRs are cherished in a way that modern Roses never can be because they have distinct, often quirky personalities that do not result from anonymous crossings.

6. OGRs are associated with the people, places, and experiences of our past and can never be replaced in our hearts by modern Roses, whatever fine physical qualities they may possess.

OGRs also help to remind us of the simple beauty inherent in the classic wild form. In 1990, Lily Shohan, a guiding light in the OGR revival, related how she won a national trophy at an American Rose Society show with a bouquet of twenty-three OGR varieties—at least fifty blooms ("How to Win a Trophy," *Heritage Roses,* vol. 15, no. 3, 1990). Later in the show, several people came up to ask her about the little white flowers with the intoxicating fragrance that she had picked from the wild to use as a dainty filler in her prize-winning bouquet. What were they? They were the clustered, newly opened faces of the humble white Multiflora Rose once widely grown as a "living fence" and now regarded as a weed: five petals loosely arranged around prominent golden stamens— the "Queen of Flowers" unadorned.

"All Roses are beautiful, but not all are fashionable at any given time," Richard Thomson wrote in *Old Roses for Modern Gardens* (1959). We are most fortunate to be living in an era when there are more OGRs available than there have been for many decades, when both old and new Roses are in fashion together.

Most OGRs are best grown as shrubs. When they have bloomed in late spring or summer, other shrubs can take up the slack. Types with long canes (6 feet or more) can be trained to grow against walls or along fences (these should be slatted for air circulation). If the side branches are pegged in an arched position to a fence or any horizontal support, they will be encouraged to bloom all along their length. Long canes also can be tied back to stout posts and grown as pillars. Heirloom perennial flowers such as Foxglove, Hollyhocks, and Lilies provide complementary upright forms in a mixed border. Low-growing Sweet Alyssum and Lamb's-ears spilling over the front edge of a bed will gracefully mark a collection of OGRs, perhaps grown on a sunny bank. The brightly decorative fall fruits and the bronzy red foliage of some types, especially the Rugosas, should be considered for their long season of interest. Nothing is livelier in the late fall and winter garden than a light carpet of snow on rosy fruit-laden bushes. Think beforehand about where you want your Roses so you won't have to move them (not impossible, but not the most pleasant job).

To Grow: Although OGRs survive neglect they thrive on attention. They prefer a heavy, well-drained soil and at least six hours of direct sun a day. They do best in morning sun in the north, avoiding having moisture linger on their leaves from morning dew. (This condition encourages fungal diseases.) The absence or presence of wind is a factor in determining hardiness, so choose a location where some shelter is available but air circulates freely. It's not a good idea, for instance, to plant Roses directly against a boarded fence. Again, this condition encourages disease and other problems.

Nothing beats Rugosa Roses for hardiness, scent, and the production of large hips.

I learned to plant Roses from a guest who showed me his simple procedure when I was planting out my first Rose ('Therese Bugnet', a Hybrid Rugosa, 1950) many years ago. Always keep Rose roots submerged in water before planting them (at least several hours). Dig a hole about 2 feet deep and 18 inches wide. To one measure of bonemeal, add four measures of rotten manure or compost. Mix this well, sprinkle it in the hole, and cover it with a mound of friable soil. Drape Rose roots over the soil, water the hole, and fill it with friable dirt, tamping down the soil to anchor the Rose in place and fill in any air pockets around the roots. Spread a shovelful of organic fertilizer—manure or compost—around the plant, being careful not to let it touch the main stem. Cover this with 2 to 3 inches of organic mulch (whatever you can lay your hands on: old sawdust, wood chips, grass clippings). This helps retain moisture during dry spells (so you won't have to wa-ter) and discourages weeds. The organic material breaks down over the season, adding its nutrients to the soil around the Rose. Renew the mulch every season in early spring. If you can't make the planting hole as deep or wide as recommended, trim roots accordingly and add extra nutrient-rich mulch.

Roses should be planted 3 to 5 feet apart, or 18 to 24 inches apart to make a hedge. Climbers should be planted 12 to 15 inches away from the surface on which they will climb.

A lot has been written about own-root roses, pro and con. My feelings are based on my experience and may not apply to everyone. Whenever possible, I purchase Roses grown on their own roots. True, they are not as mature as grafted Roses and may take several seasons to attain maturity. But I never have to worry about waking up one morning and finding thorny stalks with dog Rose bloom where I'd planted a precious antique Rose. Experts will tell you that there's no problem with the rootstock taking over the grafted Rose if—and that's a big if—the graft union (a noticeable bulge near the bottom of the stem) is planted 3 inches deep into the soil and is given a 6- to 8-inch mulch. Getting the Rose hole deep enough to bury the graft sufficiently is a problem in heavy or hard soil, with the result that the graft is damaged where winters are harsh and the vigorous rootstock takes over. Even where the graft seems to be buried, root shoots may appear in the midst of the grafted bush. These should be pulled out whenever they appear and every effort should be made to add soil and mulch near the graft union. Or you may want to buy own-root Roses to begin with.

Little pruning is necessary other than cutting out dead or broken branches or suckers

ROSE BOUQUETS

One of the rewards of growing Roses, both OGRs and more modern types, is creating lavish bouquets. Each type lends its special beauty to an arrangement. The OGRs look best in bouquets by themselves because of their more open, relaxed forms. For all types, cut flowers in various stages of opening, even buds, to add interest. Hybrid Tea blooms are usually cut when the outer petals begin to unfurl and Flori-bundas when a few blooms in each cluster begin to open. Most Roses are best cut in the late afternoon. Remove the foliage from the base of the stems, but retain as much as possible. Place the stems in cold water overnight. You can even refrigerate Roses if you need to for extended periods. Recondition them by recutting the stems and placing them in fresh cold water. Bouquets should last about a week.

(pull these out) when the plant is dormant. If the shrub becomes too portly, cut it back by a third after blooming (otherwise you will sacrifice a lot of flowers). Most OGRs will survive without winter protection, but if you are growing some at the limit of their suggested hardiness, the standard procedure for minimal protection is to heap about 10 inches of soil (not drawn from nearby plants) around the crown of the plant to protect the roots from heaving during alternate thawing and freezing. This, rather than cold temperatures, is the usual cause of winterkill. A well-planted Rose in a favored position—a sunny spot sheltered from the wind—will survive better where winters are harsh (particularly with snow cover) than one planted farther south in unfavorable conditions.

Most OGRs are easy to propagate from cuttings. Follow the procedure described on page 26. To sow seeds, refrigerate them for fourteen weeks. Chip them, then soak them overnight. Seeds require twenty-one to thirty days for germination at 65 to 70°F (18 to 21°C).

Collector's Choice:

One of the tortures of the damned must be making up a short list of OGRs, as there are so many wonderful ones to choose from. The following are proven performers in a variety of growing conditions and serve as a reliable introduction to the subject. Most OGRs are heavily scented, so only those *without* scent are especially noted. Except for repeat bloomers, OGRs begin blooming by late spring *(Rosa hugonis)* or early summer (Centifolia, Damask, Eglantine, and Gallica). A word about "recurrent" or "repeat" bloom: These synonymous terms may be misleading to the uninitiated. In my experience, they mean that

the rose will bloom intermittently or in flushes, none as full as the first bloom. After you have grown them for a while, you will note the rhythm of each type, as it seems to take a deep breath before putting forth more buds. By contrast, everblooming roses bloom without pause. I asked Rose expert Lloyd Brace, proprietor of The Roseraie at Bayfields, to recommend candidates for a listing of OGRs, which I have indicated below. Unfortunately, I could not include them all.

Wild Roses and their Close Relatives:

Rosa glauca/rubrifolia, Redleaf Rose (1814). A most delightful wild type valued for its plum-green foliage, deepening to purplish red in the fall, with bright red fruits; medium-pink single blossoms on arching stems in early June; good hedge; comes true from seed; Zone 2. Lily Shohan's choice: "The foliage is so fine in arrangements, a good contrast in the garden, and super hardy."

R. hugonis, Father Hugo's Rose (1899). Noted for its striking yellow single-petaled flowers; unscented; a blaze of color in early spring; can be trained up walls or over arches or grown as a shrub with drooping branches and dainty foliage; 6–8'; Zone 4.

R. moschata nastarana, Persian Musk Rose (1879). Described as a variation or geographical variety of the Musk Rose or a very early cross of the Musk and China Roses; loose, semidouble pure white flowers in clusters; 3–6'; a slender bush, able to withstand drought in the Midwest but probably needs winter protection to grow in Zone 6.

R. rubiginosa/eglanteria, Eglantine Rose, Sweetbrier Rose (early colonial).

Especially valued for its apple-scented foliage; small, single-petaled, unscented rosy pink flowers; often used as an informal hedge if clipped once in early spring; orange-scarlet hips; very thorny and hardy; 10–14'; Zones 3–4.

R. rugosa rubra plena (late 1800s). Tough, beautiful, and underused shrub, to 6', with semidouble crimson flowers, freely wafted clove scent, repeat bloom all summer; a great hedge, showy hips, very hardy. Disease- and insect-resistant, it grows in almost any soil.

R. virginiana/lucida, Virginia Rose (1807). Undervalued native landscaping shrub, to 6', with glossy leaves, variable pink, single-petaled, well-perfumed flowers, followed by clusters of small glossy round hips and bronze fall foliage. We have maintained a hedge for thirty years by mowing around it and cutting it back to 3' every few years. Hardy to Zone 2 and very disease-resistant. There's a seldom grown semi-double version, *R. virginiana plena/R.* × *rapa* (1820), also called the 'D'Orsay Rose'.

'Stanwell Perpetual' (1838). A Spinosissima cross with wonderful scent and rebloom till frost. Very double 3", blush pink flowers on a 4' shrub. Very hardy. A Lloyd Brace selection.

Albas: Cottage Rose (early colonial). Very hardy, disease-resistant types requiring little pruning and tolerating shade; Zone 3.

'Felicite Parmentier' (1834). Very double light pink flowers; good for hedges; performs well in hot, dry climates; 4'.

'Koenigin von Daenemark' (1826). Very double bright pink flowers with rich fragrance; great for potpourri; 4–5'. Lily's choice: ". . . is always good."

'Semi-Plena'; *R.* × *alba semi-plena* (before 1867). Semidouble white flowers, loosely arranged; bright scarlet hips; 6'.

Bourbons: China–Old Rose hybrids; valued for their repeat bloom and relative hardiness to Zone 5.

'La Reine Victoria' (1872). Cupped blooms of lilac pink, very fragrant, upright habit, to 5', repeat bloom. A Lloyd Brace selection.

'Louise Odier' (1851). Opulent, very double dark pink cupped blossoms; good for hedges; hardier than most Bourbons; 5' or more.

'Madame Isaac Pereire' (1881). Similar to 'Louise Odier', but can be used as a climber; 6'. Choice of Jeanette Dutton from San Diego, who reports that this Rose is disease-resistant and survives both drought and lack of sun in her Zone 10 garden.

Centifolia: Cabbage Rose, Rose of a Hundred Petals (early colonial). Adored for its full blossoms; "cabbage" refers to the shape of the flower and not its size, for, as someone once quipped, it could just as well have been called the "Brussels Sprout Rose." Very double medium-pink flowers; good for hedges; very hardy; 6'; Zone 3. Invaluable for potpourri, rose-petal sandwiches, and the like: "A bland uncomplicated naïve sweetness which is a pure joy" (Richard Thomson).

'Robert le Diable' (1850). Esteemed for its ability to perform well in hot weather and for its gorgeous dark color (unusual in OGRs); scarlet-pink to deep purple, as well as compact form; 3'.

China: Common Monthly, Old Pink Daily, Old Pink Monthly, Parton's Pink China

(1752). Valued for its continuous bloom, characteristic tea scent, and semidouble medium-pink flowers in clusters; 3–5'; survives to Zone 6 with protection.

'Louise Philippe' (1834). Medium-sized double, deep purplish red flowers on a bushy plant growing only to 2'; try in containers.

'Old Blush'. As described under "China."

Damask: Summer Damask (early colonial). Appreciated for its fragrance, hardiness, and fall fruits; Zone 4.

'Celsiana' (before 1750). Double light pink flowers and gray-green foliage; heady fragrance; great for potpourri; 4–5'. Lily's choice: "please include 'Celsiana', which has to be the finest of the lot and an excellent garden plant." One has to see the warm pink crinkled petals to appreciate its special beauty.

'Madame Hardy' (1832). Domed, glistening double-white flowers with green button eye and bright green foliage, a classic and a Lloyd Brace selection.

Gallica: French Rose, Apothecary Rose; *Rosa gallica officinalis* (early colonial). Semidouble almost hot-pink flowers showing numerous golden stamens, an ancient rose with a modern look; large red hips; very useful for potpourri, since the petals increase in fragrance when dried; suckers profusely, but a good hedge trimmed to 3'; very hardy; 4'; Zone 3.

'Duchesse de Montebello' (before 1838). Very double light pink flowers; 4'. Lily's choice: ". . . not typical, but is a free bloomer and excellent for cutting as well as in the garden."

'Rosa Mundi'; *Rosa gallica versicolor* (early colonial). A sport of the French Rose and the earliest know striped type; large, wide-open, semidouble deep pink and white flowers with golden stamens; good for hedges; very hardy; 4'.

'Tuscany Superb' (before 1848). Very double crimson-purple flowers; valued for its deep color, a nice contrast to the light pink types; very hardy; 4'.

Hybrid Perpetual (1840): First repeat-blooming Rose; appreciated for its disease resistance and fragrance; Zone 5.

'Baronne Prevost' (1842). Medium-pink, many-petaled flowers (large and open with a silver reverse); blooms nonstop for many gardeners; 4–5'. Lily's choice: ". . . an excellent variety."

'Frau Karl Druschki' (1901). Still regarded as one of the finest white Roses, though too much like a Hybrid Tea Rose for some OGR enthusiasts; very double white blossoms with blush center; unscented; 4–6'.

'Reine des Violettes' (1860). Smoky red-purple flowers; glossy leaves; 6–8'. Lily's choice.

Moss (1696): Perhaps a sport of the Cabbage Rose; "Moss" refers to the fuzziness around the plant's sepals, calyx, and stem, which gives it a mossy appearance and is responsible for the flower's resiny scent; the globular flowers, very pretty in bud, are highly prized for flower arrangements; very hardy; Zone 3.

'Alfred de Dalmas', Mousseline Rose. Repeat bloom, with semidouble blush pink-white flowers; suitable for a low hedge or even a container; a dainty 2–3'. Lily's choice: ". . . a good repeater."

'Mme. de la Roche-Lambert' (1851). Repeat bloom, with double dark red flowers, an especially nice change from the pinks; very hardy; 4'.

'Salat' (1854). Rose pink blooms; the best repeater among Mosses, with good hardiness. "If you have room for only one Moss, this is the one." A Lloyd Brace selection.

Noisette: This type results from crossing the old Musk Rose and the Pink China Rose; valued for its repeat bloom and flowers in clusters; frost-tender; Zone 8.

'Mme. Alfred Cariere' (1879). Semidouble blush pink-white flowers; a climber or shrub that is hardier than most Noisettes; 12–20'.

Rugosa Hybrids: Derived from *Rosa rugosa* (1845). Very tough and hardy; introduced from Japan as salt-spray-resistant, but in truth Rugosas and their offspring are resistant to everything you can throw at them: wind, drought, poor drainage, thin soil. This type has everything you could want in a Rose: fragrance, repeat bloom, brilliant fall foliage, and hips. Zone 2.

'Blanc Double de Coubert' (1892). Semi-double white flowers; especially beautiful orange hips; fine hedge or shrub; 6'.

'Hansa' (1901). Tall, vase-shaped shrub, to 7', with large, double, clove-scented, crimson-purple flowers. A nice hedge or specimen planting. Repeat bloom all summer. Very hardy.

'Roseraie de l'Hay' (1900). Double violet-red flowers; fine hedge or shrub; 6'.

Tea (1850–1900): One of the parents of the Hybrid Tea Rose, with the characteristic tea scent and repeat bloom; evergreen foliage; Zone 7.

'Duchesse de Brabant' (1857). Double pearly pink cupped flowers; 3–5'. Commonly found in old California gardens, where it thrives in humid and warm conditions, but Lily Shohan reports that a friend has been growing 'Duchesse' in a sheltered spot for fifteen years in her Zone 6 garden, a perfect example of stretching suggested zone limits by careful choice of site.

Modern Roses ✿

ROSACEAE

INTRODUCED: 1881–1950
ZONES 3–10
TYPE: Shrub/Climber/Rambler
HEIGHT: 2–20'
BLOOM: Spring–Fall
SITE: Sun/Partial Shade

Our adopted granny, a close family friend, has gone to her rest. She farmed the old-fashioned way on a backcountry farm in Massachusetts in the 1940s and 1950s. The work was arduous. On an average day, for instance, she lugged seventeen pails of water to the house, summer and winter, in a dress. "I had never seen a woman wear pants, and I didn't have any I could use even if I had thought of wearing them," she told me. During all the years of her labors on the old farm, her flowers, vines, and shrubs were a source of comfort and joy, and she became quite knowledgeable about them, remembering all her life the names of every choice cultivar.

When it came to Roses, Granny did not hesitate to declare herself in favor of the old ones. "I'm an old-fashioned person and I want old-fashioned Roses!" she would firmly declare. These, by the standard definition, are modern Roses—Hybrid Teas, Polyanthas, Floribundas, Climbers, and Ramblers—introduced from the turn of the century on.

Time has proved the value of Granny's favorites—the middle-aged Roses that form a bridge between the really ancient ones, such as the Albas, Centifolias, and Damasks, and the most modern types. Granny's Roses are of mixed parentage—some, like the Ramblers, are close to the wild types from which they were derived; some are everblooming and others bloom intermittently or only once a season; many have light to moderate or almost heavy fragrance. What they all have in common is that they have survived in a tough marketplace where, since the introduction of the first Hybrid Tea Rose, thousands of Roses have come and gone. Commenting on this phenomenon, Richard Thomson noted that "it took originality and beauty for a rose to survive among the hordes of repeat-blooming varieties," introduced since the turn of the century in ever-increasing numbers as the principles of hybridization were better understood and put into practice.

Middle-aged Roses offer, besides originality and beauty, all the qualities most cherished by heirloom gardeners: reliability, ease of culture, hardiness, and fragrance. Plant these Roses the same as Old Garden Roses and follow these rules of thumb: prune everblooming types when dormant; prune once-flowering types after blooming; space Climbers and Ramblers about 7 feet apart and all other types about 1½ to 2 feet apart. If they are grafted, make sure the bud union, where the Rose is grafted to its rootstock, is at least 2 inches below the soil surface.

COLLECTOR'S CHOICE:

'Betty Prior' (1935); **Floribunda**. Granny's choice. This type is the product of a 1924 cross between Hybrid Teas and Polyanthas, combining the best qualities of both: clusters of medium-sized, lightly fragrant flowers on long stems, hardy and everblooming. 'Betty Prior' has bright pink single-petaled flowers on bushy shrubs growing to 4 to 5'. They are quite spectacular when massed in a hedge. Prune them back to 4 to 5' in early spring, keeping only the strongest canes. Zone 5.

'Blaze' (1932), **Large-Flowered Climber**. Granny's choice. No Rose is a true climber like a vine, but if offered support, types with long, supple canes can be trained to climb. Climbers grow from 6 to 15 feet and bear large flowers (2 to 6 inches across) in loose clusters. They may bloom intermittently or all season and are effective as Pillar Roses (tied to a post for full vertical bloom). 'Blaze' has semidouble bright scarlet flowers, 2 to 3 inches across. It grows to 8 to 15 feet, blooms all summer, and has a slight fragrance. Zone 5.

'Buff Beauty' (1939), **Hybrid Musk**. Jeanette Dutton's choice. Jeanette described 'Buff Beauty', which is especially vigorous, as a survivor in her Zone 10 San Diego garden, where her Roses must survive drought and partial shade (the latter may explain their drought resistance). 'Buff' is almost everblooming, with 2- to 3"-wide double gold-cream flowers that are beautiful in bud (apricot-yellow) and have a strong musk fragrance. Growing 5 to 7' high, it makes a good pillar of bloom. It is also handsome as a shrub, with its wrinkled, leathery leaves and drooping branches. Zone 5 with protection.

'Cecile Brunner' (1881), **Polyantha**. This type, first introduced in 1875 and the result of crossing dwarf forms of the China Rose and Japanese Rose *(Rosa multiflora),* is a forerunner of the Floribunda. Also called Mignon or Sweetheart Rose, it bears small clusters of exquisite double pink flowers, yellow at their base, with a moderate fragrance. Its 3'-high shrubs make it one of the taller Polyanthas. Zone 5.

'Crimson Glory' (1935), **Hybrid Tea**. Granny's choice. This is considered one of the finest red Hybrid Teas ever introduced. It has large, double crimson velvet flowers with a clovelike scent ("That's a matter of opinion," according to Granny) and grows to a tidy 2½ to 4'. Prune it back in early spring the same way as you would Floribundas. Zone 5.

'Dorothy Perkins' (1901). A hybrid of *R.*

wichuriana and the Hybrid Perpetual 'Mme. Gabriel Luziet', it was once the most popular Rambling Rose, but fell out of favor by the 1930s because of its susceptibility to mildew. It is, however, still going strong in many old gardens, especially in the Northeast (mildew does not seem to be a problem in gardens near the seacoast). It is loved for the effortless way it covers arbors with its long, snaky canes, to 20', smothered in masses of shell-pink flower clusters (no scent) in midsummer. Lloyd Brace advises giving it good air circulation to prevent disease and cutting out two-year-old canes in August.

'Dr. W. Van Fleet' (1910), **Large-Flowered Climber**. Granny's choice. This plant's fragrant, fully double pink blooms, fading to flesh white, are 2 to 3" wide and grow on vines 15 to 20' high. It flowers once in the spring, but what a display it puts on! This was Granny's favorite Rose, the only one she took a slip from when she left the farm. Her son-in-law Hank trained it along a rail fence for prolific bloom, so great the dropped flowers literally carpet the ground. Zone 5.

'Excelsa' (1909) **Rambler Rose**. Sometimes called "Red Dorothy Perkins," this vigorous rambler grows to 15' and produces clusters of red flowers similar in shape to 'Dorothy Perkins', but showier. I've seen both trained on an arbor, where their simultaneous bloom in midsummer is breathtaking. I grow 'Excelsa' on a rustic arbor with Hop Vine.

'Frau Dagmar Hartopp' (1914), **Hybrid Rugosa**. This plant produces single-petaled medium-pink flowers that have a satiny texture and a clear color, along with large, outstanding fruit. It grows to 4'. Lily Shohan notes that it "has a lot of class and it blooms well, too." It should be grown alone as an accent plant where it can be admired in flower and spectacular fruit.

'New Dawn' (1930), **Large-Flowered Climber**. This magnificent Rose, a mutant branch of 'Van Fleet', superseded both its parent and 'Dorothy Perkins' because it offers clusters of large, double blush pink flowers 2 to 3" across. Everblooming with no disease problem, it also has nice long stems for cutting and a lovely fragrance. It has been unsurpassed since its introduction. Zone 5.

'Paul's Scarlet Climber' (1916), **Large-Flowered Climber**. Granny's choice. This is one of the most popular of all Climbing Roses, though it blooms only once in the spring. Growing 10 to 15', it puts forth profuse semidouble scarlet blooms in large clusters. Granny grew it alongside 'Van Fleet' by the side wall of the farmhouse, where they both climbed to the roof, nourished, she swore, only by an occasional handful of rusty nails. She maintained that if you grow these climbers on rusty junk, they will receive all the minerals they need to thrive. Train 'Paul's Scarlet' on a split-rail or white picket fence for a gorgeous display. Zone 5.

'The Fairy' (1941), **Polyantha**. This Polyantha is especially hardy and bears globular, light pink double flowers that bloom daintily and profusely all summer. Growing only 2 to 3' tall, it is widely used as a low hedge and for container planting. Zone 5.

'Therese Bugnet' (1950), **Hybrid Rugosa**. 'Therese' belongs to the catchall category of shrub or dooryard Roses—types that survive with little or no attention. This is an exceptional Hybrid Rugosa, growing to 4 to 6', with almost everblooming fragrant clusters of 3 to 5" lilac-pink flowers and foliage that slowly turns bronze in the fall. Developed in Canada by George Bugnet, it is very hardy, adapts well to poor growing conditions, and its dark red canes are handsome all winter. Zone 3.

"Veronica's Rambler." Named for our eighty-five-year-old gardening friend who has given us so many wonderful vigorous plants—red Gooseberries, tall pale Astilbe, scented lavender Phlox. Her Rose is in the same category: tough, vigorous, beautiful. So many ramblers have come and gone that it is difficult to put a cultivar name to this one, except that it is of Multiflora stock. More vigorous than 'Dorothy Perkins', its canes are stouter and can be tucked into the spaces of a slab fence to find their own support. It blooms a little earlier than 'Dorothy' or 'Excelsa', in masses of dome-shaped heads composed of clusters in groups of eleven with forty-four flowers packed into one head. Lightly tea-scented flowers are semidouble vivid pink with a white center, fading to lighter pink as they mature . . . a stunning companion to the dark purple Jackman Clematis that grown near it on the turkey yard fence. Older gardens still hold such treasures for the heirloom gardener, and since such ramblers are easy to propagate by cuttings they offer a wonderful introduction to the art of growing roses over arbors and along fences.

Rudbeckia hirta

ASTERACEAE

Black-eyed-Susan

INTRODUCED: 1700–1776
ZONES: 3–9
NATIVE

R. laciniata 'Hortensia'

Golden-glow

INTRODUCED: 1800–1850
ZONES: 3–10
NATIVE

TYPE: Annual/Biennial/Perennial Flower
HEIGHT: 2–8'
BLOOM: Summer–Fall
SITE: Sun

*T*here are twenty-five species of *Rudbeckia,* all native to North America. Black-eyed-Susan (an annual, biennial, or short-lived perennial, depending on its growing conditions) grows to about 2 feet on stiff stems with toothed, rather hairy basal leaves. The large flowers are perfect daisies with many golden petals, sometimes darker at their base, radiating from a brownish purple raised disk. Originating in the Midwest, Black-eyed-Susan is now naturalized in dry fields and along roadsides from southern Canada throughout the United States to northern Mexico. It is one of North America's most popular wildflowers.

Golden-glow is a long-lived, hardy perennial, double-flowered form of the Green-headed Coneflower *(Rudbeckia laciniata),* a tall plant (to 12 feet) with jagged leaves and long, drooping-petaled flowers around a dark raised cone that grows in moist ground and thickets south from Manitoba to Quebec. Golden-glow is dainty by comparison—a mere 8 feet (usually less)—with jagged leaves, double golden yellow flowers 3½ inches across, and a mass of petals, curved inward toward the center of the bloom and hiding the cone. It is often found growing as an escape around old farms and homesteads.

"I often reflect what a numerous train of yellow flowers with which your continent abounds," Peter Collinson wrote to John Bartram in the 1730s. He was referring to our bright yellow Sunflowers and Coneflowers, welcomed in European gardens long before Americans accepted them as garden subjects. "Here," complained M'Mahon in the early 1800s, "we cultivate many foreign trifles, and neglect the profusion of beauties so bountifully bestowed upon us by the hand of nature."

Green-headed Coneflower, though not grown in America until the late 18th century, was in every English cottage garden during the 17th century, having been introduced by plant collector John Tradescant, who was given roots of the wildflower by French settlers in Quebec. He passed along some roots to fellow gardener John Parkinson, who knew it as *Doronicum americanum.* It wasn't given its present name until 1740, when Linnaeus dedicated the genus to two Swedish physicians, the Rudbecks (father and son), who founded the great botanical garden at Uppsala University.

M'Mahon could take some comfort in the fact that the double-flowered Coneflower known as Golden-glow was offered to American gardeners by the early 19th century (it is advertised in G. Thorburn & Son's 1828 seed catalog), and before 1850 it was as common in American gardens as the Coneflower had been in English cottage gardens a century or more before. Annie Jack described Golden-glow at the end of the 19th century as "the darling of the ladies who are partial to yellow. It has spread itself like an epidemic over country towns and byways, and is sturdy and faithful when flowers are wanted for hardiness and careless culture. If cut off when the first flowers are over, a new crop will come from the base, dwarf but pleasing because so colorful."

Though rare now (it is becoming more available with the increasing interest in heirlooms), it is still found in older gardens. If left on its own, it will naturalize in the right spot—an open, sunny site with loamy soil—which is where I found a grand show of healthy golden blooms in late summer on an old up-and-down farm (so called locally for its rough terrain), a fitting floral emblem of the pioneers' sturdy and faithful descendants who had farmed this difficult land.

Plant Golden-glow by an old wooden shed, where the bright blooms will be shown to advantage, combined with Sweet Autumn Clematis; by the front or back door, as it so often was in the past, protected there from wind; or around a rural mailbox. Does it need staking? Not according to old-timers: "I just let it take care of itself." That's sound advice if you can manage it. At the Heritage Garden in St. John's, Newfoundland, I saw it grown at the back of a perennial border against a quiggly fence, framed by the bronze flowers of the Hop Vine, a stunning combi-nation. Recently, I've been cutting back Golden-glow midway through its growth cycle for a more bushy form (still plenty of flowers).

Black-eyed-Susan was grown in American gardens as early as the 1700s, the first *Rudbeckia* to be so honored. Its natural beauty and long blooming season (from at least midsummer to fall) could not be overlooked. It has always been a favorite flower, often dug up from the wild before seeds and plants were readily available. It was not entirely displaced in the public's affection even by the introduction of the more flamboyant (some would say vulgar) Gloriosa Daisy, with its huge yellow pointed petals painted brown and red. This variation on the Black-eyed-Susan was developed in the 1930s by treatment with the drug colchicine, a process that doubles the number of chromosomes a plant carries, resulting in stronger stems and larger flowers with richer colors. Now also regarded as old-fashioned (though it was not introduced until 1957 by the Burpee Seed Company), the Gloriosa Daisy is often variable in my experience. I was given seeds saved by an old-time gardener, and, after they self-seeded in my garden for a couple of years, I noticed flowers in the subtler form—more like Black-eyed-Susan with its simple, clean-cut beauty and appealing charm. Gloliosa Daisy blends nicely with Southernwood and Lamb's-ears in the flower border. It is very happy naturalized on a dry, sunny bank with Butterfly Weed and Wild-bergamot to create a little bit of meadow. Black-eyed-Susan also can be used to good effect when planted in tubs or containers for the patio or any open, sunny area. It is a terrific cut flower, so be sure to have plants near at hand.

Black-eyed-Susan is one of North America's most popular wildflowers.

To Grow: Both Rudbeckias tolerate heat, especially Golden-glow, which can be grown as far south as Zone 10. Both can be raised from seeds sown in a cold frame during the spring or summer and lightly covered with soil. Seedlings should be planted out the next spring after all danger of frost has passed: 2 feet apart for Black-eyed-Susans and 3 feet apart for Golden-glow. The former needs full sun and light, sharply drained soil (overrich soil produces weak plants with fewer blooms); the latter requires rich, loamy ground. Black-eyed-Susans should be cut back after blooming to prolong their life (two or three years in favorable circumstances). They should self-seed once they are established. Golden-glow is easily propagated by division in early spring every three years or as needed. It may need staking in exposed situations.

COLLECTOR'S CHOICE:

Rudbeckia hirta, Black-eyed-Susan (1700–1776). Make sure what you are buying is the humble wildflower, usually grown from seeds. Many hybrids are known loosely as Black-eyed-Susans and they usually bear large flowers, very different from the real thing.

R. laciniata 'Hortensia', Golden-glow (1800–1850).

Salvia officinalis ❀

LAMIACEAE

Garden Sage
Common Sage

INTRODUCED: 1600–1699
ZONES: 3–9

S. sclarea

Clary
Clary Sage, Muscatel Sage

S. viridis (S. horminum)

Annual Clary Sage
Annual Bluebeard, Joseph Sage, Painted Sage, Purple-top, Red-top

INTRODUCED: 1700–1776

TYPE: Annual/Biennial/Perennial Herb/ Flower
HEIGHT: 1½–3'
BLOOM: Early Summer–Midsummer
Season of Interest: All-Season Foliage
SITE: Sun

More than 750 species of Sage are widely distributed throughout the world. Three of these are of special interest to the heirloom gardener for their antiquity and use in the garden. All of them are native to southern Europe and the Mediterranean region and favor dry, stony ground. The familiar culinary Garden Sage is a perennial subshrub with woody stems; apple green to grayish green pebbly, pungent-flavored leaves; and stalks bearing white or purplish flowers in long terminal spikes, bringing the height of the plant to 2½ feet or more in favorable conditions. Clary, a biennial, establishes large rosettes of distinctive leaves—9 inches long, scalloped, nearly heart-shaped, and covered with silky down—in the first season. The second year, it sends up tall plumes of small white, lilac, or pale blue two-lipped flowers that grow from pinkish rose bracts on 3-foot stems. The whole plant exudes a strong, musky aroma. Annual Clary Sage, unscented, is slender in form, growing to about 1½ feet and bearing long racemes of showy top bracts colored deep purple, bright pink, or white with green veining; very small, insignificant flowers bloom farther down the stem in leaf axils. The genus name is based on the Latin *salvo*, literally, "I save," a reference to the healing virtues associated with the species.

Both Garden Sage and Clary were among the earliest plants grown in the New World, valued for their medicinal properties. Garden Sage, an apothecary herb from ancient times, was primarily associated with longevity, strength, healing, and fortifying, a shield against the declining faculties of old age (especially memory loss). Its ancient use to flavor such rich meats as pork is a reflection of the widespread belief in its powers to aid digestion.

Clary is a "head herb," particularly linked to soothing sore eyes (Clary comes from "clear-eye") with its mucilaginous seeds. Its leaves were used with Elder blow (flowers) in wine to copy the flavor of muscatel, hence the common name Muscatel Sage. Its distilled oil—pleasantly grape-scented—was (and still is) used as a fixative in perfumes. And with less to choose from in the vegetable line, people in the past often ate the leaves and flowers of commonly grown herbs like Clary. Parkinson described a tasty dish of Clary fritters, made by dipping the substantial leaves in batter, "made of the yokes of egges, flower, and a little milke, and then fryed with butter until they be crispe, serve for a dish of meate accepted with manie, unpleasant to none." Annual Clary Sage, often referred to as Purple-top, was credited with the same eye-healing properties as its biennial cousin.

With such a wealth of virtues to their credit, it is not surprising that all three were planted in the Wachovia Tract Medical Garden in 1760. Thomas Jefferson, ever an independent gardener, planted Annual Clary Sage as an ornamental at Monticello. By 1835 the London firm of Flanagan & Nuttings was advertising "Red Top" and "Purple Top" to sow in flower borders, but it was not until one hundred years later that herb pioneers such as Helen Fox and Rosetta Clarkson were telling American gardeners how various Sages and other herbs could be used as ornamentals.

Tender variants of the common Garden Sage—Tricolor or Party-colored Sage and Purple-leaved Sage—have been known at least since the 17th century in England, but whether or not they were grown in American gardens is not known. Although they are of interest to the antique plant collector, both are frost-tender (marginally hardy in Zone 7) and not as easy to grow as the ever-reliable Garden Sage. This sage has been much undervalued as an ornamental, probably because gardeners know it only as a cooking herb whose apple green leaves are harvested from annual plants. If left as a perennial, Garden Sage develops into a subshrub with fewer leaves for cooking (these must be harvested early in the growing season, before the flowering stem develops) but with a spike of pretty purple blooms. I regard Garden Sage as a dependable source of early color in my flower border, with its distinctive flowering plumes in early summer. The all-season grayish green leaves remain attractive, poking here and there through the soft

Garden Sage is a wonderfully useful herb and an underdeveloped ornamental.

Thomas Jefferson planted Annual Clary Sage at Monticello.

Clary was one of the first plants grown by Europeans in the New World.

yellow blooms of Lemon Daylily and Golden-Marguerite. Kept in fresh trim by annual clipping, it can be used as a low hedge, the foliage a restful point of interest among more colorful flowering plants. There are always enough leaves to flavor cottage cheese and pork and chicken dishes, as well as to make a cup or two of tea (to stimulate and fortify the brain): Steep 1 teaspoon dried leaves in 1 cup boiling water; let steep 2 minutes. This is especially good with a slice of lemon and a bit of honey added to the cup.

Clary is a plant I do not like to be without, and every spring I search the ground to find the familiar large unmistakable rosette of leaves. These biennials self-seed from year to year, and if they turn up where you don't want them, they can be replanted in their early growth. Even when they wilt after being moved, they will come back to furnish the midsummer garden with decorative stalks

of bloom attracting the attention of visitors, including hummingbirds. In my herb garden, Clary enjoys the company of Musk Mallow *(Malva moschata),* Wild-bergamot, and nearby Roses.

Annual Clary Sage is a most interesting plant that deserves more attention for its colorful, long-lasting, bright top bracts—stunning when grown in colonies in full sun, as they do at Monticello among Calendula and Corn Poppies. I first saw it growing wild in its native habitat as part of a winter carpet of bright-blooming annuals, and later as a striking massed planting of the bright pink variant. It wasn't until I returned home that I realized it was the same plant grown by Jefferson. I now grow all the colors in a harvest bed among orange and yellow Calendulas and blue Love-in-a-mist for a long season of brilliant color.

To Grow: Salvias are drought-tolerant and sun-loving. Garden Sage can be raised by seeds, planted one to two months before the last frost, to germinate in twenty-one days or sooner at 60°F (16°C). A week or so before the last frost, plant out seedlings 20 inches apart in light, even poor, sharply drained soil (all Sages perish from standing water). To keep it going as a flowering shrub, cut it back with clippers in the spring as soon as it has sprouted new leaves (so you will know which part of the plant is dead and which part you want to encourage). I have kept some plants going for many years simply by breaking apart the old plants and severely cutting them back to encourage fresh growth.

Both Clary and Annual Clary Sage can be started from seed sown in midwinter and planted out, like Sage, in a sunny spot with well-drained soil on the light side—12 inches

HOW TO USE SAGES

Annual Clary Sage stems can be cut all summer for fresh and dried bouquets. For the latter, pick stems when the flower color is brightest, tie them in small bundles, and hang them in a cool, dry, dark room until they are completely dry.

Leaves of Garden Sage can be used fresh or dried. To dry, pull the young, apple green leaves off the stalks and scatter them loosely on a cookie sheet. Dry them in a just-warm oven (at the lowest setting or after baking), stirring occasionally, until crisp. Do not cook them (you should not smell a strong aroma). Remove any stems and place the leaves, as whole as possible (to preserve the flavor), in a jar. Store the jar in a dark cupboard. Crumble the leaves to use.

apart for Clary, 6 inches apart for Annual Clary Sage. Clary is likely to self-seed; Annual Clary Sage may self-seed in most areas (in my Zone 4 garden, second-year plants have returned, though unprotected over the winter, growing up from last year's crown).

The variegated Sages can be grown as perennials in Zones 7 to 10. Elsewhere, grow them as annuals and take stem cuttings in midsummer. Carry over plants indoors, then plant them out as for Garden Sage. Their leaves can be used for flavoring the same way as Garden Sage.

COLLECTOR'S CHOICE:

Salvia officinalis, Garden Sage.
'Purpurascens'/'Purpurea'. Zones 8–10
(possibly Zone 7 in a protected spot).
'Tricolor'. As hardy as 'Purpurascens';
variable pink, white, and green.
S. sclarea, Clary.
S. viridis (S. horminum), Annual Clary Sage.
Sometimes available in separate colors.
Save seeds yourself and you can decide
where you prefer each color.

Sambucus canadensis ❧

CAPRIFOLIACEAE

Elderberry
American Elder, Sweet Elderberry

INTRODUCED: 1700–1776
ZONES: 3–10
NATIVE
TYPE: Hardy Shrub/Herb
HEIGHT: 12'
BLOOM: Early Summer
SITE: Sun

About twenty species of *Sambucus* are widely distributed in temperate and subtropical regions. The American native Elderberry grows wild from Nova Scotia to Florida and Texas, obviously a highly adaptable species. The shrub grows to 12 feet on pithy stems with arching, spreading branches (to 8 feet) bearing long, narrow leaves and showy, flat, sweetly scented umbels (6 to 10 inches across) of tiny white florets that become purplish black berries by late summer and fall. The berries hang down in great clusters—a picture of fall ripeness that is very inviting to local birds.

Since many of the uses ascribed to the European Elder *(Sambucus nigra)* were well known to the settlers, it is likely that they made similar use of the native species they found growing abundantly at the edge of woodlands in moist soils. There is a use for every part of the shrub, literally from its head (flowers and fruit) to its toes (roots), with plenty of uses in between for stems, wood, and even bark. Preparations could be made to soothe gout, dropsy, and dog bites; the juice was used as a hair dye (whether or not it washes out in the rain is unknown); and the distilled water from its flowers was used as a general skin conditioner—a complete pharmacopoeia in one bush. The settlers, who learned to tap maple trees from the Indians, also learned that the Elderberry's hollow stems could be made into little taps to catch maple sap or into whistles to entertain children.

During the 18th and 19th centuries, when more attention was given to growing ornamentals, the American Elderberry was pressed into double duty. Almost every homestead, and a good many town gardens, included a

Able to grow in almost any soil, especially damp areas, Elderberries are incredibly adaptable.

SPICED ELDERBERRY JELLY

3 pounds crabapples
2 quarts ripe elderberries with stems
2 cups apple cider vinegar
2 cups water
1/4 cup broken cinnamon sticks
2 tablespoons whole cloves
granulated sugar (see directions)

In a large pot, combine rinsed, whole crabapples and elderberries, vinegar, water, and spices. Cover and simmer until fruit is soft. Strain mixture through several layers of cheesecloth and let drip for a couple of hours or overnight. For each cup of juice measure out 1 cup sugar, cooking no more than 4 cups of juice at a time. Heat, stir in sugar, bring to a boil, and cook uncovered for 10 minutes or until a small amount of liquid sheets from the spoon (crabapples contain a lot of pectin, so don't overcook).

Makes about 2½ pints jelly.

few of these attractive shrubs to fill the blooming gap left by Lilacs. Where space permitted, it could be paired with Mock Orange and the Rosebay Rhododendron, both of which bloom at the same time as Elderberry. Neither its blossoms (Elder blow) nor its plentiful berries would go to waste. They were turned into tea, jelly, pie, juice, and wine. Nineteenth-century gardeners were advised to make an infusion of the bruised leaves to repel insects from vines. Able to grow in almost any soil, especially damp areas, Elderberries are incredibly adaptable.

Every garden with enough space should include at least one of these handsome native shrubs. When in high bloom, the Elderberry is the embodiment of early summer's long, sweet days; when in fruit it signals the end of the growing season and imminent frost. Plant it near Daylilies and great drifts of Siberian or Japanese Iris in shimmering colors, perhaps near a stream or pond, where its spreading limbs will make quite a show loaded with creamy white umbels. Massed on a sunny bank where little else will grow, the flowers and berries provide a long season of interest.

"The elder is a valuable shrub as well as a beautiful one," wrote Elizabeth Lawrence. "If you stand beside it on Midsummer's Eve, with your feet in a clump of wild thyme, you will see 'great experiences . . . from the thyme upon the height/And from the elder-blossom white/In puffs of balm the night-air blows/The perfume which the day foregoes' " *(Through the Garden Gate,* 1900).

To Grow: Elderberries thrive in fertile, loamy soil but will grow under most conditions, from moist to dry. Full sun on a rocky hillside, bank, or slope will provide good drainage, as well as some protection from early frost, since cold air flows downward. Space plants about 6 feet apart with 8 to 10 feet between rows for mass planting. Mulch the area around the bush when it is first planted. Once it is established, maintain the soil fertility with an annual mulch of organic matter and a handful of high-phosphate fertilizer. Remove suckers as they appear and replant them as desired. To keep plants shapely, cut out the oldest wood each spring. To rejuvenate an old bush, cut it off near the ground, and new growth will spring up quickly. Sow fresh seeds in the fall.

To Use: Both the flowers and the berries have many culinary uses. I add ½ cup of the fresh florets to pancake batter, substituting them for ½ cup flour (they make the pan-cakes very light); I spread the large flower heads on screens to dry for Elderflower-Mint Tea (soothing for colds); I put some flowers in cheesecloth and add to gooseberry jelly to give it a sweeter flavor. And I make jams and jellies with the berries. Our favorite is spiced jelly, great with cream cheese on toast or as a condiment with meat dishes.

COLLECTOR'S CHOICE:

Sambucus canadensis, Elderberry (1700–1776).

Note: Elizabeth Lawrence's favorite cultivar, 'Maxima', with flower clusters a foot across, is no longer commonly available but worth looking for. Explore the types available; some have larger fruits or flowers.

Saponaria ocymoides

CARYOPHYLLACEAE

Dwarf Soapwort
Creeping Soapwort, Rock Soapwort

INTRODUCED: 1850
ZONES 5–8
TYPE: Perennial
HEIGHT: 8–10"
BLOOM: Early Summer
SITE: Sun

S. officinalis ❁

Bouncing-Bet
Bride's-bouquet, Bruisewort, Crow-soap, Fuller's Herb, Goodbye-summer, Lady-at-the-gate, Latherwort, Old-maid's-pink, Sally-at-the-gate, Soapwort, Wild-sweet-William

INTRODUCED: 1700–1776
ZONES: 3–8
NATURALIZED
TYPE: Perennial Flower/Herb
HEIGHT: 2–3'
BLOOM: Summer–Fall
SITE: Sun/Partial Shade

*B*ouncing-Bet, native to Europe and Asia, is a member of the vast Pink Family. Its shaggy or ragged-petaled pink or whitish flowers grow from a long, cylindrical calyx in loose terminal clusters on thick-jointed, sprawling stems with shiny, lance-shaped leaves. Growing to about 3 feet, Bouncing-Bet is naturalized in large colonies by means of underground stolons, along roadsides, railroad banks, and ditches, in waste places, and on abandoned farmsites. It blooms during summer and fall. The flowers release their clovelike scent into the evening air to attract their pollinator, the hawkmoth.

The Latin epithet *officinalis* indicates the plant's long history of use, while its many folk names reflect the affection and interest with which it has been regarded by generations of ordinary gardeners. "Bouncing-Bet" is an apt description of the way it moves about by way of its creeping roots.

Used since Roman times as a detergent (all parts of Bouncing-Bet contain saponin, a substance that makes lather) and in the fulling process to toughen wool, it was brought to America, or seeds were sent for, in the early 18th century, perhaps for the same uses. Especially valued for its mild action in cleaning delicate fabrics, it is also soothing to the skin, which is why it may

"Bouncing-Bet" is an apt description of the way it moves about by way of its creeping roots.

have been used to treat poison ivy (a condition the settlers learned about soon enough). Double-flowered forms were cottage garden favorites in England beginning in the 17th century and soon became a favorite ornamental in America, popular all across the country from north to south, east to west, adapting to most soils and climates. Their intense fragrance on summer evenings has been described as "fulsomely sweet."

Dwarf Soapwort, from the rocky mountains of Spain to the Balkans, is very different in form. A trailing plant with oval green leaves on wiry stems, it produces a brilliant mound of bright pink, five-petaled flowers in loose sprays. In favorable conditions (sun and light, quick-draining soil) one plant can fill a square foot of space or more.

Although its leaves also make lather, Dwarf Soapwort was introduced as a garden flower in the mid-19th century. Its graceful flowing form reflected a new style in garden design—more natural, less geometric—as proposed by Andrew Jackson Downing and his successors. Like Creeping Phlox and Pinks, Dwarf Soapwort enhanced curving borders, raised beds, rockeries, and dry walls, all ways in which it can still be grown. An under-appreciated ground cover, its vivid color, trailing habit, and preference for growing in dry soil conditions make it a prime candidate for naturalizing on a dry slope. It's also beautiful at the front of a spring border with Pansies and late Tulips.

I was given a few roots of a double-flowered Bouncing-Bet from a turn-of-the-century planting at the house of a sea captain who sailed his schooner about the Maritimes, trading whatever surplus people had, even ashes from the stove. My neighbor, who now lives in the captain's rather grand house by the water's edge, called this plant "London Pride." I didn't know then that a half dozen plants in this area travel by that name.

As the roots sprouted leaves, I recognized that the new addition to my garden was a member of the Pink Family, closely resembling Sweet-William in its early growth. One evening my husband (the wildflower expert) and I were having a friendly disagreement as to the identity of the mystery plant, when, on a hunch, I went outside with my flashlight, plucked a few leaves, and rubbed them together. Voilà! A green lather. I knew at once my heirloom was *Saponaria officinalis*. Later, when it bloomed, I saw that it was the highly desirable double form, 'Flore Pleno' or 'Rosea Plena'. Regarded locally as a weed, it blooms by midsummer as a garden escape in damp spots and ditches where it found a congenial home after it was no longer wanted in the garden. Lady-at-the-gate and Sally-at-the-gate are descriptive names for the way this plant was edged out of the garden proper. I did find it still carefully tended in several older gardens, though, where it bloomed among old Phlox and Rugosa Roses, the combined scents creating a heady sweetness.

Do *not* plant Bouncing-Bet in a confined bed unless you are prepared to thin it annually (and it may be worth your while to do so). You may prefer to let it have its head where it can form a wide mat of light pink, perhaps at the end of a shrub border, in a damp spot with wild Iris and Bee-balm, or plunked on the lawn as a specimen planting and mowed around with care. This is the old-fashioned way to deal with plants that establish themselves comfortably in large clumps, and it is very effective.

To Grow: Although Bouncing-Bet grows in a wide range of soils, it is happiest in moist ground and full sun (or light shade in warmer regions, though its color won't be as bright under these conditions). Plant roots 8 to 12 inches apart in early spring or fall. Cut plants back after blooming and divide them as necessary, depending on the circumstances. To grow Bouncing-Bet from seed, sow them directly outside or in a cold frame, covering them well with soil. Germination takes about ten days when seeds are sown outside in mid-spring.

To grow Dwarf Soapwort from seed, prechill seeds for three weeks, then sow them on the soil surface twelve weeks before the last frost; germination takes seven to twenty-one days at 70°F (21°C). Plant seedlings outside in the spring in light, quick-draining soil (Dwarf Soapwort cannot tolerate lingering moisture on its crown), spacing plants 4 to 8 inches apart. Propagate by division.

To Use: To impress visitors, pick a minimum of ten fresh leaves of Soapwort *(S. officinalis),* vigorously rub them together, and you will produce a sudsy, somewhat green lather.

For more serious washing, chop roots, stems, and leaves into small pieces; soak them briefly in warm water and stir until suds form. If you chop and dry roots to use later, they should be soaked beforehand for an hour. Use about ¼ cup fresh or dried Soapwort for 1 quart of water (or as needed to form suds), and make a fresh batch after each washing. (Adapted by permission from Rita Buchanan's *A Weaver's Garden,* 1987). Presoak material you want to wash in cold water first, then lay it on a flat surface. Using a circular motion, gently rub the fabric surface with a sponge dipped in the frothy Soapwort solution.

COLLECTORS' CHOICE:

Saponaria ocymoides, Dwarf Soapwort (1850).
Saponaria officinalis, Bouncing-Bet (1700–1776).
'Rosea Plena'.

Spiraea spp. ❀

ROSACEAE

Spirea

INTRODUCED: 1800–1900
ZONES: 4–8
TYPE: Hardy Shrub
HEIGHT: 18"–8'
BLOOM: Spring–Summer
SITE: Sun/Light Shade

The most widely grown Spireas in North America are native to Asia. Vigorous growers, they range from short and mounding to tall and arching with numerous sprays of flat-topped clusters or spikes of white or reddish flowers. In some species, the flowers are tight buttons, while in others protruding stamens create a soft fuzz on the blooms. The enduringly popular Vanhoutte and Bridalwreath Spireas are synonymous with "Spirea" (and "Bridalwreath"). In mid to late spring—their branches garlanded and nearly bowed to the ground with sweet white flowers, their scent deepened by the profusion of bloom—they bespeak "old-fashioned," yet both are 19th-century introductions.

As ever more hardy shrubs were available to American gardeners throughout the 19th century, "the shrubbery" became a prominent feature of Victorian landscape design. Style principles of the period dictated plant-

Remnants of Victorian shrubberies indicate an embarrassment of riches, where the beauty of the individual shrub was lost among the mass.

ing in "small groups" (no fewer than twenty different kinds of trees and shrubs) with large specimens in the center and smaller kinds placed around them so each could be appreciated. Groupings were arranged at strategic points: at curves in a path or walkway, between site lines radiating from the house to the edges of the property boundaries, or as a screen along a fence boundary. No matter how sound the underlying advice—don't overplant—remnants of Victorian shrubberies indicate an embarrassment of riches, where the beauty of the individual shrub was lost among the mass. When carefully pruned, growth could be checked, but as enthusiasm for careful grooming waned, shrubberies declined, eventually replaced by more open lawn.

All the vintage shrubberies I've seen—no matter how overgrown—whether on humble rural farmsteads or in older suburbs, are peaceful oases, lending the landscape an old-fashioned, protected air of separation from the world beyond. In this setting, Spireas are the grace-note fillers between other shrubs and in front of evergreens. If we think of the shrubbery as a flower border—a flowing, continuous planting along walks or drives or to define boundaries—we will be able to select wisely among various Spireas (and other shrubs), for we will understand where best to plant them (at the back, middle, or front) for greatest effect. As with any well-designed herbaceous border, some irregularity in this scheme is most desirable. Tall Spireas are handsome single accents. Shorter kinds are lovely in flower borders, low foundation plantings, and rock gardens.

To Grow: Spireas grow in most soils, if well drained. They are wonderfully accommodating to site, growing even in shade, although they will produce fewer flowers than

in sun. Space large types about 4 feet apart, and smaller ones 2 feet apart. If the shrubs become crowded, remove the extras; they have fibrous roots and can be easily transplanted. Spireas benefit from pruning, and in common with most flowering shrubs, early bloomers are pruned after flowering; later bloomers are pruned in early spring before new growth begins.

COLLECTOR'S CHOICE:

Spiraea × *billiardii,* Billiard Spirea (1854). Astilbe-like, rose-pink plumes in midsummer; prefers moist, acid soil; upright form, 4–5'. Prune early spring.

S. japonica 'Albiflora', Japanese Spirea (1879). White flowers in early summer on low, compact mound to 18"; grow with red-flowering Japonicas. Prune early spring.

'Anthony Waterer', Bulmalda Spirea (before 1890). Very popular for its low growth and long flowering period in summer; large, bright crimson flowers in flat clusters; foliage tinged pink in spring; 2'.

'Coccinea'. Similar to the above but deeper red flowers; a 2–3' mound.

S. nipponica, Big Nippon Spirea (1882). Vigorous, with unusually large leaves of bluish green and white flowers in small, numerous clusters by late spring; a stiff habit, to 7'. Prune after flowering.

S. prunifolia, Bridalwreath Spirea (1843). In mid-spring, bears plentiful small, double white flowers, like buttons, on upright stems; these hold on longer than other types; leaves turn orange in the fall; to 9'. Prune after flowering.

S. thunbergii, Thunberg Spirea, Baby's-breath Spirea (1866). A rounded shrub with clusters of white flowers that appear before leaves in early spring; leaves may turn orange in fall; 5'. In the north, twigs tend to die out over winter. Prune after flowering.

S. X *vanhouttei,* Vanhoutte Spirea (before 1866). The archetypal Spirea form, vase-shaped with arching stems to 6' and clusters of flat white flowers in late spring; foliage sometimes turns reddish in fall. Prune after flowering.

Stachys byzantina

LAMIACEAE

Lamb's-ears

Lamb's–lugs, Lamb's–tongues, Woolly Betony, Woolly Stachys, Woundwort

INTRODUCTION: 1776–1850
ZONES: 3–10

S. grandiflora (S. macrantha)

Green-flowered Betony,
The-King-in-splendor

S. officinalis ❀

Betony

Wild-hop, Wood Betony, Woundwort

TYPE: Perennial Herb/Flower
HEIGHT: 1–3'
BLOOM: Early Summer–Midsummer
SEASON OF INTEREST: All-Season Foliage
SITE: Sun/Partial Shade

The Woundworts, to which group all three of these plants belong, are native to Europe and Asia, growing from a basal rosette of leaves and bearing spikes of bloom from early summer (Lamb's-ears) to midsummer (Great-flowered Betony and Betony). In Lamb's-ears, the leaves are tapered to 4 inches and quite downy, giving them a silvery cast. The flower spike is also woolly, growing on 12- to 18-inch stems and topped by a densely packed plumed head of very small pinkish purple flowers. The Great-flowered Betony, as the name suggests, bears showy rose-purple flowers in 1-inch-wide whorls on stiff 18-inch stems growing from a cluster of nearly heart-shaped scalloped leaves. Betony is a rangier, less compact plant growing to 3 feet. Its spikes of reddish purple flowers, also in whorls, grow on stems emanating from rosettes of tapered, aromatic, heavily veined, nearly heart-shaped leaves about 5 inches long. Dioscorides named the genus from the Greek word for "spike."

The Woundworts, especially Betony, an official herb of the pharmacopoeia, have a long and ancient history associated with healing virtues. From medieval times, if not well before, there does not seem to be anything that Betony did not cure, soothe, or charm. An old Italian proverb, "Sell your coat and buy Betony," aptly describes the value once placed on this musky, mint-scented herb. It was especially noted for alleviating, if not curing, all maladies of the head. When not used in this capacity, the dried herb above the root could be used for tea, as a tobacco substitute, and for a yellow dye. Although it may not have been grown in the earliest settlers' gardens, it appears twice in the plant lists of Christian Gottlieb Reuter, the surveyor for the Moravian community in North Carolina. Betony was grown in 1761 and 1764, according to his records, in the medical garden that served the community.

Lamb's-ears, with its soft, furry leaves, must have been handy to grow in a large patch by the kitchen door, to use as a Band-Aid when needed.

As a panacea, effective against both devils and despair, Betony would have been in great demand.

Great-flowered Betony, though a Wound-wort, has left no herbal account of itself worth mentioning, but it was favored in English cottage gardens as a showy plant of easy culture. It is seldom mentioned now as a subject for either the flower border or the herb garden. What a shame, since it has a great deal to offer and makes a splendid cut flower as well. Margery Fish regarded Great-flowered Betony as a long-standing friend, "just as I do bits of furniture that have been in the family for a very long time. . . . It is a good furnishing plant with its thick comfortable evergreen leaves and stiff spikes of rosy-purple. Its old name of The King in Splendour is a good one as it has a sumptuous regal look when at the height of its beauty" *(Cottage Garden Flowers,* 1961).

Lamb's-ears, with its soft, furry leaves, must have been handy to grow in a large patch by the kitchen door, to use as a Band-Aid when needed. Although I've never used it for this purpose, I'd feel lost without its handsome silvery foliage in the flower border, the rock garden, or wherever it's needed, cheerful even in the hottest weather (the down on its leaves protects the plant from wilting), the leaves glistening and shedding water in the rain. Its ground-hugging mats retain their lovely form well into the winter where they are not completely covered with snow.

I should add that for many years I failed with this plant until a friend gave me a piece from one he'd received from an old-time gardener. I have no idea if my Lamb's-ears is a tough old strain, but it's worth mentioning my experience because other gardeners, suffering from a similar failure with any number of other plants, may find a hardier or easier-to-grow strain still surviving in an old garden. This is one reason, among many, to preserve heirloom ornamentals.

All the Woundworts make an attractive ground cover, especially Lamb's-ears, if the flowering spikes are not allowed to bloom. If you want to use these for dried bouquets (as I do), cut them down as they bloom and the foliage will carry on. The silvery foliage contrasts well with most bright flowers, especially red and pink Poppies and Roses. The leaves spill over rocks, enjoying the heat and creating wide mats that defy weeds and act as a mulch for nearby plants. Great-flowered Betony, grown in groups, would be a good choice for the middle to front of the border, where the showy spikes of bloom show to their best advantage among dainty clouds of Feverfew. The taller stalks of Betony belong toward the back of the border, a dramatic contrast to the lilac-white plumes of Clary Sage or naturalize it on a dry slope with wild-flowers as I do. The Woundworts have a place in both the herb and the flower garden—if you can tell where one begins and the other ends.

To Grow: Woundworts can be grown to Zone 10, except in Florida and along the Gulf Coast. Great-flowered Betony is the hardiest, while Lamb's-ears best survives hot temperatures. Plant all types 12 to 18 inches apart. Lamb's-ears requires dry, well-drained soil and full sun where summers are hot and humid; otherwise its thick rosette of leaves may rot. Betony and Great-flowered Betony can be planted in well-drained garden soil, in sun or light shade (where summers are hot). Propagate any of these by division in early spring, or when the plants are dormant, every two or three years or as needed.

To grow Woundworts from seed, sow seeds in early spring, or when the soil temperature reaches about 70°F (21°C). Cover them lightly with soil. The plants will flower the following season.

COLLECTORS' CHOICE:

Stachys byzantina, Lamb's-ears. Zone 4.

S. grandiflora (S. macrantha), Great-flowered Betony. Zone 3.

S. officinalis, Betony. Zone 4.

Syringa vulgaris ❀

OLEACEAE

Lilac

Blue-pipe, Laylock, Lylack

INTRODUCED: 1600–1776
ZONES: 2–9
NATURALIZED
TYPE: Hardy Shrub
HEIGHT: to 20'
BLOOM: Spring–Early Summer
SITE: Sun/Partial Shade

Common Lilac is native to the mountainous regions of southeastern Europe and was introduced to the West around 1550 from Turkey. Left to its own devices, as it often is around old homestead sites, it may grow to tree size, with substantial woody stems and spreading branches that bear long, showy, fragrant panicles of lilac or white flowers in mid-May. In cultivation, bushes can reach 15 feet (shorter in some types). Blue-pipe refers to the once common practice of using the wood to make pipe stems. Lilac is derived from the Persian word *nilak,* meaning "bluish."

No one really knows when the common Lilac was first planted in the soil of the New World, but it is generally believed to have arrived during the colonial period, one hundred years before Washington and Jefferson planted it. Jefferson, an indefatigable gardener and recorder, wrote in his garden book of planting Lilacs in 1767 at Shadwell, his birthplace. In the same year he noted them among the trees and shrubs already growing at Monticello. Washington, also an enthusiastic gardener, wrote in his diary on February 10, 1786, that "the buds of the lylock were much swelled and ready to unfold."

European travelers in the New World just after the American Revolution were much taken with dooryard gardens "full of laylocks," observing that the road from Marlborough, Massachusetts, to Boston seemed a continual garden. (So much for the myth of America's lack of a gardening tradition!) While it's true that Americans seldom created grand gardens in the European style, the dooryard garden had its charms even for sophisticated travelers from abroad.

The Lilac phenomenon became a quintessentially American symbol, one with which ordinary people could readily identify, as in the famous line from Walt Whitman's poem marking the death of Lincoln: "When lilacs last in the dooryard bloom'd"—an unforgettable image of American spring across the land.

By the early decades of this century, several other species had been introduced from Asia, and lovely hybrids, most of them of *Syringa vulgaris* parentage, became available to North Americans, but still the common Lilac did not (and does not) lose its popularity, even among the most discerning gardeners. In her book *Lilacs in My Garden* (1933), the

Even when other types became available, the common Lilac did not lose its popularity.

wealthy American socialite and horticulturalist Alice Harding described the species as "the lavender plumed bush which, with its white variation . . . is used to make the tempting and rapturous hedges throughout the countryside. . . . It is the lilac which in distinction to all others comes to most people's minds when the word lilac is heard."

Mrs. Harding spent considerable time in Europe inspecting and encouraging the creation of ever-new Lilacs. Plant wizard, nurseryman, and breeder Victor Lemoine named two *S. vulgaris* cultivars in her honor: 'Mrs. Edward Harding', a red no longer considered superior, and 'Souvenir D'Alice Harding', a very double white much sought by collectors today (see "Collector's Choice").

While many of the Lemoine cultivars reached America during the early decades of this century, distribution was slow, and only a small number ever became commercially available. Walter Oakes, secretary of the International Lilac Society a decade ago, wrote, "No one now living knows what the lost cultivars actually looked like. Some of the rarest have been located and interest in them has been revived through the efforts of our members."

Even so, there are quite a few Lemoine and other heirloom cultivars available today, more than there have been in decades. But among such riches, how does one choose?

Recently, a couple from Ohio came to stay at our farm and told us the sad story of how they had planted four choice Lilacs, including the only primrose yellow type, and waited four years for them to bloom. They all produced the familiar lilac flowers of the common form. What had gone wrong?

Charles D. Holetich, who worked with Lilacs for thirty-two years at the Royal Bo-

tanical Gardens in Hamilton, Ontario, assured me that our friends probably lost their Lilacs because they had been poorly planted, under conditions where hardly any ornamental plant would survive or flourish. Lilacs, he pointed out, are suitably hardy plants from Edmonton to Montreal in the North and from Denver to Philadelphia in the South. Evidently, our friends had bought grafted Lilacs, and they had died back to the rootstock, *Syringa vulgaris,* after a hard winter. If they had been deeply and well planted, as Mr. Holetich noted, they should have survived. (Grafted shrubs should always be planted 4 to 6 inches deeper than they were in the nursery, but where winters are severe and soil problematic it's better to buy shrubs advertised as "own root.") Mr. Holetich also stressed that even if you live in a growing zone where Lilacs are not normally grown, you can succeed with them by carefully choosing cultivars that do well in higher (mountainous) elevations in the South or in wind-protected (sheltered) areas in the North. This must be so, for a friend who recently moved to Santa Fe, New Mexico, at the edge of the high desert, extols the glories of purple Lilacs blooming in early spring.

To produce blooms, Lilacs need a period of rest or dormancy, which can be brought on by either successive nighttime temperatures below 40°F (4°C) or several months of drought. Magnificent Lilacs grow in older gardens of the Sacramento Valley in California where summers are very hot and dry. (Check below for cultivars that do well under difficult growing conditions.) This group is usually referred to as French Hybrids, the result of crossing *Syringa vulgaris* cultivars, thereby producing a wider range of flower color and size of bloom, as well as extending the bloom period. (As for fragrance, even experts admit that the old common Lilac is probably the most fragrant.) Not all the French Hybrids are, in fact, French. Two of the top heirlooms on my list are 'President Lincoln', bred by John Dunbar, superintendent of parks in Rochester, New York, from 1891 to 1926, and 'Andenken An Ludwig Spath', bred in Germany.

To Grow: There are two things to remember: Lilacs need five hours of sun a day and well-drained soil. They prefer a slightly alkaline soil but grow perfectly well in acidic soil. A pH of 6.0 to 8.0 is okay. Too rich, fertilized soil produces greenery at the expense of flowers. Look around at surviving Lilacs in old gardens where they do very well with minimum attention.

If the planting site is at all soggy, mound the soil and drape the roots over it so that surface water will drain away from the plants. Dig a generous hole to accommodate the roots and plant them about the same depth as they were in the nursery, or according to planting directions supplied by the nursery. Water them well and give the plants a good shake—before and after watering—to eliminate any air pockets in the loose soil. Trim back terminal buds lightly, even though they may look fat and promising. Don't expect much the first year (or even the second or third with most types). Lilacs take patience.

Authorities usually advise deadheading (trimming off spent blooms), but this is often impractical, especially with a bush of treelike proportions. *Do* pick plenty of bouquets when your beauty finally comes of age—a painless way to deadhead and moderately thin the bush. To prolong cut flowers, trim away some of the lower bark and dip stems in near boiling water, leaving them in the water to cool before arranging.

Pruning just to keep in shape should be done after the blooming period. There are two ways to rejuvenate old Lilacs in late winter. The more drastic is to cut the whole bush to within 6 inches of the ground. A demure shrub will grow up the first season, but don't expect any bloom. Radical pruning should be attempted only if some vigorous new shoots or plants are coming up from the base of the shrub; otherwise this method is risky. The second method is the three-year plan: the first season cut out one-third of the largest of the old stems and thin the small shoots; the second year cut out another third; the third year remove the last third. That way the shrub will be gradually reduced in height without sacrificing all the bloom. Lilac experts tell me that this is the preferred plan, though I have seen the other method work.

Alternatively, you can leave your treelike Lilac the way it is, as we do. It not only makes a fine windbreak but gives us a good excuse to create a shade garden of Cowslips, Beebalm, and Hostas of all kinds beneath its aging limbs.

COLLECTOR'S CHOICE (all sold as plants):
The cultivars I have selected all have desirable characteristics of one sort or another, all are beautiful, and all have performed well, often under trying conditions in a variety of habitats. I am indebted to Roger Vick's ad hoc International Lilac Society (ILS) committee for historical data (see "Listing the Loveliest Lilacs," *Kinnikinnick,* vol. 6, no. 3).

All Lilacs are scented to a degree. The ❀ symbol denotes those rated as having the strongest scent. The numbers 1, 2, 3, and 4 represent places where cultivars have performed extremely well:

1: Royal Botanical Gardens, Hamilton,
   Ontario, Canada.
2: Arnold Arboretum, Boston, Massachusetts.
3: Leona Valley, Southern California
   (observed by an ILS member).
4: Nebraska (observed by an ILS member).

Syringa vulgaris, Lilac. Zone 2. ❀
'Alba'. White flowers. ❀

Hybrids:

'Ami Schott'(1933, Lemoine). **3, 4**; double
   cobalt blue flowers; long bloom; heat-
   tolerant; Zone 3.
'Andenken An Ludwig Spath'/'Ludwig
   Spath' (1883). **1, 3**; single purple-red
   flowers; profuse blooms in midseason;
   Zone 2. ❀
'Katherine Havemeyer' (1922, Lemoine). **2,
   3**; large, double pink flowers in early
   midseason; Zone 3. ❀
'Lucie Baltet' (pre-1888). **2, 3**; single shell-
   pink flowers; a low- and slow-growing
   type; Zone 3. ❀
'Michael Buchner' (1885, Lemoine). **1, 2, 3**;
   double lilac flowers; a heavy bloomer in
   midseason; Zone 2. ❀
'Miss Ellen Willmott' (1903, Lemoine). **2, 3**;
   double white flowers; very large trusses;
   Zone 2.
'Mrs. W. E. Marshall' (1924). **1, 3**; single dark
   purple flowers; outstanding foliage; Zone 2.
'Paul Thirion' (1915, Lemoine). **1, 2, 3**;
   double magenta flowers with silver
   reverse; a fine cut flower; Zone 3. ❀
'President Lincoln' (1916, John Dunbar). **1,
   2, 3, 4**; single blue flowers in large
   clusters; Zone 2. American bred.
'Primrose' (1949). **1, 2, 3**; single yellow
   flowers fading to creamy white; very
   unusual; Zone 2.

'Sensation' (1938). **1, 2, 3**; a bicolor with
   deep purple flowers edged with white;
   very elegant; Zone 2.
'Souvenir D'Alice Harding' (1938, Lemoine).
   3, 4; very double white flowers; Zone 3.

Tagetes patula

ASTERACEAE

French Marigold
Rose-of-the-Indies

INTRODUCED: 1776–1850

T. tenuifolia ❀

Signet Marigold

TYPE: Tender Annual Flower
HEIGHT: 6–10"
BLOOM: Summer–Fall
SITE: Sun

In the wilds of Mexico and Guatemala
where it was discovered in the 1570s,
French Marigold is a bushy annual growing
to 1½ feet. Feathery scented leaves and
single-petaled rays—yellow, orange, or reddish brown—emanate from a domed center
or crest. It was called French Marigold because it was introduced to England (as the
Rose-of-the-Indies) by Huguenot refugees.
Signet Marigolds, native to Mexico and Central America, grow to 2 feet and bear intensely
scented (citrusy) ferny leaves and tiny, single-
petaled yellow flowers. Both Marigolds are
scented, but Signets are the ones whose fragrance is considered desirable.

   Garden historians differ in their dating of
Marigolds (either French or African, *Tagetes*

erecta) in American gardens, some claiming the early settler period (1600–1699) and others taking a more cautious approach (by the early 19th century for French types). Ann Leighton recorded that by 1793 Lady Skipwith's husband had ordered striped French Marigolds. By 1808 Jefferson had heard of "the two kinds of Marigolds you gave us," and by 1812 he had sown the French kind in his own garden. There is little doubt that both the French and African Marigolds were established in America by the early 19th century at the latest, for in 1806 M'Mahon was offering choice cultivars of double-flowered types, as well as quilled African Marigolds. By the 1860s, the Signet Marigold in its dwarf form *(pumila),* had become very popular, especially prized for carpet bedding. Although each flower was small—bright yellow with brown markings—they bloomed in a great mass. In 1866 *The Magazine of Horticulture* described Signet types as "elegant . . . when fully grown, the plant will measure two feet in diameter, forming a beautiful compact bush, completely covered with flowers, and continuing in bloom until hard frost sets in."

Some people have claimed that the Marigolds of the turn of the century were virtually indistinguishable from today's. Such an idea would have been anathema to David Burpee, who took over his father's company, established in 1876. With slumping sales of the Sweet Pea, he turned his attention to improving the Marigold, boasting in later years that he took a scrawny flower of limited color range and smelly foliage and turned it into a garden Cinderella. There is no doubt that Burpee has been at the forefront of Marigold development. In 1939 it introduced the Red and Gold Hybrid Marigold, the first hybrid flower from seed to be offered for commer-

cial sale in the United States. Of the twenty-nine AAS medals awarded for Marigold introductions from 1933 to 1950, fourteen of them were for Burpee introductions, with names such as 'Crown of Gold', 'Early Sunshine', 'Golden Bedder', 'Golden Glow', 'Limelight', 'Real Gold', and 'Naughty Marietta'. The goal in Marigold breeding was to develop disease- and weather-resistant early-flowering types with more densely packed flower heads (of either the French or African type or hybrid crosses between the two) in variations on the basic gold themes. White Marigolds were not achieved until the 1970s.

The only cultivar from the pre-1950 period available today is the increasingly rare 'Naughty Marietta', a single-petaled French Marigold introduced by Burpee in 1947, winning an AAS Honorable Mention as well as an Award of Merit from the Royal Horticultural Society. 'Naughty' grows to 10 inches and bears flowers of singular charm: bright golden petals with a distinct mahogany cross in the center of each bloom. Recently, dwarf types have been introduced, but the flower type itself, so simple and satisfying in design among the increasingly densely packed colored balls of either French or African Marigolds or their hybrids, has not been improved.

'Naughty', however, did not appear out of the blue. As I learned from Jeanette Lowe, secretary of the Marigold Society of America and retired flower breeder at the W. Atlee Burpee Company, it was probably developed from crossing and re-selection, using previous bi-colors such as 'Iron Cross' and 'Legion of Honor'. I knew about 'Iron Cross' from my Dutch friend, Brother Gilbert, who remembered it well from his child-

The dwarf types of Signet Marigolds available today are probably very similar to those enjoyed by gardeners in the late 19th and early 20th centuries.

hood in Holland in the 1930s, where it was known as 'Erekruise'. 'Legion of Honor', also known as 'Little Brownie', was very popular in the early 1900s, appearing regularly in every Burpee catalog into the 1930s, until displaced by 'Naughty', which was more uniform in height and habit and bore larger flowers than the earlier introductions. Brother Gilbert carefully saves seeds of 'Naughty', which he has been growing for over twenty years. He also saves seeds from sports—some mahogany-edged, slightly ruffled, all yellow, or striped—if he considers them choice. He plants his French Marigolds in masses— bright patches at the front of his generous perennial border—or in tubs placed by doorways, sometimes paired with white Sweet Alyssum. At Old Sturbridge Village, I've seen 'Naughty' planted in the recreated Towne House garden as the most representative of early 19th-century French Marigold types.

Signet Marigolds have been least affected by Marigold development as envisioned by David Burpee. The dwarf types available today are probably very similar to those enjoyed by gardeners in the late 19th and early 20th centuries, their distinctly citrus-scented leaves regarded as anything but "smelly" by connoisseurs. Roy Genders considers the foliage of the Signets "more refreshingly aromatic than any other plant, the lemon-verbena-like perfume remaining on the fingers for an hour or more after pressing the leaves" *(The Cottage Garden and the Old-Fashioned Flowers,* 1984). In recent years, these flowers have been rediscovered as herbs, because the scented foliage and flowers can be used in potpourri, in pressed flower creations, even to flavor hot dessert sauces made with wine. The little flowers can be candied for cake decorations, too.

Signets are very useful for their colorful mounds of flowers from just a few plants blooming well into the fall—surprisingly frost-resistant (more so than other Marigolds, in my experience). If planted in tubs, they can be placed in protected areas, near buildings or taller plantings, to prolong flowering into early winter, or the containers can be moved indoors to a sunny spot. Plant Signets in rock gardens—so beautiful spilling over rocks, lighting up the garden—among evergreens in foundation plantings, or at the front of any flower border. Both cultivars listed below have been around a long time— 'Golden Gem' at least since the 1930s.

To Grow: In Zones 9 and 10, sow Marigold seeds outside almost anytime. Elsewhere, either sow seeds when the soil has warmed or start plants inside four to six weeks before the last frost. Space seedlings 6 to 12 inches apart when planted out. Signets are slow to germinate, but be patient; they're well worth the wait. You can easily remove the spent blooms of these tiny flowers by running your fingers up and down the sides of the clusters. Then you can draw your own conclusions about their scent.

To Use: I cover a handful each of Signet Marigolds (flowers and foliage), Southernwood, Mints, and Costmary with cider vinegar to make a cooling skin freshener for use in hot, humid weather. Let steep in a glass jar with a nonreactive cover for about two weeks, then strain and bottle. Dab behind ears, on neck, and on wrists.

COLLECTOR'S CHOICE (all sold as seeds):

Tagetes patula 'Naughty Marietta', French Marigold (1947). Extra-dwarf hybrids, "improvements" of 'Naughty Marietta', are crowding the original out of the market. Save seeds. This is a great butterfly flower and lovely as it is. ❧

'Harlequin' (by 1800). Single-flowered, golden-orange with variable mahogany striping; 2'.

T. tenuifolia 'Golden Gem', Signet Marigold (by 1930s). 6". ❧

'Lemon Gem'. 9". ❧

Tanacetum balsamita (*Chrysanthemum balsamita*) ❧

ASTERACEAE

Costmary
Alecost, Balsam Herb, Bible Leaf, Coast-mary, Goose Tongue, Mint Geranium, Sage o'Bedlam, Sweet Mary

INTRODUCED: 1600–1776
ZONES 4–9
TYPE: Hardy Perennial/Herb
HEIGHT: 3'
BLOOM: Late Summer
SITE: Sun

Native to southern Europe and western Asia, Costmary grows from a creeping root that produces pointed, tapered leaves up to 12 inches long—apple green and edged as if with pinking shears. Aromatic, with a refreshing balsam, lemon-mint scent, its foliage is Costmary's most distinguished feature. Where favorable conditions prevail (light soil and warm summer temperatures) it produces small yellow flowers about ½ inch across, at the top of awkward stems. "Costmary" is derived from the Latin *costus* meaning "an oriental plant," while "mary" refers to its dedication to the Virgin (its French name is Herbe Sainte-Marie).

A favorite folk herb, Costmary was once "an inhabitant of almost every garden," according to Nicholas Culpeper, the 17th-century astrologer/physician. It was planted in the first New England settlement by the Puritans, who wasted no energy on cultivating frivolities. Of limited medicinal use, it was grown primarily for scenting and flavoring, especially beer. Now, when virtually all our needs are met by commercial products, it is difficult to imagine a life where detailed knowledge of such matters was essential to the household economy. Both husband and wife knew the practical uses of every plant they grew, when to harvest it, and how to prepare it. Since beer was daily fare, on a plane with bread, its proper flavoring was essential. Costmary could also be used to flavor meats; in a pinch its young leaves could be eaten in salads or brewed like tea to aid digestion; and, when mixed with other herbs and flowers, Costmary intensified their scent—in the nature of a fixative like orris root—so it could be used in potpourri and sachets to scent rooms and bedding.

Folklore attributes another of its common names, "Bible Leaf," to the Puritan custom of using Costmary as a Bible bookmark (for which it is admirably suited). Others say the parishioners chewed the leaves to stay awake. In any case, no herb from colonial times suffered a greater eclipse than Costmary after its use declined.

Louise Beebe Wilder, who loved perfumed, old-fashioned plants, grew Costmary because "... its scent is like that of no other herb ..." (*The Fragrant Path*). She got the plant from her country neighbors in Rockland County, New York, who called it "Sweet Mary Ann," but she never described its place in her garden. It came into my life from an

> Costmary was planted in the first New England settlement by the Puritans, who wasted no energy on cultivating frivolities.

elderly man who called it "Sweet Mary," but he couldn't recall its use. He moved down the road into a shack, cut it in half, lived in one half, and stored his garden gear in the other. A strange fellow with a magnificent collection of antique flowers and herbs, he soon moved on, leaving his old plants to be overtaken by the wild.

Like the early pilgrims, I try to justify every plant in my garden, whether for practical or aesthetic need. What is Costmary good for, I asked myself? I enjoy rubbing the leaves to release their fragrance. The foliage is lovely, but, as the plant matures, leaves decrease in size and quantity, as well as quality. The plant's lax, meandering habit is not in its favor for garden design. To banish it is unthinkable, especially since Jigs likes to smell its leaves on his way to shut in the poultry every evening. How could I deny him this pleasure?

As I discovered uses for this strange plant—steeped with Mints and Southern-

wood for a cooling skin freshener, mixed with other herbs and spices for potpourri and simmering room freshener—I developed a strategy for growing Costmary at the front of a raised bed of Artemisias and double white Feverfew, where its large, basal leaves are maintained by confining the plant's growth to a ground-covering mat that sprawls attractively around a container of Lamb's-ears. Anyone passing this end of the garden can easily reach out to touch them both. I have seen striking plantings of Costmary in bloom among other herbs—with no hint of straggly appearance because of the thickness of the stand—but, in my garden, it is indispensable for its scented leaves. It would be nice to be able to compare Costmary garden notes with Mrs. Wilder.

To Grow: Costmary is grown from rhizomes (not as vigorous as Tansy, but beware its spreading nature), planted 1 to 2 feet apart in late spring or when the soil has warmed. For leaf production, plant in enriched, well-drained garden soil in full or even partial sun, and cut the plant back as soon as it starts to develop a stalk. For flowers, plant Costmary in light, sandy soil, only moderately enriched, in full sun. This will produce stronger, more upright plants. Slugs love the leaves, aphids gather around the blossom stalk, but then ants appear to take care of them. A soap spray works well (add 1 teaspoon dish detergent and a few drops of salad oil to 1 quart of water).

To Use: Cut the freshest, largest, most perfect foliage for bookmarks (press them between weighted paper). Dry smaller leaves to embellish stationery. Fresh leaves are also attractive in posies and tussie-mussies. (Costmary means sweetness in the language of flowers.) I add dry leaves freely to potpourri and simmering potpourri.

SIMMERING POTPOURRI

1½ cups broken cinnamon sticks

1½ cups dried orange peel

1 cup whole dried allspice berries

1 cup bayberry leaves (Myrica pennsylvanica), broken

½ cup whole cloves

2½ cups dried Costmary leaves, broken

¾ cup orris root or other fixative blended with 1½ tablespoons essential oils: a mixture of lemon, orange, and bayberry

Blend ingredients and store for several weeks in a jar placed in a cool cupboard; shake occasionally. To use as room freshener, add 2 to 4 tablespoons of the mixture to each 2 cups of water. Bring to a boil, then simmer. Ingredients can be strained, refrigerated, and reused.

Tanacetum balsamita, Costmary (1600–1776).
    May be listed as *Chrysanthemum balsamita.*

Tanacetum parthenium (*Chrysanthemum parthenium*) ✿

ASTERACEAE

Feverfew
Featherfoil, Fether-few, Flirtwort

INTRODUCED: 1600–1699
ZONES: 3–9
NATURALIZED
TYPE: Short-lived Perennial Flower/Herb
HEIGHT: 1–3'
BLOOM: Summer–Fall
SITE: Sun/Partial Shade

Feverfew is an upright bushy plant that can grow to 3 feet but is usually shorter. It has abundant light green, broadly segmented, pungent foliage growing along many branched sprays bearing masses of small daisylike flowers—yellow button centers, rimmed by a layer of stubbly white petals—three-quarters of an inch across. Native from southeastern Europe to the Caucasus, it has been naturalized throughout Europe and also grows as a roadside weed in North America. The common name is a corruption of *febrifuge,* from the Latin *febris,* "fever," and *fugere,* "to chase away," a reference to Feverfew's long history of treating fevers and headaches. Garden catalogs may still list this plant under the genus *Matricaria,* from whence it was moved to *Chrysanthemum* (residing before that under *Pyrethrum);* more recently it has been moved to the genus *Tanacetum.*

It is no wonder that Feverfew was among the herbs grown in early American gardens. It was so highly regarded as an antidote to headaches that it was called "the housewife's aspirin." It was used to ward off melancholy, too. An old cookbook recipe for "the dumps" includes Feverfew, Roses, Violets, Saffron, Rosemary, wine, and cider (the last two presumably in large doses).

Into the 19th century, Feverfew was still grown as a medicinal by the Shakers, who by 1850 had two hundred acres of various herbs under cultivation for seed at Harvard, Massachusetts, and Mount Lebanon, New York. Theirs was the first commercial enterprise devoted wholly to herbs and, for many years, the only seed source, as interest in "simples" declined until the herb revival of the 1930s. By 1881 Feverfew was in general circulation as a garden flower, with no reference to its herbal properties except to note that it resembled Chamomile.

The golden-leaved variety known as Golden-feather was used extensively for mass displays in Victorian bedding-out schemes, as least in England—a practice deplored by Gertrude Jekyll in the early 1900s. She warned fellow gardeners, though, not to neglect this fine plant just "because it is so common and so easy to grow." By removing its flowering stems, she dwarfed it and enjoyed the interesting foliage along the front of the border.

The double-flowered white variety, 'Flore Pleno', was described by the late 16th century. It smothers the plant in fluffy little pompoms, with the yellow centers barely evident. I first saw it growing at the Heritage Garden in St. John's, Newfoundland (at the Memorial University Botanical Garden). The pun-

All Feverfews make splendid cut flowers.

gent, rather medicinal aroma of the leaves of all types is said to discourage bees, but this does not seem to hamper the production of flowers, produced in masses from early summer to fall whether or not the spent blooms are picked off.

Feverfew is useful in the border to fill in over early-flowering bulbs, as an edging plant (especially if you dwarf Golden-feather as Miss Jekyll did), or in a mixed border among massed deep orange Calendula, Garden Sage *(Salvia officinalis),* and the purple bracts of Annual Clary Sage *(S. viridis).* All Feverfews make splendid cut flowers (try 'Flore Pleno' in bouquets with the classic single Calendula); Golden-feather's foliage is especially attractive in arrangements.

To Grow: Sow seeds indoors four to six weeks before the last frost, just pressing them into the soil. Light speeds germination, which should occur in ten to fifteen days at 70°F (21°C). Plant the seedlings 1 foot apart as soon as they have four true leaves, since they are difficult to transplant in maturity. You also can sow the seeds outside in early spring, as soon as the ground can be worked, and again in midsummer. Feverfew grows best in cool weather, so two sowings ensure an early and late crop. In northern growing regions, where summers are cool, the plants will bloom at least by midsummer and well into the fall, so two sowings are unnecessary. The site should be sunny (though Feverfew tolerates partial shade) and the soil fairly fertile and moist but well drained. If drainage is inadequate, the plants may not return the following years. To propagate Feverfew, divide the plants in the spring or cut young shoots from their base in early spring—each with a heel from the old stem—and root them in sandy soil for bloom the first year. When well estab-

lished, this short-lived perennial should self-seed, ensuring a steady supply of plants.

COLLECTOR'S CHOICE:

Tanacetum parthenium, Feverfew (1600–1699). 18".

'Aureum', Golden-feather (19th century). 12".

'Flore Pleno'. Double white blooms; 2'.

Tropaeolum majus ❀

TROPAEOLACEAE

Nasturtium
Bitter-indian, Indian-cress, Indian Nasturtium, Lark's-heel, Spanish-cress, Yellow-larkspur

INTRODUCED: 1700–1776

T. minus
Dwarf Nasturtium

TYPE: Tender Annual Flower/Herb/ Twining Vine
HEIGHT: 8–12'
BLOOM: Summer
SITE: Sun

Garden Nasturtiums are largely derived from two species of *Tropaeolum,* both native to South America. *T. majus* is a vigorous climbing plant with twisting, rather than twining, leaf stalks and outfacing bright yellow, red, or orange spurred flowers 2½ inches across. Its nearly circular green leaves grow on succulent stems to 10 feet or more. *T. minus* is a low, scrambling plant with smaller, bright yellow spurred flowers—about 1½ inches across, also outfacing—spotted orange near the center. It has shield-shaped, rather than circular, green leaves, which led to the genus name, meaning "trophy." Nasturtium flowers, stems, and leaves are spice-scented and similar in flavor to Watercress or Cress, as indicated in their common names. They also attract hummingbirds to their nectar.

Spanish explorers introduced the low-growing *T. minus* to Europe in the 15th century. By the 16th century, Gerard was sharing seeds with Parkinson, who described the flowers as "the prettiest of a score in the garden." By 1665 Nasturtiums were so well known that few European gardens were without them. The more vigorous climbing Nasturtium was introduced to Europe in the late 1600s, although Buckner Hollingsworth, in her entertaining and well-researched account of garden flowers, suggested that Parkinson was growing it by 1629, based on his description of the plant from which he picked flowers for "his delicate Tussiemussie" as having "very long trayling branches . . . if you will have it abide close thereunto, you must tye it, or else it will lye upon the ground" *(Flower Chronicles,* 1958).

There is also some discrepancy about when Nasturtiums were introduced to New World gardens. Both *T. majus* and *T. minus* are planted at 18th-century Colonial Williamsburg, and we know from the records of the Moravian community in North Carolina that both types, listed as "Spanische Kresse" and "Capper," with round leaves like those of the Marsh Mallow, were planted in the medical gardens in 1759, 1761, and 1764.

By 1806 M'Mahon carried both types. He especially recommended the climbing vine "on account of the beauty of its large and numerous orange-colored flowers, and their use in garnishing dishes." These remarks un-derscore the use of Nasturtiums as a food plant as well as an ornamental. But by the 1850s, utility had given way to aesthetics as Americans began to regard these colorful and easily grown plants solely for their beauty, especially after the introduction of interesting cultivars. These were the result of crossing the two species and adding other colors into the mix from newly discovered types (dark ruby red, for instance), resulting in 'Tom Thumb' cultivars very popular for carpet bedding. "It is said that a good bed, 6' x 20' will yield about 1,000 flowers each day," a gardening manual declared.

By the early 1870s, an ivy-leaved type with variegated foliage (cream and green) was introduced, followed in 1884 by the very choice 'Empress of India' with crimson-scarlet flowers. Hailed as a "grand novelty" and "the most important annual in recent introduction," it is still enjoyed today for its freely produced flowers and distinctive bluish-green, umbrella-like foliage, attractive even when the plant is not in bloom.

In 1928 California nurseryman J.C. Bolgier discovered what he called the 'Golden Gleam' Nasturtium in a small garden—very fragrant, double and semidouble golden trumpetlike flowers—and by 1932 ten tons of seed could not meet the demand for it among gardeners. By 1930 'Golden Gleam Hybrids' were on the market in a mixture of colors. The flowers were described in glowing terms as 2¾ to 3 inches across, sweet-scented, and in the "best brilliant colors . . . some . . . never before seen in Nasturtiums—soft primrose .. . pearly lemon." While 'Golden Gleam Hybrids' are still on the market, it is increasingly difficult

By 1665 Nasturtiums were so well known that few European gardens were without them.

to find the original golden flower offered alone or the once popular 'Scarlet Gleam' (see "Collector's Choice").

The variegated-foliage Nasturtium and 'Empress of India' are fine subjects for containers, where their distinctive beauty is highlighted. If you have a cool greenhouse, they will bloom into the winter months, and although they are not cascading types, they will overflow their containers with attractive foliage and beautiful flowers. The dwarf 'Tom Thumb' and 'Gem' types make a bright edging for a long walk, perhaps to cover the dying foliage of spring-flowering bulbs. The tall, climbing Nasturtium vine, once so popular in English cottage gardens, is returning to American-style cottage gardens. I grow it in a large keg by the garden shed, paired with white Sweet Alyssum. With a little encouragement, the sprawling stems insert themselves between the wooden slabs at the side of the building. Nasturtium flowers may be used as a tasty, peppery herb.

When choosing heirloom-type Nasturtiums, remember that the old-fashioned ones can be climbing, semitrailing ('Gleam Hybrids'), or compact dwarf types. In all of these, flowers are outfacing, rather than upfacing, as in the more modern type, but they are held above the foliage and they are spurred—an inducement to hummingbirds (the nectar is at the base of the flowers).

To Grow: The old adage "Be nasty to Nasturtiums" means don't overfeed them, or you'll get more leaves than flowers. (Don't worry, though, because even mounds of foliage are an effective and attractive ground cover). The culture of Nasturtiums is easy (a good plant for the children's garden) as long as you supply the heat they need to germinate—a minimum of 65°F (18°C)—and the cool temperatures they need for continuous bloom. In frost-free and warm growing regions, plant seeds outside in early fall for winter bloom; elsewhere plant seeds outside when the soil has warmed up in the spring. Drop several seeds every 6 inches for dwarf types and every 12 inches for climbing types. Cover them well with soil. Some protection from the hot sun will prolong their bloom. Nasturtiums don't transplant well, so be sure you plant them where you want them. Double-flowered types can be propagated by stem cuttings taken during the summer and wintered-over indoors. All types of Nasturtiums can be wintered-over and cut back to rebloom the following season (See "Wintering Annuals," page 24). Seeds of all types are large and invite collecting. Nasturtiums may self-seed, as some do every year even in my Zone 4 garden. As Parkinson noted, the climbing type will need tying to whatever support they're offered, although you can try my self-supporting slab board method.

To Use: I look forward to the day in midsummer when I pick the first Nasturtium

HERBAL CONFETTI

Pick a small handful of fresh Nasturtium flowers in different colors. Also pick young, tender leaves of Salad Burnet *(Poterium sanguisorba),* sprigs of Sweet Marjoram, a few small sprays of Fernleaf Dill, and a few leaves of 'Sweet Genovese' Basil. Inspect herbs for insects, lightly rinse with cold water, and shake dry. Gather the herbs tightly together, then, with a sharp knife or scissors, cut them up into tiny pieces. As they are cut they will assume a new life as colorful herbal confetti, which has many uses: sprinkle it over salad, tomatoes, and eggs; or mix into a cottage cheese-yogurt spread for crackers. It is delicious and beautiful in many dishes.

flowers to strew over salads, to press into cream cheese sandwiches, to stuff flowers with a dab of egg salad (especially the large 'Empress of India'), or to make into all-purpose herbal confetti. Like Rose petals, Nasturtium flowers taste like they smell . . . warm, sweet, and peppery.

COLLECTOR'S CHOICE:

❀ indicates especially fragrant types.

Tropaeolum majus, Nasturtium. single flowers; mixed colors; 6–10'.

Hybrids (all sold as seeds):

'Alaska Hybrids'. Single flowers; mixed colors; variegated foliage; dwarf type; 8".

'Double Gleam Hybrids'. Semidouble and double flowers; mixed colors; semitrailing; 12". ❀

'Empress of India'. Single scarlet flowers; dwarf type; 8".

'Golden Gleam'. Semidouble golden flowers; very fragrant; semitrailing; 12". ❀

'Scarlet Gleam' . Fragrant, double, fiery red flowers; semitrailing; 12". ❀

T. minus, Dwarf Nasturtium. Single flowers, mixed colors, 6–9".

'Tom Thumb Mixed'.

Tulipa spp. ❀

LILIACEAE

Tulip

INTRODUCED: 1600–1950
ZONES: 3–7
TYPE: Hardy Bulb
HEIGHT: 4–30"
BLOOM: Spring–Early Summer
SITE: Sun/Light Shade

*T*ulips have been called the aristocrats of the spring garden for their simple, elegant forms and brilliant flowers. Almost every known species can be found growing wild in countries bordering the Black Sea and the Mediterranean, from southeastern Europe to the Middle East. Fleshy, papery-covered, and teardrop-shaped, Tulip bulbs sprout with the onset of warm, wet weather (midwinter in their native habitat, spring in North America), sending up sturdy, broad-leaved stems, each crowned with a cuplike flower—often blotched black at its base—in various brilliant colors (most often yellow or red in the wild), with a sweet honey fragrance. Its Latin and common name refer to the flower's resemblance to a turban. Red Tulips native to Israel—vivid, large-flowered, short-stemmed—bloom in great drifts in late winter, and are considered to be the "rose of Sharon" of Solomon's Song of Songs.

The story of the Tulip's introduction to the West from Turkey, where it was discovered in 1554, is well known because of the plant's extraordinary social impact. By the time of its discovery, the Tulip was a common garden plant, and therefore already susceptible to variations in form and color. These variations aroused great enthusiasm in Europe, especially in Holland and Germany, where wealthy merchants paid enormous sums for unique varieties. By 1634 "Tulipo-mania" was in full swing, driving up the price of bulbs to fantastic heights through speculation and trading; there were more bulbs promised than could be found in all the gardens of Holland. Particularly prized were the Bizarre varieties, in which self-colored flowers changed, as if by magic, into gaudy flames of purple, rose, crimson, and gold—streaked, striped, and feathered. Such "broken" Tulips

> Tulips have been called the aristocrats of the spring garden for their simple, elegant forms and brilliant flowers.

(natural sports or mutations) are, as we now know, the result of a virus.

In 1636, Tulips were offered in the London Stock Exchange, but they were not a success and the market for them collapsed, causing economic disaster and great hardship (ordinary people had invested their life savings). As demand for them recovered—now based solely on their virtues as garden plants—Holland, with just the right soil for their cultivation, rich and deep, became the primary source of exported bulbs throughout the world. By World War II, when the country was overrun by the Nazis, Holland was sending about one hundred million bulbs annually to the United States alone.

Throughout the 16th, 17th, and 18th centuries Tulips found their way to the New World. These were mainly species or wild types, among them spidery-leaved, cream-and-red *T. acuminata; T. clusiana,* the red and white "Candystick" Tulip (still popular); dwarf *T. armena* with red flowers, edged yellow; and the Florentine Tulip, *T. sylvestris,* rich yellow and very fragrant, a favorite of Thomas Jefferson. Until hybridizing for color began in earnest, scent was the most cherished characteristic of flowers in general. Fortunately, perfume is present in varying degrees in most Tulips, regardless of their breeding.

From the 1600s through the 1800s, the most popular Tulips in American gardens were the 'Duc Van Thols', thought to have originated from *T. armena (sauveolens/schrenkii),* from southeastern Europe. Short-stemmed, from 3 to 7 inches tall, they were loved for their fragrance, early bloom, solid bright color or delicately etched variations: white edged with rose-pink; purplish rose edged with white—all sorts favored for the parlor garden. Taller types like the red single-flowered 'Keizerkroon'/'King's Crown' (1750), broadly edged with yellow, are also typical of the period.

Broken Tulips, of which Jefferson was fond, continued to amaze and delight (the cream-and-rose 'Zomerschoon' is the only one now available), as did the Parrots, sports of various types with lacinated petals, brilliant colorings, and good scent. These declined in popularity until later breeding, however, because of weak stems. The most widely grown ones today, like 'Black Parrot'—dark burgundy with black-flamed edges—are stronger-stemmed, dating from the early 1900s.

By the late 19th century, Tulips in the forms we know today—singles and doubles; early, midseason, and late—had all entered the trade, valued for Victorian massed bedding. In 1887 the Linnaean Garden on Long Island produced six hundred varieties and advised that for $500 one could buy enough to plant "a moderate-sized bed of the finest varieties" (Leighton, vol. 3). Prices, it seems, were still high for the most fashionable kinds. Increasingly, pastel shades were favored for Jekyllesque borders, rather than the brilliant sorts used in block plantings. Thus, as more and more hybrids were produced, the old tulips became harder to find. With renewed interest in Victoriana, the situation has improved (see "Collector's Choice"), but as heirloom gardeners we know that fashions are fickle. If we want to preserve them, the best strategy is to grow them.

The most memorable Tulip display I ever saw was in Madison, Wisconsin, many years ago. There, on the outskirts of the city, was a house and garden as if from the past: a long walk, leading from the front door to the property's edge, was lined on both sides with Tulips in every delightful shade, like a child's just-opened box of crayons. This planting was beautiful, and from a landscaping viewpoint, very effective: the perspective—the distance between the house and the street—was enhanced by leading the viewer's eye along the flower-lined walkway to the house, making it seem longer than it was.

More than twenty-five years ago, my young daughter and I planted fifty tulips in a rectangular piece of ground formerly inhabited by an old coal shed. With no special attention, they thrived, and today to my surprise still bloom vigorously, surrounded by a hedge of azure Lungwort, keeping company with Bleeding-heart *(Dicentra spectabilis)*, lime-colored Spurge *(Euphorbia)*, sky blue Forget-me-nots, and Creeping Phlox *(Phlox subulata)*. When I began thinning the Tulips to make room for more perennials, I threw them on the compost heap, where they began to sprout. Shamed by my husband, I replanted them in other places, where they continue to flourish. These are chiefly early single types—red, yellow, cream, and ivory—all very fragrant.

Long-lasting species Tulips are delightful for naturalizing on banks or beneath trees. Scott Kunst notes in his Old House Gardens catalog that the Florentine Tulip, Jefferson's favorite, is naturalized at the Victorian Ellwanger Garden, dating from 1867 in Rochester, New York (see "Gardens to Visit").

To Grow: Tulips thrive in enriched, well-drained soil, in full sun or filtered spring shade. Although some gardeners treat Tulips as annuals, two to three years in the ground is considered the usual survival time; five years

is unusual, and anything beyond that is extraordinary. Leave Tulips in the ground so long as their flowering is undiminished: this depends on the type, site, and soil conditions; deep planting generally encourages longer-lasting Tulips. My method is to plant bulbs in mid-fall, shoving my trowel in as deep as it will go (6 to 8 inches), inserting the bulb broad end down, then closing up the soil. I space bulbs 6 inches apart and cover them with 6 to 8 inches of soil; species types are planted 3 inches apart and covered with the same depth of soil.

Since they are planted in enriched ground, I don't fertilize Tulips until they have bloomed the following spring, when I sprinkle, then work in, bone meal around the planting. I pick off seed heads from spent blooms, and leave ripening leaves until stems can be pulled gently from the ground in early summer (by which time, other plants have grown up to cover them). At the first sign of disease (usually a virus, identified by deformed, twisted leaves) I pull out and destroy affected plants.

In Zones 8 to 10, Tulip bulbs will need pre-chilling for about eight weeks at refrigerator temperature; smaller-flowered species Tulips can be left outdoors in the ground in these areas.

To Use: Tulips are edible flowers, though their use is mainly for color (taste ranges from pealike to grassy). Shred them over fruit salads; or, after removing the pistil and stamen, stuff single-flowered cups with egg, tuna, or salmon salad, or with a fluffy dessert filling, topped with a fruit sauce.

All tulips are divided into the following categories (they grow in Zones 3 to 8 unless otherwise indicated below):

SE=Single Early. Short-stemmed, early-flowering, long-lasting in the ground.

DE=Double Early. Semidouble to double flowers, mainly short-stemmed.

T=Triumph. Single-flowered, medium-tall, midseason flowering.

DH=Darwin Hybrids. Single-flowered, long-stemmed, midseason; force well. Earlier types are referred to as Darwins (**D**).

SL=Single Late. Single-flowered, long-stemmed, late-flowering; good cut flowers; best in Zones 3–7.

L=Lily-flowered. Single-flowered, midseason, with pointed, reflexed flower petals; elegant, graceful, good for borders and cut flowers.

F=Fringed. Single-flowered, petals edged with fringes, midseason or late; variable height.

R=Rembrandt. Virus-free imitation of broken types; 20th-century introductions.

P=Parrot. Single-flowered with fringed, curled, and twisted petals; mostly late-flowering; of varying height; need to be protected from wind. Zones 3–7.

DL=Double Late. Double-flowered, late-flowering, mainly long-stemmed with rose- or peony-shaped flowers; need protection from wind; good cut flowers.

K=Kaufmanniana. Species; cultivars, subspecies, varieties, and hybrids closely resemble their wild origin; very early-flowering; foliage sometimes mottled, flowers with multicolored base, open to clear carmine red; to 8"; good for rock gardens, containers.

F=Fosteriana. Species; cultivars, subspecies, varieties, and hybrids closely resemble their wild origin; early-flowering, leaves mottled or striped; stems medium to tall; large, long flower; good for forcing or naturalizing; Zones 3–9.

G=Greigii. Species; cultivars, subspecies, varieties, and hybrids closely resemble their wild origin; mottled or striped, waved foliage; late-flowering; flower shape variable; striking in containers.

M=Miscellaneous. Species and their cultivars that don't belong to any of the above groups; good for naturalizing, rock gardens, forcing; Zones 5 or 6–10. Note: These are listed separately below.

COLLECTOR'S CHOICE:

The rare or hard-to-find antique Tulips listed below are all available from Scott Kunst's Old House Gardens; his comments are represented by "SK"; comments from bulb experts Brent and Becky Heath of Brent & Becky's Bulbs (see "Sources") are represented by "H"; all hardy from Zones 3–7 unless indicated otherwise.

'Aladdin' (1942). **L.** Narrow, yellow-edged, scarlet petals and base; ". . . like a lantern . . . glows in the garden" (H); 18–20".

'Black Parrot' (1937). **P.** Dark, glossy purple, sport of 'Phillipe de Comines'; very ruffled and frilled; 20"; "combine with 'Greuze', *Fritillaria persia,* and *F. meleagris"* (SK).

'Bleu Aimable' (1916). **DH.** Pastel lavender for the border and forcing; 24".

'Clara Butt' (1889). **DH.** Rare now, once popular; shell-pink, tall and elegant; 22".

'Cordell Hull' (1933). **R.** Deep ruby-red flames on ivory petals; 20–22".

'Coleur Cardinal' (1845). **T.** Once very popular for its long-lasting habit; deep red with plum blush; fragrant, short and stocky, to 12". ✿

'Demeter' (1932). **T.** Dark plum-purple ages to bronze-purple; reported to be long-lasting in the garden; 24".

'Diana' (1909). **SE**. Pure white, great for Jekyllian drifts; good for forcing; 12".

'Dillenburg' (1916). **SL**. Valued for its late bloom and color: a blend of peach and terra-cotta; 26".

'Duc Van Thol', Duc types. All rare antiques; extra-early, 5–7", very scented.

    Red/Yellow (1620). The original, bright red, edged gold.

    Rose (1700). White edged with rose-pink.

    Scarlet (1850). "Simple, classic, sublime" (SK)

    Violet (1700). Deep purplish rose edged with white.

    Yellow (1700).

'Duke of Wellington' (1925). **SL/D**. White; long, goblet-shaped, and elegant; 25".

'Electra' (1905). **DE**. A rare classic double; opens to purplish red, matures to deep purplish crimson; "luscious, unique, unforgettable!" (SK); 12".

'Elizabeth Arden' (1942). **DH**. Still popular, beautifully shaped rose-pink, flushed violet; oldest DH and "one of the 20th-century's major contributions to tulip history" (SK); 22".

'Fantasy' (1910). **P**. Sport of 'Clara Butt', sparked a revival of interest in these old types; flowers pink with apple-green markings; 21".

'Generaal de Wet' (1904). **SE**. Still popular for its wonderful rich amber-orange color; sport of 'Prince of Austria'; nice scent; 14". ✿

'Greuze' (1891). **SL/D**. A rare beauty with dark, rosy purple flowers. "Often gives two, even three blooms from one bulb" (SK); 23".

'Joffre' (1931). **SE**. Rare, yellow brushed with bronze; "Often gives two blooms per stem . . . and it's standing on the brink of extinction" (SK); 12".

'Keizerskroon' (1750). **SE**. Rare, because this is true to form; one of the earliest named Tulip cultivars; an old classic with bright red flowers broadly edged with yellow; 13".

'Lac Van Rijn' (1620). **SE**. Elegant; "Its form echoes that of the . . . first tulips brought to Europe from Turkey" (SK); red-purple with pointed petals broadly edged with ivory.

'Maytime' (1942). **L**. Reddish violet with narrow white edges; 18–20".

'Mount Tacoma' (1924). **DL**. Snowy white, very doubled, 18".

'Mr. Van der Hoef' (1911). **DE**. Very doubled, pure yellow, nice with dark purple Violas; 12".

'Mrs. John T. Scheepers' (1930). **SL**. A classic, still popular for its wonderful deep golden flowers; long-lived; 28".

'Orange Favorite' (1930). **P**. "Probably the most striking tulip in existence" (Genders, *The Cottage Garden);* orange-scarlet tinged with old rose, apple-green featherings on outside; nicely scented; 20". ✿

'Peach Blossom' (1890). **DE**. Pink, flushed white, very pretty; 12".

'Phillipe de Comines' (1891). **SL/D**. Rare, a reintroduction; the color of "dark sweet cherries" (SK); 24".

'Prince of Austria' (1860). **SE**. Rare; the tulip that launched Old House Gardens when the last source for this was dropped; shining red, maturing to orange, very fragrant; Scott reports it has been returning in his garden for a decade with no special care; 12". ✿

'Prinses Irene' (1949). **T**. Peachy-orange flamed with purple, fragrant; sport of 'Coleur Cardinal'; ". . . one of the most distinctive tulips of the 20th century" (SK); ". . . makes a great 'color echo' with 'Jolly Joker' Pansies" (H); fragrant; long-lasting in the garden; great for forcing; 14".

'Queen of the Night' (1944). **SL.** Deep velvet maroon; a Heath favorite; ". . . try it with *Narcissus* 'Thalia' " (H); 20–22".

'Queen of Sheba' (1944). **L.** Recent Royal Horticultural Society Award of Garden Merit winner; red edged with gold; 24".

'Red Riding Hood' (1953). **G.** One of the oldest and best of its type; brilliant red, urn-shaped flowers, mottled foliage; 12".

'Red Emperor'/'Madame Lefeber' (1931). **F.** Popular classic with glossy red flowers, long-lived; sparked interest in species tulips, important in Darwin Hybrids; 16".

'Schoonoord' (1909). **DE.** Victorian peony type, lovely in border; white with gold heart; 12".

'Van de Neer' (1860). **SE.** Soft rose-purple, at home in borders; "one of my favorite tulips . . . combine it with 'Prince of Austria' for a scintillating display" (SK); 10–12".

'West Point' (1943). **L.** Clear primrose yellow, very fragrant; a classic 20th-century tulip; "great with Grape Hyacinth and Forget-me-not" (H); 20". ❀

'White Emperor'/'Purissima' (1943). **F.** Pure white, creamy yellow base; "We have seen clumps of this tulip 20 years old!" (H); 14–16".

'Zomerschoon' (1620). Rare, true "broken" type (plant away from other Tulips to avoid spreading virus); pointed petals, shades of strawberry on cream; ". . . the most exciting tulip I have ever grown" (SK). "Which tulip . . . would be most difficult for me to give up of all that I have ever grown? I believe it would be 'Zomerschoon'," Mrs. Francis King *(From a New Garden*, 1928). Zones 4–7.

Miscellaneous (Species):

T. acuminata, Turkish Tulip (1720). Distinctive needle-pointed petals, cream-and-red flowers; 20".

T. armena/schrenkii/suaveolens (1585). Dwarf and early, red edged with yellow, gave rise to Ducs; Scott suggests planting these at the front of the border backed by purple-blue Hyacinths; 4–6".

T. clusiana, Lady Tulip (1607). Rare, the real species; narrow almond-shaped flowers, purplish red edged with white; 12–14"; Zones 6–10.

T. marjoletti (1600s? 1894?). Rare; "probably an old garden escape" (SK); cream, edged rose; late; 14"; Zones 5–7.

T. sylvestris, Florentine or Wood Tulip (1597). Graceful, almond-shaped yellow flowers with sweet violet fragrance; 8–14"; possibly Zones 4–10, but most successful in Zones 5b–8a. ❀

Valeriana officinalis ❀

VALERIANACEAE

Valerian
All-Heal, Cat's Valerian, Garden Heliotrope, Garden Valerian, Great Mountain Valerian, Wild Valerian, Setwall

INTRODUCED: 1600–1750
ZONES: 3–10
TYPE: Hardy Perennial/Herb
HEIGHT: 3–5'
BLOOM: Early Summer
SITE: Sun/Partial Shade

Valerian is widely distributed throughout Europe and northern Asia, and is a naturalized escape in North America from Minnesota to Quebec and south to New Jersey. Its fibrous rhizomes (the source of Valerian's fame) send out runners and offshoots that produce a handsome mound of dark green, deeply cut leaves similar in appearance to the precisely paired foliage of Jacob's Ladder *(Polemonium)*. In its second year, numerous wandlike stems grow up to bear a towering canopy of flowers in tight clusters of light pink to white with a heavy sweet-musk aroma. The root's smell, to which cats are attracted (as to catnip), has some of the character of the floral scent, but is generally regarded as unpleasant (Dioscorides called it "Phu"). Through various linguistic changes its ancient name "Setwall" can be traced to the Oriental drug *zedoary,* which became synonymous with "Valerian," both the drug and the plant.

For at least two thousand years, preparations from Valerian root have been used as a sedative to treat hysteria, epilepsy, depression, and insomnia, and in the Middle Ages it was also used as a spice and perfume, all uses that prevail today. The earliest herbals discuss Valerian in detail. Quoting an anonymous poet, Gerard shows how highly it was regarded: "They that will have their heale/Must put Setwall in their keale."

It seems likely that a plant so admired for its healing virtues was planted in the earliest new-world gardens, perhaps grouped with other "physick" herbs—Elecampane, Rue, Southernwood, and Tansy—and cultivated for its roots. In the early 19th century it was offered as a flower in its own right: "Garden Valerian with small white fragrant flowers" (Joseph Breck & Sons, 1845).

By the late 1800s, however, Valerian had passed into the category of "old-fashioned," a plant associated with "grandmother's garden." Its tall swaying flowers, its peculiar aroma, and its general presence had no place in stylish Victorian gardens. While Valerian was still commercially cultivated for its roots in the early 1900s, if you wanted the plant for its flowers, the best way to get it was over the garden fence, as Helena Rutherford Ely advised her readers in *A Woman's Hardy Garden* (1903), by swapping plants with someone in the neighborhood. She loved Valerian's long-blooming habit, its heavy vanilla scent, and its vigor. Just as she had taken her neighbor's Valerian, from it she had given away at least fifty roots—altogether a satisfactory transaction in the best gardening tradition.

I first came across Valerian in an older garden in early June at its height of bloom among Foxglove and white Siberian Iris. Its astonishing sweet-musk aroma filled the entire backyard, following me wherever I went, and I knew at once that I had to have this odd, desirable plant. Synonymous now with all that is most pleasing about early summer—fresh blooms, deep green grass, warm, sunny days—it pours its perfume across the garden, across our path, as we go about our summer work, its graceful stems holding aloft a mass of light-colored flowers that sway above dark crimson Peonies, Blue Borage, flaming Poppies, white Mallows, and pastel Dame's-rocket *(Hesperis matronalis),* a night-scented flower.

To Grow: Indoors prechill seeds 2 to 4 weeks, then sow on soil surface 10 to 12 weeks before the last frost. Germination takes 21 to 25 days at 70°F (21°C), or sow seeds outdoors in fall to germinate the following

By the late 1800s, Valerian had passed into the category of "old-fashioned". Its tall swaying flowers, its peculiar aroma, its general presence had no place in stylish Victorian gardens.

spring. It's easier to grow Valerian from roots set 2 feet apart in rich, moist soil, in sun or part shade. Propagate by division as needed (if you have the room a large clump is impressive). Every few years it's a good idea to renew the plant by digging it up and replanting young offshoots. To confine it to the garden, cut back plants after blooming, or it will self-sow with abandon, turning up in unlikely places (cement cracks), where it seems quite happy.

COLLECTOR'S CHOICE:

Valeriana officinalis, Valerian (1600–1750). As far as I know, no improvement has ever been offered. Pale pink or white flowers.

Viburnum trilobum ❀

CAPRIFOLIACEAE

Highbush Cranberry
American Cranberry Bush, Crampbark, Cranberry Tree, Cranberry Viburnum, Grouseberry, Mountain Viburnum, Squawbush, Summerberry

INTRODUCED: 1700–1776
ZONES: 2–8
NATIVE
TYPE: Hardy Shrub
HEIGHT: 12'
BLOOM: Late Spring
SITE: Sun/Partial Shade

The native Highbush Cranberry, one of about 225 species widely distributed throughout the Northern Hemisphere, grows primarily in the North Country (southern Canada and the northern United States), but is very adaptable to soil and climate. It bears fragrant white flowers in flat-topped cymes composed of tiny inner fertile florets surrounded by larger, showy sterile florets (the lace-cap type). The flowers, about 4 inches across, bloom in late spring. In the fall, fertile florets produce translucent red berries in heavy clusters and the plant's three-lobed leaves turn a brilliant red, extending the bush's season of interest.

There are many varieties of Viburnums. The first type grown in new-world gardens was Guelder-rose *(Viburnum opulus* 'Roseum'), with large snowball blooms composed wholly of sterile florets. Though still popular because of its ease of culture and hardiness, it is very susceptible to insect attack. For this reason, Japanese Snowball *(V. plicatum)* was considered a desirable alternative. Introduced in 1814, it also bears large snowball blooms of infertile florets along the length of its horizontal branches, but it is not as hardy as the Guelder-rose. Most of the other Viburnums were introduced in the late 19th and early 20th centuries from Asia. Although many of these are choice shrubs, none possess all the qualities that distinguish the homegrown Highbush Cranberry: beautiful flowers, hardiness, ease of culture, disease resistance, attractive fall foliage, and ornamental and useful fruits. See "Collector's Choice" for other native and introduced Viburnums.

Judging from its many folk names, the early settlers soon became acquainted with this native shrub, perhaps through the Indians. Its fruit is high in pectin as well as vitamin C. A few bushes laden with ripe berries in the fall could provide a family with enough nutritious preserves for the winter months. Highbush Cranberry was especially valued in regions where the low-growing Bog Cranberry *(Vaccinium* spp.) was not available.

In 1728 Highbush Cranberry was among the native offerings of John Bartram's newly established plant nursery. It was probably from this source that Jefferson acquired plants for his Monticello gardens, where he scattered them among other native shrubs such as Clove Currant and Rosebay Rhododendron. Despite the introduction of so many other Viburnums, the native kind is still found thriving in vintage shrubberies from the late 19th and early 20th centuries. I first saw it growing on the Bennington College campus (a former estate) in the 1950s.

Highbush Cranberry has always been highly regarded by the most tasteful gardeners. "It is beautiful," Elizabeth Lawrence told her newspaper column readers in the *Charlotte Observer,* "when the corymbs of white flowers are in bloom, and again in the fall when bunches of red berries hang from the branches. According to the books the fruits hang all winter, as the birds will not touch them, but Mrs. French says they are soon devoured in her garden in Gastonia." No wonder. As the common name Grouseberry suggests, Highbush Cranberry fruits are highly desirable for partridge, as well as pheasant and songbirds. With its spreading and open habit, there is no finer show than a bush laden with fruits in the fall with local birds enjoying them.

Highbush Cranberry is at the top of the list for creating wildlife habitats and edible landscapes with heirloom-type plants. It could be planted as an informal hedge or as a specimen, handsome with spring-flowering bulbs, or overplanted with an attractive ground cover such as Lily-of-the-valley or Lungwort.

To Grow: Highbush Cranberry will grow in almost any soil, in sun or partial shade, but it will thrive in slightly moist, enriched soil. Plant it as you would any shrub, digging a hole large enough to accommodate the roots and draping these on a little mound of soil to ensure good drainage. A top dressing of rotted manure or compost once a year is sufficient, along with a few handfuls of high-phosphate fertilizer if desired. Prune the bush as necessary in late winter to retain its shape. Hardwood cuttings can be made during the fall.

To Use: The translucent red berries should be picked before frost. The pectin-rich fruit makes a jelly with a sharper, more acid flavor than the familiar Thanksgiving cranberry jelly. A delicious condiment with chicken or turkey.

COLLECTOR'S CHOICE:

Viburnum alnifolium, Hobblebush (1776-1850). Native. A spreading, open bush; best for naturalizing, with large flat, white flowers. It grows naturally along our lane in light woodland and moist soil; to 12'; Zone 3.

V. x *burkwoodii,* Burkwood Viburnum (1924).

HIGHBUSH CRANBERRY JELLY

1 quart cranberries
2 cups water
2 cups sugar

In a large stainless-steel, wide-mouth pot combine cranberries and water. Simmer, covered, until the skins of the cranberries crack or pop. Put hot fruit through a food mill to strain out skins. Add sugar and bring mixture to a boil. Cook uncovered for 5 minutes, let settle, skim off foam, and pour into scalded jars and seal.

Makes about 2 pints jelly.

Early blooming with clusters of light pink flowers changing to off-white; 6–8' with glossy foliage; thrives in partial or deep shade. Zone 3.

V. × *carlcephalum,* Fragrant Viburnum, Fragrant Snowball (1932). Large globular flower clusters, to 5" in late spring from pink buds, deep green foliage that turns bright maroon; 6–10' in height and width. Zone 5.

V. carlesii, Korean Spice Viburnum (1902). Intense spice-vanilla fragrance, white flowers in mid-spring, to 6' tall; blue-black fruit in early summer, red foliage in fall. Plant this in slightly acid soil, in sun to partial shade along a path where the scent can be enjoyed.

V. cassinoides, Witherod, Indian Raisin (1736). Native. One of the best native Viburnums; late-blooming, with creamy white flowers in flat clusters, red to black berries and red foliage in the fall. This grows naturally at the woodland's edge along our lane, where the beauty of its clustered fruit can be observed as it changes from green flushed with pink to black in maturity. Full sun or partial shade, to 6'. Zone 2.

V. macrocephalum 'Sterile', Chinese Snowball (1844). Very large, snowball-like flowers, 3–8" wide in late spring, to 12' tall. This is a less hardy snowball type for warmer areas. Zone 6.

V. japonicum, Japanese Viburnum (1850). An upright, compact shrub, to 6', with white flowers and lustrous leaves; for warmer regions. Zone 7–9.

V. × *juddii,* Judd Viburnum (1920). A semi-snowball type with 3" flower heads from pale pink buds in late spring; a rounded shrub to 8' developed at the Arnold Arboretum. Zones 4–7.

V. lantana, Wayfaring Tree (1700–1776). Clusters of flat white flowers in mid-spring, red to black berries in summer, red foliage in fall; to 15'; a good choice for dry soil. Zone 3.

V. plicatum, Japanese Snowball (1844). An excellent snowball type with 2–3" flower clusters in late spring; to 15'. Zone 5.

V. plicatum var. *tomentosum,* Doublefile Viburnum (1814). Elegant, wide-spreading shrub with horizontal branching, flat white lace-cap flower clusters in late spring, early summer; to 10'. Zone 5.

V. prunifolium, Blackhaw Viburnum (1700–1776). Native. Flat white flower clusters in mid-spring on treelike form, to 5'; blue-black berries in the fall. Zone 3.

V. sieboldii, Siebold Viburnum (1880). A treelike type with creamy white flowers in flat clusters in late spring, to 30'. A favorite of shrub expert Donald Wyman for its attractive foliage (red in the fall) and red to black fruits in summer. Zone 4.

Viburnum trilobum, Highbush Cranberry (1700–1776). Native. Zones 3–7.

Viola odorata ❀

VIOLACEAE

Sweet Violet
Garden Violet

INTRODUCED: 1750
ZONES 4–10
TYPE: Hardy Perennial Flower/Herb
HEIGHT: 6–8"
BLOOM: Spring–Early Summer

Sweet Violets, widely disturbed throughout Eurasia, have been cultivated for millennia. Short, thick rhizomes growing from deep roots send out aboveground runners that root every 3 to 5 inches, creating new plants wherever they go. In early spring, a multitude of narrow stems arise from thick basal clumps of glossy, veined, nearly heart-shaped leaves, 2½ inches wide. Each stem holds a delicate, five-petaled purple-blue or white flower, ¾ inch across, with two upright petals like wings, and two lower petals on either side of a broader petal. This extends backward to form a nectar-rich spur. Despite each flower's relative insignificance, a single plant gains great appeal by its habit of blooming in showy bouquet-like branches.

Since ancient times, Sweet Violets have been celebrated for their beauty and used for perfume, medicine, and flavoring. As early as 320 B.C., according to Theophrastus, they were grown in special nurseries to sell in the Athens market. Gerard, Parkinson, and Culpeper, 16th- and 17th-century herbalists, praised their beauty and uses, recommending a syrup of Violets because it "comforteth the heart." Others prescribed it for headaches and sleeplessness (in fact, the plant contains salicylic acid, the active ingredient in aspirin).

Whether for use or delight, Sweet Violets were brought to the New World with the New England colonists. John Winthrop, Jr., son of the governor of Massachusetts, brought seeds—along with gunpowder, butter, ironware, and hogsheads of oil and vinegar—when he joined his father in the summer of 1631: his bill for garden seeds includes "violette seeds 2d [pence]—J. W. Jr" (Leighton).

By the 18th century, Lady Skipwith recorded growing both blue and white Sweet Violets and, later on, there were doubles (Gerard noted them much earlier). At the end of the century, hybrid "Parmas"—very fragrant doubles, less hardy than the species—of unknown origin, were introduced from Italy. They, as well as varieties of *Viola odorata,* were bred as florist's flowers for their long stems and showy, richly perfumed blooms.

Sweet Violet breeding intensified to meet the demand for cut flowers, posies, and indoor pot culture during the Victorian era. By 1860 there were four color varieties, and by 1914 over forty different cultivars of hybrid Parmas and Sweet Violets, some of which are still available.

As social conditions changed, and as greenhouse culture of exotics waned, the long-stemmed, double-flowered florist's Sweet Violets all but disappeared from commerce and their breeding virtually ceased. The hardier varieties continued to flourish in older gardens, where they were allowed to spread their mats of luxuriant foliage and produce a mass of dainty, lightly scented blooms in early summer, without permission of fashion.

Sweet Violets appeared in my garden uninvited, their roots entwined in plants we brought with us from northern Vermont to Cape Breton in 1971. They had been growing in our neighbor's backyard border since before the Second World War. By the time they were discovered, it was too late to banish them, although I certainly tried. Wherever I saw them, I pulled up the glossy-leaved clumps to make room for other, more desirable perennials. With only a vague idea of naturalizing them (a concept I knew nothing about at the time), I tossed them into a

Since ancient times, Sweet Violets have been celebrated for their beauty and used for perfume, medicine, and flavoring.

pile outside the garden, spread them out, then stepped on them to push them into a spot of damp, weedy ground. (I didn't know it at the time, but a modified, somewhat more genteel version became my standard technique for establishing vigorous plants in semi-wild settings.) I hadn't wanted them, but neither did I have the nerve to discard them altogether (true gardeners will understand).

With astonishing speed, the Sweet Violets moved into their new quarters, quickly shading out and killing weeds in their way, consolidating their position by spreading out to form a low, attractive canopy of glossy leaves. In the cool weather of early June on Cape Breton, they create a spectacular display of flowers—an accent planting beyond the garden proper—that always elicits admiration ("What are those pretty flowers?"). Elsewhere I let them run on a shady bank with Lungwort and Cowslips.

To Grow: Sow seeds in a cold frame to germinate over the winter, then set out plants in early spring, 12 inches apart. Cultivars (named varieties) should always be propagated by division to maintain their characteristics; this should be done in the spring after the plants have bloomed, or by early fall. Plants grow best in moist, humusy soil in partial shade or shade, although they will grow in sun as long as the soil is evenly moist and conditions are cool. Gertrude Jekyll maintained that Sweet Violets need to be divided every year to give the best bloom (she was talking about fancy, long-stemmed types), but her colleague, William Robinson, let them run as I do to create glossy carpets at the fringes of woods or on banks.

To Use: Sweet Violets mean modesty in the language of flowers and are nice to add to fresh tussie-mussies. I press the fresh flowers into chocolate cake frosting and use them to embellish fresh fruit cups. Their texture is crisp, their flavor lightly sweet.

COLLECTOR'S CHOICE:

Parma Violets are hardy to Zone 8 or 9.

Viola 'Duchess de Parme' (1870). Double lavender-blue Parma.

'Lady Hume Campbell' (1875). Late-blooming Parma.

'Marie Louise' (1865). Hardiest Parma; double lavender-mauve, named for Napoleon's second wife. Once very popular as a cut flower.

'Swanley White'/'Compte de Brazze' (1883). Double white with hint of blue, once the leading double-white Parma.

Viola odorata, Sweet Violet (1750). Also called "Blue Fragrant Violet."

'Alba'. White.

'Czar' (before 1897). Deep purple.

'Lianne' (1906). Pansy purple with carmine tints; blooms spring and fall, occasional summer bloom; slow spreader.

'Perle Rose' (1902). Deep coral-rose; late-flowering.

'Rosine' (1920). Pink-rose, once popular as a cut flower.

Viola tricolor

VIOLACEAE

Johnny-jump-up

Bird's-eye, Field Pansy, Godfathers-and-godmothers, Heartsease, Herb Constancy, Herb Trinity, Jack-jump-up-and-kiss-me, Johnnies, Kiss-her-in-the-fields, Ladies'-delight, Live-in-idleness, Love-in-idleness, Loving-me, Meet-me-in-the-entry, Three-faces-under-a-hood, Wild Pansy

INTRODUCED: 1600–1699
ZONES 4–10
NATURALIZED

V. x *wittrockiana*

Pansy

INTRODUCED: 1835

TYPE: Short-Lived Perennial/Biennial
    Flower/Herb
HEIGHT: 6–12"
BLOOM: Spring–Fall
SITE: Sun/Partial Shade/Shade

*V*iola tricolor is a native of Europe naturalized over much of the temperate
world. The five-petaled flowers are quite
small—¼ to 1¼ inches wide—with the top
four petals large and overlapping and the
lower one elongated to form a spur. The
whole flower resembles a miniature heart
whose face is variable in color—purple-red,
violet-blue, yellow, or creamy white, with
pencil-thin veins or whiskers radiating from
a golden center. The plant can grow as high
as 1 foot, though it is usually shorter, and has
narrow, deeply lobed green leaves. This species is considered an important parent of the
larger-flowered Garden Pansy. These hybrid
flowers vary in size from 2½ to 4 inches
across, with silky, somewhat waved petals in
shades of yellow, bronze, purple, blue, wine,
rose, and white, often with darker blotches
and veining, with a yellow eye, to 8 inches
tall. Both flowers are often referred to as Pansies, a corruption of the French common name,
pensée, meaning "thoughts" or "reflections."

Despite its diminutive size and humble
status as a wildflower, *V. tricolor* is infused
with great significance in herbal literature
and in the minds of generations of people
who regarded it with great affection (as reflected in its many delightful and witty
names). Heartsease refers to its powers as a
heart stimulant, both in the literal and figu-
rative sense. "Fetch me that flower," Oberon
orders Puck in Shakespeare's *A Midsummer
Night's Dream,* "the herb I showed thee once/
The juice of it on sleeping eyelids laid/Will
make a man or woman madly dote/Upon
the next live creature that it sees." Woe to
Queen Titania, who is made to fall in love
with an ass.

In the New World, *V. tricolor* was known
primarily as Johnny-jump-up, a purely American contribution to its colorful collection of
common names, playing on the plant's habit
of scattering its seeds like a catapult when
the pods break open, causing new plants to
spring up where you least expect them—in

The name, Johnny-
jump-up, plays on
the plant's habit of
scattering its seeds
like a catapult when
the pods break open.

CANDIED VIOLETS

*P*ick the flowers on a sunny day when they are fully opened
and dry. Remove the stems and lay the flower heads on
double sheets of waxed paper. Carefully brush one side of the
heads or petals, then the other, with an egg white beaten with
a little water. Be careful not to slop too much of the mixture
onto the flowers. Remove the flowers to dry paper and sprinkle
them on both sides with granulated sugar. Turn them periodically, changing the paper as necessary, until they are dry to the
touch. Store the candied flowers in wax-paper-lined boxes in a
single layer. Use them within two weeks or so. They make
beautiful cake decorations. Just place them in patterns on top
of the frosting, then lightly press them in.

the grass, between stones or cracks of cement, under stairs, and, of course, all over the garden. It was traditionally used in tussie-mussies, favored for its small blooms and associations with love, but its petals can also be candied or pressed for floral art. At one time, *V. tricolor* was recognized as a medicine in the U.S. Pharmacopoeia, used as an ointment for skin irritations and taken internally for bronchitis. There was no mention of its legendary uses as a heart stimulant.

FRESH FRUIT CUP

Strawberries
Raspberries
Melon
Kiwi
Sorbet (orange, mango, or lime)

Keep sorbet frozen; fruits should be at room temperature. Scoop out kiwi and melon into balls, cut up strawberries. Figure on a cup of prepared fruit per person. For each quart of prepared fruit make the following syrup:

1/2 cup sugar
1/2 cup lemon or lime juice or white wine
2 tablespoons chopped herbs: lemon balm, mints, etc.

Bring syrup ingredients to a boil and simmer, covered, for 5 minutes. Strain and cool. Add cooled syrup to fruit, and let the mixture blend for 30 minutes at room temperature, then chill until ready to serve. Spoon sorbet (about one big scoop per person) into a crystal bowl, ladle fruit syrup over it, then arrange freshly picked Sweet Violet and Johnny-jump-up flowers over the top of the sorbet-fruit sauce, inserting a bit of stem to hold each flower in place. Bring to the table and serve. Guaranteed to please.

We think of Pansies as old-fashioned, but they have not been with us very long, and might never have existed, but for the genius of those who saw in the simple beauty of the wild *V. tricolor* the possibility of something more elaborate and showy. The original Pansy may have been a chance seedling among several *Viola* species, including *V. tricolor* and *V. lutea,* which sparked breeding in England between 1800 and 1823. This effort focused on producing Show Pansies for competitive exhibition, with strict rules for their classification. By 1838, four hundred varieties had been named, but beautiful as many of them were (at least from their descriptions), they were not sturdy enough to face the rigors of ordinary garden life, and their breeding was stultified by the strictures of the Show Pansy genre. The Pansies we grow today are descendants of French and Belgian breeding efforts, which began with the English Show Pansy, and turned it into the more vigorous Fancy Pansy. These were very popular in Victorian gardens, especially for mass planting with Tulips. In its 1897 catalog, the Chicago firm of Vaughan's advertised six Pansy mixtures, among them "Chicago Parks Bedding Pansies" in separate colors of white, black, light blue, dark blue, striped, mahogany, and the cultivars 'Beaconsfield', 'Emperor William', 'Prince Bismark', 'Snow Queen', 'Goldmargin', 'Silveredge', and 'Fire Dragon', none of which have survived (light blue 'Beaconsfield' types are still offered).

We should not complain, however, for there are still older Pansy strains around, like my favorite, 'Swiss Giants', a long-stemmed, vigorous, open-pollinated type in the full range of colors and styles, solids, blotched, and eyed. They are astonishingly long-lived in the protective shade of a Rose bed, where they freely bloom almost all summer. If sheared back in midsummer they rebloom well into the late fall and early winter months. I like to mass 'Swiss Giants' in large tubs near doorways so I can benefit from their warm, sweet aroma. In my experience, the newer F_1 hybrids are less reliably perennial, and do not come true from saved seed.

It has long been observed that children seem to have a special liking for Johnny-jump-ups, drawn, perhaps, to its appealing little face, its uncomplicated beauty. Many years ago, my daughter raised a generation of 'King Henry' seedlings—deep purple velvet with a yellow eye. She planted them in a Tulip bed we shared, established on the site of an old coal shed, where the soil was deep and fertile. Our plan was simple: We divided fifty bulbs between us and planted our allotment on either side of a central path bordered with 'King Henry'. That was in 1976. Since then I have raised many lovely large-flowered Pansies, long disappeared from the garden, but 'King Henry' and its descendants of variable countenance (crossed with nearby yellow Violas) remain among the Tulips—a fitting remembrance of my daughter's first flower garden.

Several strains of Violas (besides the wild version) are worth having, among them 'Helen Mount' in the traditional colors. It has been around for decades, as has 'King Henry', but the latter is rare now and sometimes erroneously described, so be sure to save its seeds and plant it away from other types to try and keep the strain pure. (Follow suggestions for seed saving in Part 1, page 21). Plant Johnny-jump-ups in containers, as a ground cover near shrubs, in a shady bor-der as an edging plant, or along a garden path, wherever it may lead.

To Grow: Johnny-jump-ups and Pansies can be grown the same way. Either sow seeds in a cold-frame in midsummer, protect them over the winter with a light mulch, then plant them in the garden about 6 inches apart in ordinary, well-drained soil in sun, partial shade, or shade (they'll bloom longer if given protection from the sun). Or chill seeds in the fridge for two weeks (spread them on a moist paper towel, fold it up, then slip it into a sandwich bag, loosely folded). Sow the seeds on the soil surface, pressing them in, and cover the seeding container with plastic, then newspaper to exclude light. Using bottom heat, I have found germination to be rapid, within 24 hours. Both Johnny-jump-ups and Pansies decline in the heat of summer. Shear and water them and they will flower again by late summer.

COLLECTOR'S CHOICE:

Viola tricolor. The unimproved species form.

'Bowles Black' (early 1900s). Named after E.A. Bowles, who disclaimed responsibility for its origin; dark purple, nearly black, to 8" tall; not as vigorous as other types, but striking for its color.

'Helen Mount'. Similar to the wild form in colors; 7".

'King Henry'. Deep purple with yellow eye; 5–6".

'Prince John'. Pure yellow.

V. x *wittrockiana*

'Adonis' (1906–1914). Light blue with darker blue and white face, yellow eye.

'Beaconsfield'/'Lord Beaconsfield' (1880–1885). Similar to ones found in Vaughn's 1897 catalog; all blue shades, from very light on upper petals to deep purple on lower, with yellow eye.

'Chalon'. Ruffled petals, some with picotee edge in blue, yellow, mahogany, violet, and lilac shades. Cool temperatures maintain frilliness.

'Clear Crystals'. Early-flowering with smallish blooms, 2½" in solid colors of golden yellow, white, purple, scarlet, light blue, orange, and black.

'King of the Blacks' (1865–1870). All black pansies offered today are F_1 hybrids probably selected from this strain, so they won't come true from seed. The original was described as almost coal black with a yellow eye, and it reproduced true to type from seed.

'Swiss Giants'/'Roggli Swiss Giants'. Robust, large-flowered, and long-stemmed, to 8"; red shades, violet-blue, bronze shades, pure white, dark blue with blotch, white with purple blotch, wine, raspberry, orange, yellow with black blotch, pure yellow.

Weigela florida

CAPRIFOLIACEAE

Weigela
Old-fashioned Weigela

INTRODUCED: 1845
ZONES: 4–9
TYPE: Hardy Shrub
HEIGHT: 9'
BLOOM: Late Spring–Early Summer
SITE: Sun

This lovely member of the Honeysuckle Family is native to Asia, although for years it was classified with the American native shrub, Bush Honeysuckle *(Diervilla* spp.). The species name *florida* refers not to the state but to Weigela's rich flowers. In late spring or early summer, its branches bear many clusters of showy, funnel-shaped flowers, in shades of red, rose-pink, and crimson. The shrub's habit is wide and arching, but varieties like 'Foliis Purpureis', with purplish leaves, is a dwarf form, to 4 feet. Other varieties bear handsome, variegated foliage, edged pale yellow. Hummingbirds are greatly attracted to Weigela blooms.

Introduced to American gardens in the 19th century, Weigela seems to have come already packaged as "old-fashioned," in common with another late introduction, "Old-fashioned Bleeding-heart" *(Dicentra spectabilis)*. One explanation is that it fills the expected image with its graceful, arching form and flower-laden branches. On the other hand "old-fashioned" separates the species Weigela from the many larger-flowered hybrids that soon appeared on the scene.

Discovered in northern China by the great plant collector Robert Fortune, Weigela soon became a fixture in the home landscape. "This noble shrub," wrote garden authority Frank Scott, ". . . has already found a place in most home grounds from Maine to California" *(The Art of Beautifying Suburban Home Grounds,* 1870). It was loved for its beautiful display of jewel-like, glowing trumpets all along its curving stems. A single specimen shone as a lone accent by a picket fence or in the shrub border.

By 1865, Victor Lemoine, of the famous French plant nursery, began to breed Weigelas, giving rise to hybrids with larger blooms, a wider range of solid colors (in the species they tend to be mixed together), and greater hardiness. Many were produced, but few remain, among them the early-flowering 'Conquerant' (deep rose and carmine flowers) and 'Candida', still considered the best white-flowered Weigela.

Adaptable to climate—some winterkill is expected in the north—Weigela, like Spirea, was (and remains) a popular southern shrub. I first saw it on Cape Breton in a local suburban garden from the early 1950s, where it was grown apart from the extensive shrub border that lined the back and side edges of the property. By itself, it made a splendid early summer show, a celebration of the new growing season. In one of her novels of early Cape Breton life, writer Margaret MacPhail described the heroine's surprise when her thrifty mother, hardened by years of toil, chose Weigela from the traveling plant peddler's offerings. As I confronted its bright, almost vulgar flower baubles of fleeting beauty, I knew at once that Mrs. MacPhail well understood the human heart, for it was precisely for its "uselessness" in practical terms that the mother bought it, to fulfill her yearning for something impractically beautiful in her hard life. In this respect, the novelist's choice of shrub was brilliant, for not only is Weigela's beauty transient, it is not hardy enough to survive many harsh winters in Nova Scotia. Lilac would have been a sounder choice, and, in fact, it marks the remains of many old gardens here.

To Grow: Plant Weigela in enriched, well-drained soil in full sun and it will give a good show of blooms every year if it is properly pruned just after blooming. Stem cuttings taken in the summer root easily.

COLLECTOR'S CHOICE:

Weigela 'Candida' (ca. 1908). Pure white flowers with hint of green; mid-spring; 9'.

'Conquerant' (ca. 1905). Rose flowers; mid-spring; 12'.

'Dame Blanche' (ca. 1905). Blush white; late spring; 12'.

'Eva Rathke' (before 1952). Once very popular for its crimson flowers and dwarf form.

'Newport Red'/'Vanicek' (ca. 1942). Reported to be a hardier red than the later 'Bristol Ruby'; late spring; 9'.

Weigela florida 'Foliis Purpureis'. Pink flowers, purplish green foliage; valued for its lower height, to 4'.

'Variegata' (1850–1900). Light to deep rose flowers, creamy-edged foliage; 5–6'.

W. florida var. *venusta* (1905). Purple-pink flowers in dense clusters.

W. middendorffiana, Middendorff Wiegela (1850). Rarely grown, despite its yellow flowers (small, borne in 2" clusters); spring-summer flowering; relatively short stature, to 4'.

PART III

Sources and Resources

"No one can garden alone."

—ELIZABETH LAWRENCE

USDA HARDINESS ZONE MAP

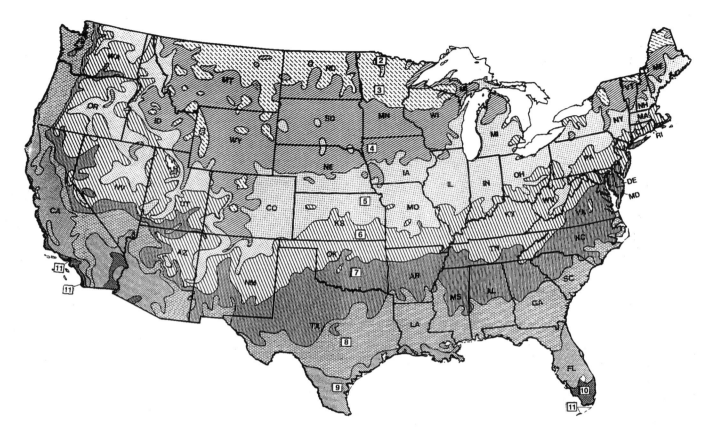

Range of average annual minimum temperatures for each hardiness zone.

Zone 1	below −50°F
Zone 2	−50° to −40°
Zone 3	−40° to −30°
Zone 4	−30° to −20°
Zone 5	−20° to −10°
Zone 6	−10° to 0°
Zone 7	0° to 10°
Zone 8	10° to 20°
Zone 9	20° to 30°
Zone 10	30° to 40°
Zone 11	above 40°

MAIL-ORDER SOURCES

THE *Andersen Horticultural Library's Source List of Plants & Seeds* makes any other source list superfluous (the 1993–1996 edition had 59,000 entries). Improved with every edition, this is the most comprehensive listing of plant and seed offerings—flowers, fruits, vegetables, trees, and shrubs—in North America. It includes a cross reference of common names and nursery and seed catalogs keyed to the plants, which are organized alphabetically by up-to-date Latin names (based on the *RHS Index of Garden Plants,* compiled by Mark Griffiths) and cultivars. You can order the Andersen Horticultural source list from Minnesota Landscape Arboretum, 3675 Arboretum Drive, Box 39, Chanhassen, MN 55317. If you have access to the Internet, Andersen's Web address is: plantinfo.umn.edu. If you want to subscribe to the publication, click on "How do I subscribe?" and it will lead you through the process of filling out the subscription form. Then you download the information to your printer, run a copy and mail it off with your check. Once you have your user code name and password you can navigate Andersen's Web site to find plants.

Not everyone has access to the Internet (I don't), so here's a listing of some of my favorite suppliers with comments. If you are a catalog reader, you will appreciate the pleasure of perusing the real, not virtual, thing. They range from simple listings to fat, glossy, illustrated publications, a world unto themselves and worth ordering just to read. To supplement the following information, you might want to check into Barbara J. Barton's most recent version of *Gardening by Mail,* one of the best general sources, easy to use, and a pleasure to read for the personality behind the listings.

Seeds

Abundant Life Seed Foundation
P.O. Box 772
Port Townsend, WA 98368
(206) 385-5660

Specializes in preserving rarely offered wildflowers, old-fashioned flowers, and herbs. Public garden.

Burpee
300 Park Ave.
Warminster, PA 18974
(215) 674-4915

A part of our horticultural heritage, established 1876; some old favorites along with the new.

Chiltern Seeds
Bortree Stile
Ulverton, Cumbria
LA 12 7PB United Kingdom

Offers seeds of 4,000 plants, well described, among them British wildflowers we grow as ornamentals.

The Fragrant Path
P.O. Box 328
Ft. Calhoun, NE 68023

Scented and unscented plants, chatty descriptions.

J.L. Hudson
Star Route 2, Box 337
La Honda, CA 94020

Unique seed company, no phone, e-mail, or Web site, just marvelous offerings of rare seed strains and the best germination information available anywhere. Carries Policeman's Helmet, open-pollinated petunias, and much else of interest.

Jo Ann's Kitchen & Garden
R. R. 1 Box 124
Essex, NY 12936
(518) 962-2849

Small selection of seeds from my own gardens, including heirloom Hollyhock strains.

Johnny's Selected Seeds
310 Foss Hill Rd.
Albion, ME 04910-9731
(207) 437-9294

Some old favorite flowers and herbs.

Jung Seed Co.
335 S. High St.
Randolph, WI 53957-0001
(414) 326-3121

A fixture of the American gardening scene since 1907; old favorites carried from year to year.

New England Wildflower Society
[see address under "Societies"]

More than 200 species offered by this nonprofit conservation group.

Park Seed
1 Parkton Ave.
Greenwood, SC 29647
(800) 845-3369

Wide selection, among them some old favorites; established 1868.

Pinetree Garden Seeds
Box 300
616A Lewiston Rd.
New Gloucester, ME 04260
(207) 926-3400

Fine selection of flowers and herbs; a friendly, appealing catalog.

Ron's Rare Plants & Seeds
415 Chappel
Calumet City, IL 60409
(708) 862-1993

Open-pollinated rare Petunia strains and much more.

Seeds of Change
P.O. Box 15700
Santa Fe, NM 87506-5700
(888) 762-7333

Open-pollinated flowers and herbs.

Select Seeds, Antique-Flowers
180 Stickney Rd.
Union, CT 06076
(860) 684-9310

Best source for antique flowers, with many dates or historical references; carries balcony and climbing Petunias, old Pansies, Poppies, Policeman's Helmet, 'Painted Lady' runner bean; also plants.

Seymour's Selected Seeds
P.O. Box 1346
Sussex, VA 23884-0346
(803) 663-3084

"From an English Lady's Cottage Garden"; includes black Poppies, black Hollyhocks, and black Pansies as well as other heirlooms, although many new types as well.

Southern Exposure Seed Exchange
P.O. Box 170
Earlysville, VA 22936
(804) 973-4703

Heirloom flower seeds (vegetable, too).

Stokes Seeds
P.O. Box 548
Buffalo, NY 14240-0548
(416) 688-4300

Excellent general catalog with some old favorites and good cultural information; established 1881.

Stokes Seeds Ltd.
39 James St., Box 10
St. Catharines, ON
L2R 6R6 Canada
(416) 688-4300

Canadian branch.

Sutton Seeds
Hele Rd.
Torquay, Devon
TQ2 7QJ United Kingdom

Large selection of flowers, herbs, and wildflowers.

Territorial Seed Company
P.O. Box 157
Cottage Grove, OR 97424-0061
(541) 942-9547

Includes heirloom strains like 'Painted Lady' Sweet Pea.

Thomas Jefferson Center for Historic Plants at Monticello
P.O. Box 316
Charlottesville, VA 22902-0316
(804) 979-5283

Plants documented in American gardens before 1900, including those grown by Thomas Jefferson at Monticello.

Thompson & Morgan
220 Faraday Ave.
P.O. Box 1308
Jackson, NJ 08527-0308
(908) 363-2225

Many beautiful seed offerings, some of them heirlooms.

William Dam Seeds Ltd.
Box 8400
Dondas, ON
L9H 6M1 Canada
(416) 628-6641

Small company with a European accent; carries some heirloom flowers as well as wildflowers and herbs.

Plants

A & D Peony and Perennial Nursery
6806 180th St. S.E.
Snohomish, WA 98290
(360) 668-9690

Wide selection of peonies including the wonderful 'Red Charm'.

Brand Peony Farm
Box 842
St. Cloud, MN 56302

Historic firm established 1862. Brand-bred heirlooms and many others in modest, informative listing with dates of introduction, basic cultural information.

Busse Gardens
13579 10th St., N.W.
Cokato, MN 55321-9426
(612) 286-2654

Fine selection of cold-climate perennials including hard-to-find fern-leaved Peony.

Canyon Creek Nursery
3527 Dry Creek Rd.
Oroville, CA 95965
(530) 533-2166

Fragrant Violets are a specialty, also heirloom Pinks.

Caprice Nursery
15425 SW Pleasant Hill Rd.
Sherwood, OR 97140
(503) 625-7241

Specialist in Peonies, Daylilies, Hostas, Japanese Iris and Siberian Iris, all choice.

Caroll Gardens
444 E. Main St.
P.O. Box 310
Westminster, MD 21157
(410) 848-5422
(800) 638-6334

Excellent comprehensive catalog that includes Roses, shrubs, and vines.

Crownsville Nursery
P.O. Box 797
Crownsville, MD 21032
(410) 849-3143

Choice selection of perennial flowers as well as flowering shrubs.

Ensata Gardens
823 East Michigan Ave.
Galesburg, MI 49053
(616) 665-7500

Japanese Iris with good information, beautiful photos.

Garden Place
6780 Heisley Rd.
Mentor, OH 44061
(216) 255-3705

Impressive selection includes old favorites.

Goodwin Creek Gardens
P.O. Box 83
Williams, OR 97544
(503) 846-7357

Wonderful selection of herbs (especially Lavenders), scented Geraniums, butterfly and hummingbird plants.

Hildebrandt's Iris Gardens
Box 4
Lexington, NE 68850-9304
(302) 224-4334

Lots of Iris as well as oriental Poppies, Peonies, Hostas, and Lilies.

Klehm Nursery
4210 North Duncan Rd.
Champaign, IL 61821
(800) 553-3715

Beautifully presented catalog features Peonies, Hostas, and Daylilies.

Logee's Greenhouses
141 North St.
Danielson, CT 06239
(203) 774-8038

Long famous for its choice greenhouse and tender plant collection; includes scented Geraniums and Parma Violets; historic firm established 1892.

Perennial Pleasures Nursery
2 Brickhouse Rd.
East Hardwick, VT 05836
(802) 472-5104

Specializes in hardy heirloom flowers and herbs before 1900; includes dates of introduction.

Rasland Farm
6778 Herb Farm Rd.
Goodwin, NC 28344
(910) 567-2705

Many herbs and scented Geraniums.

Schreiner's Gardens
3625 Quinaby Rd. NE
Salem, OR 97303
(503) 393-3232

Wide assortment of Iris, color photos, plants well described; established by the Schreiner family in 1925.

Wayside Garden
1 Garden Lane
Hodges, SC 29695-0001
(800) 845-1124

Sumptuous catalog featuring perennials, Roses, and shrubs.

We-Du Nurseries
Rte. 5, Box 724
Marion, NC 28752
(704) 738-8300

If something is rare, chances are this nursery carries it; a treasury of rock garden, woodland plants, wildflowers and more, all well described.

Well-Sweep Herb Farm
205 Mt. Bethel Rd.
Port Murray, NJ 07865
(908) 852-5390

Everything you could want in the herb line; many Lavenders.

White Flower Farm
P.O. Box 50
Litchfield, CT 06759-0050
(800) 503-9624

Long synonymous with elegance; besides the gorgeous photos, there's valuable cultural information and plant combinations; includes Roses, shrubs, and vines.

Bulbs

Alyssa's Garden
Box 6718
Fort St. John, BC
V1J 4J2 Canada

Comprehensive listing of Lilies; also includes Peonies, Siberian Iris; good descriptions.

B & D Lilies
330 P St.
Port Townsend, WA 98368
(206) 385-1738

Tops for Lilies; gorgeous catalog, informative for both beginners and experienced growers.

Breck's
6523 North Galena Rd.
Peoria, IL 61632
(800) 722-9069

Historic 1818 concern; source of assorted Dutch bulbs.

Brent and Becky's Bulbs
7463 Heath Trail
Gloucester, VA 23061
(877) 661-2852

Choice selection of bulbs, especially Narcissus, with good information, plant combinations; heirlooms are dated.

Cruickshank's Inc.
1015 Mount Pleasant Rd.
Toronto, ON
M4P 2MI Canada
(416) 488-8292

Choice selection of assorted bulbs.

Fanfare Daylilies
54 Beltran St.
Malden, MA 02148
(617) 321-3786

Period plants.

John Scheepers, Inc.
23 Tulip Dr.
Bantam, CT 06750
(860) 567-0838

Spring- and summer-blooming bulbs including species Narcissus.

McClure & Zimmerman
P.O. Box 368
108 West Winnebago
Friesland, WI 53935
(414) 326-4200

Assorted bulbs, fine listings; informative and well presented.

Old House Gardens
536 Third St.
Ann Arbor, MI 48103-4957
(734) 995-1486

*Terrific source for antique bulbs (hardy and tender), especially rare ones like **authentic** 'King Alfred' Narcissus; dates, historical information. Owner Scott Kunst's enthusiasm is infectious . . . you'll want everything.*

Sisters' Bulb Farm
Route 2, Box 170
Gibsland, LA 71028

Choice listing of southern heirloom bulbs.

Skittone Bulb Company
1415 Eucalyptus Dr.
San Francisco, CA 94132
(415) 753-3332

Period bulbs.

Swan Island Dahlias
Box 800
Canby, OR 97013
(503) 266-7711

Beautiful catalog for Dahlia fanciers (or you'll become one); photos, historical and cultural information.

Van Bourgondien & Sons
P.O. Box 100
245 Farmingdale Rd., Rte. 109
Babylon, NY 11702-0598
(800) 622-9997

Assorted bulbs as well as perennials.

Roses

The *Combined Rose List* is indispensable for anyone interested in finding sources for Old Garden and species Roses; includes dates of introduction and the Rose's parentage if known. Available from Peter Schneider, P.O. Box 677, Manuta, OH 44255.

Antique Rose Emporium
9300 Luekemeyer Rd.
Brenham, TX 77833
(409) 836-9051

Excellent source for own-root old Roses with cultural and historical information; for gardeners Zone 6 and warmer.

Corn Hill Nursery Ltd.
R.R. 5
Peticodiac, NB
E0A 2H0 Canada
(506) 756-3635

Reliable source for own-root roses, perennials, shrubs. Not everything is shipped, but arrangements can be made. Visitors are invited to extensive display gardens where nearly every species (including many hardy heirloom roses) grown at the nursery can be seen.

Heirloom Old Garden Roses
24063 NE Riverside Dr.
St. Paul, OR 97137
(503) 538-1576

Large selection, very well described. Over 1,000 Roses in display gardens.

Heritage Roses of Tanglewood Farms
16830 Mitchell Creek Dr.
Ft. Bragg, CA 95437
(707) 964-3748

Formerly Heritage Gardens; offers old and species Roses.

Lowe's Roses
6 Sheffield R.
Nashua, NH 03062-3028
(603) 888-2214

Good selection of old and species Roses all grown on their own roots; custom-propagated to order.

Pickering Nurseries
670 Kingston Rd.
Pickering, ON
L1V 1A6 Canada
(416) 839-2111

Excellent selection of old Roses; dates, general information, photos.

Ros–Equus
40350 Wilderness Rd.
Branscomb, CA 95417
(707) 984-6959

Formerly Heritage Gardens; offers old and species roses (see also Heritage Roses of Tanglewood Farms, above).

Roseraie at Bayfields
P.O. Box R
670 Bremen Rd. (Rte. 32)
Waldoboro, ME 04572-0919
(207) 832-6330

Excellent listings with dates of historic Roses, cultural information.

Royall River Roses
Forevergreen Farm
70 New Gloucester Rd.
North Yarmouth, ME 04096
(207) 829-5830

Good selection of hardy and uncommon Roses.

Shrubs & Vines

Boughen Nurseries
Box 12
Valley River, MB
R0L 2B0 Canada
(204) 638-7618

Source for hard-to-find Clove Currant called "Missouri Black Currant"; other shrubs, vines, and perennials.

Forestfarm
990 Thetherow Rd.
Williams, OR 97544
(503) 846-6963

Shrubs as well as western natives, species Roses.

Girard Nurseries
P.O. Box 428
Geneva, OH 44041
(216) 466-2881

Rhododendrons/Azaleas, choice shrubs; excellent descriptions and information.

Greer Gardens
1280 Goodpasture Island Rd.
Eugene, OR 97401
(503) 686-8266

Justly famous for the rare and unusual, which includes shrubs, vines, and Rhododendrons; splendid catalog, lots of information and valuable commentary.

Heard Gardens, Ltd.
5355 Merle Hay Rd.
Johnston, IA 50131-1207
(515) 276-4533

Choice own-root Lilacs.

Kelly Nurseries
P.O. Box 800
Dansville, NY 14437
(800) 325-4180

Many shrubs; excellent information.

Louisiana Nursery
Rte. 7, Box 43
Opelousas, LA 70570
(318) 948-3696

Specializes in "Magnolias and other Garden Aristocrats" including Azaleas, Hydrangea, flowering shrubs, many for warmer zones but colder ones are included and specified.

Roslyn Nursery
211 Burrs Lane
Dix Hills, NY 11746
(516) 643-9347

Excellent source for Rhododendrons/Azaleas, deciduous shrubs.

Wedge Nursery
Rte. 2, Box 114
Albert Lea, MN 56007
(507) 373-5225

Own-root Lilacs; descriptive listings; founded in 1878.

Woodlanders
1128 Colleton Ave.
Aiken, SC 29801
(803) 648-7522

Excellent source for hard-to-find shrubs and vines; also perennials and native plants (guaranteed nursery-propagated); basic information.

Garden Furnishings

Adirondack Designs
350 Cypress St.
Ft. Bragg, CA 95437
(800) 222-0343

The classic Adirondack chair as well as other furniture produced in a sheltered workshop situation. A not-for-profit corporation.

Bow House
P.O. Box 900
Bolton, MA 01740-0900
(508) 779-6464

Gazebos and other garden structures, eclectic offerings.

Carruth Studio, Inc.
211 Mechanic St.
Waterville, OH 43566
(800) 225-1178

Bird feeders, birdbaths, and other garden ornaments.

Country Casual
17317 Germantown Rd.
Germantown, MD 21754-2999
(301) 540-0040

Garden swings, trellis work, wooden tubs, teakwood furniture.

French Wyres
P.O. Box 131655
Tyler, TX 75713-1655
(903) 597-8322

Victorian-style trellises, window boxes, and garden accessories.

The Garden Concept Collection, Inc.
P.O. Box 241233
Memphis, TN 38124-1233
(901) 756-1649

Arbors, pergolas, trelliswork, and more in various historical styles.

Gateways
849 Hannah Branch Rd.
Burnsville, NC 28714

Garden sculpture and ornaments from hand-cast stone.

Gardener's Eden
P.O. Box 7307
San Francisco, CA 94120-7307
(800) 822-9600

Trellises and arbors.

Kinsman Co., Inc.
River Rd.
P.O. Box 357
Point Pleasant, PA 18959-0357
(800) 733-4146

Vertical plant supports.

Lagenbach Catalog
644 Enterprise Ave.
Galesburg, IL 61401
(800) 362-1991

Trellises, arbors, and various vine supports.

Plow and Hearth
P.O. Box 1090
Madison, VA 22727
(800) 627-1712

Wide selection of arbors, trellises, rustic garden furniture, and more.

Robinson Iron Corp.
P.O. Drawer 1235
Alexander City, AL 35010
(205) 329-8486

Wrought-iron ornaments made and restored.

Vixen Hill Gazebos
Main St.
Elverson, PA 19520
(800) 423-2766

Victorian and colonial-style gazebos.

Yanzum Art for Gardens
P.O. Box 8573
1285 Peachtree St. NE
Atlanta, GA 311106-0573
(800) 388-4443

Broad selection of birdbaths, bird houses, statues, and other garden ornaments.

Noncommercial Seed Sources & Exchanges

The Flower & Herb Exchange
R.R. 3, Box 239
Decorah, IA 52101
(319) 382-5872

An outgrowth of the Seed Savers Exchange for food plants, it is patterned on the same principles of sharing heirloom seeds with members. It mails its seed listing—this includes thousands of varieties of old-time flowers and herbs—to its members once a year. $10.00 membership fee ($12.00 Canadian fee; $15.00 overseas).

J.L. Hudson, Seedsman
Star Route 2, Box 337
La Honda, CA 94020

Willing to exchange seed collected from the wild or saved from unusual garden plants for credit on order; ask for "Seed Exchange" pamphlet which includes directions for collecting seed.

North American Cottage Garden Society
P.O. Box 22232
Santa Fe, NM 87502-2232
(505) 438-7038

Membership brings the quarterly publication Small Honesties *and a seed list once a year with seeds contributed by members and sold for a nominal fee. First list included vining Petunias and other treasures. A very exuberant group; publication is fun to read and full of information, plant sources. American Dianthus Society publication now merged with this one. $18.00/yr., U.S. residents; $20.00/yr., Canada/Mexico; $24.00/yr. elsewhere.*

Seeds of Diversity Canada
Box 36
Station Q
Toronto, ON
M4T 2L7 Canada
(905) 623-0353

Formerly Heritage Seed Program. Devoted to preserving heirloom flowers, vegetables, herbs, and grains. Quarterly magazine and annual seed listing. Membership $25.00/yr., Canada.

Southern Exposure Seed Exchange
P.O. Box 170
Earlysville, VA 22901
(804) 973-4703

A seed catalog as well as seed exchange (see "Mail-Order Sources"). Customers receive a gift certificate for contributed seeds of old varieties. Mostly vegetables, but a good selection of heirloom flowers with character. Seed list $1.00.

Plant Societies & Preservation Organizations

※

With few exceptions, most plant societies are *not* devoted to preserving or finding heirloom plants, but there are enthusiasts in most groups. These are an excellent source for rare seeds or plants, available only to members. I have listed only those societies with whose work I am familiar. For a complete listing, see Barbara J. Barton's *Gardening by Mail*, 5th Edition (Houghton Mifflin, 1997).

American Daffodil Society
4126 Winfield Rd.
Columbus OH 43220-4606
(614) 451-4747

Publishes a journal, historic Daffodils, letter-writing round robins, Daffnet listserve, annual conference. $30.00/yr.

American Dahlia Society
1 Rock Falls Court
Rockville, MD 20854

Publishes a journal, convention. $20.00/yr.

American Peony Society
c/o Greta Kessenich
250 Interlachen Rd.
Hopkins, MN 55343
(612) 938-4706

Bulletin, convention, seeds.

California Garden and Landscape History
   Society
P.O. Box 1338
Sebastopol, CA 95473

Newsletter, tours. $20.00/yr.

Canadian Gladiolus Society
c/o Heidi Haines
189 Trudeau Drive
Bowmanville, ON
L1C 1B9 Canada

Formed in 1921, the oldest of the world's national or international Glad organizations; a 100-plus page annual publication includes a comprehensive rating of Glad cultivars, including antique types.

The Canadian Wildflower Society
Unit 12A, Box 228
4981 Highway #7 East
Markham, ON
L3R 1N1 Canada
(905) 294-9075

Publishes a magazine devoted to wild flora of North America. Members attend conventions, trips, and have access to plants and seeds.

The Garden Conservancy
Main Street, Box 219
Cold Spring, NY 10516
(914) 265-2029

Formed in 1989 under the sponsorship of the Tides Foundation to preserve fine gardens by transferring them from private to public ownership. It is worth quoting from its brochure for its relevance to the whole issue of preserving ornamentals, a subject that has not yet been seriously addressed: "Left untended when their creators can no longer maintain them, gardens quickly succumb to nature's ravages. . . . While Americans have rallied to protect our wilderness lands, historic buildings, and endangered plants and animals, no single advocacy group has arisen to preserve our rich heritage of garden works of art." Gardens are selected for sponsorship by the Conservancy on the basis of their aesthetic, horticultural, and design value.

Heritage Rose Foundation
1512 Gorman St.
Raleigh, NC 27606

Newsletter, annual meeting. $10.00/yr.

Heritage Rose Group
c/o Beverly Dobson
1034 Taylor Ave.
Alameda, CA 94501

Publishes quarterly Heritage Roses, *always full of interesting articles by members about Old Garden Roses. Regional groups. $6.00/yr. to U.S. members; $7.00/yr. to Canada.*

Historic Iris Preservation Society
c/o Andree Wilson
15 Bracebridge Rd.
Newton Centre, MA 02459
(617) 232-4823

Informative newsletters, plant-finding services, round-robin letter writing. $5.00/yr.

International Bulb Society
c/o Dave Lehmiller
550 1H-10 S, #201
Beaumont, TX 77707

Interested in tender bulbs and species. Publishes journal, newsletter, e-mail discussion group. $30.00/yr.

New England Garden History Society
300 Massachusetts Ave.
Boston, MA 02115

Newsletter, journal, tours. $45.00/yr.

New England Wild Flower Society, Inc.
Hemenway Rd.
Framingham, MA 01701
(508) 877-7630

Devoted to the preservation of native flora. A range of activities for members, including participation in plant sales, field trips, courses. See "Gardens in the Woods" under "Gardens to Visit," page 311.

North American Gladiolus Council
c/o Robert Martin
RFD #1, Box 70
Belgrade, ME 04917

Publishes a journal, shows, convention. $15.00/yr.

North American Lily Society
c/o Robert Gelman
P.O. Box 272
Owatonna, MN 55050

Quarterly bulletin, bound yearbook, participation in Lily seed exchange. $20.00/yr.

Solon Heritage Flower Society
Box 224
Solon, IA 52333

Enthusiastic group raises awareness of heirloom flowers.

Southern Garden History Society
Drawer F
Salem Station
Winston-Salem, NC 27108
(919) 723-3688

Works toward restoring and gathering history on southern gardens. Publishes bulletin, meets annually in different areas of the South. $20.00/yr.

Species Lilies Preservation Group
c/o Maureen Barber
335 Sandlewood Rd.
Oakville, ON
L6L 3R8 Canada
(905) 827-5944

Fascinating journal, seed exchange for Lily enthusiasts. $7.00/yr. for U.S. members; $9.00/yr. in Canada.

Wakefield and North of England Tulip
    Society
c/o Wendy Akers
70 Wrenthorpe Lane
Wrenthorpe, Wakefield
West Yorkshire, England WF2 OPT

Newsletter, shows. Even if you can't attend, you can read about them and learn a lot about Tulips. $6.00 U.S./yr.

Gardens to Visit

❧

VISITING SOMEONE ELSE'S GAR-
DEN—no matter how large and
grand or small and humble—can
give you a new perspective on your own. The
following fall into both categories, as well as
in between, and illustrate themes stressed
throughout this book regarding native flora,
herbs, and various types of heirloom plants and
their place in the garden. Readers will see that
certain specific areas like Rochester, New York,
and Atlanta, Georgia, are so rich in historical
plantings that it would be well worth the time
to spend several days in the area.

ALABAMA

Ordeman Shaw House & Garden
310 N. Hull St.
Montgomery, AL 36104
(334) 240-4500

Period grounds from 1850s.

ARIZONA

Century House Museum & Gardens
240 Madison Ave.
Yuma, AR 85364
(520) 782-1841

*Wide variety of plants and flowers, established in
1890.*

CALIFORNIA

Descanso Gardens
1418 Descanso Drive
La Canada, CA 91011
(818) 952-4400.

Famous for Roses and Camellias.

Empire Mine State Historic Park
10791 East Empire Street
Grass Valley, CA 95945
(916) 273-8522

*About 90 old-type Roses are planted in the for-
mal gardens and on the landscaped grounds of a
former mining center, which includes the Empire
Cottage (English manor home), Gardener's
House, and Greenhouse. The original Rose Garden, developed in the early 1900s, has been restored and organized into 11 basic groups according to their dates of discovery. The walking tour
begins with the French Rose and moves onto the
Damasks, Albas, Centifolias, and so on, to include
types introduced before 1929, such as our
Granny's favorite, 'Paul's Scarlet Climber' (1916).*

Fioli
Canada Rd.
Woodside, CA 94062
(650) 364-2880

Sixteen-acre formal gardens, 1917 estate.

Los Angeles State and County Arboretum
301 North Baldwin Avenue
Arcadia, CA 91006
(213) 446-8251

More than 5,000 plants, old favorites and new; historic area includes an 1885 Queen Anne cottage and an old-fashioned Rose Garden.

Mission San Diego de Alcala
10818 San Diego Mission Road
San Diego, CA 92108-2498
(619) 281-8449

Mission gardens in California are dated from 1769, when the first of 21 Spanish missions was founded. Typical flowers include Jonquils, Madonna Lilies, Hollyhocks, and Roses in a charming setting with several courtyards.

Octagon House
2645 Gough St.
San Francisco, CA 94123
(415) 441-7512

Nineteenth-century period garden.

Santa Barbara Mission
2201 Laguna St.
Santa Barbara, CA 93105
(805) 682-4713)

Restored 1786 cloistered garden.

Connecticut

Bates-Scofield House
45 Old Kings Highway
Darien, CT 06820
(203) 655-9233

Eighteenth-century period gardens featuring shrub Roses, herbs, medicinal plants.

Bowen Cottage
Rte. 169
Woodstock, CT 06281
(860) 928-4074

One of the oldest parterre gardens in New England.

Brookfield Craft Center and Historical
   Museum
Brookfield Center
Brookfield, CT 06804
(203) 740-8140

Colonial herb and flower garden.

Putnam Cottage
243 E. Putnam Ave.
Greenwich, CT 06830
(203) 869-9697

Authentic 18th-century kitchen garden, includes plants dated to 1690.

Delaware

Winterthur Gardens
Winterthur, DE 19735
(302) 888-4865

Famous for naturalistically styled garden.

Washington, DC

Dumbarton Oaks and Gardens
1703 32nd St. NW
Washington, DC 20007
(202) 339-6410

Spectacular early-1900s garden designed by Beatrix Farrand, especially brilliant in spring and fall.

Georgia

Atlanta Historical Museum
130 W. Paces Ferry Rd. NW
Atlanta, GA 30305
(404) 814-4000.

Twenty-six-acre complex of homes and gardens from authentic 19th-century garden to 1920s formal vistas.

Green-Meldrim House
14 West Macon St.
Savannah, GA 31401
(912) 233-3845

Authentic Victorian 1850s garden.

Historic Savannah Foundation
111 Barnard St.
Savannah, GA 31401
(912) 233-7787

Source of information about many local historic gardens.

Isaiah Davenport House
324 E. State St.
Savannah, GA 31401
(912) 236-8097

Restored 1821 period garden.

ILLINOIS

Abraham Lincoln Memorial Garden and
    Nature Center
2301 E. Lake Dr.
Springfield, IL 62707
(217) 529-1111

Eighty-acre garden, 5-mile trail featuring native plants from Lincoln's childhood.

Pettengill-Morron House Gardens
1212 W. Moss Ave.
Peoria, IL 61606
(309) 674-1921

Hostas, fragrance gardens, wildflower walk are featured in this 1868 Second Empire house and grounds.

INDIANA

James F. Lanier House and Garden
W. 511 First St.
Madison, IN 47250
(812) 265-3526

Grounds laid out in 1840 feature a rare 19th-century greenhouse.

Sullivan House Garden
304 W. Second St.
Madison, IN 47250
(812) 265-2967

1818 Federal-style estate features large-scale domestic gardens.

IOWA

Terrace Hill
2300 Grand Ave.
Des Moines, IA 50312
(515) 281-3604

1869 mansion features native trees and shrubs as well as flower gardens.

KENTUCKY

Farmington
30333 Bardstown Rd.
Louisville, KY 40205
(502) 452-9920

Fourteen-acre garden features pre-1820 plants.

Liberty Hall
West Main & Wilkson Sts.
Frankfort, KY 40601
(502) 227-2560

Eighteenth-century garden features old Roses and Boxwoods.

Locust Grove
561 Blankenbaker Lane
Louisville, KY 40207
(502) 897-9845

1789 estate features restored gardens.

LOUISIANA

City Park
Lelong & City Park Aves.
New Orleans, LA 70124
(504) 483-9386

Huge garden with Roses, Camellias, Azaleas, and a floral clock garden.

Longue Vue Gardens
7 Bamboo Rd.
New Orleans, LA 70124
(504) 488-5488

Early 1940s gardens organized by color with wildflower area.

Rosedown Plantation & Gardens
P.O. Box 1816
St. Francisville, LA 70775
(504) 635-3332

Restoration of the 30-acre site was begun in the 1950s under private ownership. The 1830s gardens include the Herb Garden and Medicinal Garden. The tour also includes the 16-room mansion.

MARYLAND

William Paca House and Garden
1 Martin Street
Annapolis, MD 21401
(301) 269-0601

William Paca was a signer of the Declaration of Independence whose Colonial house and grounds were preserved from destruction in 1965 when the site was being considered for a high-rise office complex. The formal hedged gardens are beautifully restored and include herbs, flowers, and shrubs such as Columbine, Loosestrife, Calendula, Southernwood, Mountain-laurel, and Roses.

MASSACHUSETTS

Chesterwood
4 Williamsville Rd.
P.O. Box 827
Stockbridge, MA 01262
(413) 298-3579

Restored gardens of sculptor Daniel Chester French span late 19th- to early 20th-century; summer home.

Gardens in the Woods
New England Wild Flower Society, Inc.
Hemenway Road
Framingham, MA 01701

Plunked in the middle of a wall-to-wall suburb of flowerless lawns and foundation plantings, the garden comprises 45 acres of rolling hills, ponds, and trails beautifully planted in native flora and wildflowers in striking combinations, blooming from spring through fall. Visitors can buy plants, including such desirable heirloom natives as Flame Azalea, Maidenhair Fern, and Virginia-bluebells.

King Caesar's Garden
King Caesar's Rd.
Duxbury, MA 02332
(781) 934-2378

Restored estate from 1808 features rare Iris reticulata.

Mount Auburn Cemetery
580 Mt. Auburn St.
Cambridge, MA 02138
(617) 547-705

Historic garden cemetery with rare old trees.

Old Sturbridge Village
Sturbridge, MA 01566
(508) 347- 3362

Established in 1946, Old Sturbridge Village has helped to set the standard for such restorations, in this case an early 19th-century New England village on 200 acres. The village includes charming dooryard and formal gardens, one of which features the Child's Arbor, with climbing vines as described in Joseph Breck's 1933 children's book. Period plants of interest include Golden-glow, Jerusalem-cross, Garden Balsam, Bee-balm, Everlasting Pea, and Hop Vine. A compact Herb Garden displays 300 varieties of herbs, which are well labeled. Guides are very helpful and knowledgeable. Note the meticulous staking job on many flowers.

The Arnold Arboretun
Jamaica Plain, MA 02130
(617) 524-1718; 524-1717

Established in 1872, this is the oldest public arbo-retum in America, with 7,000 varieties of orna-mental shrubs and trees on 265-plus acres. A visit here is a must for the shrub enthusiast. Flowers and foliage vary from week to week, beginning in the spring with Lilacs (the famous Lilac Walk), fol-lowed by masses of blooming Azaleas, and ending with brilliant autumn foliage. This very important resource offers classes and student programs.

MISSISSIPPI

Governor's Mansion
300 E. Capitol St.
Jackson, MS 39201
(601) 359-6421

Restored 1838 Greek Revival mansion, formal perennial beds, gazebo.

The Oakes
823 N. Jefferson St.
Jackson, MS 39202
(601-353-9339

Greek Revival cottage and restored garden.

NEBRASKA

General Crook House
30th & Fort Sts.
Omaha, NE 68111
(402) 455-9990

1878 Italianate house with Victorian garden.

NEW HAMPSHIRE

Celia Thaxter Garden
Appledore island
Isles of Shoals

Restoration of poet Celia Thaxter's 19th-century "Island Garden" began in 1977, guided by Vir-ginia Chisholm and the local garden club. Several Old Roses, Hop Vine, and "Traveler's Joy" Clematis were found suviving on the site. The re-construction is very much in the Thaxter spirit with a different assortment of flowers every season as Celia planned it herself. A visit to the restored garden must be arranged in advance through the Shoals Marine Laboratory, Cornell University, G-14 Stimson Hall, Ithaca, NY 14853-7101; (607) 255-3717. Their Web site is www.sml.cornell.edu.

To protect the fragile ecology of Appledore Is-land, a limited number of visitors is allowed on Wednesdays from late June to late August. Reser-vations are accepted beginning in April.

Fuller Gardens
10 Willow Ave.
North Hampton, NH 03862
(603) 964-5414

Colonial Revival garden features formal areas, wildflower walk, hedge topiary.

Gilman Garrison House
12 Water St.
Exeter, NH 03833
(603) 778-7183

Seventeenth-century home with 18th-century addi-tions, restored grounds featuring several period gar-dens.

Governor John Langdon Mansion
143 Pleasant St.
Portsmouth, NH 03801
(603) 436-3205

1784 colonial estate with extensive gardens.

Moffatt-Ladd House and Garden
154 Market Street
Portsmouth, NH 03801
(603) 436-8221

The house was built in 1763, and the gardens were designed in 1862. Both are now maintained by the National Society of the Colonial Dames of America. The garden, on 2 1/2 acres, features brick walks, rose arbors, an herb garden, and old-fashioned perennials.

New Jersey

Acorn Hall Memorial Garden
68 Morris Ave.
Morristown, NJ 07960
(973) 267-3465

Restored Victorian garden.

Frelinghuysen Arboretum
53 E. Hanover Ave.
Morristown, NJ 07962
(973) 326-7600

Formerly Whippany Farm. A Colonial Revival mansion from 1891 with 127 acres of formal and informal gardens, fields, and woodland.

Israel Crane House Gardens
110 Orange Rd.
Montclair, NJ 07042
(973) 744-1796

Seventeenth-century kitchen garden and herb area.

Tempe Wicke House
Jockey Hollow, Tempe Wicke Rd.
Morristown, NJ 07960
(973) 539-2016

Restored Colonial garden.

New York

Boscobel
1601 Rte. 90
Garrison-on-Hudson, NY 10524
(914) 265-3638

Restored 36-acre early 19th-century garden.

Genesee Country Village & Museum
Flint Hill Rd.
Mumford, NY 14451
(716) 538-6822

Recreated historic gardens from pioneer era to Victorian elegance. Heirloom vegetables, Shaker garden of medicinal plants.

George Eastman House
900 East Ave.
Rochester, NY 14607
(716) 271-3361

International Museum of Photography and Film in George Eastman's restored mansion. Four restored gardens with more than 300 historic varieties of perennials, bulbs, ground covers, trees, and shrubs.

George Ellwanger Perennial Garden
625 Mt. Hope Ave.
Rochester, NY 14620
(716) 546-7029

Established by the cofounder of the famous Ellwanger and Barry Nursery in 1867. One-acre garden with Roses, Peonies, and perennials is at its peak in early May.

Old Westbury Gardens
P.O. Box 430
Westbury, NY 11568
(516) 333-0048

Pre-World War II estate gardens in the grand style: classical symmetry and vistas, borders with Delphinium, Foxgloves, a Boxwood garden and Lilac garden.

Rochester Historical Society, "Woodside"
485 East Ave.
Rochester, NY 14620
(716) 271-2705

Enclosed perennial garden created in 1917 with period garden structures.

Rochester & Monroe County Parks
Rochester, NY 14620
(716) 428-6770 (Maplewood Park)

Historic area for horticulture; by the late 1860s Rochester was known as the "Flower City." The combined acreage of public parkland owned and maintained by the city of Rochester and Monroe County totals more than 11,000 acres. May is the Highland Park Lilac Festival (many historic varieties, some bred by John Dunbar, superintendent of parks in Rochester from 1891–1926). June is the Maplewood Park Rose Festival.

Sonnenberg Gardens
151 Charlotte St.
Canandaigua, NY 14424
(716) 924-5420

Turn-of-the-century estate with rock, Pansy, and moonlight gardens, 2,600 Rose bushes, 20,000 annuals, and wildflowers.

Stone Tolan House & Museum
237 East Ave.
Rochester, NY 14620
(716) 442-4606

Early 19th-century farmstead and tavern, heirloom perennials, herbs, native plants on 4½ acres.

The Cloisters
Metropolitan Museum of Art
Fort Tryon Park
New York, NY 10040
(212) 923-3700

Three gardens in the Cloisters display ancient herbs and flowers—among them the Madonna Lily, Florentine Iris, Damask and French Roses, and Betony—in a very peaceful setting. To study these and other heirloom-type plants, in-depth tours for garden groups are available Tuesday through Sunday by reservation from May through June and September through October. For the general public, garden is available Tuesday through Sunday at 1 P.M. during the same months. No advance reservations are necessary. Contact the Cloisters Education Department for group arrangements and fees (phone number above, plus extension 126).

Wave Hill
675 West 252nd Street
Bronx, NY 10471
(212) 549-2055

A 28-acre Hudson River estate with turn-of-the-century (1890s) gardens that include many old-fashioned perennials and herbs.

NORTH CAROLINA

Biltmore Estate & Gardens
One N. Pack Square
Asheville, NC 28801
(808) 274-6333

Twelve thousand acres unique for their scope and beauty. Extensive formal gardens, Azaleas, walled garden, Italian garden.

Old Salem, Inc.
Drawer F, Salem Station
Winston-Salem, NC 27108

A restored Moravian community on 40 acres. Buildings date from 1760 to 1840 with authentic plantings on small home plots: Hop Vine, Roses, Lilacs, and many of the herbs and flowers listed in Christian Reuter's records—altogether about 1,000 types. Group garden tours can be arranged by writing to the Tour Coordinator at the above address; telephone (919) 721-7344; in North Carolina, telephone (800) 441-5305.

Sarah P. Duke Memorial Gardens
Duke University
Box 90341
Durham, NC 27708
(919) 684-3698

Formal gardens, perennials, flowering shrubs.

Tryon Palace Gardens
610 Pollock St.
New Bern, NC 28562
(252) 514-4900

Ornate Colonial gardens, clipped hedges, floral parterres, kitchen garden.

Ohio

Western Reserve Herb Society Garden
11030 E. Blvd.
Cleveland, OH 44106
(216) 721-1600

Established in 1969, its purpose is to convey an understanding of the design and uses of herbs throughout history. There are well-maintained terrace, knot, fragrance, medicinal, culinary, Rose, and dye gardens, as well as a trial and cutting garden.

Pennsylvania

Bartram's Garden
54th Street and Lindbergh Boulevard
Philadelphia, PA 19143
(215) 729-5281

John Bartram, "curious gardener" extraordinaire and 18th-century plant explorer and botanist, established his plant nursery in 1728. You can see the Seed House where he stored native plants before shipping them to Europe. The 17-acre garden displays many of the plants he and his son William collected and grew, including many shrubs and flowers. The restored stone house is of interest, too.

Old Economy Village & Gardens
14th and Church Sts.
Ambridge, PA 15003
(724) 266-4500

Nineteenth-century intentional community gardens.

Wick
6026 Germantown Ave.
Philadelphia PA 19144
(215) 848-1690

Three acres of 18th- and 19th-century gardens with Boxwood borders and Old Garden Roses.

Rhode Island

Chateau Sur Mer
747 Bellevue Ave.
Newport, RI 02840
(401) 847-1000

Mid 19th-century grounds in the landscape style with rare and unusual trees and shrubs.

John Brown House & Courtyard Garden
52 Power St.
Providence, RI 02906
(401) 331-8575

1786 historic house and gardens.

Wanton-Lyman-Hazard House
17 Broadway
Newport, RI 02840
(401) 846-0813

Seventeenth-century restored gardens.

South Carolina

Drayton Hall
3380 Ashley River Rd.
Charleston, SC 29414
(843) 766-0188

1730s plantation estate and gardens.

Texas

San Antonio Botanical Center
555 Funston Place
San Antonio, TX 78209
(512) 821-5115

The 33-acre site includes the Old-Fashioned Garden of annuals and perennials and the Herb Garden with plants used by the Texas settlers.

Vermont

Park-McCullough House & Gardens
P.O. Box 388
N. Bennington VT 05257
(802) 442-5441

Restored Victorian gardens.

Virginia

Colonial Williamsburg
P.O. Box Drawer C
Williamsburg, VA 21387
(804) 229-1000

The site and gardens are so well publicized that there is no need to describe them except to point out that visitors should watch for the following plants of interest: Canterbury-bells, Cornflowers (Bachelor's-button), Morning-glories, Feverfew, Golden-Marguerite, Sneezewort, and the Tawny and Lemon Daylilies among the flowers, and Mountain-laurel, Tatarian Honeysuckle, native Rhododendrons, and Old Roses among the shrubs. There is much to see in the formal gardens of this ultimate in 18th-century restorations.

Monticello
Charlottesville, VA 22902

Years of work by the Garden Club of Virginia and the Committee of the Thomas Jefferson Memorial Foundation have restored Jefferson's gardens according to plans dating from about 1807. The gardens include many native shrubs, as well as period annuals and perennials such as Roses, Primroses, Pinks, and Poppies. Plants for sale at the Jefferson Center's Plant Shop include Hollyhocks propagated from naturalized stands at the estate. Future plans include the propagation and distribution of many more heirlooms from the 18th to early 20th centuries.

Mt. Vernon House & Gardens
Box 110
Mt. Vernon, VA 22121
(703) 780-2000

George Washington's carefully restored landscape with flower gardens, kitchen gardens, trees, and shrubs laid out in the English manner. "The whole plantation, the garden, and the rest prove well that a man born with natural taste may guess a beauty without having ever seen its model" (1798 visitor to Mt. Vernon).

The Anne Spencer House & Garden
1313 Pierce Street
Lynchburg, VA 24505
(804) 845-1313

Very charming restored garden of Harlem Renaissance poet Anne Spencer, born in 1882. With little means at her disposal and working with a small area behind her house (45 by 125 feet), she brilliantly created the illusion of space. There are many period shrubs, vines, and flowers, as well as middle-aged Roses such as 'Blaze' (1932) and 'Betty Prior'. The house and garden were placed on the National Register of Historic Places in 1976 after the poet's death. Well worth the visit.

Canada

British Columbia

The Butchart Gardens, Ltd.
Box 4010, Station A
Victoria, BC
V8X 3X4
(604) 652-4422

The garden as spectacle. Jenny Butchart, the wife of a cement manufacturer (with the factory on the grounds of the estate), set out to prettify the place including the creation of the now-famous Sunken Garden on the site of an old limestone quarry. Now these gardens are spread out over 50 acres, with mass plantings of bright period annuals and perennials from the early 20th century, among them Godetia, Nicotiana, Nasturtiums, Annual Phlox, and much more. Complete with light shows and a tea shop.

Newfoundland

The Memorial University Botanical Garden
Mount Scio Road
St. John's, NF A1C 5S7
(709) 737-8590

This is a gem of a botanical garden, developed over 20 years by Bernard S. Jackson. Of special interest is the Heritage Garden of perennials, all grown from actual plants found in Newfoundland gardens and grown before 1940. Among the most spectacular finds is the Fair Maids of France (Ranunculus aconitifolius 'Flore Pleno'), a charming double-flowered white Buttercup, traced back 150 years to a Norwegian whaling captain. This is probably the same flower that Sir Peyton ordered by the dozen for Lady Skipwith in 18th-century Virginia. Guided tours by appointment.

NOVA SCOTIA

Annapolis Royal Historic Garden
P.O. Box 278
Annapolis Royal, NS B0S 1A0
(902) 532-5104

Ten acres of theme gardens on an historic site, representing English, Acadian, and Indian heritage. Of special interest are the 3,000 Roses of all types and classes from old to new, the impressive Rose Maze, the Herb Garden, the Victorian Garden of mainly annual flowers, and the Governor's Garden, dating from the early to mid-18th century.

ONTARIO

The Katie Osborne Lilac Garden
Royal Botanical Gardens, Box 399
Hamilton, ON L8N 3H8

The world's largest collection of Lilacs, 770 different varieties, presided over for the past 30 years by Charles Holetich, former president and active member of the International Lilac Society. This is a great place to study heirloom Lilacs.

BIBLIOGRAPHY

Entries marked with an asterisk (★) are particularly recommended for their gardening information.

Abraham, George. *The Green Thumb Garden Handbook*. Englewood Cliffs, N.J.: Prentice-Hall, Inc., 1961

American Cottage Gardens. Brooklyn Botanic Gardens (BBG) Record/Plants & Gardens, vol. 46, no. 1 (1990).

American Garden Heritage. BBG Record/Plants & Gardens, vol. 23, no. 3 (1968).

American Gardens: A Traveler's Guide. BBG Record/Plants & Gardens, vol. 42, no. 3, (1986).

Andersen Horticultural Library's Source List of Plants and Seeds, comp. Richard T. Isaacson. Chanhassen, Minn.: Andersen Horticultural Library, 1989.

Anderson, A.W. *How We Got Our Flowers*. New York: Dover, 1966 (reprint of 1951 edition).

Art, Henry W. *A Garden of Wildflowers*. Pownal, Vt.: Storey Communications, 1986.

The Audubon Society Field Guide to North American Wildflowers, Eastern Region. New York: Alfred A. Knopf, 1979.

Baily, L.H. *Gardener's Handbook*. New York: Macmillan, 1942.

Barton, Barbara J. *Gardening by Mail*, 5th Ed. Boston: Houghton Mifflin Co., 1997.

Bender, Steve, and Felder Rushing. *Passalong Plants*. Chapel Hill: University of North Carolina Press, 1993.

Berrall, Julia, S. *The Garden*. New York: Viking, 1966.

Betts, Edwin M., and Hazlehurst Bolton Perkins. *Thomas Jefferson's Flower Garden in Monticello*. Rev. ed. Charlottesville: University Press of Virginia, 1986.

Bowles, E.A. *My Garden in Spring*. Portland, Or.: Timber Press, 1997.

Bridgeman, Thomas. *The Kitchen Gardener's Instructor*, 1857; excerpts reproduced in facsimile in *The Herb Grower Magazine* vol. 14, no. 4 (1962): 24–27.

Bubel, Nancy. *The New Seed-Starters Handbook*. Emmaus, Penn.: Rodale Press, 1988.

Buchanan, Rita. *A Dyer's Garden*. Loveland, Colo.: Interweave Press, 1995.

———. "Getting Started with Dyeing," BBG Record/Plants & Gardens. vol. 46, no. 2. (1990).

———. *A Weaver's Garden*. Loveland, Colo.: Interweave Press, 1987.

Christopher, Thomas. *In Search of Lost Roses*. New York: Summit Books, 1989.

Clarkson, Rosetta E. *Herbs: Their Culture and Uses.* New York: Macmillan, 1942.

★Crockett, James Underwood, et al. *Annuals* (The Time-Life Encyclopedia of Gardening). New York: Time-Life Books, 1971.

★———. *Bulbs* (The Time-Life Encyclopedia of Gardening). New York: Time-Life Books, 1971.

★———. *Perennials* (The Time-Life Encyclopedia of Gardening). New York: Time-Life Books, 1972.

★———. *Roses* (The Time-Life Encyclopedia of Gardening). New York: Time-Life Books, 1975.

★———. *Wildflower Gardening* (The Time-Life Encyclopedia of Gardening). New York: Time-Life Books, 1977.

Culpeper, Nicholas. *Culpeper's Complete Herbal.* London: W. Foulsham & Co., Ltd. (facsimile reprint, n.d.)

Dobson, Beverly R., and Peter Schneider. *The Combined Rose List.* Dist. by P. Schneider, Mantua, Ohio, 1998.

Dowden, Anne Ophelia. *This Noble Harvest.* New York: Wm. Collins, 1979.

Ely, Helena Rutherford. *A Woman's Hardy Garden.* New York: The Lyons Press, 1999; (reprint of Macmillan Co. 1903 edition).

Ernst, Ruth Shaw. *The Naturalist's Garden.* Guilford, Conn.: Globe Pequot Press, 1987.

Fairchild, David. *The World Grows Round My Door.* New York: Scribner's, 1947.

Favretti, Rudy J. *Early New England Gardens: 1620–1840.* Sturbridge, Mass.: Old Sturbridge Village, 1966.

Favretti, Rudy J., and Joy Putnam Favretti. *Landscapes and Gardens for Historic Buildings.* Nashville, Tenn.: American Association for State and Local History, 1978.

★Fell, Derek. *Annuals: How to Select, Grow and Enjoy.* Los Angeles: HP Books, 1983.

Fish, Margery. *Cottage Garden Flowers.* London: W.H. & L. Collingridge. Ltd., 1961.

———. *A Flower for Every Day.* London: Faber & Faber, 1965.

★———. *Flowering Shrubs.* BBG Record/Plants & Gardens, vol., 37, no. 1 (1981).

———. *Gardening in the Shade.* Reprint London: Faber & Faber, 1983 (originally published 1964).

Foster Gertrude B. *Herbs Our Heritage.* Falls Village, Conn.: The Herb Grower Press, n.d.

Foster, Gertrude B., and Philip Foster, with Cathleen Maxwell. *Herbs for a Nosegay.* Falls Village, Conn.: The Herb Grower Press, 1966.

★Foster Gertrude B., and Rosemary F. Louden. *Park's Success with Herbs.* Greenwood, S.C.: George W. Park Seed Co., Inc. 1980.

Foster, H. Lincoln. *Rock Gardening.* Reprint. Portland, Ore.: Timber Press, 1982 (originally published 1968).

Fox, Helen Morgenthau. *Gardening with Herbs for Flavor and Fragrance.* New York: Macmillan, 1933.

Freeman, Margaret B. *Herbs for the Medieval Household.* New York: Metropolitan Museum of Art, 1943.

Friend, Rev. Hilderic. *Flowers and Flower Lore,* vols. 1 and 2. London: George Allen & Co., Ltd., 1883.

★Gardner, JoAnn. *Herbs In Bloom.* Portland, Ore.: Timber Press, 1998.

★———. *Living With Herbs.* Woodstock, Vt.: Countryman Press, 1997.

———. "Overwintering Annuals." *Horticulture Magazine* (October 1988).

———. "Restoring Heritage Flowers." *Atlantic Advocate* (July 1990).

★———. *The Old-Fashioned Fruit Garden.* Halifax, N.S.: Nimbus Publishing, 1989.

Genders, Roy. *The Cottage Garden and the Old-Fashioned Flowers.* London: Pelham Books, 1984.

Gerard, John. *Gerard's Herball, The Essence thereof distilled by Marcus Woodward from the Edition of Th. Johnson, 1636.* London: Bracken Books, 1985.

Gleason, Henry A., et al. *The New Britton and Brown Illustrated Flora of the Northeastern United States and Adjacent Canada.* New York: New York Botanical Garden, 1952.

Gray, Asa. *Gray's School and Field Book of Botany.* New York: Ivison, Blakeman & Co., 1887.

Grieve, Mrs. M. *A Modern Herbal,* vols. 1 and 2. New York: Dover, 1971 (reprint of 1931 Harcourt, Brace edition).

Griffiths, Mark. *RHS Index of Garden Plants.* Portland, Ore.: Timber Press, 1995.

★*Ground Covers and Vines.* BBG Record/ Plants & Gardens, vol. 34, no. 2 (1978).

Growing Annual Flowering Plants. Washington, D.C.: USDA Farmer's Bulletin, no. 1171, 1939.

Halifax Seed Company catalogs, Halifax, N.S.: 1926, 1930, 1945.

★Harper, Pamela, and Frederick McGourty. *Perennials: How to Select, Grow and Enjoy.* Los Angeles: HP Books, 1985.

Peter Henderson & Co. Flower seed listing. New York, 1891.

Hibberd, Shirley. *The Amateur's Flower Garden.* Portland, Ore.: Timber Press, 1986 (reprint of 1871 edition).

★Hill, Lewis, and Nancy Hill. *Bulbs.* Pownal Vt.: Storey Communications, 1994.

★———. *Daylilies.* Pownal Vt.: Storey Communications, Inc., 1991.

★———. *Successful Perennial Gardening.* Pownal, Vt.: Storey Communications, 1988.

Hill, May Brawley. *Furnishing the Old-Fashioned Garden.* NY: Henry N. Abrams, Inc., 1998.

———. *Grandmother's Garden.* New York: Harry N. Abrams, Inc., 1995.

Hollingsworth, Buckner. *Flower Chronicles.* New Brunswick, N.J.: Rutgers University Press, 1958.

———. *Her Garden Was Her Delight.* New York: Macmillan, 1962.

Hortus Third. Comp. and ed. by the Staff of the Liberty Hyde Bailey Hortorium. New York: Macmillan, 1976.

Hottes, Alfred C. *A Little Book of Climbing Plants.* New York: A.T. De La Mare Co., 1933.

———. *The Book of Shrubs.* New York: Dodd, Mead & Co., 1958.

———. *How to Save Your Own Vegetable Seeds.* Uxbridge, Ont.: Heritage Seed Program, 1990.

Huxley, Anthony. *Huxley's Encyclopedia of Gardening.* New York: Universe Books, 1982.

Hyams, Edward, with Jan de Graff. *Lilies.* London: Thomas Nelson & Sons, Ltd., 1967.

Ingwersen, Will. *Classic Garden Plants.* London: Hamlyn Pub. Group, Ltd., 1975.

Jabs, Carolyn. *The Heirloom Gardener.* San Francisco: Sierra Club Books, 1984.

Jackson, Bernard S. "Newfoundland's Heirloom Flower Garden." *Garden* (November/December 1986).

———. "Oxen Pond Botanic Park." *Garden* (November/December 1981).

Jackson, Bernard S., and Valerie Baines. *Mindful of Butterflies.* Sussex, England: The Book Guild Ltd., 1999.

Jekyll, Gertrude. *Annuals and Biennals.* London: Country Life, 1916.

————. *Colour Schemes in the Flower Garden.* London: Country Life, 1911.

————. *A Gardener's Testament.* London: Antique Collector's Club, 1982 (first published by Country Life, 1937).

Johnson, Marjorie P., and Montague Free. *The Concise Encyclopedia of Favorite Flowers.* New York: Doubleday, 1953.

King, Mrs. Francis. *From a New Garden.* New York: Alfred A. Knopf, 1930.

Klimas, John E., and James A. Cunningham. *Wildflowers of Eastern America.* New York: Alfred A. Knopf, 1974.

Krauss, Helen K. *Geraniums for Home and Garden.* New York: Macmillan, 1955.

Kunst, Scott G. "Daffodils: The Glory of the Post-Victorian Garden." *Old House Journal* (September/October 1989).

Kunst, Scott G., and Arthur O. Tucker. "Where Have All the Flowers Gone?" *The Journal of Preservation Technology Bulletin,* vol. 21 (1989).

Lacy, Allen, ed. *The American Gardener: A Sampler.* New York: Farrar, Straus & Giroux, 1988.

Lawrence, Elizabeth. *Gardening for Love.* Durham, N.C.: Duke University Press, 1987.

————. *The Little Bulbs.* New York: Criterion Books, 1957.

————. *Through the Garden Gate.* Chapel Hill: University of North Carolina Press, 1990.

Leighton, Ann. *American Gardens in the 19th Century: "For Comfort and Affluence."* Amherst: University of Massachusetts Press, 1987.

————. *American Gardens in the 19th Century: "For Use or for Delight."* Amherst: University of Massachusetts Press, 1987.

————. *Early American Gardens: "For Meate or Medicine."* Amherst: University of Massachusetts Press, 1986.

Loewer, Peter. *The Evening Garden.* New York: Macmillan, 1993.

Logan, William Bryant. *The Gardener's Book of Sources.* New York: Penguin Books, 1988.

Marranca, Bonnie, ed. *American Garden Writing.* New York: PAJ Publishers, 1988.

Martin, Tovah. *Once Upon a Windowsill.* Portland, Ore.: Timber Press, 1988.

Michael, Pamela. *All the Good Things Around Us.* New York: Holt, Rinehart & Winston, 1980.

Mitchell, Henry. *The Essential Earthman.* Bloomington: University of Indiana Press. 1981.

Newcomb, Peggy C. *Popular Annuals of Eastern North America 1865–1914.* Washington, D.C.: Dumbarton Oaks, 1985.

Nuese, Josephine. *The County Garden.* New York: Scribner's, 1970.

Olkowski, William, Sheila Daar, and Helga Olkowski. *Common-Sense Pest Patrol.* Newtown, Conn.: The Taunton Press, 1991.

One Hundred Finest Trees and Shrubs for Temperate Climates. BBG Record/Plants & Gardens, vol. 13, no. 3 (1957).

Painter, Gilian. "Herbal Irises." *The Herb Grower* (Spring 1983).

Peterson, Roger Tory, and Margaret McKenny. *A Field Guide to Wildflowers of Northeastern and North-central North America.* Boston: Houghton Mifflin, 1968.

★Phillips, Harry, R. *Growing and Propagating Wild Flowers.* Chapel Hill: University of North Carolina Press. 1985.

★Phillips, Rodger, and Martin Rix. *The Random House Book of Shrubs.* New York: Random House, 1989.

Plowden, C. Chicheley. *A Manual of Plant Names.* New York: Philosophical Library, 1970.

Reader's Digest Magic and Medicine of Plants. Pleasantville, N.H.: Reader's Digest Association, 1986.

Reynolds, Joan, and John Tampion. *Double Flowers: A Scientific Study.* New York: Van Nostrand Reinhold, 1983.

Rockwell, F.F., and Esther C. Grayson. *The Complete Book of Bulbs*. Philadelphia: J.B. Lippincott, 1977.

———. *The Complete Book of Roses*. New York: Doubleday, 1958.

Rockwell, F.F., Esther C. Grayson, and Jan de Graaf. *The Complete Book of Lilies*. New York: Doubleday, 1961.

Rodale's Illustrated Encyclopedia of Herbs. Emmaus, Penn.: Rodale Press, 1987.

Roots (Journal of the Historic Iris Preservation Society). vol. 2, no. 2 (Fall 1989); vol. 3, no. 1 (Spring 1990); vol. 3, no. 2 (Fall 1990).

Sanecki, Kay N. *The Complete Book of Herbs*. New York: Macmillan, 1974.

Sanford, S.N.F. *New England Herbs*. Boston: New England Museum of Natural History, 1937.

★Scott, George Harman. *Bulbs: How to Select, Grow and Enjoy*. Los Angeles: HP Books, 1982.

Seals, Joseph. "Heirloom Blooms." *National Gardening Magazine* (August 1986).

Seymour, E.L.D., ed. *The Wise Garden Encyclopedia*. New York: Wm H. Wise & Co., 1954.

Shohan, Lily. "How to Win a Trophy." *Heritage Roses,* vol. 15, no. 3 (1989).

Slate, George L. *Lilies for American Gardens*. New York: Schriber's, 1947.

Snyder, Leon C. *Trees and Shrubs for Northern Gardens*. Minneapolis: University of Minnesota Press, 1980.

Steele Bros. Catalog (flower seed list). Toronto, 1878.

Strayer, Nannette M. "Wakefield." *The American Herb Grower Magazine,* vol. 1, no. 5 (December 1947–1948).

Stritikus, George R. *List of Recommended Period Plant Materials for Alabama Gardens*. Montgomery, Ala. (self-published): 1986.

Stuart, David and James Sutherland. *Plants from the Past*. New York: Viking, 1987.

Thomson, Richard. *Old Roses for Modern Gardens*. New York: Van Nostrand Reinhold, 1959.

Traill, Catharine Parr. *The Canadian Settler's Guide*. Toronto: McClelland & Stewart, Ltd., 1969 (reprint of 1855 edition).

Tucker, Arthur O. *Antique Plant Newsletter,* vol. 1, no. 1 (1989).

———. *Antique Plants: Old Cultivars of Ornamentals for Today's Gardens*. Private collection of Dr. Arthur O. Tucker, n.d.

Vaughn's Autumn Bulbs & Plants, 1897. Reprint no. 2, 1996, Antique Bulb Catalog Collection, by Scott Kunst. Ann Arbor, Mich.: Old House Gardens.

Von Baeyer, Edwinna. *Rhetoric and Roses: A History of Canadian Gardening*. Markham, Ont.: Fitzhenry & Whiteside, 1984.

Webster, Helen Noyes. *Herbs: How to Grow Them and How to Use Them*. Boston: Ralph T. Hale & Co., 1942.

———. "Lavenders", *The American Herb Grower*, vol. 1, no. 3 (Aug./Sept. 1947): 4–8.

Weishan, Michael. *The New Traditional Garden*. NY: The Ballantine Publishing Group, 1999.

★*Western Garden Book*. Menlo Park, Cal.: Sunset Books, 1977.

Whiteside, Katherine. *Antique Flowers: A Guide to Using Old-Fashioned Species in Contemporary Gardens*. New York: Villard, 1989.

Wilder, Louise Beebe. *The Fragrant Garden*. New York: Dover, 1974 (reprint of *The Fragrant Path*, Macmillan, 1932).

———. *The Garden in Color*. New York: Macmillan, 1937.

Williamson, John. *Perennial Gardens*. New York: Harper & Row, 1988.

Woodstock, H., and W. Stern. *Lilies of the World*. London: Country Life, 1950.

Wyman, Donald. *Shrubs and Vines for American Gardens*. New York: Macmillan, 1969.

———. *Wyman's Gardening Encyclopedia*. New York: Macmillan, 1971.

LIST OF COMMON NAMES

✤

Annual Clary Sage	*Salvia viridis (Salvia horminum)*	Cottage Pink	*Dianthus plumarius*
Azalea	*Rhododendron* spp.	Cowslip	*Primula veris (P. officinalis)*
Bachelor's-button	*Centaurea cyanus*	Daffodil	*Narcissus* spp.
Balsam	*Impatiens balsamina*	Dahlia	*Dahlia* hybrids
Beach Wormwood	*Artemisia stelleriana*	Dame's-rocket	*Hesperis matronalis*
Beautiful Clarkia	*Clarkia pulchella*	Dutchman's Pipe	*Aristolachia macrophylla/A. durior*
Bee-balm	*Monarda didyma*	Dwarf Box 'Suffruticosa'	*Buxus sempervirens*
Bellflower	*Campanula* spp.		
Betony	*Stachys officinalis*	Dwarf Nasturtium	*Tropaeolum minus*
Black-eyed-Susan	*Rudbeckia hirta*	Dwarf Soapwort	*Saponaria ocymoides*
Bleeding-heart	*Dicentra spectabilis*		
Bouncing-Bet	*Saponaria officinalis*	Eastern Columbine	*Aquilegia canadensis*
Box	*Buxus sempervirens*	Elderberry	*Sambucus canadensis*
Butterfly Weed	*Asclepias tuberosa*	Elecampane	*Inula helenium*
		European Columbine	*Aquilegia vulgaris*
Canna	*Canna flaccida,*	Everlasting Pea	*Lathyrus latifolius*
	Canna indica,		
	Canna X *generalis*	Feverfew	*Tanacetum parthenium*
China Aster	*Callistephus chinensis*		*(Chrysanthemum parthenium)*
Chives	*Allium schoenoprasum*	Forget-me-not	*Myosotis* spp.
Clary	*Salvia sclarea*	Four O'Clock	*Mirabilis jalapa*
Clematis	*Clematis* spp. and hybrids	French Marigold	*Tagetes patula*
Climbing Hydrangea	*Hydrangea anomala petiolaris*	Fringed Bleeding-heart	*Dicentra eximia*
Clove Currant	*Ribes odoratum*		
Clove Pink	*Dianthus caryophyllus*	Garden Lupine	*Russell Hybrids*
Corn-flag	*Gladiolus* spp.	Garden Sage	*Salvia officinalis*
Cosmos	*Cosmos bipinnatus*	Garlic Chives	*Allium tuberosum*
Costmary	*Tanacetum balsamita*	Giant Snowdrop	*Galanthus elwesii*
	(Chrysanthemum balsamita)	Glad	*Gladiolus* hybrids

Glossy Abelia	*Abelia × grandiflora*	Orange Daylily	*Hemerocallis fulva*
Godetia	*Clarkia amoena*	Oregon Holly-grape	*Mahonia aquifolium*
Golden Currant	*Ribes aureum*		
Golden Marguerite	*Anthemis tictoria*	Pansy	*Viola × wittrockiana*
Golden-glow 'Hortensia'	*Rudbeckia laciniata*	Peegee Hydrangea	*Hydrangea paniculata* 'Grandiflora'
Goutweed	*Aegopdium podagraria* 'Variegatum'	Peony	*Paeonia* spp.
Green-flowered Betony	*Stachys grandiflora (Stachys macrantha)*	Petunia	*Petunia × hybrida*
		Phlox	*Phlox* spp.
Highbush Cranberry	*Viburnum trilobum*	Policeman's Helmet	*Impatiens glandulifera*
Hollyhock	*Alcea rosea*	Poppy	*Papaver* spp.
Hollyhock Mallow	*Malva alcea fastigiata*	Pot-marigold	*Calendula officinalis*
Honesty	*Lunaria annua/L. biennis*	Purple Foxglove	*Digitalis purpurea*
Honeysuckle	*Lonicera* spp.		
Hop Vine	*Humulus lupulus*	Ribbon Grass	*Phalaris arundinacea picta*
Horsemint	*Monarda punctata*	Rocky Mountain Garland	*Clarkia unguiculata*
Hosta	*Hosta* spp.	Roman Wormwood	*Artemisia pontica*
Hyacinth	*Hyacinthus orientalis*	Rose Campion	*Lychnis coronaria*
		Roses	*Rosa* spp. and groups
Imperial Morning-glory	*Ipomoea nil* 'Scarlet O'Hara'		
Iris	*Iris* spp.	Scarlet Runner Bean	*Phaseolus coccineus*
		Scented Geranium	*Pelargonium* spp.
Japanese primrose	*Primula japonica*	Signet Marigold	*Tagetes tenuifolia*
Jerusalem-cross	*Lychnis chalcedonica*	Sneezewort	*Achillea ptarmica*
Johnny-jump-up	*Viola tricolor*	Snowdrop	*Galanthus nivalis*
		Southernwood	*Artemisia abrotanum*
Lady's Mantle	*Alchemilla mollis/A. vulgaris*	Spanish Fennel Flower	*Nigella hispanica*
Lamb's-ears	*Stachys byzantina*	Spirea	*Spirea* spp.
Lavender	*Lavandula angustifolia*	Sweet Alyssum	*Lobularia maritima*
Lemon Yellow Daylily	*Hemerocallis lilioasphodelus (H. flava)*	Sweet Cicely	*Myrrhis odorata*
Lilac	*Syringa vulgaris*	Sweet Pea	*Lathyrus odoratus*
Lily	*Lilium* spp.	Sweet Violet	*Viola odorata*
Lily-of-the-valley	*Convallaria majalis*	Sweet Woodruff	*Galium odoratum (Asperula odorata)*
Lovage	*Levisticum officinale*	Sweet-William	*Dianthus barbatus*
Love-in-a-mist	*Nigella damascena*		
Lungwort	*Pulmonaria* spp.	Tulip	*Tulipa* spp.
Maidenhair Fern	*Adiantum pedatum*	Valerian	*Valerian officinalis*
Mock Orange	*Philadelphus coronarius*	Virginia Creeper	*Parthenocissus quinquefolia*
Monkshood	*Aconitum* spp.	Virginia-bluebells	*Mertensia virginica*
Moonflower	*Ipomoea alba*		
Morning-glory	*Ipomoea purpurea*	Weigela	*Weigela florida*
Mountain-bluet	*Centaurea montana*	Western Bleeding-heart	*Dicentra formosa*
Mountain-laurel	*Kalmia latifolia*	White Runner Bean	*Phaseolus coccineus* 'Albus'
Musk Mallow	*Malva moschata*	Wild Lupine	*Lupinus polyphyllus*
		Wild Mallow	*Malva sylvestris*
Nasturtium	*Tropaeolum majus*	Wild-bergamot	*Monarda fistulosa*
Nicotiana	*Nicotiana alata*	Winter Currant	*Ribes sanguineum*
Nutmeg Flower	*Nigella sativa*		

INDEX

※

Beach Wormwood, 79–81

Beales, Peter, 5

Bearded Iris, 56, 57, 151–52. *See also* Iris (*Iris* spp.)

Bear's Foot. *See* Lady's Mantle

Beautiful Clarkia, 51, 96–97

Bee-balm, 15, 23, 38, 42, 43, 45, 46, 48, 187–90

Bellflower, 18, 40, 43, 56, 88–91

Bergamot. *See* Bee-balm

Bethlehem-sage. *See* Lungwort

Betony (Woundwort), 43, 261–66. *See also* Green-flowered Betony; Lamb's-ears

Bible Leaf. *See* Costmary

biennials, 10. *See also* specific biennials
American cottage garden, late 1800s to early 1900s, 53
butterflies, planting for, 39
colonial gardens, 1600-1700, 43
evening garden, 40
native flora in natural garden, 1700-1850, 46
parlor garden, late 1700s-1850, 49

Billy-buttons. *See* Wild Mallow

Bindweed. *See* Morning-glory

Bird's-eye. *See* Johnny-jump-up

Bishop's Weed. *See* Goutweed

Bitter Fitch. *See* Nutmeg Flower

Bitter-indian. *See* Nasturtium

Black Caraway. *See* Nutmeg Flower

Black Cumin. *See* Nutmeg Flower

Black-eyed-Susan, 22, 39, 45, 46, 48, 250–52

Black Hollyhock, 54, 70

Bleeding-heart, 10, 25, 53, 54, 113–15. *See also* Fringed Bleeding-heart (Wild Bleeding-heart)

Blew Bindweed. *See* Morning-glory

Blew-bottle. *See* Bachelor's-button (*Centaurea cyanus*)

Bloody-butcher. *See* Lungwort

Bloody-fingers. *See* Purple Foxglove

Blue Barberry. *See* Oregon Holly-grape

Blue-cowslip. *See* Lungwort

Blue Flag Iris, 35, 39, 46, 56, 151. *See also* Iris (*Iris* spp.)

Blue Funnel Flower. *See* Virginia-bluebells

Blue Lungwort, 46. *See also* Lungwort

Blue Mallow. *See* Wild Mallow

Blue Monarda. *See* Wild-bergamot

Blue-pipe. *See* Lilac

Blue-rocket. *See* Monkshood

Boerner, Gene, 5

bones, garden, 32–33

Border Carnation. *See* Clove Pink

Border Phlox (*Phlox paniculata*), 39, 40, 224–26

Border Pink. *See* Cottage Pink

borders, 36

Bouncing-Bet (Soapwort), 15, 18, 40, 42, 43, 46, 257–59

Bourbon Rose, 53, 54, 244

Box, 42, 44, 48, 83–85

Boys-and-girls. *See* Lungwort

Bridal-wreath Spirea. *See* Spirea (*Spirea* spp.)

Bride's-bouquet. *See* Bouncing-Bet (Soapwort); Sneezewort (*Achillea ptarmica*)

British Myrrh. *See* Sweet Cicely

Bruisewort. *See* Bouncing-Bet (Soapwort)

Buffalo Currant. *See* Clove Currant; Golden Currant

bulbs, 10. *See also* specific bulbs
colonial gardens, 1600-1700, 44
evening garden, 40
parlor garden, late 1700s-1850, 48, 49
propagating and preserving, 27, 29
sources of, 299–300
storing, 30
Victoriana, 1850 to early 1900s, 49–51

Bunch Pink. *See* Sweet-William

Bush Balsam. *See* Balsam

Buttercup, 35

butterflies, planting for, 39–40

Butterfly Flower. *See* Butterfly Weed

Butterfly Milkweed. *See* Butterfly Weed

Butterfly Weed, 23, 39, 45, 46, 48, 82–83

Buxus sempervirens (Box), 42, 44, 48, 83–85

Cabbage Rose, 44

cake recipes
Louise Hyde's Sweet Cicely Coffee Cakes, 193
Vera's Poppy Seed Cake, 208

Calendula (*Calendula officinalis*), 11, 23, 29, 36, 39, 43, 56, 85–86

Calico Bush. *See* Mountain-laurel

Callistephus chinensis, 49, 51, 87–88

Campanula spp. (Bellflower), 18, 56, 88–91
glomerata 'Alba,' 40, 90–91
medium, 40, 43, 91

Canada Lily, 43, 167. *See also* Lily (*Lilium* spp.)

Canadian Columbine. *See* Eastern Columbine

Candelabra Primrose. *See* Japanese Primrose

Candied Violets (recipe), 287

Candlemas Bells. *See* Snowdrop

Canna (*Canna flaccida, Canna* x *generalis, Canna indica*), 35, 50, 51, 91–94

Canterbury-bells, 40, 42, 43, 48, 88–91

Cape Marigold. *See* Calendula (*Calendula officinalis*); Pot-Marigold

Carnation. *See* Clove Pink

Catawba Rhododendron, 44, 46, 51. *See also* Rhododendron (*Rhododendron* spp.)

Cat's Valerian. *See* Valerian (*Valerian officinalis*)

Centaurea cyanus. *See* Bachelor's-button

Centaurea montana (Mountain-bluet), 39, 56, 57, 94–96

Chebols. *See* Chives

Cheese. *See* Wild Mallow

Cheese Mallow. *See* Wild Mallow

Chibolls. *See* Chives

Chigger Flower. *See* Butterfly Weed

Children-of-Israel. *See* Lungwort

China Aster, 49, 51, 87–88

Chinese Chives. *See* Garlic Chives

Chinese Hollyhock. *See* Hollyhock; Wild Mallow

Chives, 11, 23, 39, 42, 43, 72–74

Christmas-cowslip. *See* Lungwort

White Lily. *See* Madonna Lily

White-pipe. *See* Mock Orange

White Runner Bean, 54, 220–21

Wild-bergamot, 39, 43, 45, 46, 187–90

Wild Bleeding-heart. *See* Fringed
    Bleeding-heart (Wild Bleeding-
    heart)

Wild Fennel. *See* Nutmeg Flower

Wild-hop. *See* Betony (Woundwort)

Wild Iris. *See* Blue Flag Iris

Wild Lupine, 46, 173–76. *See also*
    Lupine

Wild Mallow, 11, 182–84

Wild Pansy. *See* Johnny-jump-up

Wild Petunia, 54. *See also* Petunia
    (*Petunia* x *hybrida*)

Wild Roses. *See* Roses (*Rosa* spp.)

Wild-sunflower. *See* Elecampane

Wild-sweet-William. *See* Bouncing-Bet
    (Soapwort)

Wild Valerian. *See* Valerian (*Valerian
    officinalis*)

wind, prevailing, 33

wine recipes
    Cowslip Wine, 229
    May Wine, 120

Winged Tobacco. *See* Nicotiana
    (*Nicotiana alata*)

Winking-Mary-budde. *See* Calendula
    (*Calendula officinalis*); Pot-
    Marigold

Winter Currant, 47, 236–39

wintering annuals, 24–25

Witches'-gloves. *See* Purple Foxglove

Wolfsbane. *See* Monkshood

Wood Betony. *See* Betony (Woundwort)

Woodbine. *See* Virginia Creeper

Woodland Forget-me-not. *See* Forget-
    me-not

wool, dye for, 75

Wooly Betony. *See* Lamb's-ears

Wooly Stachys. *See* Lamb's-ears

Woundwort. *See* Betony; Lamb's-ears

Yarrow, 18, 23

Yellow Daylily. *See* Lemon Yellow
    Daylily

Yellow Flag Iris, 15, 35, 46, 56, 151. *See
    also* Iris (*Iris* spp.)

Yellow-larkspur. *See* Nasturtium

Yellow Tuberose. *See* Lemon Yellow
    Daylily

Yerger, Meg, 5

Youth-before-old-age. *See* Goutweed

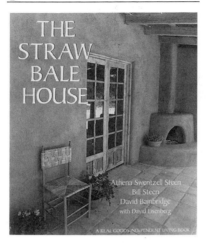